Aleksandr Nikolaevich Engelgardt's
Letters from the Country, 1872–1887

Aleksandr Nikolaevich Engelgardt's

LETTERS FROM THE COUNTRY, 1872–1887

Translated and edited by
CATHY A. FRIERSON

New York   Oxford
OXFORD UNIVERSITY PRESS
1993

Oxford University Press

Oxford   New York   Toronto
Delhi   Bombay   Calcutta   Madras   Karachi
Kuala Lumpur   Singapore   Hong Kong   Tokyo
Nairobi   Dar es Salaam   Cape Town
Melbourne   Auckland   Madrid

and associated companies in
Berlin   Ibadan

Published by Oxford University Press, Inc.,
200 Madison Avenue, New York, New York 10016

Oxford is a registered trademark of Oxford University Press

Library of Congress Cataloging-in-Publication Data
Ėngel'gardt, A. N. (Aleksandr Nikolaevich), 1832–1893.
[Iz derevni. English]
Aleksandr Nikolaevich Engelgardt's Letters from the country,
1872–1887 / translated and edited by Cathy A. Frierson.
p.   cm.
"Consists of 12 separate letters which first appeared in
the Russian journals 'Notes of the Fatherland'
and 'Herald of Europe' "—Pref.
ISBN 0-19-507620-6 —ISBN 0-19-507621-4 (pbk.)
1. Peasantry—Russia—History—19th century.
2. Peasantry—Russia—Social conditions.
3. Agriculture—Economic aspects—Russia.
[1. Russia—Social conditions—1801–1917.]
I. Frierson, Cathy A.
II. Title.   III. Title: Letters from the country,
1872–1887.   HD1536.R9E5413   1993   305.5′633—dc20   92-39426

2 4 6 8 9 7 5 3 1

Printed in the United States of America
on acid-free paper

For my son,
Isaac Tennant Josephson,
whose joyful presence marked
all the stages of
the production of this work.

Preface

Aleksandr Nikolaevich Engelgardt's first letter "From the Country" appeared in the May 1872 issue of the literary-political journal *Notes of the Fatherland,* published in St. Petersburg. It was an immediate hit, and the following letters, published over the next ten years, were the most important work of this progressive publication. *Notes of the Fatherland* was closed down by the government in 1884, but a final letter by Engelgardt appeared in the liberal *Herald of Europe* in 1887. These letters constituted the centerpiece of debate about the peasant and Russian agriculture in Russia's post-Emancipation era. Engelgardt provided an eyewitness account of the state of agriculture and the success of the land reform, relations between the gentry and the peasantry, the structure of rural existence, and the moral climate in the villages near his estate of Batishchevo in Smolensk Province. For contemporary, educated Russians, Engelgardt was the undisputed authority and best source of information on the countryside. As the agricultural editor of the neo-Slavophile journal *Rus'* conceded in 1881, there was no one in Russia who could match Engelgardt's knowledge, force of argument, and precision in presentation, and for that reason, the letters stood beyond criticism during the first ten years of their appearance.[1]

The letters continued to enjoy unusual popularity as a collected volume. The first eleven letters appeared as a separate volume in 1882; the twelfth letter was added to the third edition in 1897. Four subsequent editions have appeared, with the most recent being the seventh, a centennial edition published in 1987. For Soviet historians, Engelgardt was required reading for serious study of this period, not least because of the attention Lenin devoted to his writings. For Lenin, Engelgardt was one of the best of the Populist observers of developments in the countryside, and he drew on the letters from Batishchevo both in his study of the development of capitalism in Russia and in his criticism of Populism as an ideology and revolutionary movement.[2] A century after their first publication, Engelgardt's letters have again become a resource for would-be reformers who are looking back on the post-Emancipation era as a possible standard against which to measure their own goals and programs.[3]

This is the first English translation of Engelgardt's *Letters from the Country*. It is an abridged version, intended primarily for use in the classroom as a source on the social history of rural Russia in the post-Emancipation period. I decided to translate this text because it includes observations about virtually every aspect of post-Emancipation rural life and thus serves as an excellent primary source for students to use with recent studies by Soviet and Western scholars on the social history of rural Russia. Engelgardt's letters also enjoy the advantage of being fun to read due to his intensely personal style and sharp wit.

I have used the texts of the letters as they first appeared in *Notes of the Fatherland* and *Herald of Europe*. Approximately half of the complete letters appear here, including the passages in which Engelgardt described the life of the peasantry who lived around his family estate. Most of the remaining passages (which I have translated but have chosen not to include in this edition) concern gentry farming in post-Emancipation Russia and Engelgardt's important experiments with phosphate fertilizers during the final years of his life. These include valuable information for the student of Russian agriculture but are unlikely to be of great interest to students exploring Russian social history. I have also omitted many passages where Engelgardt repeated himself, sometimes within one letter, often from one letter to the next. I have indicated short deletions by ellipsis points in brackets. Engelgardt also made frequent use of ellipsis points, but the brackets will identify mine. Longer omissions, of several pages, are identified and described in bracketed notes within the translation. I have also provided section subtitles within each letter and in the table of contents to facilitate selection of passages according to subject.

Engelgardt's letters posed certain problems in translation. The most serious was his use of expressions peculiar to Smolensk during his residence there. V. N. Dobrovolskii's dictionary of Smolensk colloquialisms, which dates from the same period, was a great help, although Dobrovolskii also often cited passages from Engelgardt's letters in lieu of a definition of terms. I have also consulted with Soviet linguists and specialists on the peasantry, who were able to clarify several points, although they were also unable to explain some of Engelgardt's references and expressions. The second major challenge in the translation was distinguishing between Engelgardt's and the peasants' speech. Engelgardt did not report peasant speech as less formal than his own, and he himself adopted peasant expressions. It was consistent with Engelgardt's depiction of the peasantry as intelligent and rational that he did not debase their speech. I decided, therefore, to follow his lead and make minimal distinction between educated and uneducated voices in the text. I have followed the Library of Congress system of transliteration. In transliterating names, I have omitted the soft sign, so that Avdot'ia becomes Avdotia, Savel'ich becomes Savelich, and so on. For such transliterated terms as *baba, muzhik, artel', volost',* and *zemstvo,* which have entered the vocabulary of Western specialists of the Russian peasantry, I have italicized their first appearance and provided a definition in an endnote. They appear in roman letters in subsequent instances. The exception to this rule is the term *krug,* the definition of which, although it appears in the glossary, is too lengthy to include at each point where Engelgardt uses it. Because it is an uncommon term that also carries so much weight in Engelgardt's analysis of gentry-peasant relations, I decided to retain italics throughout the text when it appears.

I am indebted to several individuals and institutions for their assistance and support of this project. The translation was supported by a National Endowment for the Humanities Translation Grant. Steven Hoch, who began a translation of Engelgardt in 1980 but decided not to pursue the project, was generous enough to give me his photocopies of the letters, and of biographical and critical materials that he had originally gathered. Rutgers University supported my research by providing leave time and financial support through a Henry Rutgers Fellowship. The International Research and Exchanges Board supported my research for the introductory essay and consultation with scholars in Moscow, Leningrad, and Smolensk. The Central State Archive of Literature and Art, Pushkin House, and the State Archive of the Smolensk Region granted me generous access to their materials related to Engelgardt. Several individuals assisted me with problems of translation. These included Valerie Wattenberg, Raymond Miller, Ekaterina Kontor, Monika Greenleaf, and Olena Bochko. Vladimir Akimovich Volkov of the Institute for the History of Science and Technology in Moscow directed me to materials related to Engelgardt's career as a chemist. Mikhail Naumovich Levitin enabled me to work with materials in Smolensk. Melissa Stockdale, Richard Pipes, Samuel Baron, Paul Josephson, Richard Wortman, and numerous members of the Department of History at the University of New Hampshire read and commented on the introductory essay. At Oxford University Press, Nancy Lane's support of this project has been essential to making Engelgardt's letters available in English. David Roll offered valuable advice on how to abridge and annotate the text, and Paul Schlotthauer made the tedium of repetitive proofreading more pleasurable by being an accessible and positive interlocutor during numerous telephone conferences. I would also like to take this opportunity to thank the woman who made this project possible by helping me care for my son, Ofelia Otero. Finally, thank you to Paul, who built the study.

Durham, N.H.   C. A. F.
May 1993

Contents

Letter XI, 228

Letter XII, 239

Notes, 256

Bibliography of Related Works, 269

Glossary

Arshin: Measure of length, equal to 28 inches, or 71 centimeters.

Chetvert: Dry measure, 5.95 bushels.

Chetvert: Land measure, one half of a desiatina.

Desiatina: Land measure, 2.7 acres, or 1.092 hectares.

Garnets: Dry measure equal to 3.28 liters.

Krug: "By the *krug*": When peasants took on gentry land after the Emancipation to cultivate for the full agricultural cycle, using their own horses and tools, and providing their own food.

Osmina: Dry measure, 11.55 pecks, or about 3 bushels.

Pud: Weight equal to 36 pounds.

Sack: Approximately 275–300 pounds.

Sazhen: Just less than 84 inches.

Shtof: Unit of liquid measure equal to 1.23 liters.

Vedro: Liquid measure, 3.25 gallons, or 12.30 liters.

Vershok: Measure of length, 1.75 inches.

Verst: Measure of length equal to 0.66 miles, or 1.067 kilometers.

Aleksandr Nikolaevich Engelgardt's
Letters from the Country, 1872–1887

Introduction

I went to visit A. N. Engelgardt for the first time around 9:00 in the morning, if memory does not fail me, in the winter of 1878–1879. He had already finished his tea and an open notebook lay on his table. He was obviously working on it, but he greeted me standing in the middle of his office. His powerful figure created a singular impression: he was tall, broad shouldered, splendidly built. His large head was covered with long and graying hair, he had a small beard, while his eyes, with a gray steely glint, had an immobile and slightly majestic gaze. His sheepskin coat lay on the armchair, but he was himself dressed in a simple flannel shirt and wide trousers, tucked into black leather boots. . . . I should add that my host's office was not covered with wallpaper and its log walls recalled a tidy peasant izba. He had quite an effect in his peasant dress.

A. I. Faresov, *Semidesiatniki* (1905)

This tall, powerful figure, dressed in peasant clothes, working over his notebooks in an unadorned room reminiscent of a peasant hut, stood at the conjunction of social and intellectual currents in post-Emancipation Russia. The room was part of a family estate in the village of Batishchevo, Dorogobuzhskii District, Smolensk Province. The house was a modest, drafty structure, the site of Aleksandr Nikolaevich Engelgardt's internal exile, imposed on him in 1871 by the tsarist government. A prominent St. Petersburg chemist, he had been banned from all locales with institutes of higher education as a result of radical student gatherings at the St. Petersburg Agricultural Institute during his tenure as rector there.

Granted the privilege of selecting his residence within the Empire, Engelgardt chose a neglected family estate where he could put his training in agricultural chemistry to the test. Chemist, exile under police surveillance, practicing farmer—these were the roles he assumed in 1871. He quickly took on two others: author, and advocate of the peasantry. As Engelgardt stood to greet his visitor after eight years of residence in Batishchevo, his peasant shirt, pants, and boots signaled his immersion in rural Russia, while his pen and notebooks signaled his role as the most important eyewitness reporter on the countryside, whose writings on the world around his estate were transforming educated society's comprehension of the Russian peasant and his world.

Aleksandr Nikolaevich Engelgardt's letters "From the Country" were the most insightful, thorough, and entertaining eyewitness account of rural Russia in the post-Emancipation era. Published individually in the leading progressive journal of the day over the period 1872–1882 with a concluding letter appearing in the journal of the liberal intelligentsia in 1887, they explored village culture, peasant-gentry relations, and agriculture in a period of heightened concern about the so-called peasant question in Russia. They were commissioned by M. E. Saltykov-Shchedrin, who, as editor at *Notes of the Fatherland*, recognized that the reading public was grappling with the question of the future role of the newly emancipated peasantry in Russia's economic, social, and political development. Saltykov-Shchedrin astutely guessed that Engelgardt would be able to provide just the kind of fresh information from the countryside that readers were hungry for, while Engelgardt would need the added income that the journal would pay for his contributions.[1]

For the student of Imperial Russian culture, and for anyone interested in peasant studies, in land reform, in the rural world's experience in a period of rapid economic and social change, these letters offer valuable access to history from below, from the village street, the gentry manor, the local court of justice, the train station, and the tavern. Western students of Russia will find the sharp observations of an engaged and energetic intellectual who attacked the problems of farming in Russia with a vengeance, and in the process came to know the countryside intimately. Engelgardt's readers come to know specific peasant individuals as emblematic of broader types and are able to read his reports of specific developments as typical of general trends in agriculture and society. In addition to the primary themes of rural society and farming in Russia, Engelgardt also offered biting and detailed criticism of efforts by the state and educated society to reform and improve rural governance, providing entertaining vignettes of relations between the peasantry and local officialdom. These letters thus both inform and illustrate. They bring history alive in the fullest sense of the word, while attuning the contemporary, urban reader to the peculiarities of the economic and social imperatives of the late-nineteenth-century village in the wake of reform.

Aleksandr Nikolaevich Engelgardt

> The secret of my influence lies in the fact that I believe in myself and never doubt what I say.
>
> A. N. Engelgardt, as quoted in A. I. Faresov, *Semidesiatniki* (1905)

Engelgardt was a member of the landed nobility and an accomplished chemist. He was born into a noble family of Smolensk Province in 1832 and spent his youth largely on a family estate at Klimovo. At the age of sixteen he entered the

Mikhailovskii Artillery School in St. Petersburg, which boasted one of the few truly modern chemical laboratories in Russia, as well as one of the leading lights of the early study of chemistry in Russia, N. N. Zinin.[2] Upon completion of his degree in 1853, he began service in the military, working for the next thirteen years in the casting division at the St. Petersburg arsenal, supplementing his academic preparation with a trip to Germany to study steel production in the Krupps establishment.[3]

He maintained an active life outside his work at the arsenal, joining in the vibrant intellectual life of the capital and continuing to develop his scientific interests. Chemistry during these years was picking up momentum as a national science in Russia, and Engelgardt was very much a part of this development.[4] He cofounded Russia's first journal of chemistry, opened the first private chemical laboratory in St. Petersburg, and participated in the founding of the Chemical Society at St. Petersburg University.[5] In 1864 he began teaching part-time at the St. Petersburg Agricultural Institute. In 1866 he left military service to become a full-time member of the chemistry faculty and to direct the institute's chemistry laboratory.

In each of these undertakings, Engelgardt displayed a high level of commitment and a decidedly pragmatic approach, characteristics that would also dominate his rural experience after 1871. In the editors' remarks in the first issue of *The Chemical Journal of N. Sokolov and A. Engelgardt,* he joined N. N. Sokolov in declaring the practical goals of the journal, as well as of their private laboratory founded two years earlier. Rather than concentrate solely or even primarily on theoretical questions, Engelgardt and Sokolov considered the dissemination of established scientific knowledge their first objective as a means of developing a critical number of young chemists in Russia who could then devote their work to theoretical discoveries.[6] Similarly, in the curriculum he developed for students of chemistry at the Agricultural Institute, Engelgardt insisted on the essential goal of applied science, on the mastery of chemical knowledge for the purpose of improving agricultural practice.[7] In both of these instances he displayed his concern that science serve Russia's scientific and economic development. To educate, to improve, to serve: these three goals would characterize his entire adult life.

While Engelgardt was not a chemist of the stature of his peer Dmitrii Mendeleev, he was prominent and engaged in leading scientific circles of his day and active in bringing scientific knowledge to the public.[8] Engelgardt demonstrated an early interest in agricultural chemistry. His work in this area, particularly in mineral fertilizers, influenced his initial approach to farming in the first years of his residence in the countryside, and later developed into his primary occupation.[9] In the end, his reputation as a scientist would result from his experimentation with phosphates that would earn him the title of first chemical agronomist in Russia.[10]

From the earliest stages of his professional career, Engelgardt worked to bring science to the public through activities outside his formal obligations. In addition to founding the journal and laboratory with Sokolov, he wrote popular articles on science for such nonscientific journals as *Rassvet* (Dawn, a journal for young women), *Uchitel'* (Teacher), *Artilleriiskii zhurnal* (The Artillery Journal), and various newspapers.[11] He also gave a series of well-attended public lectures at the Agricultural Museum in Petersburg.[12] His urge to make knowledge available was coupled with exceptional self-confidence.

This self-confidence pervades his letters from the country, never allowing the reader to forget the author, his opinions, his particular passions and prejudices. He pithily dismisses his fellow chemists as "eunuchs"; the two leading editors at the journal *Rus'* as "know-nothings"; local officials as variously stupid, absurd, and vain; petty merchants and peasant exploiters as parasites, leeches, and trash. His authorial presence enlivens his account and distinguishes it from similar efforts by other educated residents of the post-Emancipation countryside. Despite his sharp tongue and merciless criticism, Engelgardt retained the friendship and respect of former students, colleagues, and counterparts in the public debate about agriculture in Russia, maintaining an active correspondence remarkable both in its scale and in the warmth of sentiment evident on all sides.

Engelgardt was thus an exceptional figure in post-Emancipation Russia on several counts. He was a member of the privileged nobility and had secured a superior education. He was a prominent chemist in a time when he could take a leading part in the establishment of Russian chemistry. He was a popular and effective teacher at a leading institution of higher education, as well as an evangelist for science among the broader public. He moved in progressive circles in the capital and gained influence through his unique talents and strengths. From a hundred years' distance, Engelgardt still has the power to captivate and convince through the power of his prose. While one may easily imagine that his overweening self-confidence often may have seemed challenging to his peers, his enduring impression is one of an active, charismatic personality who devoted his life to endeavors larger than himself. Before he reached the age of forty, he had over seventy publications and an apparently shining future before him. In 1871, however, his life took an unexpected turn, throwing him out of the capital and its intellectual milieu into the wastelands of Smolensk Province and the company of the uneducated, dark, and simple peasantry of an especially impoverished region of Russia.

The departure from St. Petersburg took the form of enforced internal exile. The noble chemist Aleksandr Nikolaevich Engelgardt wound up in the rural backwoods because of indiscretion on his part as rector of the St. Petersburg Agricultural Institute. Engelgardt was named rector of the institute in 1870. In that capacity he was responsible not only for matters of administration and curriculum but also for student affairs. The students' weekly Saturday evening gatherings for supper, entertainment, and discussion thus fell under his purview. Engelgardt often attended these gatherings, especially the discussion groups.

Most authors who have described these events dismiss any impropriety in the students' meetings, but the Soviet historian P. Ia. Nechuiatov found evidence in the archives of the Imperial government that indicated there was indeed cause for concern by the state's security organs. Reports by agents of the Third Department internal security police quoted radical statements and general sympathy for revolutionary causes. One report included the description of a toast, "To the French Republic, to the success of the red banner, and to revolution in general."[13] One student involved later wrote that he believed the affair was the work of an agent provocateur who was able to invent such a scandal because of Engelgardt's well-known radical views.[14]

While enthusiastic talk on the part of institute students was unlikely to have any further consequences, Engelgardt could not have been unaware of the reaction they could provoke on the part of a government that had witnessed an attempt on the life of the Tsar in 1866 and a growth in radical sentiment among students in the capital.[15] He himself had had a brush with the authorities during student demonstrations at St. Petersburg University in 1861 and had been in jail for two weeks as a result.[16] His own early sympathies for progressive ideas were so well known that a group of five conspirators, including N. G. Chernyshevsky, approached him in 1862 to join a revolutionary organization, promising him the postrevolutionary post of Minister of War. He wisely declined the offer.[17]

The surveillance reports on student activities at the institute led the government to call for Engelgardt's arrest. A group of gendarmes arrived in the dead of night on December 1, 1870, seized him in his apartment next to the chemistry laboratory, and took him to the Peter and Paul Fortress. Arrests of several students and his colleague P. A. Lachinov followed. In the investigation over the next month, Engelgardt was identified as the individual most responsible for the "disturbances" at the institute because of his position as rector.[18] He was sentenced to exile from Petersburg and all university cities in the Empire. He was also denied the right to travel abroad. Operating within these restrictions, he chose to return to his family's estate in Batishchevo, Dorogobuzhskii District of Smolensk Province, which he had last visited fifteen years earlier. In those fifteen years, Russia had undergone the emancipation of the serfs and the major land reform that accompanied it. These events influenced both the world Engelgardt would find in Batishchevo and his own expectations of his experience there.

Emancipation and Land Reform

I left St. Petersburg convinced that everything had changed in the last ten years, that the folk were moving rapidly forward. . . .
A. N. Engelgardt, "From the Country, IV" (1874)

When Engelgardt departed from St. Petersburg in January 1871 for his family estate, he was embarking on a journey into a countryside where the effects of the Emancipation of 1861 were still taking shape a decade later. While the name of the keystone legislation of the Reform Era emphasized its act of liberating the Russian serfs from personal bondage to their masters, the Emancipation was equally a land reform, indeed, one of the great land reforms in history. The men who designed Russia's Emancipation legislation decided to liberate the serfs with land, which in turn required that landowners relinquish some of the land they had possessed and from which they had derived their income through the uncompensated labor of serfs living on their property.[19] This basic feature of the Emancipation—peasants received land and gentry landowners lost land and free labor—generated a series of complicated financial and legal arrangements to provide the landowners with compensation for the land and labor they gave up.

First of all, peasant recipients of land had to pay for it. They did so not as individual landowners but through the institution of the peasant commune, an administrative unit intended to oversee the collection of payments on the land and of tax obligations in the villages under its jurisdiction. After a two-year transitional period during which land settlements were to be worked out, peasants entered a legal status called "temporary obligation." In this position they were to pay their former master rent for the use of the land they received. They were to remain in this status until they had entered an arrangement to redeem or pay off their obligation to the landowner for the full assessed value of the land. To go on redemption, as this was called, peasants were essentially given a mortgage on the land by the state. At the time of the land settlements between landowners and their liberated serfs, the state set the cost of redemption and paid the landowner 75–80 percent of the assessed value of the land through redemption certificates. The state then turned to the peasants and assigned them a forty-nine-year note on the land, which peasants were to pay off in annual redemption payments. Peasants also had to pay the landowner the remaining 20–25 percent of the land's price directly. In 1861, redemption was described as optional, but in 1881 it was made compulsory for all former serf owners. In the meantime, peasants who were not on redemption continued to pay rent, which was set according to the land's assessed value.[20] These arrangements applied to former proprietary serfs; state peasants and peasants on appanage lands received different terms of emancipation and land reform. The majority of the peasants in Smolensk Province in the area of Engelgardt's exile were former proprietary serfs.

Peasants considered this arrangement a profound betrayal of their expectation that they, as the people who worked the land and brought forth its fruits, should receive possession freely. Gentry landowners, on their part, were anxious to minimize their losses in the land settlements they made with their former serfs. They did so by (1) trying to grant peasants as little good plough or arable land as possible; (2) retaining control of critical forest and pasture lands; (3) securing inflated land valuations on the land they did cede; and (4) hemming the peasants in with lands that the peasants had to have to survive in farming, which the former masters could then "rent" to their former serfs in exchange for the peasants' labor they had previously enjoyed at no cost. The overvaluation of the land was so great that one historian has aptly termed it a "personal ransom" that peasants paid for their personal liberty.[21]

The process of working out these land settlements across the Empire took several years and required the agency of a special official, the peace mediator, whose mandate was to bring the peasants and landowners to agreement. When all was said and done, the peasants received their mortgaged property in the form of land allotments that varied in size and value according to the location and quality of the land. Approximately 30 million serfs became free subjects of the Tsar, and over 33 million *desiatina*s, or almost 90 million acres, of land changed hands.

In and of itself, the Emancipation of the Russian serfs in 1861 was a monumental reform. It took on added importance as the first in a series of reforms that launched autocratic and Imperial Russia on a path of social, legal, and economic transformation. Educated Russians viewed 1861 as one of the great turning points in their culture's history and their era as one of progressive promise. By 1871, when Engelgardt entered his period of exile, the Emancipation had been followed by reforms of the judicial system, of municipal government, and by the introduction of locally elected boards of self-governance, the *zemstva*. Having tracked reforms in the countryside through the reports of local correspondents to newspapers and journals in Moscow and St. Petersburg, Engelgardt had reason to hope that his journey would bring him to a rural Russia that reflected the progressive and optimistic currents of thought and activity prevailing ten years into the era of the Great Reforms.

Dorogobuzhskii District, Smolensk Province

Everything was covered with snow, everything was frozen, and if it were not for the smoke coming out of the snow-covered izbas which flashed by along the sides of the track, it would have been possible to think you were riding through uninhabited tundra. I looked at these little izbas and I wondered how they could live there, how I was going to live, what I was going to do, how I would farm, if from the first day I already felt that I did not have the strength to endure this terrible cold.

A. N. Engelgardt, "Iz derevni, IV" (1874)

Dorogobuzhskii District, Smolensk Province, became the setting for Engelgardt's future activity and the letters he wrote to *Notes of the Fatherland* and *Herald of Europe*. It was a suitable location to serve as a case study on Russian agriculture, for it lay at the crossroads of two major economic regions, was primarily a grain-producing area, and revealed many of the characteristics of gentry and peasant farming in the post-Emancipation period.

Engelgardt's letters accurately described the patterns of farming and landholding in the region. Cultivation in the province continued according to the traditional methods and crops of the pre-Emancipation era. The vast majority of households continued to farm according to the three-field system for the entire period up to the turn of the century.[22] In this system, arable land was divided each year into three fields: one for summer crops, one for winter crops, and one left fallow. This meant that one third of the available plough land always lay fallow. Only 58 percent of the land in Smolensk Province was under cultivation in 1881, a result of the reduction of farming by gentry landowners, extensively described in Engelgardt's letters.[23] Rye was the primary crop. In Dorogobuzhskii District hemp was the chief commercial crop, although flax began to take hold in the 1890s, not least because of Engelgardt's efforts in this area.[24]

The distribution of land in Smolensk Province and Dorogobuzhskii District illustrated a general trend in central Russia, the shift of landholding out of gentry hands on a grand scale, and much of the land the landowners sold was bought by peasants.[25] Following the Emancipation in 1861, peasants in Smolensk Province received among the largest land allotments in the Central Industrial Region, which included such other provinces as Moscow, Vladimir, Tver, and Iaroslavl. In 1877, former proprietary serfs (as opposed to state peasants, peasants on crown lands, and house servants) held allotments of 4.01 desiatinas[26] on the average, whereas those in Moscow Province held only 2.96.[27] Former proprietary serfs constituted 93.7 percent of the peasants in Dorogobuzhskii District. The maximum allotment for the district, 4.5 desiatinas, was the highest in the province, and fully 85.7 percent of the peasants received this amount or more.[28]

However, the "generosity" of the landowners in granting these allotments was a recognition of the inferior quality and low value of the land. Many calculated that the excessive payments in land they could receive through the redemption process would provide greater income than the land itself. In a process whose efforts Engelgardt describes fully and elegantly in his letters, the landowners protected their financial interests by slicing away critical pasture, forest, and meadowlands from the peasants' pre-Emancipation holdings. These lands were known as "cutoffs." Almost two thirds of the peasants of Dorogobuzhskii District lost these valuable lands and found themselves compelled to provide labor for their previous landlord in exchange for their use.

The setting for Engelgardt's letters thus exhibited many of the key features of post-Emancipation Russian agriculture and the position of the freed peasantry: large tracts of abandoned gentry lands, peasant lands of poor quality, cultivation through the three-field system of farming, de facto dependence of the peasantry on gentry landowners due to the role of "cutoffs," and the accelerated transfer of land from the gentry to the peasantry twenty years after the Emancipation. Engelgardt took note of all of these developments and offered anecdotes and analysis to explain their importance for developing Russia.

The Letters: Their Context and Impact

These are not articles following a certain style or a set pattern; they are simply, one can say, a conversation: a "good man," a farmer, sits during his free time and holds forth in a friendly way. He is not constrained by the subject or its treatment, and immediately following a page full of the deepest and liveliest humor, one comes upon another where the author, the rascal, is raised to sincere pathos. . . .

Sergei Sharapov, "Schastlivyi ugolok" (1881)

Engelgardt's first eleven letters appeared in *Notes of the Fatherland*, the premier progressive journal of the day. It was one of several so-called thick journals that published literary works, articles on economic and political issues, and translations of foreign literature. These journals had been central to the emergence of the Russian intelligentsia in the first half of the nineteenth century and continued to serve as a forum for public debate over issues of national importance. Each prominent thick journal had an identifiable position in the spectrum of nineteenth-century Russian social and political thought. *Notes of the Fatherland*, under the direction of the "poet of the people" Nikolai Alekseevich Nekrasov and the liberal satirist and critic Mikhail Evgrafovich Saltykov-Shchedrin, was the home of Populist literati, zemstvo activists, ethnographers, and legal scholars. *Herald of Europe*, in which the twelfth letter appeared following the government's closing of *Notes of the Fatherland*, was consistently the organ of liberal members of Russian educated society.

At the time Engelgardt's letters were appearing in *Notes of the Fatherland*, the journal had a readership of roughly one hundred thousand.[29] This readership was made up largely of "a curious middle stratum of specialists and administrators, many of whom worked for central and local government authorities."[30] Materials on the peasant question, and Engelgardt's series in particular, were of great interest to the middle layer of Russian society and government as these elements "struggled with the conditions of Russian backwardness, as their attempts to improve life in the cities and the countryside or merely to live what they considered a civilized life collided with the policies of autocracy."[31] As R. J. Ware has stated, the journal "existed to educate and enlighten the elite that they might then go out and bring education and enlightenment to the people."[32] Radicalized students and rural activists also looked to the journal for inspiration and support.[33] The readers of *Notes of the Fatherland* were thus seekers; they sought information on rural Russia and guidance on how to make use of that information.

Engelgardt's letters "From the Country" offered a full measure of both in an inviting style. They had significant impact on the public debate over the "peasant question" and the "agrarian question" during his lifetime, and continued to serve as an authoritative source on rural social and economic systems into the twentieth century. Much of their influence resulted naturally from the fame of the author, a man who counted among his correspondence major figures in the world of Russian science and letters. They were equally influential due to their reception as accurate and true in an intellectual climate where positivism, empiricism, and an interest in Darwinian theory dominated intellectual life.[34] Finally, the fact that Engelgardt continued to publish articles on science and agriculture at a dizzying pace ensured that his descriptions of life in the countryside would find a ready audience who would take his account seriously.

The most obvious group to be influenced by Engelgardt's letters were the eighty or so young members of the intelligentsia who heeded his summons to the countryside and went to his estate to learn the practice of farming by living and working side by side with the peasants of Batishchevo. Several students wrote reminiscences of their experience and of the impact of Engelgardt's ideas

on their personal decisions.[35] Engelgardt's fellow chemists in Petersburg continued to follow his activities, to assist his experimentation with phosphates, and
to visit him on the estate.[36] His writings were also discussed at the highest levels
of the Imperial government in early 1881 when Lachinov and Mendeleev
approached the Minister of the Interior, General Loris-Melikov, about lifting
Engelgardt's punishment, and Loris-Melikov's comments revealed his familiar-
ity with the letters and Engelgardt's activities in general on Batishchevo.[37]

The letters were clearly the mainstay of *Notes of the Fatherland* during the
1870s. Saltykov-Shchedrin wrote Engelgardt a steady stream of pleas to write,
write, write *anything* for the journal to publish, so critical were the letters to the
success of the journal during these years.[38] The rival Slavophile journal, *Rus'*,
was equally anxious to publish Engelgardt's work, despite the fact that he
openly ridiculed Sergei Sharapov, then agricultural editor of the journal, as a
"know-nothing."[39] The success of the editions of the collected letters further
attested to the authority they held in public opinion during Engelgardt's life and
following his death.

For Lenin and Soviet historians, the primary value of Engelgardt's letters was
their description of the emergence of the figure of the *kulak,* the impoverishment of the peasantry through gentry control of cutoff lands, and the dissolution
of patriarchal structures, particularly the communal, extended household. Even
Lenin, however, paused to admire Engelgardt's style and to recognize this
aspect of the letters as the key to their enormous popularity and authority.[40]

While Engelgardt has traditionally been identified as a Populist, indeed
serving as a case study for Richard Wortman's study of Populism, his peers
were less quick to categorize him as such. Sharapov went so far as to say that
he belonged to no political camp, that he was clearly not a liberal, a conserva-
tive, or a socialist of any description.[41] The difficulty in finding a pigeonhole
for Engelgardt resulted from both his positive and negative statements in the
letters and elsewhere. While his defense of the peasantry and advocacy of
communal systems of agriculture suggested he was a Populist, his harsh criticism of peasant women, of kulaks, of the exploitative urges of the average
peasant, and his refusal to attribute a superior, naturally communal morality
to the peasantry made such a pat label inappropriate. Similarly, his attitude
toward liberal, would-be progressive reforms seemed wholly critical, even
disparaging at first glance, but the attentive reader will recognize that Engelgardt was very much a proponent of enlightenment, education, and expanded
local self-governance, as long as such reforms were introduced in the spirit of
partnership with the peasantry rather than tutelage over them. Thus, in his
defense of the ability of the peasants to innovate and to prosper, he took on
the prominent liberal K. D. Kavelin, who had joined in the general chorus of
criticism of the peasant by repeating the charge of his "laziness, drunkenness,
and untrustworthy character. . . ."[42]

The unique authority of Engelgardt's letters during his lifetime and as a
historical document since was enhanced by this lack of a solely political
agenda and his consistent grounding in the specific, the observed, the empirical. Much of the information about life around Batishchevo that he includes in

the letters came from his farmer's journal, in which he recorded developments on the estate in short entries at the end of each day. These notes and the statistics they contained were especially valuable in Engelgardt's preparation of the final two letters, in which he evaluated agricultural and economic progress in villages surrounding his estate.[43] As an eyewitness account written by an observer thoroughly committed to the principles of scientific objectivity and empiricism, the letters offered contemporaries and continue to provide historians and students anecdotal evidence of the best sort.

As a critique of the popular views of rural life propounded not only in the capitals of Moscow and Petersburg, but equally in the reports of local correspondents from the provinces, Engelgardt also issued an important caveat to historians on the accuracy of the press as a true reflection of life in the countryside. By contrast, his was the privileged vision, he explained, born of intimacy with the land and the people who worked it, and his very insistence on the limited nature of his observations did much to ensure the authority and influence of his account. Throughout the letters Engelgardt displayed a hidebound skepticism about virtually everything. In this he was similar to Henry David Thoreau at Walden Pond, who hailed nature in an era of industrialization and growing population density in New England. In the same spirit, Engelgardt declared that, in an era of nascent industrialization, urbanization, and professionalization, the future of Russia lay in the countryside and in the hands of peasant landowners. He made it his mission in these letters to debunk popular notions of Russia's progressive development, hopes for reform originating in state commissions, zemstvo boards, and professional societies, and schemes to bring more scientific, rational farming to Russia.

The Letters: Major Themes and Contributions to the Study of Rural Russia

> I am not a statistician, I am not a political economist, or a publicist, but just a farmer who farms, moving in a little village and describing what I have observed. Everything that I write relates to that small locality I know; if it turns out that it is the same in other places, then that is because the same conditions give birth to the same phenomena. Therefore, I ask the reader to be undemanding toward these village sketches.
>
> A. N. Engelgardt, "Iz derevni, VII (Okonchanie)" (1879)

As a reporter from the countryside, Engelgardt was not consistent in his appraisal of the conditions or the residents there over the course of his letters. During their fifteen-year span, Engelgardt experienced contradictory reactions and took varying lessons from his observations. The letters do not constitute a smoothly evolving position on the "peasant question" but rather Engelgardt's incremental epiphanies in the countryside. His shifting portrayal of the peasants around his estate, ranging from positive images of his housekeeper, steward, and manservant to harshly negative portraits of peasant women and village usurers, frustrated some of his readers who looked to him for a more stable vision of "the peasant."[44]

He offered contradictory appraisals not only of "the peasant" but also of the "agrarian question," that is, of prospects for and appropriate approaches to agricultural reform. Here again, he began with a nearly unalloyed respect for the practical wisdom of the peasant, only to return at the end of his life to a renewed faith in applied science in the form of mineral fertilizers as a panacea for Russian farming. Engelgardt did not acknowledge his changing opinions; no doubt he saw no need to do so. Instead he persisted in avowals of his fealty to the facts as he saw them and to the empirical data he religiously recorded at the end of each day's labor. By offering such fluid analysis to his readers, he conveyed the critical message that there was no one truth about the Russian village as it evolved in response to the changing conditions of the post-Emancipation era.

Engelgardt's letters "From the Country" closely followed the developments in his life on his estate, which was made up of three major activities. The first in order of importance and the length of time it constituted his primary occupation was managing his farm and turning it into a profitable enterprise over the period 1871–1883. The second was engagement in the Populist movement as a prophet and teacher who both summoned young people to the countryside and offered his estate as a training ground for would-be educated agriculturalists, primarily in the late 1870s. The third was research and experimentation with fertilizers, especially mineral fertilizers and phosphates in particular, beginning in 1884 and continuing until the end of his life. Throughout his twenty-two years on Batishchevo, Engelgardt was a prolific writer. Each area of activity spawned a considerable amount of record-keeping, correspondence, and published work on his observations and results.

In the letters, these interests shaped his observations and focus. The first three letters were the most descriptive, dwelling on vignettes of rural life, on peasant personalities, village customs and institutions. As he later wrote, his education in the ways of the peasantry came as a by-product of his farming interests, the necessity of working with peasants nearby to turn his neglected family estate into a profitable enterprise. Engelgardt's preoccupation with farming was clear from the opening lines of the first letter to the closing lines of the twelfth. He soon discovered that his life as a landowner whose income came from his estate was as closely defined by agricultural concerns as that of any peasant. The cycle of his daily life, from one season to the next, emerged in response to the climate, the soil, the crops he chose to plant, and the livestock he decided to raise. His total immersion in farming made Engelgardt an insider in the rural world, to the extent that this was possible for an educated member of the nobility. It also brought him face-to-face with the problems and requirements of Russian agriculture in the northern non–Black Earth Region. His dependence on farming income was one very compelling motivation to involve himself with the farm; his determination to disprove the naysayers of Russian society who dismissed the possibility of farming was another.

The challenge that awaited Engelgardt on Batishchevo when he arrived in the winter of 1871 was enormous. He found the estate in nearly total neglect, the manor house and farming structures in serious disrepair, the neighboring peasants disheartened and in extreme poverty. His estate contained 618 desiatinas of land, of which he found only 88 to be under cultivation.[45] He found few livestock and consequently little manure. He also found that the peasants continued to farm according to the three-field system.[46] He had frequently heard complaints in Petersburg about the impossibility of making a go of farming in Russia, especially in the non–Black Earth Region. He described these complaints: "But why is it that it is impossible to farm and do well? Always and everywhere, the answer to this question is the same: it is impossible to do well because workers are expensive, they work badly, they get drunk, they don't fulfill their contracts, they are lazy, and so on. In other words, it is impossible to manage because we do not have serfdom."[47] Engelgardt refused to accept this explanation and placed his hopes in a more rational system of farming that would alter the face of Russian agriculture. To succeed he had to involve himself actively in every aspect of farming, live a modest life, and establish positive relations with the neighboring peasants on whose labor he depended.

The separation from his urban, professional existence and the reality of a neglected estate in the dead of winter made Engelgardt's first year on Batishchevo one of psychological and physical challenge and adaptation. He had to make an abrupt transition from the public sphere of high culture to the private sphere of the mundane concerns of living off his farm. Having spent all of his adult life in the stimulating world of educated, privileged, and powerful men living and working in the capital of the Russian Empire, he now found himself living with the laboring, uneducated men and women who inhabited Russia's villages. His concerns shifted from scholarly journals, lectures, and societies to pickled cucumbers, pot cheese, manure, and flax fleas. The mundane details of village life became his focus and provided the material for the information he provided in the letters. Engelgardt conveyed the atmosphere of rural life most effectively by describing his own daily routine, his dress, diet, interests, tasks, and social interaction. He lived an isolated life, shaped primarily by the climate and the demands of farming. His wife, Anna Nikolaevna Engelgardt, remained in St. Petersburg with their three children. She was a prominent feminist who supported herself by translating foreign literary works, which appeared in the same journals as her husband's articles. It is unclear when they became estranged, or why. Engelgardt once offered her residence and complete independence from his interference on the estate when he heard through mutual acquaintances that she was having financial difficulties, but she refused.[48] The children often spent school vacations with their father in Batishchevo, and his daughter, Vera, would eventually take over its management. Visitors arrived throughout his twenty-two years of exile, and in the late 1870s young students lived as agricultural workers on the estate. For the majority of his exile, however, and particularly in his first year, Engelgardt found his only companions to be his house servants, his dog, and his cats.

The deepest impressions during his first year were of cold, poverty, and the need to alter the system of farming on his estate in order to survive, much less to prosper. His adoption of peasant dress represented one example of his vulnerability to the climate. More evocative and convincing, however, was his description of the pleasure of sitting out in the sun on a January day following four months of nearly total darkness. His daily routine followed the sun. Farming was an all-consuming, demanding occupation that required the total commitment of Engelgardt and his peasants in order to eke out an existence in the harsh, miserly environment in which they lived.

The challenge of this struggle and the fragility of the systems which the rural population had developed through generations of labor emerged as central elements of his eyewitness account. Engelgardt's approach was clearly shaped by Darwinian theory, especially the concepts of natural selection and the struggle for existence. In the early letters, and particularly in the first two, he focused on the struggle for existence against material or natural conditions and explained many peasant customs as adaptive behavior in that struggle.[49] Psychologically shaken by the physical challenge of winter in the provinces and intellectually prepared to perceive systems for survival, Engelgardt stressed environmental factors in shaping the peasant mentality. In the first letter we find the outline of Engelgardt's vision of the peasant economy as a subsistence economy that functioned according to an internal logic or rationale, which made him one of the first exponents of the model of the peasant as a rational economic actor.

He stressed here the fragile equilibrium of subsistence and the constant presence of the specter of hunger. His lengthy description of the custom of begging for crusts of bread among the peasant population served to illustrate both the tenuous nature of their lives and the community system of mutual aid that evolved to protect each member from starvation. This system of begging for crusts of bread was one example of the many institutions of village life that reflected the essential pragmatism of the peasants. The practical knowledge of the Russian peasant gained Engelgardt's admiration quickly and fully. He offered fond portraits in his first letter of the peasants who figured most prominently in his daily life on Batishchevo, from his housekeeper to the children of his herdsman, and explained their special virtues. Avdotia's domestic know-how, Ivan's managerial skill, the "old woman's" golden touch with the animals, little Andrei's bravery, all of these qualities contributed to the Russian peasants' ability to survive in the closed world of the village.

Furthermore, Engelgardt presented their practical knowledge as superior to that of book learning. Throughout the first eight letters he maintained that the peasants' knowledge, acquired through experience, was much more valuable than the volumes on agriculture written by German and Russian experts that he had brought with him to the estate. "Why is it," he asks in the third letter, "that a vibrant chord is felt in the articles on horticulture and market gardening, but from articles on agronomy, there is only the smell of moribund, castrated inertia?"

In the second letter, Engelgardt's description expanded to include two important post-Reform local institutions, the local organs of self-rule (the zemstvo) and the justices of the peace. In passages saturated with sarcasm, he narrates his visit to the local assembly of electors for noble delegates to the zemstvo, where the chief occupations were eating and drinking. He concludes his description of this trip with a sketch of a meeting of the justices of the peace to consider cases sent up for appeal. Here, Engelgardt concludes, display and staging were the primary concerns of the judges, who overwhelmed but did not serve the peasant plaintiffs or impress upon them any respect for the law. Even as early as his second year in the countryside, thus, Engelgardt had taken on the peasants' perspective, viewing both the zemstvo and the justices of the peace from the vantage point of the needs and concerns of the village, rather than from that of educated society and its lofty aspirations for reform.

The fourth and fifth letters, while still heavily descriptive and continuing the theme of criticism of would-be enlightenment of the peasants and agricultural reform (in this case through an agricultural exhibition), were transitional, marking Engelgardt's shift to a more analytical approach in his advocacy of the peasantry. Whereas the first three letters strove to impress upon the urban reader the challenges of subsistence farming as an example of the struggle for existence, in the fourth, Engelgardt began to explore causes for the peasants' poverty beyond environmental factors, and approached the topic of the failure of gentry farming in the post-Emancipation era.

In response to the widespread complaints about the instability and high cost of paid labor, that is, the cost of paying the peasants rather than enjoying their labor for free as under serfdom, Engelgardt turned the tables and indicted not the peasants but gentry landowners for the decline of Russian agriculture following the Emancipation. He ridiculed their objections to what he termed "extraordinarily low" wages and raised the issue he would explore fully beginning in the ninth letter—the leverage the landowners enjoyed through their control of cutoff lands, and their lazy, negligent attitude toward farming in general. In this letter as well, Engelgardt hinted at a weakness he perceived in the peasant economy, namely, peasant resistance to collective labor, "lack of unity in their actions." While his gentle, affectionate descriptions of the eccentricities of his servant, Savelich, and of his dog, Lyska, maintained the atmosphere that Sharapov described of the gentleman farmer's pleasant chat, the fourth and fifth letters reveal the tensions that Engelgardt was beginning to feel as he farmed for profit and depended on peasant labor to meet that end. These tensions are especially clear in Engelgardt's description of peasant women who processed flax for him on the estate, and thus served as an essential factor in his success or failure. He ascribed to them features he excoriated and was anxious not to find among the male peasants: individualism and lust for money.

The sixth letter marked a caesura, as it were, in the development of this theme, which would reach its climax in the seventh letter. The sixth letter offered the rural inhabitant's perspective on developments in the Balkans leading up to the Russo-Turkish War, on mobilization, and on peasant attitudes toward the war. Here Engelgardt was entering a public debate about the level of the peasants' comprehension of the war effort and of their conscious patriotism, a debate in which Tolstoy, in *Anna Karenina,* and Dostoevsky, in *Diary of a Writer,* were the other prominent contributors. Engelgardt's conclusion was that peasants were both highly confused about the diplomatic details of the war and sincerely patriotic about the national cause. His tone shifted on the peasant woman, offering an alternative to the image of the baba as individualist—the baba as victim, victim of the war effort both through the loss of the men in her household and through the failure of the state to provide any support in their absence. Here Engelgardt moved abruptly from biting criticism of the horse levy in Smolensk to the pathos of the abandoned wife and mother.

The seventh letter offers Engelgardt's most extended defense of populist principles in the series. He opens with a discussion of one example of the Russian peasant labor cooperative called the *artel',*[50] presenting it as a model of the virtues of collective effort rather than individual pursuit of profit in labor. He continues his advocacy of collectivism over individualism in his analysis of extended peasant households. His discussion of the advantages of large households, made up of several generations working and living together as one economic unit, was consistent with the attitude held by most educated Russians that large families prospered, while small families almost inevitably fell into financial ruin.[51] Like his contemporaries, Engelgardt was alarmed by the increase in family divisions, in the hiving off of younger sons and brothers into nuclear family units, living and farming separately. While lacking the type of statistical analysis that would dominate this discussion in the press, Engelgardt's explication of this issue was one of the best in exploring the personal concerns of the various actors. His conclusions on this subject were striking in their harsh portrayal of peasant women as the agents of disintegration of the patriarchal household as an economic unit and of the morality of the village as a whole. While he made a rather feeble effort to provide the economic rationale for the financial motivations of the female peasant, he revealed again his aversion to individualism and the urge for money, and contributed to a widespread negative view of peasant women as the agents of destruction in the Russian village.[52] In the second half of the seventh letter, Engelgardt's Populism took the very recognizable form of urging educated young Russians to return to the land, to join him in the countryside, where they could learn to "work like muzhiks" and become part of his new model for farming in Russia: collectives of educated Russians working side by side in efficient agriculture with peasants. The seventh letter thus consists of Engelgardt's rather peculiar admixture of admiration for certain peasant institutions because of their collective spirit, aversion to evidence of individualism in the village, and hope that educated Russians might join in his enterprise and then serve as model farmers for peasants after having learned how to work like peasants themselves.

Something very important was happening in Engelgardt's mind and in his reporting from the countryside. He was moving away from the peasants. While he maintained optimism over the peasants' ability to adapt and to move Russian agriculture forward, he was becoming increasingly convinced of the need for the educated example to serve as a model for would-be peasant innovators. Although he had by no means fallen back into the arms of agronomy, or of gentry farming as he observed it around him, he had returned to a reliance on education, reason, and the leading role of the educated classes in Russia. While in his remaining letters he would continue to mock local officialdom and bureaucratized forms of tutelage over the peasantry, in the seventh letter he had already stepped onto the path that would lead him back to science and away from simple farming for profit.

He diverged from this path in the eighth letter to make his contribution to the tradition of describing the farce of local bureaucrats in rural Russia and to offer a public confession of his decline into alcoholism as a product of his subjection to the surveillance of such petty figures. True to his self-assigned role as curmudgeon, he ridiculed the efforts of zemstvo activists, agronomists, entomologists, and administrators to teach peasants how to take care of themselves. He remained true in the letters to his skepticism toward bureaucratic measures for reform, although he would himself serve as a zemstvo delegate responsible for agricultural issues from 1884 to 1886.[53]

The final four letters represent Engelgardt's gradual removal of himself from the village and back into his scholarly persona. He returned to a more detached, rational, analytical approach to rural life and questions of Russian agriculture. While the ninth through twelfth letters did not contain the entertaining vignettes of the earlier letters, they did offer valuable essays on factors shaping Russian farming, the rural economy, and gentry-peasant relations. For students of land reform, these are the most informative of the letters. They also contain some critical sections on such issues as the peasants' attitude toward the land and private property in general; an extensive sketch of the village strongman and usurer, the kulak; and descriptions of several villages that successfully innovated through the assistance of the Peasant Land Bank after it was established in 1883.

In the final two letters, Engelgardt returned to one of his primary scientific interests of twenty years earlier, the value of mineral fertilizers for farming in Russia. He moved between the eleventh letter in 1882 and the twelfth in 1887 from a nearly total dismissal of their potential role to unmitigated enthusiasm for their applicability to the non–Black Earth Region in Russia. In the intervening years, he had taken up the exploration of phosphate deposits and had begun a series of experiments on his estate that constituted his main activity until the end of his life. The letters conclude on a generally optimistic note as Engelgardt focuses on the successes of the application of mineral fertilizers and of peasants who innovate and invest in land they are able to purchase as private property. There is no proper closure in the final letter, which instead trails away in a characteristic ellipsis. This suggests that Engelgardt thought he might publish some more letters from the countryside, but by the late 1880s, public interest had begun to veer away from the "peasant question" to other avenues of Russia's development.[54]

Conclusion

Recalling how my friends expressed their regrets over my misfortune when fate threw me into the country, I involuntarily smile. Now I thank fate . . . Here in this free air, in these open spaces of fields and forests . . . here, in the country, I have come to know the sweetness of freedom, I have found peace, happiness, I have felt the earth under my feet, I have become a son of my native land, I have come to know her strength, her power, her wealth, her invincibility.

A. N. Engelgardt, *O khoziaistve* (1888)

At the end of his life, Engelgardt found himself fully in the embrace of the Imperial government again, primarily because of his work with mineral fertilizers. Twenty years to the day after he received his dismissal from his position at the Agricultural Institute from the Ministry of State Domains, he was awarded a stipend of five thousand rubles by the same ministry to support further experimentation on his estate.[55] Engelgardt died two years later, on January 21, 1893, as he prepared to dictate some instructions to his daughter about one of his experiments. His old steward, Ivan, was also present, having rushed to his bedside because "I wanted him to die in my arms."[56] Despite rapid deterioration of his health, and of his circulation in particular, Engelgardt remained active until the end, demanding to be driven around the various fields during the last days of his life. Engelgardt as an elderly man, with flowing hair, bouncing over cultivated land in a simple wagon to inspect the progress of his crops, gesturing with hands that had already gone numb, is an appropriate image. For he was a rare example of persistent optimism, energy, and engagement. In a memorial speech delivered at the Historical Museum in Moscow, Sergei Sharapov termed this quality joy, a seemingly limitless joy in life in all its manifestations.[57]

Following Engelgardt's death, Batishchevo became a state-run agricultural experimental station. It continued to serve this function under the Soviet government until it was completely destroyed by German troops during World War II. As part of the recent revival of interest in Engelgardt, a memorial statue of him is under construction in Batishchevo. Engelgardt's numerous writings, and his twelve letters "From the Country" above all others, constitute the most enduring monument to his life and service. Through them, readers come to know Russia, the Russia of the peasant hut, the rye field, the threshing barn, the country kitchen, the peasant wedding, the gentry assembly, the crowded train station during mobilization for war, and the village court. Through his eyes, we gain an intimacy with rural Russia of the 1870s and 1880s, with its particular challenges and promise.

Letter I

✉ In this first letter, Engelgardt draws his readers into life on his estate by describing the details of one winter day, introducing several peasant characters living on his estate, and presenting and analyzing two institutions of village life.[1] The structure of the letter, like the structure of Engelgardt's life on his estate and of his peasants' life as well, is cyclical. He opens and closes the letter with his descent into sleep filled with dreams about projects for improving farming on his estate. He thus frames his account with the interests that have come to consume him and to define his daily life: firewood, grain, livestock, and manure. He conveys to his educated peers in such places as Moscow and St. Petersburg the transformation he has undergone during his first year on Batishchevo. One important symbol of that transformation is his shift to peasant dress. This shift carried special resonance in Russian culture, where dress was coded to signal the individual's membership in a particular social estate. That Aleksandr Nikolaevich Engelgardt, professor of chemistry and a member of the nobility, was stomping around his estate in a sheepskin coat and felt boots was a metamorphosis that broke numerous social conventions. Equally important, however, Engelgardt reveals his transformed sensibilities as a rural inhabitant who follows the cycle of the sun as closely as his peasants must in organizing their life as farmers.

In addition to presenting the setting of his new life, Engelgardt introduces several peasant characters who live and work for him on Batishchevo. In Engelgardt's description, these figures possess particular skills that contribute to the success of his farm. By devoting as much space as he does to the peasants on his estate, he gives them legitimacy and authority. His respect for their skills is encapsulated in the statement he makes about his housekeeper, Avdotia: "It is I who am learning from her." In this way he establishes a theme that will run throughout his letters from the countryside: peasants are practiced, knowledgeable, even superior farmers from whom educated specialists have much to learn.

In the final two sections of the letter, Engelgardt offers vignettes of daily life in the village, which establish a second central theme of the letters: the fragile equilibrium of the peasants' subsistence farming, which both encourages systems of mutual aid and injects economic considerations into personal relationships. The custom of begging for crusts of bread, practiced widely by ordinary peasants in times of want, he explains, is a constant necessity in the tenuous economy of peasant farming in post-Emancipation Russia. While Engelgardt was neither the first nor the last observer to describe this practice, his description was one of the most effective in conveying an image of peasant Russia as a population of near-starving people consigned to alternating roles of charity and begging to survive the frequent disasters of drought, crop failure, and famine.

The economic imperatives of such subsistence farming also do much to explain the incident Ivan recounts to Engelgardt during his evening report. Khvorosia's tale reveals not only the rather flexible sexual mores of the village but also the economic considerations attached to them. Khvorosia's primary significance to her husband is clearly not as his monogamous sexual partner but as a partner in the labor of the family economy. When one of her lovers beats her, the village elders order him to compensate her husband by paying him money and providing a female laborer to replace her until she is able to work again. It should be noted that Khvorosia receives no compensation for her injuries.

The letter closes with Engelgardt's solitary evening in his house. Despite transformations in his dress and daily habits, he remains isolated ultimately from his peasants, turning to a French novel and a dinner where his only companions are his cats, to whom he tries to teach the proper manners of refined dining. He leaves his readers with a final impression of the cold and dark closing in on him, broken only by his dog's signal that the wolves are edging toward him in the night.

⊠ ⊠ ⊠

Daily Life with the Peasants on My Estate

You want me to write you about our rural way of life. I am fulfilling your request, but I warn you, that I absolutely cannot think, speak, or write about anything else except about farming. All of my interests, all of the interests of the people I see daily, are focused on firewood, grain, livestock, manure . . . Nothing else matters to us.

On February 5, I celebrated the year anniversary of my arrival in the countryside. This is a description of my winter day.

. . . After supper, I go to bed, and as I fall asleep, I dream of how in three years I will have thirteen desiatinas[2] of clover on the meadows where I now grow flax. In the dream, I see a herd of Kholmogor cattle,[3] bred from a bull promised me by a certain livestock dealer, grazing on the stubble of the clover. I wake up thinking about how to buy hay a bit more cheaply.

I wake up, light a candle, and knock on the wall—that means the master has awakened and he wants his tea. "I hear you!" Avdotia answers and she begins to putter with the samovar.[4] While the baba[5] sets up the samovar, I lie in bed, smoke a cigarette, and daydream about what an excellent plot of land there will be when the woods I have just sold are cut down. Having had my daydream and my cigarette, I put on my felt boots and sheepskin coat.[6] My house is rather poor: when you heat up the stoves, it is impossibly hot by evening, by morning it is cold, there is a draft from under the floor, a draft from the door, the windows have frosted over; it is just like being in a peasant izba.[7] At first, I wore a German suit, but I quickly came to the conclusion that would not do and began to wear felt boots and a sheepskin coat. They are warm and comfortable. Finally, the baba, yawning, brings in the tea. She is dressed, just as I am, in felt boots and a sheepskin coat.

"Good morning, Avdotia. Well, how are things?"

"Oh, so-so."

"Is it cold?"

"Not especially. The weather's a little stirred up."

"Did Ivan go to the cattle yard?"

"He went out a while ago. Probably already fed them."

"Why was Lyska barking last night?"

"God only knows. Probably nothing. The wolves are probably coming up close."

I order lunch. Avdotia, the wife of the steward, Ivan, is my housekeeper. She fixes my meals, does the laundry, she handles the household matters. She also milks the cows, manages the dairy, makes the butter, strains the curd for pot cheese. Avdotia is the most important person on my female staff, and all of the other peasant women are under her command, with the exception of "the old woman,"[8] who is the mistress of the dining hall.

Lunch is ordered. The baba leaves. I drink my tea and daydream about how good it will be when the low areas on the wastelands and empty fields are cleaned out this spring, which will improve the mowing and bring more hay.

I continue to drink tea, smoke, and dream. The steward Ivan has arrived; he's wearing felt boots and a sheepskin coat.

"Hello, Ivan. Well, and how are things?"

"Everything's fine, praise God. We fed the livestock. The brown and white pied cow calved."

"Oh? Safely?"

"Praise God. She had a normal delivery. We put it in the small cattle shed."

"And is it a female?"

"A female, a little brown and white pied one. A nice calf."

I get my notebook out of the desk and record the newborn calf in the list of current cattle: "No. 5, 1872: a brown and white pied female calf born on February 8, 1872 to No. 10" and look on the calendar to see when the calf will be six weeks old, and I note that in the book.

"So, they ate the evening feed well?"

"They ate it up, only the grass was left. The horned stock'll really eat the hay from the wasteland, you'll see for yourself: nothing'll be left over but grass, 'cause there's no straw in it."

"Why was Lyska barking last night?"

"Oh, it was nothing. Probably the wolves were coming close."

Silence. There is nothing else to discuss. Ivan, waiting as long as politeness requires and seeing that there is nothing else to say, takes the tea dishes and goes out to drink tea with Avdotia. [. . .]

Morning has broken. The confectioner, Savelich, has come to heat up the stoves. At my house, a confectioner heats up the stoves, a real confectioner who knows how to make real confections. This confectioner wound up here by chance. Sometime, about fifty or sixty years ago—in his old age, the confectioner himself has forgotten how old he is—Savelich studied the confectioner's trade in one of the best confectionaries in Moscow. He was a pastry chef in one of the Moscow clubs, then he was taken to the countryside by a landowner where he held various jobs: he was cook, driver, bartender, the footman, dishwasher, he was in charge of the stoves, and so forth. Savelich did not manage to marry, he did not settle down with a family and a house-hold, he did not acquire property—when he was with his masters he always received board—as he grew old, he went deaf, and in an unfortunate acci-dent, he lost his jaw.[. . .] Eleven years ago, Savelich was emancipated and since then, he has lived more and more around the church. At first he was a church elder, then he went with a prayer book to collect for the church. For the last two years, Savelich has lived like a fly-by-night, making ends meet from day to day, somehow or other. In the summer and fall, he hired himself out to the *muzhiks*[9] to guard the church, then each household in turn gave him food and paid him five *kopeks*[10] a night. And sometimes he made fruit pre-serves for merchants in town, for which he also got small change. But in the winter, the most difficult time for Savelich, he lived on the savings he had earned in the summer. He took room and board with some muzhik he knew, and in exchange for the room, helped the muzhik with household chores: he went for the water, he chopped firewood, he rocked the cradle. An old man in the house is never superfluous. He fed himself by his confectioner's trade: in the summer, he would buy several pounds of sugar with his small savings, make it into fruit drops, and carry them around to the villages (without a trader's permit, of course). He would give some old woman candy for her grandchildren, she would feed him. Of course, he always ate badly, sometimes he would go hungry, but he says that he never asked for charity. Savelich wound up at my house in this way: I went by the cottage where the workers live sometime during the high fast last year and I saw a tall, thin, bald, old man, emaciated from bad food, sitting in only a shirt and shaking tobacco into a wooden dish. "Who's that?" I asked. "Oh, the old man," the head of the house replied, "he came because he knew us; I gave him tobacco to grind in exchange for lunch with us." Toward evening, while reporting on the farm, the steward began to talk about the old man; he said the old man was a former house serf, that he was a confectioner, that he had lived with gentry, that he knew proper ways. He asked permission to invite the old man to the Easter holiday of breaking the fast, "and he can help Avdotia prepare the holiday table in exchange," the steward added. I, of course, agreed. Avdotia was ecstatic that the old man would come before the holiday and help her prepare everything properly, as it was done for gentlemen. That everything should be proper, as among the gentry, that was Avdotia's hobbyhorse.

When I settled in the countryside, I resolved not to retain drivers, or cooks, or footmen, that is, all that constitutes the accoutrements of landlords' houses, all that was one cause of the financial ruin of the middle gentry who did not know how to manage their lives any differently after the Emancipation than before. Which was one of the reasons why the gentry abandoned their farms and ran off into service.[11] Having settled in the countryside, I set about my life in a new way.

I found a steward on my estate; the steward, of course, had a wife who managed his household, prepared his meals, washed his laundry. I moved the steward with his baba from their izba to the house and made Avdotia my housekeeper, cook, laundress. There was nothing for me to teach her about domestic agriculture, that is, the dairy, feeding the cattle, and so forth—it is I who am learning from her and I must confess that I learned rather more from her than from books which say that "the milk cow has a light head with thin horns, thin legs, a long and thin tail, soft and tender skin and coat, in general, the whole appearance is *feminine* and so forth." But in kitchen matters, I helped her somewhat. With my assistance (I'm not a chemist for nothing; even in cooking matters I can understand the essential), Avdotia, who possesses unusual culinary skills and diligence, and also the knowledge every baba has on baking bread, making cabbage soup and meat pies, began to cook for me splendidly, as well as making various supplies for the winter: pickles, marinated mushrooms, fish and crayfish conserves, preserves, creamy cheeses. I explained to her that in making syrup from berries, the most important thing is to boil them to the point that, because of the acidity, the crystallized sugar becomes winelike and the syrup thickens so much that no fermentation can take place; I explained that there will be no spoilage in preserves, no mold in pickles, and so forth, as Pasteur showed, if no bacteria of lower organisms fall out of the air into them; I explained the influence of high temperature on bacteria, albumen, and so forth. Avdotia understands all of this splendidly.[. . .]

The confectioner arrived three days before the holiday; he cut up the lamb; I went to the station and bought wheat flour, sandalwood, raisins, and almonds. The cooking began. The confectioner cut decorations for the Easter cake and leg of lamb out of different colors of paper; I, with a fellow chemist friend who had come for a visit from Petersburg for the holiday, made a rose out of rose-colored tea paper, perfumed it with excellent perfume, and put it in the Easter cake. Everything came out wonderfully: the Easter cake, the cheese pudding, the suckling pig, the lamb, and most important, everything was proper and we did not fall on our faces in front of the priests. Avdotia was at the height of bliss and walked around with a shining face, dressed in a bright tunic. Only the confectioner slipped up; he tried to make some kind of sweet English torte, but the torte did not turn out, that is, it turned out very badly. When he noticed the next day that everything had been eaten except for the English torte, the confectioner became so embarrassed that, without saying a word, he went off somewhere and hid.

In the summer, the confectioner lived somewhere at a church, not far away, about ten *versts*[12] from me. I forgot completely about him. Only in August, when I needed a watchman for the winter crops, the potatoes and peas, did I remember the confectioner. Why not, I thought, take him on for the winter—you know he won't eat you out of house and home, and he'll do anything around the house. Since August, the confectioner has lived with me and has turned out to be a very useful person: in the fall, he guarded the peas and potatoes, he drove stray horses off the winter crops, of course he did not catch one trespassing horse (he's old, his body has failed and lost its force because of meager food), but, even so, he is a field watchman. The muzhiks are wary, so do not let their horses loose needlessly, and if one wanders onto the field accidentally, the old man will run it off. In the fall, he caulked the house and put on the storm windows. Now he heats up the stoves, helps Avdotia, cleans up the rooms, disciplines the kittens if they need it, cleans the clothes, washes the dishes, and sometimes he makes candy.[. . .]

Besides the steward, I also have a herdsman, Petr, with his wife Khivra and their children. The herdsman has seven children.[. . .] This entire family, down to and including Soloshka (the youngest), works without rest from morning to night simply to feed themselves.

Petr himself pastures the cattle in the summer from May first to October first; in the winter from October first to May first, he feeds and waters the cattle. His two oldest sons, Varnai (14 years) and Andrei (10 years), help him with this work. In the summer, the herdsman, rising at dawn before the sun is up, drives the cattle into the field and with the help of his two oldest children (there are now 100 head of cattle) pastures them (the younger one, Andrei, usually carries a gun to ward off the wolves). At eleven o'clock, he drives the cattle back to the yard, where they stand until three o'clock. At four o'clock, he drives them into the field again and returns home for the night. And so it goes, day in, day out, for the entire summer, on workdays and holidays, in the heat, rain, and cold. There are no holidays for the herdsman in the summer or in the winter; for him holidays are distinguished from other days of the week by the fact that then and on Sundays he gets a serving (1/100 of a *vedro*)[13] of vodka before his afternoon meal. In the winter the herdsman, again with the help of his two oldest children, feeds and waters the cattle. Rising before daylight, he gives them their first feeding; when it grows light, the babas milk the cows, after which the herdsman waters them, driving each stall to be watered separately. After the watering, he gives them their second feeding, eats lunch, and rests. Toward evening, he waters the cattle a second time and gives them their third feeding for the night. At night during the winter, the herdsman does not have any real peace because, despite freezing cold and blizzard, he must go into the stalls several times to check the cattle, and when the cows begin to calve (in December, January, and February), he must constantly watch over them and always be alert, because it is his responsibility to take the calf and put it in a warm izba. The older sons help with the feeding and even the ten-year-old Andrei works as hard as his strength allows—he harnesses the horse, he helps his brother to put the hay on the wagon—the herdsman Petr himself at this time carries feed to the young cattle because it is necessary to choose the hay for them and one cannot give this task to the children—he leads the horse and distributes the feed among the stalls and puts it in the troughs. Of course, Andrei, as far as he is able, carries small loads of hay; but if only you watched how he bravely walks between the cows, how he shouts at the bull and how the bull fears him, because Andrei carries a knout! [. . .]

The herdsman's wife, Khivra, milks the cows along with Avdotia and the milkmaids, waters the calves, feeds the lambs, prepares meals for her large family—how much bread alone she must bake—she washes and sews for the children. Her older daughter, Aksiuta (12 years), and her younger daughter, Soloshka (6 years), help her with these chores, the younger one's special responsibility is to watch after little Khivra, whom she rocks in the cradle, carries around the yard, amuses, and nurses. Prokhor (8 years) also helps around the farm: he chops wood, and because he is not terribly strong, it takes him all day to chop enough firewood to heat up one stove. Only Pavlik and little Khivra do not do anything.

For all of this the herdsman receives 60 rubles a year, 6 sacks and 6 measures of rye, 2 sacks of oats, 1 and ½ sacks of barley; I cover the feed for the cow and the sheep. He has a small garden which he must cultivate himself; he receives an area for planting one measure of flax and one osmina of potatoes; he receives two portions of vodka—for himself and his wife—on Sundays and holidays, pot cheese, skimmed milk, as much split wood as it is my pleasure to give because this is not included in our agreement. Because the herdsman needs no less than 11 sacks of rye per year for his family, he must buy an additional 4 sacks and 2 measures of rye, which costs 34 rubles according to current prices. Thus, out of his 60-ruble salary there remain only 26 rubles for the purchase of grain, out of which he pays 20 rubles quitrent for his farmstead (formerly, when he had fewer children, he paid 40 rubles), and 6 rubles a year remain for the purchase of salt, hempseed oil, and clothes.

It's not much, as you can see. Hard labor like the herdsman's and his whole family's is not paid well. From this example, you can see that the situation of the peasants of this area, who received 4.5 desiatinas of allotment land,[14] is hardly bright. For, if there were any kind of possibility whatsoever that Petr could live off his allotment land, he would not, of course, have ended up with such low pay as a herdsman, where he has no rest day or night.[. . .]

Once I have looked over everything in the cattle yard, after chatting with the herdsman and his wife, having admired the children, the calves, the lambs—you cannot imagine how sweet little Pavlik is when he plays on the floor with the lambs—I go back to the house. Avdotia, all flushed, excited, in an oblivious mood, in fact even angry, fusses over the stove where everything is boiling and bubbling.

"I'll give you your lunch. It's ready."

"Fine."

Avdotia sets the table and serves lunch. After she serves the food, she stands and waits nervously to see what I will say, is it good or not. She becomes especially nervous if she serves me some new dish: at these moments she is in the same kind of excited state as a pupil at an exam, as a chemist who is burning some newly discovered substance. She stands and watches me to see what will happen. Usually everything is always very good. Then Avdotia is at the height of bliss. If it happens that I have guests, then I even begin to feel sorry for Avdotia: she becomes so nervous that she gets a nervous headache.

Avdotia's entire life is consumed by the household she runs. Taking everything to heart, from failed butter to a badly washed stocking, she is constantly nervous, suffering, or rejoicing. She is impossibly stingy and guards my property as if it were her own. She is impeccably honest. She is frank, straightforward, she never lies, she is proud, conceited, and hot-tempered beyond belief; she has always been free and she does not have any of those failings which distinguish former serfs: she has no slavishness, servility, falsehood, no cowed attitude, fear, subservience.[. . .]

After lunch, I smoke a cigar, I drink punch, and daydream . . . Starting in January, when the sun begins to be springlike and to warm up, after lunch I go out on clear days and sit in the sun. If you sit on the porch, on the sunny side, you can even get warm. It is not so cold, about minus 8 to 10 degrees; it is quiet. The sun shines brightly and warms up. It is fine. You need to live through October, November, December alone in the country, the awful months when it is dark the entire day, when the sun is never visible in the sky, and if it even peeps through, it is dim, cold, sometimes there is a freeze, then a thaw, then rain, then it drizzles so much there are no roads: either mud or heaps, icy conditions or thaw—in order to come to appreciate a good sleigh ride in December and the first ray of sun in January.[. . .]

But we, who have sat without light for three months, already feel the approach of spring in February and revive. On practically the first clear, sunny day everything comes alive and tries to make use of the life-giving light of the sun. At noon, when it begins to drip from the roof in the warmth, the chickens, ducks, and all living things spill out into the yard to warm in the sun, the sparrows rush up and down there between the large birds and twitter gaily. The cow, driven out for watering, stops in the sun, blinks, and warms herself. In the stall, all of the cattle push against the window which faces the sunny side. The bulls, sensing the approach of spring, bellow, grow angry, and tear the manure with their feet. You seat yourself on the porch in your sheepskin coat, turning your face to the warm sunlight, you smoke, you dream. It is fine.

Village Poverty and Charity: Crusts of Bread

Having warmed myself in the sun, I set out for the second time around the farm and go first of all to the "old woman." The "old woman" is an old

peasant woman who is about seventy years old and then some—she remembers the destruction[15] and loves to tell how the babas impaled a Frenchman
with oven forks, which does not prevent her, however, from viewing the
French amiably because, she says, the French are a good people—she is
seventy years old, but she is still healthy, brave, energetic, active. The "old
woman" is the mistress of the dining hall where everyone eats except for the
herdsman who runs his own household with his family. The old woman bakes
bread and prepares meals for the dining hall, she cares for the swine, ducks,
and chickens, which are all under her command. She takes care of sick cattle,
and every animal who falls ill in the cattle yard is transferred to the care of the
old woman, whose jurisdiction includes the stalls built at the side of the dining
hall. It is the old woman, as the mistress of the dining area, who hands out
"crusts."

I don't have a properly organized distribution of baked bread from a scale
to the poor as it is done, or, to put it more accurately, as it was done, in some
manor houses. On my place, the old woman simply gives out "crusts" in the
dining hall, just as crusts are given out in every peasant household where
there is bread—as long as a peasant has his own grain or grain he has bought,
he will give out crusts down to the last loaf. I did not offer any instructions, I
did not know anything about these crusts. The old woman herself decided that
"we" must give out crusts, and she does so.

In our province, even in good harvest years, rare is the peasant who has
enough of his own grain to last until the next season: almost everyone must
buy grain, and those who have nothing with which to buy grain send their
children, old men, and old women to beg for "crusts" around the community.
This year there was a complete crop failure in everything: the rye came up
badly and was full of straw, weeds, grass; the spring wheat failed utterly, so
that, for the most part, there was a return only of seeds. There was not enough
fodder because of the failed crop of spring thatch and the bad harvest of grass
because of drought. And that is the most difficult for the peasants because,
when there is not enough grain, one can still feed oneself in the commune
somehow or other with crusts, but you can't send a horse into the commune to
beg. It is bad, so bad, that it can be no worse. Children were out after crusts
even before Kuzma-Demian [the feast day of Saints Cosmas and Damian]
(November first).[. . .]

The peasants had eaten all of their grain long before winter Nikola [the
feast day of Saint Nicholas the Miracle-worker, December 6] and had begun
to buy grain. I sold my first sack of grain to a peasant in October, and the
muzhik, as you well know, buys grain only when they have kneaded their last
pound of flour at home. Every day at the end of December as many as thirty
pairs would go about begging for crusts; they would walk and ride, children,
babas, old men, even healthy children and young married peasant women.
Hunger will drive a man to anything; if he hasn't eaten, he's ready to sell his
soul. It is shameful for a young man or girl, but there is nothing to be done but
to put on a pouch and go beg in the commune. This year, not only children,
babas, old men, old women, young men, and girls went for crusts, but even

many heads of households. There is nothing to eat at home—do you understand this? Today they ate up the last loaf, out of which yesterday they gave crusts to people who came by begging, they ate it and went out into the commune. There is no grain, there is no work, everyone would be happy to work, they would be happy to work just for grain but there is no work. Do you understand—there is no work. And the members of the St. Petersburg Assembly of Landowners say that "the sorest point in the economy currently is the indisputable costliness of working hands"?[16] [. . .]

"Someone begging for crusts" and "a beggar" are two completely different types of people who ask for charity. Someone begging is a specialist; asking for charity is his trade. He usually has neither house, nor possessions, nor farm, and constantly wanders from place to place, collecting grain, eggs, and money. The beggar sells all the natural produce he collects—grain, eggs, flour, and so forth—turning it into money. The beggar usually is a cripple, a sick man, a man not capable of work, a weak old man, a fool. The beggar is dressed in rags, he asks for charity loudly, sometimes even persistently, he is not ashamed of his trade. A beggar is a man of God. A beggar rarely goes among the muzhiks: he operates more around merchants and gentry, he goes from city to city, large villages, markets. In our area, real beggars are rarely seen—there is nothing for them to get.

Someone begging for "crusts" is something completely different. He is a local peasant. Offer him work and he will take it up on the spot and will not go out after crusts anymore. Someone begging for crusts is dressed like every peasant, sometimes even in a new coat, only with a canvas bag over his shoulder; the peasant begging with him may not even take a bag. He is ashamed and arrives as if he happened to stop by for no special reason, by chance, as if to warm up, and the mistress of the household, taking pity on his shame, will give something to him imperceptibly, as if by chance. Or if he arrives at lunchtime, she invites him to sit at the table; in this respect, the muzhik is surprisingly tactful, because he knows that he may himself have to go begging for crusts. Someone begging for crusts is ashamed to beg and, entering the cottage, having crossed himself, silently stands at the door, after saying to himself, usually in a whisper, "For the love of Christ, please give." No one pays any attention to him, everyone is busy with something or conversing, laughing, as if no one were there. Only the mistress goes to the table, takes a small crust of bread, from 2–5 square *vershok*s,[17] and gives it to him. He crosses himself and leaves. The same size crusts are given to everyone—if it is 2 vershoks, then 2 vershoks go to everyone; if two come at once (those begging for crusts, for the most part, go in pairs), then the mistress asks: "Are you collecting together?" If they are together, then she gives 4 *vershok*s, if they are separate, then she cuts the crust in half.

Someone begging for crusts has a household, a farm, horses, cows, sheep, his baba has good clothes—it's just that he doesn't have any grain right now; next year when he has grain, not only will he not go begging, he will himself give out crusts, and even now, if, having gotten by with the help of crusts he has collected, he finds work, earns money, and buys grain, then he will himself give out crusts. A peasant has a household, allotment land for three souls, three horses, two cows, seven sheep, two pigs, hens, and so forth. His wife has her own supply of fabric in a trunk, the young bride has fine clothes, and her own money, the son has a new sheepskin coat. Beginning in the autumn, when there is still a supply of rye, they eat pure bread in abundance, and if the head of the household has been very frugal, they will even have adulterated bread through the autumn—I have seen peasants like this. Beggars come, they give out crusts. But then the head of the household notices that the grain is running short. They eat a little less, not three times a day, but two, and then one. They add chaff to the bread. If there is money, a little something left over from selling hemp to pay taxes, the head of the household buys grain. If there is no money—he miscalculates somehow—he will try to get some ahead through work, he'll borrow. One can see the kind of interest they pay for this by the fact that the owner of the neighboring inn who trades in vodka, bread, and similar items which are essential for the muzhik, and who gives out these things on credit, himself borrows money on speculation for purchases—for example, a whole wagon of rye, and pays two rubles interest for one month on fifty rubles, that is, 48 percent. What kind of percentages does he take himself? When a muzhik has used up all of his grain and there is nothing else to eat, the children, old women, old men put on sacks and go to beg for crusts in neighboring villages. Usually, the young children return home for the night, the older ones return when they have gathered more crusts. The family feeds itself on the collected crusts, and what they do not eat, they dry in the stove as a reserve. Meanwhile, the head of the household busies himself trying to find work, and getting grain. The mistress feeds the cattle—she cannot leave the house, the older children are ready to go to work almost just for grain. If the head of the household comes by some grain, the children no longer go for crusts and the mistress again hands out crusts to others. If there is no way to get grain, the babas and young girls go out following the children and old men, and in the worst case (this happens with those who live alone) the heads of households themselves. It can happen that only the mistress remains in the household to look after the livestock. The head of the household no longer walks. He goes on horseback. That way they get out further, sometimes even into Orel Province.[18] Now in the middle of winter, we often meet a cart loaded down with crusts, and on it there will be a muzhik with a baba, a young girl or boy. Begging on horseback, he collects crusts until he has properly filled the cart. He dries the gathered crusts in a stove when anyone lets him spend the night in a village. Having gathered crusts, he returns home and the entire family lives on them, and the head of the household works around the house or for someone else at this time, if an opportunity arises. When the crusts begin to run out, they hitch up the horse again and go begging. Some feed themselves this way the whole winter and even gather a reserve for the spring. Sometimes, if there is a reserve of gathered crusts in the house, they will give out some to others. In the spring, when it warms up, the children will go out again after crusts and wander around the neighboring villages. The heads of household must work in the spring, that is when it is hard to make ends meet.

There is nowhere to get anything except on credit, and in the spring there are taxes to pay again. When it becomes warmer, the mushrooms come up, but one works badly on mushrooms alone. It is all right if it is only grain that is lacking. If there is no grain, then you can make your way in the commune *somehow* until spring. No one will die of hunger, thanks to this system of providing mutual aid through giving out crusts of bread. This autumn, one baba who was already out of grain in October said to me, "There have been lean years when we thought that we would all die from hunger, but we didn't die. If God provides, we won't die today; no one is starving to death." But it is worse when there is not only no grain, but also no feed for the livestock, as now. You can't feed the livestock in the commune.[. . .]

It is a *sin* not to give a crust when you have grain. For that reason, even the "old woman" began to give out crusts, without conferring with me, and I think that if I had forbidden her to give crusts, then she would have scolded me and would probably have even refused to live on my place.

The old woman gives everyone the same size crusts of bread—she gives crusts that are a bit larger only to soldiers (veterans, those on indefinite leave, those on leave) because it seems that soldiers are forbidden or were formerly forbidden (I don't know this for certain) to beg for charity.

My Natural Healer: The "Old Woman"

The "old woman" is the commander—I can't call her anything else—in the dining hall, which also includes the swine and poultry. The old woman is always bustling about and it seems that she doesn't sleep even at night. She is extremely compassionate and loves every animal beyond reason. Nevertheless she has everything in order—the hens, the ducks, the swine. All day long she feeds them, waters them, strokes them. Although all of the ducks are gray, the old woman knows each one by face. In the summer she also considers it her duty to count the chicks and ducklings, she gets muddled up keeping track and is excessively upset by it all. If a chick or duckling disappears—a kite[19] has taken it off—the old woman will search and search, counting all the birds ten times (and I have more than a few birds—last year I ate 83 chicks) and when all of her searching turns out to be in vain, she will come, embarrassed, to inform me that a duckling has disappeared, she cries, she says that she did not keep a good enough watch on them, and asks me to dock her pay (she receives one and a half rubles a month). The old woman also has the swine on her hands and she is also constantly occupied with them: either she is washing the piglets or feeding them or driving them out into the sun, or to the water to bathe. Finally, a child born to one of the milkmaids is under her care. She keeps him in the cradle right there in the dining hall and even finds time to fuss over him. But more than that she drills the mother to make sure that she nurses when she should, washes the baby more often, and does not rock him too much, and so forth.

The old woman knows what each bird, each animal needs down to the last detail. She takes excellent care of the cattle. If an animal falls ill, it is taken immediately to the old woman. Just watch, in a week or two, it will have recovered. It is simply amazing. And the old woman does not use any kinds of medication, except sometimes she prepares a poultice of herbs or smears the cows' tongues with a honey caustic. Usually, she takes the cow into a warm cottage, in extreme cases she even keeps it with her for the night next to her bed—she sprinkles it with holy water from three villages (at Epiphany, water is brought from three different villages and guarded all year; the farm cannot get by without this water because one must sprinkle each newborn calf and lamb with it), she fumigates it with a candle, washes it, and begins to feed it first with this, then with something else; she'll give it some hay with chaff in it, baked bread, oats with chaff, oatmeal, flour water, clear water. She'll look after it, scrutinize it, pamper it, observe what the cow eats—just watch and it will have recovered.[. . .] Most important, the old woman does all of this somehow by sight, simply, without measuring feed, without figuring how much protein, hydrocarbons, and so forth are needed. I have to confess that I don't even have scales on my place on which it would be possible to weigh stock and feed. Everything is measured by sight—everyone is already used to doing it this way. "This is 27 *arshin*s,"[20] the carpenter will say: I'll measure and it comes out 27 arshins and a quarter, it's not even worth it to measure, because a quarter means nothing. The herdsman and his wife think that the old woman "divines," that is, that she can tell fortunes; but this is nonsense. The old woman, simply, as the muzhiks say, "understands animals"; she knows their nature in detail, she loves animals, she commands enormous experience, because she has lived among cows, sheep, swine, and hens for fifty years. The old woman cures the animals with pure air, sunlight, appropriate feed, soft bedding, attentive care, tenderness; she studies the personality of each animal, and accordingly, puts it in either these or those hygienic conditions, feeds it with this or that fodder. I believe in the old woman's know-how so much that if she says, "God will provide, it will pass," I am completely convinced that the animal will recover. I trust the old woman sooner than the veterinarian, who thinks that his medications are the key to the specific cure for illness.[. . .]

After I have looked over everything at the old woman's, I go for the second time to the cattle yard. The cattle have been watered for the second time and are getting their fodder for the night. I look to see if the second feeding has been eaten up, and how the stock are taking their evening feeding. I watch the calves being watered and the cows being milked.

Evening falls. I return to the house to drink tea. It is Savelich's duty to prepare the samovar for my return, because Avdotia is with the cows at this time. There has not yet been an instance when the confectioner has been late with the samovar. I come into the kitchen, the samovar is boiling. Savelich has taken care of this.

Village Justice

During evening tea, I get a report. First of all, Avdotia appears and reports how much they have milked, what condition the cows and calves are in, which cows are about to calve, which ones are due, what kind of problems one cow or another has, and so on and so forth. Since there is nothing to do in the evening in the winter, the report can be lengthy, detailed, and thorough. Ivan appears after Avdotia and tells me what has been done on the farm today, what will be done tomorrow. I talk with him as necessary every day: we confer on the present, discuss the past, make recommendations for the future. He also shares village news with me.

"There was a court session in the village today, Aleksandr Nikolaevich."[21]

"About what?"

"Yesterday Vasilii nearly beat Efer's wife Khvorosia to death."

"Why?"

"Well, because of Petr. The muzhiks have been noticing for a long time already that Petr (Petr, a peasant from another village, works here in the mill) has been hanging around Khvorosia. Everybody wanted to catch them, hadn't managed to, but today they caught him. (The muzhiks watch out for the babas of their village, so they don't amuse themselves with outsiders; it's no big deal if they go with men of their own village, that's the husband's affair, but with outsiders—they had better not.) It was Ivan's doing. They noticed at lunch-time that Petr wasn't in the tavern and that Khvorosia wasn't there either. They guessed that they must be in Moreech's cottage, he's not home, only the old woman. Everybody in the village went down to Moreech's place. It was locked. They knocked, the old woman opened up, Khvorosia was sitting there, but nobody else. But Ivan found him. He pulled him out from under the bench. Everyone started laughing."

"So what did the husband, Efer, do?"

"Nothing. Petr gave Efer some vodka. But then it was Vasilii who got furious."

"So what was it to Vasilii?"

"What do you mean, what's it to Vasilii? Everybody knows he's been sleeping with Khvorosia for a long time, and now she's taken up with Petr. Toward evening, Vasilii watched out for Khvorosia, and as soon as she went to get water, he jumped out from a corner with a log, he grabbed her; then he beat her and beat her. If the women hadn't heard her, he would've beaten her to death. They carried her home near death, she was black and blue all over. Now she's lying on the stove, she can't even turn over."

"So how did it end?"

"Today the commune gathered at Efer's place. They tried Vasilii. They found him guilty. They decided that Vasilii has to pay Efer ten rubles, and send him a woman to work for him 'til Khvorosia's better, and that he has to give the commune a half vedro of vodka for the trial. They drank the vodka right in front of me."

"But what about Khvorosia?"

"So-so, she's lying on the stove, moaning. They also beat up Listar. Listar got drunk and began to bully Kuzia. So Panas asks him, Why are you being a bully? So Listar boasted: Why shouldn't I be a bully—I don't owe the tsar or the landlord a thing. So! Panas says, so you want to get some of the landlord's money out of me. Bang! in the snout! Then Kuzia got mixed up in it, Efer, Mikhalka—everybody fell on Listar; and they beat him and beat him—and Mikhalka is saying to him the whole time: Don't go after someone else's wife, don't do it—they beat him bloody. I said to them: Why are you doing that, fellows, all of you ganged up against one. That's what he needs, they say; we know why we're beating him."

Ivan has left, tea is over. It's boring. I sit by myself and read novels by Dumas which a neighboring landlord gave me. Avdotia, Ivan, Savelich, having finished tea, get ready to go have supper. "We're going to supper," Avdotia says, coming in to turn back the bed, "and I've put your supper in the dining room." Everyone has gone to the dining hall. I go into the dining room. The cats, knowing that I'll give them tidbits after supper, run in after me. I have two cats—a big black and white male and a black, yellow, and white female. I got this kind of national-colored female as an experiment. They say that only females can be black, yellow, and white and that there can never be a male of those colors. They say that when a male cat who is black, yellow, and white is born, then it will mean that the end of the world is near. I want to see if this is true. The first sign of the end of the world is, as is well known, the appearance of a large number of moaners, that is, people who moan constantly; the second is the birth of a black, yellow, and white male kitten. After the Emancipation Edict a multitude of moaners appeared. I want to see if a black, yellow, and white male kitten will be born.

The cats are trained so that when I sit down to supper, they jump up on the chairs placed in a circle around the table where I dine: one sits on my right side, the other on the left. After my vodka, I eat and teach the cats patience and good behavior, to sit properly and not to put their paws on the table, to wait until the grown-ups have finished, and so forth.

Meanwhile there is a storm outside, a blizzard, the kind of weather about which we say "even if I don't eat for three days, I'm not moving off the stove."[22] The wind whines, I hear the broken bark of Lyska, "gaoo, gaoo," which is melancholy, and in half a minute, again, "gaoo, gaoo," and so it continues endlessly. Which means that the wolves are wandering nearby.

After I finish supper, I go to bed and dream . . .

Letter II

✉ Engelgardt's second letter from Batishchevo is more fragmented than the first and offers several short descriptions of a variety of aspects of his life in the countryside.[1] He opens by briefly continuing the theme of the marginality of the peasants' economic existence and stressing their dependence on the local gentry even after the Emancipation. He then turns to the local peasant thief, Kostik, and recounts an episode involving him as a vehicle for describing peasant attitudes toward the volost courts and other more formal judicial institutions. Engelgardt's message here was his contribution to a debate among educated Russians about the desirability and feasibility of developing understanding of and respect for the law among the peasantry. The volost court referred to in this letter was a court of peasant judges established by the Emancipation legislation to handle petty civil disputes in the countryside. Its court of appeal was the individual justice of the peace in the area and, above him, the assembly of justices of the peace in the province.

In explaining the peasant plaintiff, Matov's, approach to apprehending the thief, securing witnesses, and getting them all to the volost court for his trial, Engelgardt stresses the economic considerations of peasant attitudes toward justice. The plaintiff's goal is compensation for his loss. The witnesses' goal is to lose as little work time as possible. Through an efficient investigation and timely rewards for his witnesses, the plaintiff achieves his goals. Furthermore, having paid his due, the thief is free and welcome to move about the local community after the trial. Engelgardt recognized and applauded the fundamental pragmatism of the peasants' approach to justice. At the end of the letter he returns to this theme by offering an ironic description of an assembly of the justices of the peace. Engelgardt highlighted the pomp and circumstance of the proceedings, while conveying his doubts that such an approval would have any positive effect in developing so-called legal consciousness among the peasantry.

In a similar vein, Engelgardt also deflates the image of the much-hailed institution of the *zemstvo*. This was an elected council of local self-governance that took on many public works responsibilities after the Emancipation. Engelgardt's account of the election of gentry delegates to the provincial zemstvo board points again to the pomp and circumstance, the socializing, wining and dining, and general frivolity of this occasion. With his ironic treatment of the justice of the peace and the zemstvo elections, Engelgardt is introducing a refrain that will sound throughout his letters: reform programs dominated by the gentry have high display value but little true impact on the peasantry.

Of the remaining topics treated in this letter, Engelgardt's discussion of the fate of a young peasant girl who dies for lack of adequate medical care offers another piece in his emerging portrait of the position of peasant women in their families and community. Like Khvorosia in Letter I, Aksiuta in Letter II represents an economic entity for her family. As an unmarried daughter, she is a burden whose illness and death elicit no great sense of loss. Instead, her death causes resentment over the fact that she does not die in the autumn at the end of her work season for the family but in the spring, after the family has borne the expense of feeding her all winter. This vignette emphasizes again the fragile equilibrium of the peasant economy, and therefore the force of economic considerations in the personal relationships of the peasant household.

✉   ✉   ✉

The Peasants' Poverty and Dependence on Local Gentry Landowners

In my first letter I described my winter day for you. Or specifically, taking tea in the morning, then the stroll in the cattle yard, lunch, my visit to "the old woman" and to the cattle yard, evening tea and reports, supper . . .

And so it is day in and day out.[. . .]

Of course, not every day passes exactly the same way. It happens that someone will come by, but of course, on business, and always about one and the same thing. "A muzhik has arrived from Pochinko," Avdotia reports. I go into the kitchen. A muzhik bows and says:

"Hello, Aleksandr Nikolaevich."

"Hello. What is it? Some grain?"

"I could use some rye."

"A sack?"

"A little sack would do."

"Eight rubles."

"Couldn't you go a little cheaper?"

"No, any cheaper is impossible. Take some from the back for fifty kopeks less."

"What do you mean, some from the back? I'll take the good stuff. Take the money, with pleasure."

The muzhik takes out eight greasy one-ruble notes and goes with the steward to the storeroom to get the grain—muzhiks tend to have one-ruble notes (paper rubles) most of all. Three-ruble and five-ruble notes are also common, a red note (ten rubles) is a rarity, a twenty-five-ruble note is even more rare, and only *artel's*[2] have one-hundred-ruble notes.

"A muzhik has arrived from Diadino," Avdotia reports. I go into the kitchen.

"Hello, Aleksandr Nikolaevich."

"Hello. What is it? Grain?"

"I could use a little grain."

"An *osmina?*"[3]

"That would do."

"Four rubles."

"I don't have any money. Let me work for it. Aren't there any bushes to clear?"

"There's no clearing to be done. The work has all been put out, there's only a half desiatina of flax left."

"I know. We'd have done the flax."

"That's not possible. You are alone with a wife and daughter, you have only a pair of horses. You couldn't do it."

"But I do have a pair of horses."

"Not possible. You couldn't finish it. Flax, as you know yourself, requires a lot of effort, and it must be done on time."

"Yes, but we'll do it. If you take it on, you can't not finish it. We'll put our own work aside and we'll do it on contract. I'll borrow a neighbor's horses. Only now we need to get by."

"No, it's not possible. You can't do it. You do not have the manpower to work flax. And furthermore, you live far away, more than seven versts away. Then I'd have to look for you. It's impossible, it's not convenient."

"All right, it's not convenient. It's hard with flax when you're alone. That's true—you won't be able to do it. Things are bad: I don't have any grain, and I don't want to go begging for crusts. And now they're threatening to sell my livestock for arrears. What's a man to do?"

The muzhik leaves to try his luck someplace else.[. . .]

And so it is every day. A muzhik comes: give some work, give some grain, give some money, give some firewood. This year, of course, is not typical because of the bad harvest and the lack of fodder, but even in good years it is bad for the muzhik toward the spring because he does not have enough grain. And furthermore, with the construction of the railroad, even the cost of firewood is going up inordinately. In three years the price of firewood has increased by five times, and, as you know, the muzhik does not have firewood on his allotment land. The peasants also do not have meadows in their allotment, or very little meadowland, so that for hay and pasture, he is dependent on the landlord. Around here there is also no work around the house because the gentry let their estates go after the Emancipation, neglected the fields and meadows, and ran off into service (seeing as many positions have opened up now and pay excessively large salaries), wherever they could: some into state service, some into the zemstvo.[. . .] The gentry do not farm, they have abandoned their land, they don't live on their estates. So what is left for the

muzhik to do? There's no work around the house. What remains is to abandon the farm and go into hired labor in towns where the landlords have
gathered for service. And this is what the muzhiks are doing . . . But I will
talk about this in greater detail later.

The Peasant Thief Kostik and the Volost Court

If a muzhik comes by, it means that he is asking for grain or work. I know only
one muzhik who never asks for either work or grain—if he ever asks for
anything, it's gunpowder, but, even so, he always offers money for the powder; with this muzhik, I never discuss farming, which does not interest him in
the least.

This muzhik, his name is Kostik, is a specialist. He is a hunter and a thief.
His business is hunting and stealing. Mainly he hunts for wolves and foxes—
he catches them with traps and poisons them. In the spring he shoots grouse
and duck, gathers bones for fertilizer for me, does various chores—whatever
you ask—watches the grouse's mating places and so forth. He works as a thief
at any time of the year. He steals wherever and whatever falls into his hands.
Kostik has a household, he has a plot of allotment land; now, however, he has
lost his farm, because he has sold his last mare and his hay. He sows, reaps,
even takes on the processing of half a shock of flax (not on my place, of
course, but at some landlord or other's), but he is a bad farmer. Thus, more
and more he lives hand to mouth. Kostik is a drunk, but not like the drunks
you find in cities among the factory workers or bureaucrats and in country
towns—the landlords, priests, house servants, drunks who have drunk away
their mind and conscience, who have lost their humanity. Kostik loves to
drink, to carouse; he is as much a drunkard as the people who have fallen in
love with Shneidersha, who dine and drink at Dusot's.[4]

In general, I should remark that dissolute habitual drunks are very rare
among muzhiks who live in the village. I have already lived in the country for
a year and I have not seen any real drunks with swollen faces, dull minds, or
shaking hands among the muzhiks. Upon occasion, muzhiks, babas, young
girls, even children drink, and drink quickly, will even drink themselves drunk
(I say "even" because a muzhik has to drink a lot to become drunk—two
glasses of vodka is nothing to a baba), but they are not drunks. Indeed we also
drink—look at Eliseev's, Erber's, Dusot's,[5] and so forth—but you know that
this is also not dissolute drunkenness. Having read in the newspapers about
the unusual rise among us of drunkenness, I was surprised by the sobriety
which I have seen in our villages. Of course, they drink upon occasion, during
Easter Week, on Nikola [the feast of Saint Nicholas, May 6], on the Feast of
the Holy Virgin, weddings, christenings, funerals, but no more than we also
drink upon occasion. I have had occasion to be at both peasant assemblies and
at the assemblies of landowner deputies—and truthfully, I cannot say where
they drink more. It is true that the peasants drink a larger number of half
shtofs,[6] but you must take into account that it is nothing for a muzhik to drink

a half shtof—he'll become animated, but that's all. He'll sleep it off and be back behind the plough. I am completely convinced that the various measures against drunkenness—that there be no tavern by the mill, that the tavern be a certain number of sazhens[7] away from the volost administration offices[8] (what is it to a muzhik to go several sazhens—even I will go 15 versts to the station for a beer, which we don't have in the village), and so on and so forth—are unnecessary, tentative, and useless measures.

I often treat peasants to vodka, I give out a lot of vodka, but I have never seen anything bad come of it. They drink up, they have a good time, they sing songs, someone may even fall down, sometimes they even start to fight. I positively can say that they do nothing worse than what we encounter at Erber's. For example, during the rye harvest, I give the reapers two glasses of vodka each in the evening: it's part of the farm account. There should be four reapers per desiatina (I pay by the desiatina), but only two come or three (I do not fine them); but if there are refreshments, then six will come and they will do half a field in one day—and that's that. They drink two glasses each in rapid succession (to get the effect most quickly), they have a bite to eat, they sing songs and go around the villages making merry, making a lot of noise of course, they'll be a bit more obliging with their buddies (and is it not exactly so at Erber's?), but the next day, as soon as the dew dries, they will go to work as if nothing had happened.

I have already said that Kostik is a hunter. It was on this account that I got to know him. We got together because he was the first person in the village from whom I heard a chemical term. Soon after my arrival in the country, when firewood, grain, and manure had not yet displaced cresol, introphenol, antratsen, and so forth from my mind, Kostik came to sell me a hare and asked me—we had talked about hunting—to get him some strychnine to poison foxes, which, in his words, works splendidly. I won't deny that to hear the word strychnine was for me, who was used to talking about diphenyl-amines, letitsines,[9] and so forth, extraordinarily pleasant, just like hearing a native word in a foreign land. It seems to me that the word strychnine was the reason that I immediately felt a special disposition toward Kostik, expressed, of course, through my treating him to vodka in addition to paying for the hares. After that, Kostik began to bring me grouse, ducks, and rabbits; in the spring he collected bones for me—he did not carry the bones himself, how-ever, but sent them with a boy, because it was not right for the household head to do so, not proper, to sell such an unimportant item—he cut firewood for me before Easter Week in order to earn a few half shtofs for the holiday.

I already said that, in addition to hunting, Kostik is a thief. He is a cheat and a thief, but he is not a malicious thief, but a good-natured, good one. He swindles, cheats, dodges if he can—rogues teach honest men to be on their guard—but he swindles benevolently. He'll steal if something is lying around (if you aren't careless, you won't tempt a thief), but more often by chance, without a preconceived goal, because it is not possible to call a theft premedi-tated when it happens just because the occasion arises. Kostik is always ready to steal if there is an occasion, if something is lying about: if a muzhik stands gaping, Kostik will take a hammer out from under his belt and will immediately give the victim something to drink and will even treat him. If he is caught, he'll give back the stolen goods or pay for them; if the peasants catch him stealing, they'll beat him up, but he will not be offended. It seems to me that Kostik likes the sheer process of stealing, he loves to pull a fast one on a smart operator.

But this year Kostik did not have any luck stealing, probably he did not manage to steal anything on Annunciation. It is well known that thieves begin to steal on Annunciation for luck for the whole year, exactly as horse dealers deal on St. Boris's Day (May 2) in order to deal profitably for the rest of the year. Now Kostik has fallen into steady theft so that he has lost even his last mare; I don't know how he will even farm his land.

Once in the autumn, I was going to watch the threshing when I saw Matov galloping up. Matov is a merchant-kulak,[10] who buys and sells everything, the owner of a coaching house about six versts from my place. Having caught sight of me, Matov, who had already galloped past my house, stopped and jumped off the horse.

"Hello, sir."

"Hello, Vasilii Ivanovich. What's up?"

"I was coming to see you, sir. You said that you've got some bulls for sale."

"I do."

"Let's go have a look."

"Fine."[. . .]

I think that it was not about the bulls that Matov has come; but it is impossible not to show him the bulls. We go to the cattle yard. The peasants drive out a bull. Matov looks at him, feels it, as if he actually wants to buy it. I ask fifty rubles for the bull; he offers fifteen, meanwhile one hide costs eight. There is nothing to discuss. It is obvious that he does not need the bull. We return to the house.

"Sell me two sacks of barley, sir."

"I can't."

"Be so kind, and sell. I don't have anything to feed the pigs."

"I can't, I need it myself."

"Well, then, good-bye."

"Good-bye."

Matov unties the horse and, putting his foot in the stirrup, turns to me.

"I'm completely worn out today."

"How's that? And where are you riding from, look how you drove the horse."

"I'm out on business. I'm looking for a thief; someone stole four hides from me day before yesterday."

"So who do you think it was?"

"There's a muzhik here in Babino, his name is Kostik, you don't know him. I think it was him. He was at my place on the third, in the evening, when the hides disappeared, and now he hasn't slept at home for two days already. He's out getting drunk somewhere. It seems like I've been around to all of the taverns, and he's nowhere to be found."

"Kostik? I know him, in fact he was here today."

"Kostik? When?"

"It was not long ago at all, he came by to ask for some gunpowder."

"Gunpowder? Aha, he's . . . Well, so he shouldn't be far away now—no doubt he's in the tavern in Dubovo."

Matov jumped up on the horse and galloped off to Dubovo. "Well, I think this one will catch him." I went on to the threshing and told Ivan about my encounter with Matov.

"It was Kostik who stole them."

"How do you know?"

"Well he came here to see me on the threshing floor today. He asked me for some blanks. I told him we didn't even have much gunpowder. He insists, sell me some, he says, I'll give you ten kopeks for each one. But I laughed and said: come on you don't have money. I do, he says. Well then, show me. He shows it to me; he actually has three one-ruble notes. Look, I say to the workers, bet him that he doesn't have any money in his pocket. He showed the money to everyone. No doubt he stole Matov's hides and has already sold them somewhere. Where could he get money from!"

"That's Kostik's business, said one of the workers: Evmen and I ran into him yesterday early in the morning when we were on our way to threshing. We watch and see that Kostik's carrying something on his back, I even touched it, it was something soft. What's this you're carrying? we ask. Things, he says, I hired out to carry them from the station to Ivanovo. And so it was hides he was carrying. He sold them in Slitia. That's where he got the money. Now Matov'll catch him, he's getting drunk in Dubovo for sure."

Matov caught Kostik and filed a complaint with the volost authorities. After a while, my steward, thresher, and the workers were called as witnesses to the volost court. Kostik went to trial. At first Kostik denied it, but in view of the clear evidence, he confessed that he had stolen four hides from Matov, of which he had hidden two in the forest, and had sold two to the owner of the posting inn. Matov and Kostik came to an agreement, as it was explained to me, by which Kostik had to return the two hides hidden in the forest and to pay for the two others, which he had sold. Kostik also paid the witnesses, it seems, and treated them to vodka.

Recently on my way to the station, I went by Matov's to have a drink of vodka. I saw that Kostik, drunk, jovial, and on the friendliest of terms, was chatting with Matov, who had already had one or two.

"Hello."

"Hello, Aleksandr Nikolaevich. Greetings, sir," Kostik said, pleased to see me.

"Hello, Kostik, what are you doing here?"

"Oh, we're drinking up profits: I sold a mare to Vasilii Ivanovich."

"So, you have settled for the hides?"

"No, we took care of the hides before," Matov said, "and now I paid money for the mare. Please, Fimia, give the little sir something to eat."

"The host should begin."

Matov poured a small glass of vodka, crossed himself, blew into the glass (to drive out the devil who sits in vodka), said, "to your health," drank it up in a gulp, and, filling the glass up to the rim, gave it to me with a bow.

"So, to your health."

Kostik began to tell me about his failures at fox hunting this year, and complained especially about the fact that he had not succeeded in taking a single poisoned fox this year. And this was all because he did not have any strychnine.

To tell the truth, isn't this fascinating? The main thing is it is simple. It is practical.

Someone stole Matov's hides. First of all, he ponders who could have stolen them. As the owner of the tavern and the posting inn who buys everything around the villages that he can use, seeds, hides, flax, combs, he knows every muzhik thoroughly for twenty versts in the district, he knows all the thieves. Having considered all the circumstances of the case and having suspected Kostik, he, without a word to anyone, tracks him and finds out that Kostik has disappeared from home. Suspicion becomes certainty. "It's him," Matov says and rides around the taverns to find out where the hides have been sold and where Kostik has been drinking. He happens by my place—he was riding past, happened to see me, why not ask—finds important witnesses who have seen money on Kostik (and everyone knows that Kostik cannot have money), who have seen Kostik with the hides. Having found witnesses, and promised them that he will not take the business any further than the volost court, and will not drag the witnesses around the courts, and thus having ensured that Kostik will not get off, Matov complains to the volost authorities. Matov, Kostik, and the witnesses are called to the volost—it's not far for the witnesses to go to the volost and they were not dragged away from their work, because the court was held in the evening. The witnesses identify Kostik and he, seeing that there is no way to get off, confesses. The case ends with a settlement and everyone is satisfied. Matov got back the hides Kostik had not managed to sell, no doubt he received twice as much for the ones Kostik has sold, and moreover, if you please, pinched something out of the owner of the posting inn who bought the stolen hides from Kostik. Kostik either paid the witnesses or treated them to vodka, but most important, they were not dragged around the courts; just to go to the volost, and in the evening at that, or on a holiday (the volost judge, you see, is also a muzhik, and knows that one needs to work on the weekdays), is nothing to the witnesses. Kostik is satisfied because once the theft was discovered, it is better for him to pay for the stolen goods than to sit in jail. We are satisfied because if Kostik were to do time in jail, then he would be turned from a petty thief into a serious thief.

It would have turned out completely differently if Matov, instead of finding the thief himself, had complained to the police, as the gentry do for the most part, and especially the gentry women. The constable[11] would have arrived, he would have written up a report, have made an inquest, and there, in all probability, the matter would have ended. What means does a constable with a few officers have at his disposal to uncover such acts of theft? Even if the constable had not 24 but 100 hours in a day and if he could get by without any sleep, even then he would not be able to uncover the innumerable quantity of such petty thefts. The constable has the time only to collect taxes from the landlords: he writes and writes, he orders his officers, he himself comes by . . .

Suppose that the landlords call the constable, usually without having found out anything about the theft, and they do not present any kind of information, they cannot even say anything regarding their suspicions. But Matov, it would seem, having found out everything ahead of time and having witnesses, could have filed a complaint with the justice of the peace and, in general, wherever appropriate. Not at all. Matov, as a practical man and one who fears the courts himself, knows very well that if the witnesses only knew that Matov would be going to court along with Kostik and would drag them, the witnesses, around the courts, then they would hide and would not say anything. In fact, imagine that if, as a result of Matov's complaint, the witnesses, that is, the steward, the thresher, and workers, had been summoned somewhere over 30 versts away to the constable, justice of the peace, or to an assembly—would they thank Matov? Imagine the position of the master: the steward, who has the entire farm on his hands, the thresher, without whom the threshing cannot go forward, and the workers are called to be witnesses! All work must come to a halt, the entire estate must remain without supervision, and in the time when they are giving testimony, they could not only thresh, but also carry the grain from the threshing barn. Yes, and who will begin to keep the kind of steward or livestock man who does not know the wise rule: "Hear no evil, see no evil, speak no evil," who does not know how to remain silent, who chatters unnecessarily, who meddles in others' affairs, who will be dragged as a witness to the justice of the peace, to the assembly of justices of the peace, or to the regional court? Just understand what this means for the master if, even for one day, they take his steward or livestock man. Just understand what it means if the muzhik is torn from his work at the time when it is not possible to take even five rubles for a day: leave as a witness and leave the field not planted on time. Yes and even if it is not work time, it is very pleasant to set out as a witness for more than 25 versts in minus 25 degree temperatures or, to go to town to the assembly of the justices of the peace as a witness, having to live by begging in Christ's name. Add to this that the muzhik fears the court and always worries that they will put him, the witness, God preserve us, in jail, or that they might flog him. Matov would not have discovered the theft at all if the witnesses had not known him to be a practical man who would not drag them around the courts. And what good would it have been for Matov to take Kostik to court—they would have put Kostik in jail, and what would Matov have gotten? The skins would have still disappeared. Kostik would have shut up completely at the court and would not have returned the hides or have told to whom he had sold them. Matov would have been left with nothing, would have lost a lot in the eyes of the peasants, which would not have resounded well on his trading business. Isn't it better to settle everything amicably, fairly?

Here, fortunately, many cases end this way.[. . .]

The Question of Public Health in the Countryside

"Incidents," which disturb our domestic calm and make us think and talk about something else, are very rare, although, out of boredom, we are glad of any incident. I said above that the muzhiks come by usually with a request about work, grain, and firewood, but there is one more subject about which they often come to ask—medicine. As soon as someone falls ill in the village, they come to me for medication. Although I do not practice medicine and do not know how to treat people, still, even so, they turn to me for medicine. You, they say, are a literate man, a scholar, you understand everything more than we, give us something.

And I give them castor oil, Epsom salts, birch mushrooms, pepper vodka, tea, whatever turns up. It helps.[. . .]

As for getting care if one falls ill, it is very bad in the countryside not only for a peasant but also for a landlord who is not wealthy. There is a doctor in town over 30 versts away. You fall ill. You must send to town in a troika or, at the very least, on a pair of horses, in a decent coach with a driver. If the doctor comes, one must pay him 15 rubles for the visit, and if that's too little—10 rubles more. One must take the doctor back to town and bring back the medicine. Add everything up—how much that makes, and the important thing is that one must have a coach, horses, a driver. But, as you know, in the case of serious illness, one visit is not enough. It is obvious that a doctor is currently accessible only to the rich gentry, who live in the old manner, who have carriages, drivers, and so forth, that is, for individuals who have retained their old estate, for individuals who have held onto money or redemption certificates,[12] who still have forests, who still have many portions of land on which they farm, or for individuals who, living in the countryside, are employed in some salaried position. The gentry who are not wealthy, those, for example, who had 300 redemption soul peasants, who rent small estates, petty officials who run separate farms, priests, owners of posting inns, and those who are similarly well-to-do, when compared to the peasants, cannot send to town for the doctor. These, for the most part, use good *feldshers*,[13] that is, those having a reputation in the region, primarily from the house servants, feldshers who ran apothecaries and hospitals on the estates of rich landlords during serfdom. However, even such feldshers are also inaccessible to the mass of our poor peasants, because one must give the feldsher three rubles for a visit with his medicine, and sometimes even five rubles. Only very prosperous peasants will go to such feldshers. After this come the second-rate feldshers who practice the simplest, self-taught methods, old men, old women, and everyone who has even the slightest notion. There remain also chance doctors: some kind of physician or medical student who has come home for a visit with relatives, and so forth. If a muzhik gets sick, he'll keep going, he'll try to get over it as long as he has the strength. If he collapses, then he'll go to bed. If it is very bad, then they will send for the priest, he'll receive communion and stay in bed. If there are means to do so, he'll find a feldsher or old man, and if not—he'll simply lie or send to ask for something from someone of the gentry who has medicine. Some are cured, some recover. Others die. They lie and lie until they die.

The worst is when, having recovered, having lain it out, they get sick again. And they rarely get up the second time because, not having managed to recover completely, they begin to work, they come down with a cold (I will note, by the way, that the peasants have no privies and the most terribly sick man crawls out or is carried outside to take care of his needs, no matter what the weather), and, most important, they don't receive good food, why speak of good food, they don't receive even barely tolerable food.

I have a worker named Khima from a neighboring village. In her household—and this household is poorest of the poor, they have already been without grain since the Feast of the Holy Virgin—there were besides a daughter, a young, pretty girl Aniuta, the husband–head of household, and three children, who all went out after crusts this winter. In the fall, at a wedding, Aksiuta[14] came down with a serious cold. She developed a cough, began to cough up blood, and went to bed. They sent for the priest. Aksiuta got sicker and sicker. They went for some kind of former house servant who, they say, can help. He gave her a potion—it was sour, very sour, Khima told me—and it helped. Aksiuta began to recover and might have gotten well if they had given her nourishing food, a comfortable place, and protected her from catching a cold. But then Khima came to me.

"What do you need, Khima?"

"I came about my daughter."

"And what of your daughter?"

"She's doing better. She's walking about. Only she can't eat bread made with chaff. She chews and chews, but then she spits it out—she can't swallow it. She sent my little boy, let mama, she said, ask the master if he won't give me some potatoes."

Adulterated, chaff bread is prepared out of unwinnowed rye, that is, a mixture of rye with chaff, ground directly into the flour, out of which bread is made in the usual manner. This bread is a doughy mass, permeated with thin needles of chaff; it has no special taste, it's like ordinary bread, its nutritive value is, of course, less, but its most important disadvantage is that it is hard to swallow, and someone who is not accustomed to it cannot swallow it at all. If he does swallow, then he'll begin to cough and cough and feel some kind of uncomfortable sensation in his mouth. And this is the kind of bread, or even worse—dry, chaff-filled crusts that were collected a month ago, that one should feed a recovering invalid? How can she possibly recover?

Soon Aksiuta, who had begun to recover, got worse again. Without having gotten well, she began to carry water, to brake flax, to look after the animals.

She came down with a cold and went to bed again. Everyone in the village decided that Aksiuta was going to die. Her mother, who loved and pampered Aksiuta very much, reacted to this very cold-bloodedly, that is, with that, if it is possible to express it this way, lack of feeling with which one starving man relates to another. "And so she will die, so what—it's all the same, we'd have to marry her off in the fall, she would leave the house; if she dies, the expense will be less." (It costs less to bury someone than to marry someone.)

Aksiuta was in bed all winter and died in March. Every misfortune falls to the poor man. She could have already died in the fall, but instead, there was expense all winter, and toward spring, when she could have worked, she died. Girls are given in marriage to peasants in the fall, mainly because, what kind of economic sense would it make to give a girl away after feeding her all winter, before the start of work—it's the same as selling a milk cow in spring.

[Engelgardt discusses the need for more medical personnel in the countryside, particularly young, dedicated, "humane" doctors and midwives.]

The Rural Clergy

Every month priests arrive at my place. "Priests" does not mean priest in the plural. By the word "priests" the peasants mean everyone belonging to the clergy, everyone who wears long hair, and a special priest's frock; this means the priest, the deacon, the sexton, the sacristan,[. . .] and everyone serving in the village. At Easter or at Christmas, where the custom exists, a whole flock of such church folk go about the parish behind the priest. The word "priests" has exactly the same meaning as the word for carrion crows. Carrion crows, grackle, crow, jackdaw, magpie, this whole feathered kingdom are "carrion crows." I like it when the clergymen come. Priests are at my place every month to bless the water in the cattle yard. This custom has existed from of old (from the earliest times, as the deacon says), for the water in the cattle yard to be blessed every month. On the first of every month, or thereabouts, the priests arrive—the priest, the deacon, two or three sextons—they perform the blessing of the water in the cattle yard—in the yard, in the stall, or in the izba—and walk around the entire yard singing the anthem "God Save Your People," then the priest goes into each stall and sprinkles holy water. If I am home, I usually attend the service and then I invite the priests in to have a bite and drink tea. We eat, drink tea, converse. I love to converse with the priests and find these conversations useful and instructive. First of all, no one knows the life of the simple people in all of its subtleties as the priests do; whoever wants realistically to know the daily life of the people, their situation, customs, morals, rights, notions, good and bad sides, whoever wants to get to know this unknown, enigmatic creature called a muzhik should, not limiting himself to his own observations, seek the information that he needs precisely from priests. In the given locality the priests are invaluable in this regard, because they know the situation of each peasant in their parish in detail.

Second, after the peasants, no one knows the local practical aspects of farming as well as the priests. The priests are our best practical farmers—they are even above the peasants in this regard and it is precisely from them that one can learn the practice of agriculture in a given locality. Farming constitutes the principal source of income for priests. And what will the junior deacon, even the deacon, live on, how will he raise his children, of which he always has a lot, if he is not a good agricultural manager?[. . .] I don't know how it is in other places, but here there are many churches, the parishes are small, the peasants are poor, the priests' income is insignificant. Just how small the priests' incomes are, here, at least, is evident from the low pay that the priests receive for services. For the monthly blessing of the water in the cattle yard, I pay three rubles a year, which means that the priests receive 25 kopeks for each visit. These 25 kopeks are divided into 9 parts, thus each part is 2¾ kopeks (with ¼ kopek remaining each month). The priest receives 4 parts, that is, 11 kopeks . . . [. . .] It is clear that, given such meager incomes, the priests support themselves mainly by their farms, and why it is that, if a sexton, for example, is a bad manager, he'll be done for. I have noticed that junior deacons, especially older ones, are always the very best farmers—by natural selection as in everything.

My Trip to the Zemstvo Elections

Sometimes I go to visit landlords, or I should say, landladies, because now it is primarily noblewomen who remain on the estates and run the farm. At first I talked with landlords mostly about farming, which is the most interesting topic for us.[. . .] But soon I became convinced that it was completely useless to talk to landlords about farming, because they, for the most part, understand very little about it. I'm not even talking about theoretical knowledge—to date I have not yet met a single landlord who would know where vegetation gets nitrogen or phosphorous, who might command even the most elementary knowledge of natural science and consciously would understand what he does on his farm— but this is what is surprising, that he lacks even practical knowledge. You must understand, there is none whatsoever. At least the muzhik understands practice and has a healthy understanding in farming matters.[. . .]

I take a ride to the railroad station. There, 100 sazhens from the station, there is an inn which is always full of people—people buying and selling firewood, petty officials, firewood inspectors, wood loaders, haulers. This inn is our Dusot's, with the single difference that instead of hearing, as you would at Dusot's, "comme elle se gratte les hanches et les jambes,"[15] here we constantly hear: "He took five for each log. They sold it for 6.80 on the spot. He owes me 70 per desiatina; that's a likely story, I say."

All of our trade focuses on firewood. Now there is talk only about selling forests. The entire station is crammed with firewood, all of the freight cars are filled with firewood, firewood is moving along all of the roads leading to the station, firewood is being felled in all of the forests within 25 versts of the station. Forest land which had no value for us whatsoever until now has become a business. The owners of the forests, the gentry, have cleaned up their affairs. Firewood will enable them to support themselves for another decade, even those who are running their farms according to agronomy. Those who are a bit more prudent, having sold their forest, buy bonds and will live off of the interest, being convinced that it is not an entirely noble business to work in farming. Despite the capital which is flowing to us along the railroad, agriculture is not improving in the least because capital alone is not enough to run a farm.

Look, this is how it is. I constantly sit at home in the countryside, I don't go farther than 15 versts away, and I have only been in my own district town once. It is understandable that I cannot write about anything else except farming. In the letters which will follow, I intend to describe for you the condition of farming among the gentry, the condition of farming among the peasants, and the economic relations between gentry and peasants.

I said that I constantly sit in my village and do not go anywhere farther than 15 versts . . . I don't want to sin, once I was in the neighboring district at an assembly of zemstvo electors[16] for the election of landowner delegates. I went to this assembly because I wanted to visit with my relatives and acquaintances who were supposed to attend the assembly—I am myself a native of that district. There was nothing of interest at the assembly. They elected delegates. They would read the name, patronymic,[17] and last name, they would shout: "We invite you to vote, we invite you to vote," and they would begin to place the ballots, who had received the majority, who had received the minority of the vote. But if there had been anything of interest at the assembly, I would not have been aware of it, because, well, judge for yourself: One of my rich relatives had asked me to come to the assembly; he also sent a proper carriage with horse and driver for me. Toward evening, I arrived at my relative's. We dined, we drank Rhine wine and burgundy; there are still gentry in our area at whose houses one can find ale, Rhine wine, and a bottle of some other sparkling drink. The next day, we got up at dawn and set out. Having gone around 12 versts—it was cold because this was in September— we ate and drank. At the posting inn where a change of horses awaited us, we ate and drank while they harnessed the horses. We had not covered the 8 versts or so to town when we caught up with an old acquaintance, a peace mediator,[18] so we put a rug on the ground and ate and drank. We arrived in town before lunch and stopped at the hotel. Of course, we ate and drank before lunch (which we had not ordered). Many people gathered for lunch, at the "table d'hôte" (what real Europeans we are!), all of the rich landowners (and how they were dressed! what velvet morning coats!). Of course we drank after lunch. We had punch after lunch, after which we sat out the evening. We wined and dined. The meeting was the next day. The election of delegates took place in a rather large hall on the top floor of the hotel, in the same hall where the "table d'hôte" was held. Through a room from the hall there was a buffet where it was possible to eat and drink; this is what refinement means! right here, a buffet is set up, because it's safe; no one will get drunk! But look at the muzhiks. Here you have the volost administration but the tavern must be 40 sazhens away because, so they say, it cannot be otherwise, the muzhik will get drunk right away if the tavern is alongside the volost administration, and here, therefore, one must go 40 sazhens. The election lasted long after midnight. There was no time and no place to eat, everyone snacked. The next day the election of the candidates for delegates took place. After that, we dined in true fashion and drank well. On the third day, there were no public service obligations, but in the evening there was a ball in the same hall. We danced. We dined. We drank. I fear, however, that my expression "we drank" will be taken incorrectly. I made a slight slip: precisely, I drank, and perhaps two or three others, while the rest were occupied with serious business—the election of the delegates.

On the fourth day there was an assembly of justices of the peace. My God, what a wonder that was and how different from the department offices! A large, bright, splendid room with wonderful furniture for the public, a place where the court sits, splendidly made, all of the judges were in glittering frock coats, covered with awards and various medals—all of them were former members of the militia in the Western Region before the Emancipation. Excellent. They took up the case of some muzhik who had stolen a horse. He was a small muzhik in bast shoes,[19] in a thin homespun coat, he made such a contrast with the splendor of the court—but that is fine: splendor inspires respect in the masses for the occasion; abroad the university and in general educational institutions are, for the most part, the most splendid buildings in town. But I think that this was somewhat frightening for the muzhik. For you know that it is a real misfortune to land in court, saints alive. The muzhik stands and they address him from one side, then another, and all of this politely in the formal form of address (and this is even more frightening). The prosecutor offered his opinion, he spoke angrily. They went out, they came in again: to prison, they said, but they shortened the sentence. Move on to the next case. Excellent.

This new judicial system is a surprisingly good thing. The most important thing is this system is good because it is fast. A man sits a year, maybe two while the investigation takes place and the indictment is prepared, and then all of a sudden the trial happens, and in one day everything is settled. They convicted him—he went back to prison, only now it will be punishment, and when he was sitting in jail before it was not punishment, but only a measure to preclude any way for the accused to escape from investigation and trial. If they acquitted you, then you are free, live where you like. If the authorities permit, of course. Splendid.

Letter III

✉ Engelgardt's third letter displays the degree to which he has penetrated rural relations during his first two years on Batishchevo and the extent to which he has taken on the local perspective.[1] Having focused earlier on peasant personalities and village vignettes, Engelgardt now turns to description and analysis of the peasants' attitudes toward contractual relationships, private property, and agricultural innovations. He concludes the letter by stressing again the fragile equilibrium of the peasants' subsistence economy and its impact on their worldview and behavior.

Engelgardt introduces two types of unpaid labor arrangements that peasants in his area undertake for local gentry and for each other: work done "out of respect" and work done "for damages." Both arrangements are characteristic of rural communities in which labor has not yet fully become a commercial commodity requiring cash compensation through a formal contract, but rather something a peasant may offer as a deposit against his or her own potential future needs or as a form of compensation for damages caused by the family's livestock through trespassing on neighbors' fields and gardens. In either case, peasants in the area around Engelgardt's estate prefer informal systems of mutual aid and compensation to his "German" or "St. Petersburg" approach of calculating a cash payment and making a formal agreement. As will become clear in future letters, not all work is suitable for this arrangement, and agricultural labor during the farming season in particular requires a formal arrangement with set compensation in cash or grain. But for tasks that peasants can do after their farm labor is complete, working "out of respect" or "for damages" is a well-established element in the network of relationships in the community.

In discussing his strategy for dealing with trespassing on his estate, Engelgardt also addresses the question of the peasants' attitudes toward private property. His emphasis on this point derives from the debate in educated society about the peasants' "legal consciousness." For jurists, officials, and others hoping to develop respect for formal law among the peasants, the vision of "the law" was predominantly a classical liberal one stressing the inviolability of private property as the sine qua non of individual protection under the law.

51

Therefore, many educated Russians were anxious to develop respect for private property among the peasants and to receive information on the current level of that respect. Engelgardt's appraisal was thus a partial response to that anxiety and desire for information.

His lengthy account of his experience with flax fleas and of the response of his steward, Ivan, is similarly a contribution to the societywide debate about agricultural innovations and the ability of peasants to participate in them. In this episode Engelgardt reveals his frustration as a chemist caught between the recommendations of German agronomists and the fatalism of his steward, who freezes when confronted by something entirely new to his knowledge of farming. This letter offers the first hint that the bloom may be fading on Engelgardt's infatuation with the practical know-how of the Russian peasant.

Engelgardt returns at the end of this letter to the tenuousness of the peasants' existence and offers accounts of two peasants to illustrate how constant economic pressures constrain and define them. Here we meet a peasant mother, Panfilikha, who thanks God for the death of one of her children, for her life is made easier by having one less mouth to feed. Engelgardt describes the trials of one Dema, who cannot meet all of the competing obligations to various landowners he has undertaken in an effort to survive a hungry winter. He portrays both Panfilikha and Dema as caught in the tight web of subsistence farming that can both harden the heart and demean the spirit.

⌘　⌘　⌘

Work Done "Out of Respect"

September. Indian summer has arrived. The forest has broken out in motley colors, the leaves on the trees have become brittle and are rustling as they do in autumn, but they have not yet frozen—there has been no frost. The sky is gray, a fine autumn sprinkle is drizzling, if there is a bit of sun, it shines through the clouds, and it is not very warm. It is damp; but thank God for that because, "if the weather is foul in Indian summer, then the autumn will be dry." We are waiting for frost from day to day; we in the country are always waiting for something: in the spring we wait for the first warm rainfall, in the autumn—the first frost, the first snow. Although we do not need the frost at all, it is impossible to have autumn without frost, it is somehow unsettling if there is no frost, we always think that something bad will come of this. Something exceptionally good happened this year: spring began in the first days of April and autumn has not yet begun in September, there have been five months without frost. "Will this lead to any good?" the "old woman" grumbles, "no, there is no frost, but then it will really get us! Everything is God's will," she adds, having suddenly remembered that it does not do to grumble, "everything is God's will, God is not without mercy, He is merciful, He knows better than we the reason of things."

But now even Indian summer has come to an end.[. . .] According to the calendar, autumn has come but there has still been no frost at all, it has become tedious even. Finally, on the Day of the Exaltation of the Cross [September 14] there was a real frost; it really set in during the night. I awoke in the morning and it was bright, clear, gay. I looked through the window, everything was white, the sunflowers hung their heads dejectedly, the leaves on the nasturtiums, the bean plants, and the morning glories had gone black—only the peas and the bluebonnets were still standing. After the frost the forest quickly became bare: the leaves on the laurels and aspens froze; after another frost, so did the birch trees. The leaves are flying so that with every day it becomes lighter and lighter in the woods, the fallen leaves rustle under your feet, the summer birds have flown away, the winter ones have gathered in a flock, the hare has begun to go white, and the first winter guests, the titmice, have begun to appear around the house.[. . .]

Once you begin to get used to it, even in autumn it is fine in the country, but most important, one is free here.

The cattle were brought in from the fields long ago. The horses have free rein, they wander untethered wherever they want. The peasants are happy, the grain came up well, the heavy labor in the field is over. Of course, even now the muzhik is not without work, but the day is short and the night is long—work does not tire him out so much during the day and there is time to rest at night; the bread is pure, plentiful. The sounds of gay fall wedding songs come in from the gardens and the barns; the women have already decided who should marry whom, and in their songs they accordingly match the names of boys and girls whose time has come to marry this autumn.

In the living quarters it is now obvious that it is autumn, there is the special smell you sense in autumn, entering a posting inn or a clean izba of a prosperous muzhik, priest, or merchant: the smell of onions, peas, dill, and so on. Onions are piled in one corner, in another beans and nasturtium seeds are ripening on frames. In the dining hall, the entire floor is covered with corn and sunflowers, all of these things are now ripening here. On the windows, on the tables, on the shelves are laid out flower and vegetable seeds, samples of hay, flax, and grain. Bunches of dill, thyme, and parsley hang on the walls.

We are harvesting the garden produce now. Avdotia has completely forgotten about me. She is so occupied with the garden and the flax—it is Avdotia's responsibility to deseed the flax and to decide if it has retted long enough—that she is ready to leave me without lunch. She runs by in the mornings.

"Today, Aleksandr Nikolaevich, I'll make you cabbage soup with mutton."

"And what else?"

"I'll roast some mutton."

"Could you not at least cook a duck with mushrooms, and not mutton, mutton, and more mutton, Avdotia?"

"Whatever you order," Avdotia says, beginning to get angry, "you always wait 'til too late, today the women are chopping cabbage, and now you want a duck . . . You can order what you will, only don't ask about the garden produce. I'm happy to make you a duck, but that means that we'll leave the cabbage. We've just wasted our time baking the pies."

"Well, all right, fine, roast some mutton, only don't forget to put in some garlic."

"I won't forget," Avdotia answers happily and she runs out quickly into the dining hall, from which her ringing voice is heard momentarily, "You, girls, go get the cabbage and I'll just turn the flax."

After about half an hour already, Avdotia runs to me with two handfuls of flax.

"Which flax is this?"

"From the Troshchenko fields. I deseeded it yesterday; in my opinion, it has retted long enough; it's really thick. The fine flax has not retted quite long enough, but the thick flax is done, please have a look yourself."[2]

"So, we shall take it up."

"It's your decision, but, in my opinion, it is time to lift it—some of it is already ripe in the retting, it's getting weak."

Avdotia runs into the garden, where her voice is heard again:

"You, girls, as soon as you have gathered the cabbage, eat lunch, and then begin to chop it, while I fix the master something to eat."

Avdotia prepares the meal, but her thoughts are far away, in the izba where they are chopping the cabbage. As soon as the meal is ready, she gives it to me to eat at barely eleven o'clock and without waiting until I have finished, having ordered Savelich to clear everything, runs into the dining hall to treat the women to vodka and pies, because the peasant women have come to gather the garden produce "out of respect."[. . .]

During the garden harvest, Avdotia displaced me completely, as though I were not even the master; it reached the point that she even moved into the house with her cabbage. While I was waking up one morning, I heard some kind of noise on the other side of the wall, they were pulling something, they were moving about.

"What's that?" I asked Avdotia.

"Why, they're going to chop the cabbage in the kitchen."

"Which cabbage?"

"The white cabbage; we're going to chop and shred the white cabbage for you. It's dirty in the dining hall, and for you, we need to do it more cleanly, and so I thought that we could chop it in the kitchen."

"And where am I to go?"

"Go out to the field for now, and in the evening you'll be able to sit all alone. It'll be fun, the babas will be playing songs, I called for the best players, we'll do 'The Drake.' "

"And will you sing 'That the rye should be full, that my wife will mow standing up, not breaking her back?' " I laughed.

"We'll play this one too." Avdotia is ready to agree to anything as long as I don't forbid them to shred the cabbage in the house: she wants terribly for the cabbage to turn out well, so that it won't be any worse than at neighboring gentry houses.

Of course I gave them permission to chop the cabbage in the house. Avdotia occupied all of the rooms and was ready to put some kind of tub in my office, but I defended the office. It was gay in the evening. Avdotia put the girls in the two clean rooms to shell the beans and go through the onions; in the kitchen, on Avdotia's territory, they chopped and shredded the cabbage. The babas and unmarried girls sang songs, and finally, having finished with the cabbage, left to dance. Avdotia directed everything, and even her husband, the steward Ivan, did not interfere with anything because cabbage is a woman's business. Everything came out very well; they chopped and shredded two enormous tubs which they then put in the kitchen. The next day I left to go visiting and returned after several days. I came into the rooms and there was the most horrible stench, it was impossible to breathe freely.

"Why does it stink so in here, Avdotia?"

"Saints preserve us!"

"You cannot even come into the house."

"I don't know. There's no such thing, it hardly smells of cabbage, it's marinating, it's fermenting. That's all it could be."

In fact, it was the cabbage fermenting.

Women from two neighboring villages gathered all of the garden produce on my place "out of respect"; they gathered only the potatoes "for damages."

Work done "out of respect," like that done at work bees, is done for free, without pay; but, of course, there must be refreshments, and vodka above all else, of course. When she plans to chop the cabbage, to clean beets, and so forth, Avdotia invites, "asks," the peasant women to come "to help." No one ever refuses, one or two women come from each household early in the morning. They have some vodka, they bake pies, they prepare the best possible lunch, and if there is something to make it from, they make a meat aspic without fail—that is the best treat. These people who offer their assistance always work excellently, especially the women since they never work for a daily wage. Everyone tries to do the best possible, to stand out, so to speak. The work is accompanied by gaiety, jokes, laughter, songs. They work as if they were playing, but, I repeat, splendidly, just as if they were at home. This is not even considered working, but "helping." A baba from a prosperous household, especially now in the autumn, will not go to work as a day laborer, but "out of respect," "to help," to "a work bee," she will come and work superbly, completely willingly, efficiently, even better than a baba from a poor household, because in a prosperous household where there is a good master, even the women are in order, they know how to do everything, and moreover, they are stronger because they live on good food. You cannot even say that it is only the vodka which brings them because even those women who do not drink vodka come. It even happens that they will arrive without having been called, having found out that there is some kind of work to be done. Of course, this all happens because, even now, the muzhik is always dependent on the neighboring landowner; the muzhik needs a little firewood and a little meadow, and pasture, and sometimes he needs to lay his hands on a little money, maybe he will have to seek advice about something because all of us walk under God—and suddenly, God save us, someone will be called to court—how can you not show respect to the nobleman just in case! And in the village, well, it is the same thing: everyone goes "out of respect" to the rich muzhik through a "work bee" because it just may happen that they will have to turn to him for help for one thing or another. I have noticed that the richer the village, the more prosperous and thoughtful the peasants, the more they will try to have good relations with the landowner who is their nearest neighbor. The prosperous muzhik is always polite, respectful, ready for any small service—what does it cost him to send a woman for a day or two when the fieldwork is done? Of course, he will not hire himself out for nothing, but if the price is right, advantageous, then even he will take on work and will work excellently.[. . .]

Two years ago, when I arrived in the village, that first spring, my dam washed away in the river's flooding and the road was spoiled. So I, as a Petersburger would, thought that it was impossible to drive on it. Of course, I soon became convinced that it is possible to go on any kind of road, because if you cannot go in a cart, then you can go in the front of the wagon—in the spring the peasants usually ride on the cart's front, where they put a small basket on the axle, and it is always possible to go by horseback or on foot. But then, when I was still a novice, when I heard my steward propose to a passing landlowner who wanted to cross to the other side of the river that he ride on our horse, and when, furthermore, he insisted that this was completely safe because the horse is smart, careful, experienced, knows the road, and swims where it is deep—I was extremely embarrassed and decided to mend the road as soon as the water fell and to patch the break in the dam. According to my calculations, it should not take more than twenty cubic meters of dirt to repair the dam and road, and if you hire navvies, or common laborers as they are called around here, then the work would run about thirty rubles; but there were no common laborers nearby, and it seemed to me, as a Petersburger, that it would not do to leave the road in such condition and that it was essential to repair it immediately. That is why I asked the neighboring peasants and proposed that they take this work on. The peasants asked one hundred rubles for the job. I offered thirty, I offered fifty, and they flatly refused. "We won't go any lower than one hundred rubles," they said. So, I thought, they are putting the squeeze on me. They know that I can't hire common laborers anywhere, and that is why they are pressing me.

You see, I had taken it into my head then that it was absolutely necessary to repair the road immediately and that the peasants, knowing this, were squeezing me. Now, as I write these lines, that distress seems ridiculous because now, if the road goes bad, I just say coolly: summer will come, God will bring good weather, the road will repair itself, and let anyone who wants to clear it now. And besides, who in the world drives in the spring? Why drive at such a time? They may call you to the justice of the peace—go ahead, summon me—to the justice of the peace if you like, he is also a man, he understands that I have no power against the forces of God. The justice! As if he has a better road than mine on his estate? Everybody knows that you can get through on a village road anyway. Somehow we get by, it is possible to drive on a cart—you will survive.[. . .]

I repeat, now I have gotten used to all of this; I know that one should not drive in the fall and the spring, and even in the summer, setting out on the road, one should cross oneself—but then, as a novice, I got terribly upset. It was necessary to clear the road, and the peasants were demanding an unimaginable price for the job—one hundred rubles. What was I to do about this? The peasants were really stubborn about the one hundred rubles.

The next day, the first peasant who befriended me when I arrived in the country came to see me. This peasant had been taken out of the village during serfdom and taken into house service as a servant boy in the house where I lived until I was fifteen. We were friends in our childhood and sometimes played, ran, and fought together back then. Then, I was sent to St. Petersburg, and Stepka wound up in cooking, he was a cook for one of the young lords with whom, as he expressed it, he knocked off two campaigns: the Hungarian and the Crimean. After the Crimean War, Stepan[3] received his freedom, he served for a long time in St. Petersburg at one of the gymnasiums[4] there. In the end he got sick, lay for eight months in the hospital, and when he had recovered, on the doctor's advice, returned to the village—his household was prosperous—where in several years he became a complete peasant, he learned to plough, reap, thresh.[5] He died this winter—he was a very smart man, an honest worker, an excellent head of household, he got along well with others, he understood everything, and enjoyed enormous respect in the village. When I arrived in the village, Stepan came by to congratulate me on my arrival; I was very glad to see him, we began to reminisce about old times, how we climbed the dovecote together, how we stole cherries, and how we teased the old gardener, Osip. I, of course, treated Stepan to both a little vodka and tea. Afterward, Stepan would sometimes come to my place on holidays to spend an evening chatting: we drank tea, we talked about St. Petersburg, about old and new times, about farming. Stepan explained a lot about rural relations to me, he gave me a lot of good advice. "Now it is possible to farm even better than before when there were serfs," Stepan would say. "Now everything has become more expensive, especially since they brought the road in; don't worry that there won't be enough workers, don't be afraid that the land will lie fallow, they'll work all of it; do it so that it will be profitable for both you and the muzhik, then everything will turn out well for you."

"And how am I to do this?"

"You've got to be a farmer for this. If you make yourself a farmer, then everything'll be fine, but if you don't turn yourself into a farmer, then it's not worthwhile to live in the country. Just do everything the way folks in the country do, and not the way you do in St. Petersburg. You can't do it any other way here. You'll see for yourself."

After the conversation with the peasants about repairing the dam and road, Stepan came to see me the next day and brought me a hare.

"Look, I've killed a hare, a gray one, and I've brought it to you, Aleksandr Nikolaevich."

"Thank you, this is splendid, roast it yourself and we shall eat it together."

Stepan roasted the hare, we drank, sat down to eat, and of course talked about the break in the dam. I complained that the peasants were squeezing me and demanding one hundred rubles for work which was worth thirty rubles at the most.

"You didn't handle that right, Aleksandr Nikolaevich," Stepan said. "You want to do everything with money the way you do in St. Petersburg; that's not the way we do things here."

"But how else?"

"Why do you have to hire them? Just call them to help you, everyone'll come out of respect for you, and they will repair both the road and the bridge. Of course, give them a glass of vodka each."

"Yes, but is it not easier, it would seem, to work for money? The deal is cleaner that way."

"Well, Germans might think that's easier, but the way we do things, it doesn't turn out to be any easier. As neighbors, we shouldn't take your money, but everyone'll come 'out of respect,' take my word."

"Fine, let us assume that I call for assistance. I will need good refreshments, and you know yourself that I do not have any household equipment, I don't even have tables."

"You don't need any of that. Everyone knows you haven't set up housekeeping yet, so they'll have breakfast at home before they come, you give each one of them a glass of vodka, and you should come yourself, as the master, to the job. The question here isn't vodka, they'll come 'out of respect,' you only need the vodka to make the work more cheerful."

"It seems to me that it would be much easier to do it for money. This is a time when there is no fieldwork, it's all the same, they would just be lying on the stove. Am I not offering them a good price?"

"Of course the price is good, but a muzhik'll do it more quickly 'out of respect.' That's why they demanded such an absurd one hundred rubles. Look, listen, I myself would absolutely not do this kind of job for money, but 'out of respect,' of course, I'll come, and there are a lot of folks like me. Out of respect, all of the rich ones'll come; what'll it cost us to send a man and horse from each household? This is free time, it's all the same, we're just hanging about."

"But wait, isn't all farm work done for money?"

"Farm work's different. You can't do that any other way."

"I don't understand, Stepan."

"Look! Your dam washed away, the road's ruined, that, you see, is from God. How could anyone not help as a neighbor? And if, God save us, someone's barn burns, it's not likely you wouldn't help with some wood, would you? Your dam's been ruined—you immediately hire for money, that means you don't want to live as a neighbor, it means you're going to do everything the German's way, with money. Today you need to repair your dam, you pay money; tomorrow we need something—we'll pay you money. It's better to live as neighbors—we help you, and you don't turn us down. Of course we can't live without you: we need a little firewood, some meadow, and we don't have any place to pasture our livestock. Both for us and for you it's better to live as neighbors, fairly."

"Well then, fine."

"They only did one thing badly, they asked you for money, the fools; they should've said straight out: 'Excuse us, Aleksandr Nikolaevich, why should we do this for money, we'll come out of respect.' If you had sent to our village, this is what we would've said. So you try this: say you're willing to give them one hundred rubles, and see how they scratch their heads. If they take one hundred rubles from you, then you won't forget they squeezed you; then already, this means we won't live as neighbors. Then you'll tell them they can't pick mushrooms; of course, the mushrooms won't be any use to you, they'll rot, you'll even have to hire a guard, but a muzhik can't get by without mushrooms. You'll also tell them they can't gather young heather, and you won't give them moss for building, and you won't let them pick berries, and if they even let their livestock get *onto* your land, you'll grab it and put it in a stall. You can squeeze the muzhik from all sides. You won't return your one hundred rubles, of course, and the muzhik won't be able to get any support from you; and quarrels and unpleasantness will break out between us. That's why it is better to live as neighbors, fairly: we'll help you and you won't turn us down. They're fools for asking for money, our village would never have done this. Send tomorrow, Aleksandr Nikolaevich, to our village and ask for people to come to a work bee."

I heeded Stepan and sent my steward to ask in the two neighboring villages for help repairing the dam and clearing the road. The next day, twenty-five men showed up, all of the splendid big fellows came, because even the rich peasants had sent their children, with twenty-five horses, and they did everything in one day. Since then, we have begun to live as neighbors and soon it will already be two years without any unpleasantness whatsoever.

Trespassing and the Peasants' Sense of Private Property

I said above that my potatoes were gathered "for damages." The question of trespassing is considered an important one in farming and last year it was brought up for consideration by the St. Petersburg Assembly of Landowners. "The second widespread evil in Russia (the first evil was the high cost of working hands)"—the assembly said—"is trespassing on both meadows and fields, especially where there are numerous small landholders. Fines lead only to unpleasant conflicts, and for the most part they are not an option since the peasants are not always in a position to pay for trespassing. Could not some measures be suggested which are more lasting and mutually beneficial for neighbors?" the assembly asked.[. . .] I would like to make my contribution and describe how I have set myself up in regard to trespassing.

I will begin with the fact that I work my farm as a business to which I give my soul, by which I live (and not only in the material sense) and that I cannot adopt a casual attitude to damages caused by trespassing. My flowers, my vegetables, my flax, my clover,[6] and my grain are so dear to me that if someone offered for my cabbage twice what it is worth, if only I would allow pigs to root freely in my garden, I would not agree to such a bargain. If my estate were in an area where there were military maneuvers, and my fields were trampled down each year, and even if they paid thrice the value for the trampling, I would still abandon the farm. I say all of this so that you will not think that I take trespassing lightly.[. . .]

The peasants also are very strict about trespassing. It is well known that peasants are the most extreme when it comes to owning private property, and not a single peasant will give up a single one of his kopeks, not a single shred of hay. A peasant is merciless if someone tramples his grain; he will pursue the trespassing to the last degree, will take a poor man's last shirt, he will beat him up if there is nothing to take, but he will not excuse damage caused by trespassing. In precisely the same way, the peasant recognizes that one must not trample someone else's grain, that he must pay for the damage, and if there really is damage, then the peasant will pay and bear you no grudge if you take a fair fine. Of course the peasant does not nurture an unconditional respect for other people's property for the sake of principle, and *if it is possible,* he will let his horse loose in someone else's field or meadow, exactly as he will chop wood in another's forest, if possible, will take someone else's hay, if possible—it's all the same if it is the landlord's or a peasant's—just as he will not do any of another man's work if it is possible, he will try to pile all the work on his partner; for this reason peasants avoid as much as possible joint or wholesale labor. If you hire, say, four men to dig a ditch by the job with a set price by the sazhen, they will not dig the ditch together, but will divide it into four sections and each one will dig his section separately. *If it is possible,* the peasant will let his animals loose on a landlord's field, of this there is no doubt. If he is caught trespassing, the peasant, although he recognizes instinctively that he should pay for the damage, will, of course, come to the landlord and ask him to forgive the trespass, he will say that the horse accidentally jumped over, and so forth, in the hope that the lord, out of simplicity, that is, out of stupidity, not as a farmer, but as a man who does not value his property—it's well known what a lord is!—will rant and rave, but will forgive.

Of course, if the lord is simple, he is not a farmer, and he does not file suit for the damages, then the peasants will trespass in his meadows and fields, and will let their horses loose in the garden. Why not feed the horses in the lord's field if he is not going to seek damages? Why not let the horses loose, without supervision, if this is possible? Why should the peasant worry about someone else's property if the master himself is not concerned?

I cannot agree in any way with the St. Petersburg Assembly "that fines lead only to unpleasant conflicts." There will be no unpleasant conflicts if the master demands compensation for his property, if he takes a fine that is consonant with the actual damage, just as a muzhik takes from another muzhik, one village takes from another village (I have not yet seen a case where a muzhik would not take from another muzhik for trespassing or another village would not take from another—and there are no unpleasant conflicts between two muzhiks or two villages because of this), if there is no carping, no whining, no extortion, no desire to use fines to make the peasants do some kind of work under conditions which are not profitable for them, no so-called striving to teach the peasants to execute and respect the law, and so on.[7] The sources of unpleasant conflicts are usually whining, extortion, and disputes.

"I do not want your horses on my land! Don't you dare let your horses loose on my pasture!"

"So! You don't want to work for me, well then, I will pressure you. You're not going to be able to show your face anywhere. I'll hire five watchmen . . . ."

A war will break out, and since the muzhik does not like trouble and especially does not like courts, he will usually give in; but I think that if the muzhik dug in his heels, the lord would have to concede because just as much as the muzhik needs pasture and so forth, the landlord needs working hands.

If you penetrate the position of the peasants, if you get to know rural daily life, if you discard the concepts you have borrowed from German books about agriculture, then even the question of trespassing will be decided rather simply. Of course, when the peasants become prosperous, when they plant clover, enclose their fields with live hedges, and feed their stock in the summer in their stalls, then there will be no trespassing. But now it is necessary to arrange matters to fit with local circumstances. Peasant livestock is always pastured with a herdsman; the herdsman is usually bad, of course, but with a herdsman all the same. If he does not let the livestock graze on purpose, there will be no serious damage.[. . .] It does happen that because of the neglect of the herdsman one cow will break free from the herd and will go onto a meadow or into the grain; this, of course, calls for a fine. The peasants, of course, demand this fine from their herdsman if he trespasses even on their fields, just as they will file suit for a fine—and if there is nothing to take, they beat him. If the damage is done by cattle who are under the care of a herdsman, then it is impossible not to take a fine because a village herdsman, seeing that the lord does not demand compensation for trespassing, will think that he is simple, that is, a fool, and one should teach a fool, and he will simply feed his cattle on the lord's meadow.[. . .] Damage by cattle, sheep, even swine, as long as the garden does not border the village directly, happens rarely when the herdsman knows that you keep a sharp lookout and do not pardon trespassing.

Horses are another matter. Horses are not pastured with the livestock. Having finished with feeding, the peasant will leave his horses to feed, and will go take a rest himself. Supervision of the horses is given in this case to the children, and each household looks after their own horses, and of course, *only their own,* so that if a boy from the Panasovs', taking care of his horses, sees that the horses from the Semenov household have gone into someone else's grain, he will not drive them out: "Look out for your own horses yourself, what business is it of ours." At night, the horses are driven into a night field where, again, each household looks after its own horses. It is from the night field that the horses more often than anywhere else fall into trespassing; in the evening, the boys who are usually made responsible for keeping an eye on the horses in the night field keep a good watch on the horses, and the horses, until they finish eating, do not go far. But then the boys, having played about, fall asleep at dawn, and the horses get loose. Therefore, more often than not, it is the horses which trespass; but if there is good supervision, if the elder or watchman goes around the fields and pastures every day, if the master himself is in the fields often and sees for himself what has been trampled, and having seen, does not let the elder go, if he does not give the seized horses back for free, then it is not possible to say that trespassing happens often. The horses of prosperous peasants, strict masters, who have many good horses, rarely cause damage, because the master himself goes into the night field, or sends "an old fellow"—in a rich household there is almost always some old fellow or other, the grandfather or uncle of the head of the household, because prosperous peasants live to very old age for the most part—or a worker, or if there are boys, then the boys of a strict master do not play around and do not let the horses get loose.

For a peasant, a fine is not as important as the loss of time when the horse turns out to have been seized: you have to look for it, find it at the lord's house, wait until they give it back. Besides, it is shameful: that's a fine master if he cannot look after his horses. For you know that if a horse can go into someone else's field, then it could just as easily be stolen.[. . .]

Since I know the proverbs, "rogues teach honest men to keep on their guard," "if you don't leave things lying around, you won't tempt a thief"; since I know that everyone considers it his responsibility to "teach the fool," since I know from experience that if I do not take a fine, the peasants will trespass on the fields and meadows—they will drive their horses to feed on my meadow or on my oats—I always strictly demand compensation for trespassing. And since the peasants usually do not have money, and I do not want to take money, anyway, because a fine is taken essentially to cause fear, so that they will be wary and not let their horses loose idly, then the steward will return the horse that has been caught trespassing—on an unmowed meadow or in the grain—to the peasant for something as a surety: a jacket, a belt, a cap. In the spring, when the peasants let the cattle into the field, usually many horses stray the first time: they drive several of them back, take sureties, the peasants begin to watch their horses more carefully. The peasants will watch them carefully for around three or four weeks, there will be no trespassing, then they will let their guard down; again we will drive several animals back, take sureties, again they will begin to keep a stricter watch—and this is the way it goes all summer. In the autumn, when the peasants have less work, the steward will call all those from whom he has taken sureties to dig potatoes or gather the garden produce "for damages," and will return their goods upon the completion of the work. It is interesting to note that when we call those who have committed trespassing to dig potatoes for a day or two—I do not have many potatoes—not only those whose horses were caught trespassing, but also those whose horses were not caught come. This year, one neighboring village, where the majority of the peasants are prosperous, without being called, sent one baba from each household to dig potatoes, although not one horse was caught trespassing all summer from this village. The deposit is obviously taken only "for a warning"—if you do not keep a close eye on your horses, then it is possible according to the law to take a money fine—which is why if you "call," all of the neighbors will come to dig potatoes in the fall, even without that.[. . .]

It seems to me that trespassing is only an imaginary "evil," and that the view of the St. Petersburg Assembly is not entirely correct on this subject. The matter is much more simple if you look at it from up close. If the landowner himself knows every desiatina in his field, if he looks over the field often, if he knows how to assess how great the damage caused by trespassing is, if he regards trespassing calmly and does not whine, does not extort from the peasants, if the watchman is strict, then there will be no unpleasant conflicts. It is written and said that the first evil is the high cost of workers; the second evil is damage caused by trespassing; the third evil is the workers' failure to honor contracts. In fact it does not turn out to be so; workers are cheap, so cheap that the worker never earns enough to have a piece of meat for lunch, a bed at night, boots, and even a little leisure. Damages due to trespassing?— but with trespassing, as I said above, *the landlord* can always solve the problem. The failure of workers to observe contracts?—but why is it that prosperous peasants, when they hire workers, never make any contracts and no problems arise? Of course, the muzhik does not relate to the gentry in the same way that he does to another peasant; of course, the muzhik has a certain kind of hidden feeling toward the gentry . . .

The muzhik is not able to pay his taxes, but who levied them? The lords, the muzhik says. Who is selling property for arrears? Again, the lords. The justice of the peace sentenced the peasant to three and half months of jail for stealing two loads of hay; the muzhik asks to write a complaint to the assembly of justices of the peace and can in no way understand that it is not possible to complain about the fact that the justice sentenced him to three and a half months of jail for two loads.

"Three and a half months for just two loads?"

"Yes, there is such a law."

"Forgive me, where is such a law? Look, judge for yourself, is this fair!"

"You must understand, it is written in the law."

"What kind of law is this? Who was it who wrote this law? The lords wrote all of this."

And so it is in everything. Everything—the demand for arrears, the demand that they repair the road, the requirement that they send their children to school, recruitment, the decisions of the courts—all of this comes from the lords. The muzhik does not know "laws"; he respects only some kind of divine law.[8] For example, if having caught a muzhik with a load of stolen hay, you take the hay back, give him a thrashing, and tell him not to steal, then that is fine with him; if a kulak, having bought some hemp, finds a handful of it to be rotten and gives the muzhik a thrashing and tells him not to trick him, it is nothing; this will all be just. But here is this law that you can get three and a half months in jail for a load of hay—that means that the lords decreed that the muzhik be locked up.

Living in the country, farming, living in the closest relations with the muzhik, you constantly feel this secret feeling, and it is this that makes rural life difficult in the extreme . . . You must agree that it is difficult to live in a society where everyone has a hostile attitude to you, if not as an individual, then as a lord. But, however, well, we'll leave it . . .

Peasant Fatalism and Attitudes toward Agricultural Innovation

This year we are having a harvest unlike any we have had for a long time; everything came up beautifully, even the mushrooms and nuts. God, in his mercy, did not let Kassian look on us, and it is well known that "everything will wither if terrible Kassian even glances at it."[9] For this reason, there is only one holiday in four years for the merciless Kassian, while there are two each year for Nicholas the Good Miracle Worker. But the summer this year was awful for the farmer, especially the hot-tempered and immature one. Can you believe that I nearly went out of my mind this summer? This is what the problem was.

Having taken up farming two years ago, I quickly calculated that to farm in the old way, that is, to plant rye and oats, to keep livestock for manure and feed them with whatever was left from half of the harvest, in a word, to practice agriculture as it was practiced in this area by the majority of the gentry who did not concern themselves with farming and who earned their money through state or zemstvo service—was not worthwhile. A simple calculation quickly showed that it was necessary to change the system of farming, to introduce new grains, to improve the livestock. I will not talk here about various considerations of this subject, that would take us too far afield; I will only say that I began from my first year to introduce flax. The peasants, of course, were against this innovation, they said that flax would not grow here, that I would not find anyone willing to work it, that the flax would ruin the soil, and so forth.[. . .] Last fall, I selected four desiatinas of abandoned meadow to put in flax; birch groves had grown on some of them. Beginning in the autumn, we cleared the birches, we burned the roots, we threw the ashes on each desiatina and turned the meadows for the winter. The spot was excellently chosen, because of the old manure the land was superb, the work was carried out masterfully. The meadows froze up splendidly over the winter and were beautifully lush in the spring. The day for planting was excellent; we could not have planted and covered it any better. We planted the flax on the second, third, and fourth of May; on the evening of the fourth of May, when the last flax had been covered, a warm soaking rain fell, which made the soil good and wet and flattened the ploughed soil firmly; the fifth was cloudy; it rained on the sixth; on the seventh sprouts began to appear. On the morning of the eighth, looking over the flowers and vegetables in the garden, I was struck by the fact that all of the young leaves on the rhubarb seemed to be full of holes. I looked closely and I saw that small, dark brown, shiny jumping bugs were sitting on the leaves—earth fleas that I had not seen before, completely different from the earth fleas with the gold stripes on their back which we know well, which eat the sprouts of turnips and radishes. After I had looked over one garden, the small one near the house, the landlord's, as the steward calls it, because I work this one myself and am raising various, lordly vegetables in it, I went to another, the peasants' garden, where, on my place, by the way, there was a small portion of flax planted. This flax was planted before that in the field, it had come up nicely and was already a vershok high. I looked at the flax, and the same earth fleas which were on the rhubarb were on the flax, and were eating the young leaves. So what is this that has befallen us? I thought. And I ran to the field.

I glanced at the flax and nearly fainted. Imagine, the entire field was covered with an incalculable quantity of earth fleas which had attacked the young shoots of flax; several fleas sat on each plant gnawing away at the young leaves. There were fewer fleas in the lower area, where it was wetter, where the flax had already grown; where it was drier, where the flax had trouble coming up, that was where the wretched flea was gnawing. The flax was perishing before my eyes. So, I thought, this is the end; in two or three days they will eat it all, so there's your flax for you, there's your innovation. They'll say that we told you that flax would not grow here, that even our grandfathers did not work with flax. The question here was not money, of course; the loss of the one hundred rubles paid for the cultivation of four desiatinas would not have ruined me, but the business would drag on, and with the introduction of anything new, the first thing is success. If one thing comes out well, another, a third, then you get respect and trust in your knowledge. "That, my chap, is a good head," they would say, "that is a farmer." And they would already look at each new thing with less mistrust, and if in the course of several years everything goes well, then you can earn so much trust that they will take up any novelty.

It is understandable why I was so shaken by this unexpected misfortune.

What was I to do? Having had my fill of seeing how the fleas were eating the flax, I ran home.

"Well, Avdotia, our flax has failed."

"God preserve us!"

"Yes. I already told you that it has failed. Where is Ivan?"

Avdotia was frightened; she thought that her husband, the steward Ivan, had done something wrong.

When I found Ivan, I took him to the field of flax without a word.

"Do you see? What is it?"

At first Ivan could not understand what I was asking him about. I pointed at a flea.

"I see, now I see, there are little insects."

"Yes, little insects, and do you see, that these little insects are eating the flax?"

Ivan was dubious, but after he looked more carefully, even he agreed that, in fact, the insects were gnawing away at the leaves on the flax.

"That's nothing."

"What do you mean, nothing? Do you not see that they are eating it, and well, they are eating everything. Our flax will perish."[. . .]

But in this case, Ivan was not convinced that the fleas could really eat up all of the flax. "Because there are few insects this summer."

That day I ran ten times to look at the flax—and they were gnawing away.[. . .]

I simply thought that I would go out of my mind. Wherever I went, whatever I did, everywhere there seemed to be fleas. I would drink tea, begin to think, and a cloud of fleas would be jumping before my eyes; I would throw down the unfinished glass and run to the field, they would be gnawing. I even lost sleep: I would lie down, I would just fall asleep and a myriad of earth fleas would appear before my eyes, they would be jumping, turning: look how they grow, grow, grow to be as big as elephants . . . It was stuffy, hot; tormented by the nightmare, I would jump up. It would be getting light. I would put on a robe and run to the field. The dew had not dried yet, it seemed there were fewer fleas, they had taken cover, were sitting in clumps on lumps of earth; the flax had perked up, revived by the dew. Soothed, I returned to the house and fell asleep. After waking up rather late, I called Ivan.

"Well, what?"

Ivan shrugged his shoulders. At first he considered this a trifle, "since they are insects and there are not many of them." But seeing that the fleas, having fallen on the first leaves that came out of the earth (the seed lobes), and had eaten them clean, so that the root was drying up, he became convinced that the fleas were really ruining the shoots, and he also began to have some doubts. But I could see what he was thinking: there is a reason for this.

"Are they eating it?"

"They are gnawing away, it was better in the morning, they must be afraid of the dew, but now they've set to it again. And where do so many of them come from?"

"Our flax is failing."

"It is God's will."

"What are we going to do?"

Ivan does not say anything, shifts from one foot to the other, and trying to turn my thoughts away from the flax, starts a conversation about planting oats, for which the weather is so propitious. Ivan, as an experienced man, who has already long served as a steward, who has rubbed elbows with gentry, is always concerned about the good humor of the lord.[. . .] Now Ivan, thinking to turn my thoughts away from the flax, applied himself to another aspect of the farm.

"How well the cattle are eating! The new cow, the one you bought recently, should calve soon. If only God would give us a female!"

I remain silent.

"The land is giving a good yield this year. Rarely is there such a planting. How the rye's ripening! If God does everything, the harvest will be excellent."[. . .]

What do I care about the rye? I did not go to the rye field even once during the entire spring; what do I care about the oats? I run out again to look at the flax. They eat away, the leaves do not even manage to return before a whole bunch of fleas sits on them and gnaws.

What was to be done? I dug up all my books, looking for methods to destroy fleas. The Germans proposed many methods. "For its elimination—that is, the flax flea—sprinkle the shoots of flax with ashes," I read in one book. I call Ivan.

"Ivan, you still do not believe that the fleas will eat up the flax, but even in this book it is written that the flea destroys shoots of flax. The Germans have noticed it, and you say that it has never happened."

"It's never happened, as much flax as I've planted."

"So, you see, you do not believe it!"

"Why not believe it, everything happens—look at what happened at the noblewoman B.'s—you know yourself—this spring the magpies were set loose."

At first Ivan did not grant the fleas any kind of significance whatsoever, but then, having become convinced that the insects were actually eating the shoots, and that the flax would fail as a result, he claimed that these were not real fleas—there had never been anything like them before—that these were not simple insects, but some kind of curse laid on by evil people out of envy, just as magpies and rats could be a curse. In fact, something like this happened at one of my neighbors' this spring—magpies were set loose. For no reason whatsoever, in the spring, when the livestock were already weak,[10] could hardly stand, a multitude of magpies appeared, which began to fly in the stalls and to peck the cows' backs: they would come into the stall, would sit on the cows' backs and set to pecking—all of the cows' backs were wounded in a most horrible way. No matter what they did, nothing helped (look what happens when you introduce Simental cattle here!);[11] the peasants tried to drive them away, they shot at them, someone suggested that they send for the old men,[12] finally the noblewoman sent for a priest to read a high service. Then, several weeks later, having met a priest at one of the rich landowners on his nameday, I told him about the magpies. "This happens; the real question is *what kind of magpies*, if they are a curse, then this is bad," the priest said thoughtfully. On our place something also happened recently: rats appeared in the stalls of one of the Polish tenants, they ran over the cows, they ate their hides, they made nests on their backs; he worried and worried over them, and even though he was a Catholic, he called the priests to sprinkle the cattle with holy water, which he had not done before.

"In your opinion, these fleas are a curse? Everything is a curse with you." I began to get angry: "If the cattle die, if the stall won't stand right, if a cow gets sick, it is because someone put a spell on them."

"After you live in the country a bit, Aleksandr Nikolaevich, you'll get to know for yourself that everything can happen. You can't protect yourself against an evil man."

"Well, why are we blabbering away, in the book it says that they eat the flax. I only know that if we don't do anything, then our flax will die."

"But what is there to do, Aleksandr Nikolaevich?"

"They advise sprinkling ashes on it. What do you think?"

"Well . . ."

"To eliminate them, sprinkle the shoots of flax with ashes," I read slowly from the book.

Ivan is silent.

"So why aren't you saying anything?"

"Show me how. We could try it: maybe the women have not raked out all of the ashes from the stoves already, we may find some."

"They haven't raked it all out, they haven't raked it all out! Go look!"

Ivan leaves. Indeed, where are we to find the ashes to sprinkle four desiatinas? Again I begin to rummage through the books: "In other localities, spread flowers of sulphur [a common fungicide] mixed with water on the shoots. Equally useful in this case is flooding the shoots with water in which guano has been mixed." But it is impossible to get guano here, but why not try flowers of sulphur? I call Ivan.

"Look here, Ivan. Of course we will not get enough ashes now for four desiatinas, but it says here in the book that flooding the shoots with flowers of sulphur mixed in water is good. What do you think?"

Ivan is silent.

"We could send to town to buy the flowers of sulphur. We could mix two barrels, that would be enough to water it—you have seen how they spray the highway?"

Ivan is silent.

"Why are you not saying anything? Haven't you seen how they spray the streets in Petersburg?"

"It's possible to fit the barrels, we'll make the planks out back."

"Well, then, let's fit them; you know that will do, you have noticed yourself that the flea does not like moisture, and here there is the sulphur water besides."

"We'll need a lot of water, Aleksandr Nikolaevich."

"Of course, but you know very well yourself, that nothing gets done without a lot of work; it is only too bad that the book does not say how much flowers of sulphur is needed per desiatina. I think that two puds[13] will be enough."

Ivan is silent.

"We'll send Sidor to town today, tomorrow evening he'll be back, let him go on the light brown horse, it goes faster, and we'll fit two barrels in the meantime."

"As you order, we can send Sidor."

"Only, will he get flowers of sulphur there?"

"He'll get whatever there is; if they don't have any in the shops, then he can get it in the apothecary. I got it at the apothecary for the dogs—they put a good-sized portion in a packet for ten kopeks."

Silence. I leaf through the book. Ivan shifts from foot to foot.

"If he can't get flowers of sulphur, then he can get saltpeter; there is always saltpeter in the shops."

"Saltpeter? What do you mean, saltpeter?"

"Why the kind that you put in salted beef, so that worms won't get in it, worms are afraid of saltpeter. Borax is also good, it helps with cockroaches."

"No, that is not necessary. Go on."

Ivan leaves. I rummage through the books again: I look to see if there is not something in the market-gardening courses. "For the elimination of these insects, frequent dousings with water are effective, as well as sprinkling lime or tobacco; the substance recommended by Bushe has also proven to be especially effective, namely: sprinkling ground wormwood; others favor the sprinkling of garlic water." None of this will do; how am I to sprinkle water here—the first one will dry up while we go to the second; there is no lime, there is no wormwood, and you cannot even always get enough garlic for the cucumbers. Could you really spread tobacco? It will not do: when you crush it, and then spread it, it would be awkward, it would get all in your eyes. I begin to go crazy, I curse the Germans, and even more the Russian compilers of scholarly guides on agriculture. "Mix flowers of sulphur in water and spread it on the shoots." How clever! And probably they make students learn all of this and flunk them and do not grant academic degrees if they do not know ways to destroy this harmful insect, this scourge of agriculture . . .

Again I dig through my books—still going by books out of old habit—I leaf through them again, my eyes even become dim from the intense attention; and look, it seems there is an appropriate method: "Make two frames one foot high in the row, attach a strong canvas to them, smear both sides with a very sticky substance, for example, tar or birdlime. Add handles of three feet length to the front part of the frame, and on the back, attach small twigs. When you run these frames several times along the row, many of these jumping bugs will get stuck to the sticky surface of the canvas." It seems that this would be good; this was proposed for gardens, but, I thought, if you make the frame larger, covered with a large canvas, smear it with tar and carry it on wheels to the field, then the fleas would jump and become stuck to the tar. Excellent, I think, when it collects a lot of fleas, then one can clean the frame, smear it again with tar, and take it to the field again. And we will not throw the fleas away, as many as are caught, but put them in the compost, after all the Germans use May bugs in compost, which they simply catch with their hands. I ran to the field, the flax was covered with fleas, I hit the ground with my cane, the fleas jumped. Excellent, I noticed at what height they jumped. That is how high we will build the frames.

Having run back home, I call Ivan and tell him about the frames.

Ivan is silent.

"But you see, this, it seems, will work. We will build the frames on wheels, you understand, we will smear them with tar, and take them along the field."

Ivan is silent.[. . .]

"So why are you not saying anything? You tell me, what do you think? Surely, it won't be hard to build the frames? It's not difficult?"

Ivan is silent.

"So why are you keeping quiet? You know they are gnawing away."

"They're eating, just think, they've eaten the whole border on Kuzin's desiatina. That's how they're gnawing."

"So?"

"Whatever you order, only in my opinion, Aleksandr Nikolaevich, it would be best of all to call for the priests to say prayers. God is not without mercy, He'll give some rain, and everything will be fine; you've noticed yourself that the flea fears God's dew."

In several days, I had been driven utterly to distraction. I had gone without sleep or food, I lost weight and even began to talk nonsense, I wanted to write the Moscow Committee for Agricultural Consultation . . .

What was to be done? I thought and thought, and finally, having sent all of the Germans to the devil, both the original ones and the translated ones, I decided.

"Well, Ivan," I said, "I've decided: if there is no rain tomorrow, if the fleas do not diminish, then we will plant another crop, we'll harrow again well, we'll plant again, it's not too late."

At first Ivan opposed such a decision, but I beat him down on all points which consisted mainly of the fact, that maybe, God would provide, and we could avoid this. Finally, I offered him this ultimatum: if there were still no rain for several days, then the fleas would eat the flax, therefore we should send for seeds; if even you, Ivan, an old and experienced farmer, think that it is not necessary to replant the crop, then let it be according to you, only you take the flax; both the profits and the losses will be yours. If you take the flax on for yourself, then you can do whatever you want: you can send for the priests, for the old men, whatever you want.

Ivan went out into the field, looked at the flax for the hundredth time, and returned with his answer:

"No, we'll leave it as it is, we won't plant again."

"So that means that you are taking the flax for yourself? Fine—you have until tomorrow; think about it, take a close look."

That day, Ivan went out several times to the flax. In the evening, when he came with his report, I immediately noticed that he was beginning to have doubts. Having heard out his report about work on the farm, I did not say a word about the flax. Ivan himself brought it up.

"So what is there to discuss here? In my opinion, the flax will probably fail, we should plant again, and if we can't get flax seeds, then we'll plant oats; but if you take the flax for yourself, give me your final answer tomorrow, then it will be your decision."

The next day, I did not go look at the flax. Ivan noticed this.

"Aleksandr Nikolaevich, why didn't you go to look at the flax today?" he said.

"And why should I look at it? In my opinion, there is nothing to look at—we need to plant again; but if you take it for yourself, then let it be your decision."

But I saw that Ivan was growing leery. Avdotia had been on him. I kept silent.

"Today, they ate up even more."

"So, how is that?"

"I've decided too, we should probably plant again."

"So, if we have to plant again, then we'll plant again. Fine, get ready and get going. If we cannot get flax seeds, then we will plant oats or we will leave it under the winter crop for next year."

After his lunch, Ivan left to go sixty versts to get the seeds. It was a hot and sultry day, but toward evening, it began to cloud up from the west, and toward night, clouds came which broke into such a pouring rain that the wood chips were floating. The next day a winter wind blew, it became cold, a light rain drizzled all day; the fleas disappeared and the flax began to revive—how could it have been so simple? When Ivan returned with the seeds it was not necessary or possible to plant. It rained, the fleas died, the flax revived, recovered, and the harvest came out well.[. . .]

It turned out that we worried about the fleas for nothing—the flax harvest was excellent. When it came time to scutch, I was hardly allowed to show myself at the scutching: the old thresher Pakhomych would not allow me to pass. The moment I stepped into the threshing barn Lavren immediately said:

"Just look, lord, how much flax we carried from Demin's desiatina, and you were saying in the spring that the flax would fail. You wanted to replant it, you thought about going against God. You wanted to correct God's business, but look at how much flax the merciful Father produced. That's the way it is, lord."

"Still, Pakhomych, you saw for yourself that the fleas were eating the shoots; if it had not suddenly rained, then we would have had to plant again."

"What fleas? You dreamed up fleas!"

"But you saw them yourself!"

"I saw. Everything is God's will, which means that this was also necessary. God ordered that the flea exist, that means it must exist. But you wanted to plant again, you thought about going against God, you wanted to correct him. No, lord, everything is God's will; if God produces, then fine, if He does not produce, then you can't do anything."

"However, even the muzhiks say, 'For manure you would even steal from God.' "

"That's the way it is, no, everything is God's will. Live a bit, you'll see. Look, this year we thought that we would all die of hunger, but here we are alive, we're eating the new harvest and drinking new vodka. That's the way it is. God is not without mercy."

God is not without mercy, the folk say, there has not been such a year for a long time. God is not without mercy.

The Subsistence Nature of Russian Agriculture

Once, in the spring, in the midst of the thaw, returning home after looking over the fields, I met the baba Panfilikha from a neighboring village. She was carrying a bundle on a cart.

"Greetings, Aleksandr Nikolaevich."

"Hello Panfilikha, what are you carrying?"

"Oats from the state store. They gave out one osmina to each household, there's nothing to feed the animals with."

"How can that be, there is no hay?"

"What hay, there's no straw, we've taken the last bit from the roof. There was nothing to spread, so praise God, they gave an osmina to each of the poorest souls."

"It is a bad business, but surely we will let the animals into the fields soon!"

"It's God's will. The Lord is not without mercy—he took one of my children, it's much easier."

"Which one?"

"The youngest, I buried him a couple of days ago. God is not without mercy, he kept an eye on us orphans and sinners."

I am not making this up; I am reporting facts. If you do not believe me, remember what a baba answered at the Tver[14] provincial commission which had examined, in regard to my article, the question of artel dairy workers.

"It's you, sirs," the baba said, "who are squeamish about children; with us it's not that way: if they live, fine, if they don't, then 'God be with them.' "

"So what trouble was the little one for you—wasn't he still nursing, he did not need bread?"

"Of course, a nursing baby didn't need bread, but you know it was a strain on me too, and what kind of milk comes from chaff bread, you know yourself. And he interfered with my going for crusts of bread, you send your older ones and sit at home with the nursing baby. Wherever you go with him, it's cold, he whines. Now that God has taken him, it's become easier for me. You know yourself how good Panfil is at making them, but he doesn't know how to feed them. It's bad. It is God's will; yes God is not without mercy." And the baba hit the filly with a knout.

This spring the peasants were totally lost. There was no grain, no fodder; even the rich ones had to buy grain; they took all of the straw from the roof, they fed the sheep with sauerkraut, whoever had any left over—we'll get by ourselves on sorrel soup in the spring—they even used the flax seeds, those who had some left over for planting; they crushed them and spread the cuttings. Each one thought not so much about himself as about the animals, how to maintain the cattle until they could be put out to pasture. At the end of March and the beginning of April, the situation was terrible; if the spring had been typical, then most of the animals would have had to be destroyed for lack of feed, but God is not without mercy! Spring came so early this year that even the old people do not remember one like it.[. . .]

I repeat, the situation was terrible. The peasants who were poorer sold or pawned everything that was possible: both future grain and future labor. They paid enormous interest on the money they borrowed, thirty kopeks a ruble and more for six months. The muzhik will try before all else to borrow, even at high interest, if only to get by, and then only when there is nowhere to borrow will he take on work. In April, a rather prosperous muzhik who did not have enough grain came by one day to ask me to lend him some money for two sacks of rye.

"Aleksandr Nikolaevich, lend me fifteen rubles till the Feast of the Holy Virgin [October 1]; I'll pay you back on time, as soon as I sell the seeds, and as interest, I'll clear a desiatina of meadow."

"I cannot. But if you wish, clear three desiatinas of meadow, and I will give you five rubles per desiatina. With the money all up front."

"I can't do it, Aleksandr Nikolaevich."

"But you know that I am giving a good price, five rubles per desiatina; you know yourself what kind of meadow it is; if I get one hundred puds it will be cause to praise God."

"The price is good, it's just not good for me. If I take on clearing three desiatinas of meadow, it'll mean that I have to leave my own mowing, which'll ruin my farm. I would rather take the money now only as a loan, then, God willing, I'll sell some hemp around the Feast of the Holy Virgin, then I'll happily mow your desiatina."

In fact, it is very often much more profitable for the peasant to borrow money and give a lot of interest, especially in labor, than to obligate himself to work for the borrowed money, even at a high price for the labor. In certain circumstances, the muzhik cannot take on work for you, although you would give him an inordinately high price, let's say two rubles a day, because, having taken on your work, he must leave his own farm, ruin his farm, and it is understandable that a peasant will hold onto his farm, no matter what kind it is, with hands and teeth. When a muzhik needs money, he pays enormous interest, only to be able to get by, and then, God will bring a bit of grain, there will be a little hemp. If a muzhik has to borrow money with high interest, that is still not totally bad; but it is bad when a muzhik does not have the strength to take on work. This year there were many of even this kind, who were willing to take on any kind of work if only the money was up front. There was no grain, there was no fodder, there was nothing to eat for oneself, there was nothing to feed the cattle, no one was giving out loans, this is when the muzhik rushes about from side to side. For one he will take on a piece of land for the full planting season working with his own horse and plough, for another a desiatina of flax, for a third, to clear the meadow, as long as he receives the money up front, he will buy a little grain, "to save his soul." The situation of a muzhik who has, "saving his soul," taken on a lot of work in the winter, is the most difficult in the summer: they tear at him from all sides—go there to plant, there to mow, there is no end of work, and his own rows stand.

It is morning. A beautiful spring morning, there is dew, the air smells wonderful, the birds are beginning to awaken. The sun has not yet come up, but Aurora is no longer asleep "and from subterranean darkness she runs with a bright torch." The muzhik Dema got up before sunrise, ate a bit of bread, tied his horse to the plough in the yard, is thinking of going to his own field— he has ploughed everyone's fields, and his is still lying unploughed, but Dema had not managed to get his horse up before the steward from Bardino— having galloped over to get out those who had obligated themselves to work in the winter, namely here—knocked on the gate.

"Hey, Dema!"

"What is it?"

"Get down to the harrowing. Why haven't you been down to harrow yet— the others have left, and still you haven't shown up."

"Let me off, Gavrilych, my own field is still unploughed, I swear to God."

"What do I care about your field? Get over to harrow, I say."

"Don't you have a conscience, Gavrilych? For God's sake, my field is not ploughed—everyone else has already turned theirs over, and mine is lying untouched."

"Get going. Get going. You obligated yourself, so get going, and if you don't then Sidorych (the volost elder) will be quick to pull your pants down."[15]

Dema scratches himself, but there is nothing to be done—he obligated himself for work, he has to go, the volost elder is no joker, and the steward won't leave anyway. The steward waits while Dema harnesses the horse to the harrow and goes out onto the road.

"So, get going, and, look here, you harrow well, I'll be back by and by." Having summoned Dema, the Bardino steward galloped to another village to dig up some Panas or other.

Dema heads off to Bardino to do the harrowing and thinks about his unploughed field.

"Wait, Dema, where are you going?" the Fedino steward, who is also out digging up people for work in Fedino, meets Dema. "Why haven't you come to plant the flax yet, you know that I called for you yesterday."

"I was on my way to your place, Pavlych, but Gavrilych just came by, he forced me to go to Bardino to harrow."

"So what do I care about the steward from Bardino! You know you made a deal to work on our place on the flax, so you have to work. You know that we don't pay shavings either. So what do we care about the steward from Bardino! Come plant the flax, everyone else has left, only you aren't there. Get going, and if you don't, you know . . . Sidorych won't have to think for long."

"I swear to God, Pavlych, the steward from Bardino was just here, he forced me to harrow, he's threatening me with the volost elder too."

"What business is that of ours! Get going, get going, hitch up the cart."

The steward from Fedino, in order not to let Dema get away, waits until he hitches the horse and ceremoniously leads him to Fedino, but the lord is already in the courtyard, getting angry.

"Why are you so late, Dema? You see what kind of quiet morning it is, perfect for planting, go start planting."

"But I was hurrying, Mikulaich, the horses were in the pasture, the mare took off on the way, she ran and ran, I barely caught her—if I hadn't the wolves would eat her—that's why I'm late. I'll plant right away, it won't take me long to plant, I'll finish by evening, may God only let it grow."

The next day, Dema harrows in Bardino, and his field stands unploughed. No, this is really the last straw when the muzhik must take on work that he is not in a position to do—then his whole farm is neglected and, look, in a few years he will be completely ruined. But what is he to do? He has "saved his soul," he did not die from hunger over the winter . . .

[Engelgardt here describes his frustration in trying to find useful advice in his library of materials on agronomy, and his general conclusion that the science of agronomy offered little to the practicing farmer. He then provides further detail about the early spring and his reaction to it.]

This year, the peasants, as I wrote in the first letters, endured a terrible winter, no grain, no feed. Only the unusually early spring saved the livestock. When the cattle went into the field early, there was less worry; one had only to feed oneself until the new harvest, but it is this that is most difficult. In the winter, the poorer ones fed themselves in the commune on crusts of bread; now, when the working season has arrived, there is no time to go for crusts of bread, and no one is giving them out because everyone has used up his grain. They managed somehow. Those who planned ahead, as Avdotia says, began to store grain for the work season in the winter already, they saved up their own grain and went out after crusts of bread. In the spring, some sold their extra livestock and bought grain, some obligated themselves for labor and used the advance to buy grain, some took out loans until the new harvest; but there were also many who got by from day to day. A muzhik will come by a pud of flour somewhere, put himself in debt, will do some kind of work, will sell a lamb, some time will pass, he'll work, then he'll go hungry for a day or two, running around to find someplace to get even a pound, even a half pound, he'll begin to work as a day laborer somewhere—it is good if he can even find daily labor—he'll earn a pound of flour and sit at home again, will plough his own field. Of course, this is not a matter of good bread; the baba will mix the bread in the evening, it won't manage to rise, she needs to eat, to feed the children, so she'll make flat cakes, and then she'll simply make mash. On a holiday, he'll run out after crusts of bread, he'll send the children to neighboring villages, and then he'll manage this way and that around his fellow villagers who have grain. He'll earn something—they'll feed him, give him a bit of grain; another time he'll simply go by someone's place during lunch, he'll say that he hasn't eaten today; they'll feed them, then during the harvest, he'll help in the mowing, he'll work for them a bit. While the women . . . "And what on earth are you going to do," Avdotia says— "and . . . not die from hunger!"[16]

The mushrooms came up, it became a little easier, but it was some help even so. This year, the mushrooms appeared early and the crop was unusual;

of course you can't work much on mushrooms alone without bread, but still you can get by until you get some bread, and they are also a good supplement with bread—it is still better than dry bread alone. Mushrooms grow in my woods in abundance. At dawn's first light in the summer, all of the babas from the neighboring villages run to my woods after mushrooms, so that there are surely as many as one hundred and fifty people in my woods each day. Of course, the babas have already ransacked the entire woods and gathered all of the mushrooms by dawn, they especially like the white ones, so that nothing remains by morning. Avdotia, as a baba, as a Korobochka,[17] out of greed, was always trying to convince me to reserve the woods, that is, to forbid anyone from gathering mushrooms in them. I did not agree to this. It seems to me that there is no gain for the landlord in forbidding the gathering of mushrooms on his holdings, to say nothing of the fact that the hungry peasants feed themselves solely on mushrooms, and that this is just the kind of prohibition that leads to unpleasant conflicts. It is well known that the peasants, not only here, but even in Germany, do not recognize the forest as private property and do not consider poaching wood to be theft. Even according to formal law, chopping wood in another man's forest is not considered theft, so what are you to say about mushrooms![18][. . .]

A mushroom grows by itself, no one plants it, no one tends it, no one even knows where it will grow; it is impossible to protect a mushroom—if you did not take it today, then tomorrow it won't be good for anything; you can't wait for it to grow; it's also not possible to intervene to keep it from growing in a certain place, and it is also wrong to cut mushrooms the way you cut forest to use the land. Thus, if even the forest is not recognized as property, a theft of the forest not as theft, then you cannot even put stealing mushrooms on the same level as poaching wood. It is obvious that the mushroom grows by God's will for general use, and to forbid mushroom gathering is somehow shameful. Of course, the owner of the forest can forbid mushroom gathering in his forest, but that already means that he takes the pickings . . . but even if you do not take into consideration the, so to speak, elusive quality of such property as mushrooms, there is still nothing to be gained by a prohibition. If you forbid mushroom gathering, then this will inevitably place the owner in a battle, so to speak, with the peasants, which is unprofitable.[. . .]

However, I also got some use out of the mushrooms. Someone poached some wood in one of my groves; peasants from a neighboring village cut down ten birches and ruined one spruce for drying. I called them to my place:

"They cut the forest?"

"We can't know, Aleksandr Nikolaevich."

"You went past, did you see?"

"We went past, we saw."

"Was it done by people from your village?"

"We can't know."

"What do mean, we can't know? If there is going to be wood poaching then I won't allow mushroom gathering, tell the women this."

"We understand, Aleksandr Nikolaevich; rest easy."

Since then, there has been no wood poaching.

Thus, with mushrooms, a pud of flour gotten somewhere, always going hungry, never eating his fill, the poor peasant gets by until the next harvest. If I were an artist, a painter, how many typical pictures I could present at the Academy's exhibition! Here is the muzhik Dema, he has a wife and two children, the entire spring he lived from hand to mouth however he could. Soon the new harvest will be in, but Dema ate the last crumb of bread day before yesterday and ran out to find even a pud of flour. Having run around all day yesterday, he couldn't get it anywhere, neither on loan, nor through labor. Today, along with some others, he came to me to hire himself out to clear the meadows. Look at this group: the two well-fed ones bargain, but the hungry Dema is seized by impatience and the fear that I will deny him work if he does not agree to my price; he pushes the well-fed Babur with his elbow: take it. It is all the same to Dema what wage I offer as long as he can get a loaf of bread today, and tomorrow a pud of flour. If I knew how to paint, I would paint a "reaper," but not the kind that they usually paint. There would be the most narrow field, scraggly rye, the sun would burn, a baba in only a shift, wet with sweat, with a groggy face gone dark from hunger, with dried-up blood on her lips, mowing, beginning to reap the first sheaf—but she will not even have any bread tomorrow, because she won't have time to grind it. She will already be satisfied with kasha[19] made from steamed rye.

Life is hardest of all for the muzhik just before the new harvest. Look, look, not today, perhaps tomorrow the rye will ripen enough that it will be possible to eat green kasha, but still there is no bread; it is hard to get even a pud of flour at this time because each one saved enough grain only to last to the next harvest. If the year is bad, everyone is stingy.

But now at last they have ground the first rye and taken the new grain to the mill, barely one out of a hundred returns from the mill without having gotten drunk. And that is understandable: a man has gone hungry for a whole year, and now there is bread to one's heart's content—until the Feast of the Holy Virgin, at least. For us, who have never gone hungry, for us, who take a stroll before lunch in order to stimulate the appetite, of course, the position of the starving peasant who has made it to the next harvest is not entirely comprehensible. But just imagine that Dema who a week ago was running about, bustling to and fro, bowing, falling on his knees before the owner of the mill begging for a pud of flour, is now happy, proud—even the devil is not his equal—is sitting on a cart in which two sacks of new pure grain are lying! The owner of the mill who a week ago, despite his supplications, did not lend Dema a pud of flour, now meets him gently, respectfully, calling him by his patronymic, Pavlych. Dema, having nodded to the miller, gets out of his cart slowly, takes his sacks down and gets in line—the new harvest has swamped the miller—when his turn comes to pour his grain, he goes into the miller's cottage, out of which come songs and cries of those who have been drinking behind the mill. "Ah! Greetings, Demian Pavlych! Greetings, Dema! So, you've brought your new grain?" Well, judge for yourself how can one not drink here! Just comprehend the joy of a man who has fed himself all winter on crusts of bread, who has gotten by somehow in the spring, partly by feeding himself on mash alone from rye flour and mushrooms, when suddenly this man has a *whole* sack of pure grain, *a whole sack!* Inside the izba, those who have been drinking behind the mill call Dema to their table. Dema asks for a glass of vodka, a loaf of wheat bread, some pickles; they give him the vodka and the snacks with respect, without asking for money ahead of time, as it is usually done, because his rye is at the mill. Vodka acts quickly on an empty stomach; after one glass, Dema is tipsy and asks for more vodka. In half an hour, Dema is already drunk . . . When he wakes up, he'll pay up with rye . . .

[Engelgardt here discusses the futility of existing bureaucratic measures designed to prevent the sale of vodka at the mills.]

Having had a taste of the new harvest, the peasants celebrated, and now it is already full harvesttime, a superb autumn. But the peasants did not rejoice for long. Around the Feast of the Holy Virgin, the authorities began to demand arrears, various taxes, and all of the newspapers are to blame: they proclaimed what the harvest was like and now they've set in like never before. Formerly, they waited until Andrian [Saint Andrew's Day, November 30], when the peasants sold their hemp, but now they've set in beginning with the Feast of the Holy Virgin. Usually in the autumn, having sold a bit of hemp on time, some seed, extra livestock, the peasants pay back their private debts, but this year, all of the debtors asked to wait until hemp time; and that's nothing, every day, first one, then another comes by to ask for a loan—they put down hemp as a deposit or rye, or take an advance for future labor—the volost is leaning heavily on them.[20] In order to pay off their taxes now, they have to sell their livestock immediately, their hemp, and the price is bad. The muzhik would have waited until the prices rise—but that's not possible, they are demanding money, the volost officials are squeezing them, they are threatening to do an assessment of their property, they are promising to put those in arrears to work. The buyers, knowing this, held back, lowered prices, stopped going around to the villages; take it to him at home, at the posting inn, where he will take it on his scale, will give something back, and here he has his vodka . . . and how can he not drink! It is bad. And there is a good harvest, but the poor peasant still barely recovers. Labor is also a bit cheaper, especially piecework, sawing firewood, for example, because there is nothing to pay them with—just go to work. There are no kind of prices at all for livestock, they won't give a ruble and a half for a pud of beef. In the spring they struggled and struggled somehow to feed the livestock, and now they are getting less for it than it cost to feed them last spring. It's a bad business. A poor harvest is bad. A good harvest is also bad . . .

Letter IV

✉   Engelgardt's fourth letter is a rather diffuse, rambling affair that touches briefly on two aspects of the peasants' work habits, then shifts to discuss his trip to an agricultural exhibition, which in turn prompts him to contemplate the various transformations he has undergone during his three years on Batishchevo.[1] The one common thread running throughout the letter is Engelgardt's self-conscious skepticism about urban conceptions of the village, coupled with his own deepening understanding of the realities of life in the countryside.

He opens by defending the peasants against widespread charges of laziness and dishonesty. He offers his observations about the rhythm of peasant labor and stresses the incredible amounts of energy that peasants farming in Russia's miserly climate must expend in order to survive. On the question of the peasants' honesty, he argues that they are no worse, and perhaps are even more trustworthy, than members of the educated society on this score. Having defended the peasants, however, Engelgardt introduces the coda for what will become a major theme in his remaining letters: individualism in peasant farming. As a Populist who advocates collective farming, Engelgardt finds this aspect of village culture extremely frustrating.

The bulk of the letter, however, is devoted to Engelgardt's trip to a provincial agricultural exhibit, which is roughly similar to an American state fair without the amusements. His trip to the city of Smolensk forces him to confront his peculiar position as an educated member of the nobility living among the peasants who has come to recognize the falseness of urban concepts of the countryside, yet who continues to be "drawn to town." Both en route to the exhibition and at the event itself, Engelgardt is reminded of the distance between newspaper accounts of developments in the countryside and the true nature of things. Like his earlier descriptions of the zemstvo elections and the assembly of the justices of the peace, his account of the agricultural exhibition pops the balloon of educated illusions about improvements in the countryside. Engelgardt effectively deflates any image of progress in rural Russia, whether through gentry or peasant initiative.

Engelgardt's confrontation with the amenities of "civilization" in Smolensk also provokes self-examination. He reminisces about his initiation into the life of the countryside and his adaptation to it. In these reflections he launches into a discourse on patterns of dress in Russia and proposes slightly modified peasant dress as a useful model for all Russians. While this proposal is interesting in and of itself, it has the further value of suggesting the extent to which dress made the man in late Imperial Russia.

⊠ ⊠ ⊠

"Rogues Exist to Teach Fools to Be on Guard"

Spring. Again the grackles[2] have arrived, again the streams have begun to flow, again the larks have begun to sing, again the peasants are without grain, again . . .

"What do you need, Foka?"

"I need a little osmina of grain; there's no grain anywhere, there's nothing at all to eat."

"How are you going to pay me back?"

"I'll pay you back with money. I'll pay you back by Easter, my brother will send it from Moscow."

"And if he does not send any?"

"Then we'll work it off, whatever you tell us to do."

"Well, then, fine, I have a lot of work this year, I will lend you the same as I have lent 'to everyone else.' "

"We thank you."

"Go get your horse."

"My horse broke down hauling lumber, I'll carry it myself."

"As you wish, bring your sack."

"I've got it."

Foka, grinning, takes a sack from under his shirt: he came confident that I would not turn him down, practically no one is turned down this year, and only out of politeness, to show that he was not going into his own storehouse, he hid the sack under his long coat. Foka filled it up and put the four-and-a-half-pud sack on his shoulders.

"And what do you need, Fedot?"

"I need a little grain."

"But you have already taken some!"

"It won't be enough; I need two more sacks before the new harvest."

"And how will you pay me back?"

"I'll pay you with money in the fall: half before the Feast of the Holy Virgin, the other before Nikola. I'll clear a desiatina of meadow to set the deal."

"Why promise so much labor ahead, or do you want to tie up the money?"

"What do you mean, tie it up, we'll pay it back. All the same, no one'll give a loan without a pledge of some sort, it's better to do a favor for you.

Year before last, I took two sacks from the priest in P., that was for a pledge, too; I mowed his garden, it was more than a desiatina, and his grain was even bad, it was mixed up with straw. My brother and I got together and decided that it was better to borrow from you than to take something from someone else; that way the business is closer by, the mowing will be right near our village, you mow early; it won't cost us anything to clear a desiatina, it's better to work for the lord who's your neighbor."

"Well, fine, then, but I will make it easier for you—I will give you the rye for six and a half."

"We thank you for that."

"Go get your horse."

"We also need about an osmina of barley. I'll work for you for the barley."

"What kind of work?"

"Whatever you order, we'll gather the flax, we'll brake it; maybe you'll send some to town. I'll take it."

"Fine, I will lend you what I have lent 'to everyone else.' "

"We thank you."[. . .]

This year, practically no one is refused; I'm giving everyone grain on loan this spring, some for money, some for labor, some for a repayment of grain, some with a pledge, some without, depending upon the circumstances. Because, in the first place, I myself now have plenty, and no one is buying grain, and in the second place, I got to know the peasants and the peasants know me, in the third place, I put the farm on a new system and I have all kinds of work.

Yes, last year, my farm succeeded beyond my expectations. I had a good harvest of everything. Judge for yourself—here is a table comparing my harvests for 1871 and 1872.

Harvested	in 1871	in 1872
Rye	110 sacks	202 sacks
Oats	145	265
Barley	13	38
Wheat	0	19
Flax seed	6	18
Flax	34 puds	128 puds

Everything produced twice and sometimes three times what was produced in the preceding year.[. . .]

Last year (1872) we had a good harvest. Of course, the peasants did not have enough grain to last to the new harvest, but even so, it was not like it was in 1871 when both rye and the spring crops failed. The wealthy peasants had more rye than they needed for their own subsistence, the prosperous peasants had enough grain to last until the new harvest, those who used to buy beginning in March had enough to last until June, those who usually began to buy in January had enough to last until March, and so on. The gentry also had a good rye harvest—everyone wants to sell it, they must sell, because rye constitutes the main source of income on gentry farms, but meanwhile, the price is low, and most important, nobody is buying.[. . .]

The peasant who cannot get by on his own grain, who buys grain for his own subsistence, prays to God that grain will be cheap. But the landowner, the merchant-landowner, and the wealthy peasant all pray to God that grain will be expensive.[. . .]

The peasant's well-being depends totally on the rye harvest because, even given an excellent harvest, the mass of peasants will not have enough of their own grain and will have to buy some. The less rye the peasant has to buy, the cheaper the rye, the better for the peasant. The landowner, on the other hand, always sells rye, and receives his main income from it in the current system of agriculture. Consequently, the more expensive rye is, the greater the demand for it, the better it is for the landowner. The mass of the population wants grain to be cheap, but the gentry merchant-landowners and the wealthy peasants want grain to be expensive.[. . .]

In the course of two years, I have come to know the neighboring peasants and they have come to know me; a certain mutual trust has been established, although each one of us always remembers the proverb "Rogues exist to teach fools to be on guard."

In general, relations are not bad. I never hold back their pay in money, I don't shortchange them, and if we have not agreed about a price, then I do not extort from them, but pay fairly; if I am not home or am occupied with guests, Ivan takes care of the pay. But on other gentry estates, the muzhik comes for his money—"Not now, the lord or lady is sleeping; come another time," "Not now, the lord is busy with guests, come a third time," "We don't have the cash, wait until I sell some grain." Paying cash fairly is the first thing, but that is still not enough. It is essential to know how to value labor, to know what costs what, and if it should happen that the muzhik injures himself or, out of need, from hunger, takes on work for too low a price, which often happens, then you need to look into the matter and calculate fairly so that you will not take a loss, but the muzhik will be satisfied. If the muzhik does not meet his obligations, if he abandons the work, denies his obligation, then again you need to look into the matter, and to work it out sensibly. There will always turn out to be some kind of good reason: the family situation of the muzhik has changed, prices have risen, the work is beyond him, in general, something of this sort; deception is rare in these cases. I never take anyone to court; I have not yet complained to the justice of the peace once, nor to the mediator, nor to the volost court,[3] and furthermore, I lend money and grain without receipts for the most part, I give out advances without conditions—and so far, not one of the peasants has deceived me. Peasants do not like courts and if someone goes to court often, complains about every trifle in the volost offices, or to the justice of the peace, the peasants will not work for him. A peasant will never default on a debt—at least it has never happened with me—and if he cannot pay on time, he will ask for an extension, and once he has gotten on his feet, will pay it back or work it off. And in regard to fulfilling labor agreements, I cannot complain that they have been at fault. So far everything has been done on time on my place, but, of course, one must be on one's toes and at the same time one should remember that every peasant has work in his own field.

Honesty and Industry of the Russian Peasant

If you listen to what various newspaper correspondents say, then it seems impossible to run a farm. The muzhik is a drunkard, and a thief, and a fraud, he does not fulfill his agreements, he doesn't pay back his debts, he walks off from his work having taken an advance, he's lazy, works badly, ruins farm instruments, and so forth and so on. There is none of this; at least, soon I will have been farming three years already and I have seen nothing of the kind. Of course, I will not try to prove that the muzhik is the model of honesty, but I do not find that he is worse than we educated people are.

Try to lend money to each of your acquaintances who asks for a loan and see how they pay you back. Will many of them pay on time? Won't many of them forget that they owe you? Living in St. Petersburg, I reached the point that, with extremely rare exceptions, I either did not lend money at all or, if I did lend it, I wrote the money off as an expense because I did not expect to be paid back. But with the peasants I have not had a single incident of deception. Of course, I always know ahead of time whether the muzhik can pay me back. If he has nothing to pay me with, I suggest that he borrow in exchange for labor, I give him an extension, I sometimes even lend him more money so he can get over the hump and give him a chance to pay back the loan. Of course, the muzhik is simple, he does not know that one can default on a debt if there is no receipt, he fears the courts like fire, he doesn't rely on knowing how to talk before the judge, he's afraid of saying the wrong thing, of landing in jail and so on. No matter how innocent the muzhik is, he always fears that anyone with money can prove him guilty, and furthermore, he usually does not know himself if he is innocent or guilty, and if he is guilty, what kind of punishment he can receive. It is hard for him to know this, because different courts judge according to differing laws.[4] For example, the justice of the peace will not do anything special about the failure to repay a loan, he will simply order repayment of the loan. But in the volost, probably, they'll give you a flogging besides. The justice of the peace will put you in jail for two months for stealing two loads of hay; but in the volost the most they will do is put you under arrest. How can the muzhik not be afraid of this? But it is not enough that the peasant is simple and does not know any tricks (he fears God), he is still tied to the land and is always anticipating his needs. If you do not pay money back today, then tomorrow they will no longer give you any, and who knows what you may need tomorrow—money, grain, hay, firewood, etcetera, etcetera. No, in regard to paying back debts, the peasants are much more prompt than people of our class, and I have never had to worry as much about getting repayment from the peasants for grain I have sold them on loan as I formerly had to worry about getting money from various publishers for articles.

It is said that the muzhik is a thief; the stewards, the clerks, the day laborers—it is said that all of them are thieves. I will say it again: I have not noticed a single case of theft on my place so far. The steward has money and grain and possessions within reach, but there is no stealing. Avdotia sells pot cheese, milk, I cannot keep track of her, but I am sure that she gives me everything in full. I rely on Sidor as well in everything. The steward has no time to go to the storehouse, he sends a male or a female worker to give grain to a buyer, to take flour for the calves, and so forth, and in the storehouse everything is safe and sound; there is not only grain, but also nails, iron, lard, and ham—and no one steals anything. Of course, supervision, accounting is essential, of course, everything depends on the selection of people, on the *spirit* which has been established in the house, but this is why it is not possible to say that theft is *developed* among the peasants.[. . .]

It is the same with laborers; people complain that our workers are lazy, unscrupulous, that they work badly, do not fulfill contracts, and abandon the work after taking an advance. In this case also, everything depends on the master, on his attitude toward the worker: "It is well known that the day laborer lives on good food and a gentle word." Of course, there are lazy people also, there are also diligent ones, but I am utterly convinced that you cannot accomplish what you can accomplish with our workers with any other workers. Our worker cannot, like the German, work steadily every day in the course of the year—he works in spurts. This is already his essential characteristic, a quality that has been created through the influence of those conditions under which fieldwork takes place here, which, as a result of climatic conditions, must be done in a very short period of time. It is clear that there, where the winter is short or does not even exist, where fieldwork goes on practically the entire year 'round, where there are no such quick changes in the weather, that the nature of labor is completely different than it is here, where often you get only what you grab.

It is under these same conditions that the character of our worker, who cannot work evenly and precisely like the German, has been formed. But when the occasion arises, when it is required, he can accomplish an incredible amount of work, that is, of course, if the master knows how to inspire the necessary energy in him to do this. People who say that our laborer is lazy usually do not *grasp this peculiarity of his character,* and seeing in him sluggishness and imprecision in his work, thoughtfully compare him to the German, who is always conscientious and precise in our eyes, and consider our worker to be an unscrupulous sloth. I completely agree that the kind of worker *we imagine the German to be* is extremely hard to find among Russians, but it would be hard to find the kind of workers among the Germans who could accomplish what all of ours are capable of when the occasion arises, for example, during mowing.[. . .]

Just observe the execution of any kind of difficult labor (a man digs, mows, pulls heavy loads) and you will see that our worker, even if he is working unsupervised, always does the work in spurts, that is, in bursts of energy, and therefore he stops constantly in order to regain his breath. A lord will see this and, not paying attention to how the man is working, but noticing only that he rests every minute, thinks that he is being lazy. Meanwhile, to write, for example, is not really difficult work, but I cannot write a page without stopping several times to have a smoke. People pass judgment about the laziness of the laborers but they themselves do not know the scale of work, or they measure it in terms of the quantity of work which a man can fulfill only in exceptional circumstances. Everyone knows that a horse can run twenty versts in an hour if he exerts himself, but that he cannot run two hundred in ten hours. It is precisely the same with the worker: he can carry one and a half cubic meters of dirt in a wheelbarrow in a day, but he cannot move fifteen cubic meters in ten days.[. . .] It always seems to the master that the peasants have not done enough, because he always wants them to do the maximum of work, but does not know the pace of work. Of course, the peasant who is working for himself at mowing or threshing will do an awesome amount, but then if you observe how he punishes himself at this time, you would not know the man. Furthermore, in the autumn, after the gathering of the harvest, he rests as a hired hand never rests, from whom employers demand that he *always* work at full strength, and whom they consider a sluggard if he does not constantly produce the maximum of labor.

No, *our laborer is not lazy,* if a master understands labor, knows what it is possible to demand, if he knows how, when it is necessary, to inspire energy and does not constantly demand superhuman exertion.

Of course, serfdom left its stamp here as well; under its influence a special method of work took shape called work "for the lord" (the peasants will even say about flies that bite fiercely in the autumn: "In the summer the fly works for the lord, but he works for himself in the autumn"), but now there is already a whole generation of young people who have not worked on *barshchina.*[5]

Again, I do not want to idealize the muzhik. Of course, if the master is bad, if there is not a good spirit on the farm, if the master is concerned only that "the peasant does not run off from his job," if the worker always feels that "you don't wear yourself out for the lord," then he will also be lazy and will adopt a very lax attitude toward his task. But in this regard I do not find that the muzhiks are any worse than we educated people.

Go into any office and observe how the bureaucrats work; ask if there are many bureaucrats who diligently fulfill their responsibilities. I do not know what others think, but no matter how often I looked into it, it always turned out that the majority viewed their duties apathetically, they only wanted to kill time and receive their salary. And why just bureaucrats! Are there many professors in the university who work diligently, who do not take up superfluous places, and who do put their soul into the work they have taken up?

But we want workers, illiterate people who have received no education whatsoever, who have struggled their entire lives in want, receiving pay which hardly assures them their daily bread, to be the models of honesty, industry, and diligence![. . .]

I do not know about other people, but I am satisfied with my farm laborers; they work excellently even without supervision. If I come up, no one is without work, if they were smoking—they continue to smoke, if they were chatting—they continue to chat, if they were resting—they continue to rest, and when they turn to work—the work flies; but I will talk about this in greater detail on another occasion.

[Engelgardt describes the new jobs on his estate due to his innovations.]

Individualism in Peasant Farming

I settled on the farm two years ago. Having had a look around and taken in the conditions of my estate, I saw that it was impossible to farm as before, to farm as the majority of our gentry farmers farm. . . .

[Engelgardt describes the failings of gentry farming in the post-Emancipation era.]

Having penetrated the condition of the peasantry, their relations to the gentry, having become familiar with wages for labor, having come to understand the agreements by which pay for labor is determined, and so forth, I became convinced that the existing system of agriculture continues only because labor is incredibly cheap, because the peasant cultivates the landowner's fields for extremely low wages only out of need, because of his impoverished condition. Since such an order of things cannot last long, and because a man who is free will go hungry a year, two, three, but finally will find some escape for himself, then for me it became indubitable that the time will come, and it will come quickly, it is already coming, when the peasants will not work the land for such low wages as they do now. It is clear that the old system of agriculture must then be destroyed and replaced by a new, different one.

The result of my research about wages for labor was the article "Is It the High Cost of Working Hands That Hurts Our Economy?" which appeared in No. 2 of *Notes of the Fatherland* for 1873.

In this article I proved factually that the cost of working hands in Russia is extremely cheap; that the peasant who works the lord's fields by the job barely earns, literally, a loaf of bread, that it is not the high cost of workers that hurts our economy, but something else.[. . .]

I wanted to show in my article, first of all, that our pay for agricultural labor is extraordinarily low, that for the most difficult farm work, the worker does not receive even as much as he needs to have enough food to keep his body in a normal state, that there is no profession that would reward labor more poorly than the difficult work of the agriculturalist. I think I proved this; I think the figures I presented, figures I can document, convinced everyone that agricultural labor in Russia is extremely cheap. Then, I tried to trace the cause of such cheap labor; precisely why the peasants currently work the gentry fields for such low pay; I showed that the reason for this, above all else, is the need for meadows, forest, pasture, and so forth, and then poverty and the inability to pay taxes. I stopped there, but I should have added that there is yet another reason for the poverty of agriculturalists—that is lack of unity in their actions. This independence in their actions is very important, and I intend to discuss it in detail in a special article. Now I want only to show what I mean by the words "independence in their actions."

The peasants live in separate households and every household has its own separate farm which it also manages through its own supervision. I will clarify with an example: In the village one half verst away from me, with whose daily life I have become familiar in detail, there are fourteen households. Every day in these fourteen households, fourteen stoves are lit, fourteen mistresses prepare food, each one for her own household. What an enormous waste of labor, food products, heat, and so forth! If all fourteen households baked bread and prepared food together, that is, had a common dining hall, it would be enough to heat two stoves and to have two mistresses. And the bread would be cheaper and less food would be used. Furthermore, in the winter, every household must have a man to look after the cattle, while for all of the village's cattle two men would be enough; every day during mowing, fourteen men are busy with drying grain in the barns; the grain lies in fourteen small storehouses; the hay in fourteen haylofts, etcetera. For me, a landowner, for example, everything is much cheaper than for the peasant because everything is done together, in common. On my place, all twenty-two workers eat at one table and one housekeeper prepares their food in one stove. All of the cattle stand in one yard. All of the hay, all of the grain is put in one storehouse and so forth. My wage laborers, of course, do not work as hard as peasants do for themselves, but since they work in an artel, in many cases, for example gathering hay and grain, threshing, and so forth, they do more than the same number of peasants working alone for themselves could do . . . But I will need to discuss this in greater detail another time, if only to show that every year the independence of peasants' actions becomes greater and greater, so that many tasks which were still done together several years ago by the whole village are now done separately by each household. I think that the peasants will soon divide even the land by household and destroy communal landholding.

[Engelgardt continues to discuss the failings of gentry farming.]

A Visit to the Local Agricultural Exhibition

But in the meantime, let me describe how I went to the agricultural exhibition put on by our agricultural society in the provincial capital this autumn.

After receiving an announcement that there would be an exhibition of agricultural products, agricultural tools and machines, cattle, and horses in our provincial capital, that during the exhibit there would be sessions of our agricultural society to discuss various questions affecting local farming, I was very glad to have this opportunity to exchange ideas with practicing farmers and scholars of agronomy, by the opportunity to see the results of improved farming, and I decided to go to the exhibition.

[Engelgardt discusses the difficulty of gentry farming and his own sense of inadequacy in his first attempts on his farm.]

The entire trip cost about thirty rubles. Of course, for this amount of money, one could cultivate an extra desiatina of flax and make a profit of fifty rubles. But science is not free for anyone and furthermore, the thirty rubles used for the trip could give a return of thousands if we learn something and learn how to put it to good use.

More than anything else, I was counting on meeting farmers and members of our society. For us agriculturalists, at least for those who did not know how to set themselves up in some kind of civil service job, agricultural questions are the most vital ones now. Everyone complains and moans, it is clear that under such circumstances everyone would seize the opportunity to discuss questions that interest him with other people.

[Engelgardt describes what he hoped to find at the exhibition in terms of agricultural information.]

I am ashamed to say that I also wanted a change of scene; I wanted to see civilized people who wear frock coats, and not homespun coats, who drink champagne, and not vodka, who eat various fines herbes, and not adulterated bread, who receive a proper salary, and do not pay any taxes, who do not fear not only the volost administrator, but not even the constable.

Perhaps I'll even see those whom the constable himself fears. I wanted to pass over a carriage way, and to walk on a sidewalk, and to hear some music, to stop by the club, to go to the theater, to see women who wear pretty boots and clean gloves. It's a strange thing, it seems that I have already grown accustomed to the countryside, soon it will be three years that I have seen only homespun coats, bast shoes, badly wrapped heads, I have been smelling cabbage, manure, whey, I have heard only, "Eh, Proska, you little whore, go slop the pigs." "What?" "Go slop the pigs, you shit," and so on. It would seem that I should have grown accustomed to it, but no, I am still so drawn to the town. If only I could be at Erber's for just an hour . . . to drink a glass of wine with an acquaintance, to eat ten oysters, to chat, to sit with women who do not smell of manure and sour milk as the milkmaids do.

The packing began. I had to transform myself completely. At home in the autumn, I always wear high boots, a red flannel shirt, and a sheepskin coat, an outfit that I came to logically in the country, an outfit that is extremely comfortable and even attractive, because the bright red color makes a pleasant change in contrast with the gray sky, the gray weather, the gray buildings, and gray ploughed fields. But I could not bring myself to show up at the exhibition in such an outfit, even though it would seem that this country costume would be very appropriate for an agricultural exhibition, because this could be taken as being pretentious, or something worse. One must dress in town clothes when one is in town.

By custom, every member of the gentry arriving in the provincial capital presents himself to the authorities, therefore one must take tails and black pants. For paying calls, dinners, meetings, one needs a frock coat. For daily attendance at the exhibition, a suit. I also had to take a fur coat, an overcoat, galoshes, fine underwear, in a word, a multitude of things which make up the wardrobe of a civilized man. I gathered many, many various things. Sidor, who was going with me as my "man," also had to become familar with the name and use of each item. I gave this task over to Savelich, who, as an experienced man who had even served a general in St. Petersburg, knows what's what.

[Engelgardt describes the preparations for the trip and the peasants' surprise that they have not been asked to send anything to the exhibition.]

We set out in the wagon early in the morning. I took along the worker Nikita in addition to Sidor; he was supposed to drive the horses back from the station and to take back our, that is Sidor's and my, country clothes in which we had decided not to appear in town. We had to go fifteen versts on the wagon to the station along the most disgustingly dirty road and of course it was impossible even to think of riding there in city clothes.[. . .]

We arrived at the station, we changed clothes, entered the station, waited for the train. It was Europe, civilization: gendarmes were strolling along the platforms, officers in red caps—true Hussars—were running about, artillery men were handling the luggage. There was a buffet in the waiting room, various vodkas, some hors d'oeuvres, a bit of caviar and fish. I went up to the stand and asked for two glasses, one for myself and the other for Nikita, we drank, had a bit of bread, I tossed down two five-kopek pieces. "That's not enough, fifty kopeks, please." "Fifty kopeks for two glasses!" Nikita interjected. "Keep quiet, friend," the waiter said to Nikita, "this is not a tavern, there are gentlemen here!" Nikita was struck dumb. Europe! A half a verst from the station they give you a bottle, but here you get only two ounce glasses for the same price, and they aren't really full ounces at that.

The train arrived. Sidor and I got on, I, the lord, in second class and he in third. Two gentlemen were sitting in the compartment talking.

"Look, they write from A.," said one, "that the peasants of S., G., and P. volosts decided to build public schools in their volosts . . ."

"Yes, but what does one school per volost mean?"

"Of course, it's not enough, but it is still gratifying to see that the peasants are striving for education and, recognizing its necessity, are sacrificing their hard-earned money for the construction of schools."

Aha, I thought, these are city gentlemen and probably from St. Petersburg! They still don't know that anything is possible in Russia, that if the authorities wished it, the peasants of any volost would make a contract about their desire to open not just a school in their volost, but a university or a classical gymnasium! I wanted to talk a bit with gentlemen who believe what is written in the *News*.[6] I wanted to test myself because three years ago when I was in St. Petersburg, I also believed everything that is written in newspapers, I believed that the peasants were striving for education, that they were building schools and donating their money for them, that there were charities for orphans, that there are hospitals, and so on and so forth. In a word, I not only believed that in such and such volost the peasants resolved "to establish a school," but, according to the correspondent's own judgment, that "it is gratifying to see how the people are striving for education," etcetera.

Yes; three years ago, I believed all of this. But in the countryside I soon learned that many things are not like this and that one cannot believe the *News*. I reached the point that I stopped reading newspapers and only wondered for whom they were written.

I left St. Petersburg convinced that everything had changed in the last ten years, that the folk were moving rapidly forward, and so on and so forth. You can imagine my surprise when, soon after I settled in the country, a muzhik came to me once requesting that I stand up for him because his son was being taken to school out of turn.

"Stand up for me, they're making trouble for me," he said, "they're demanding that my son go to school out of turn. My son served his time in school last winter, they're making him go again this year."

"Yes, but how can I act on your behalf in this kind of question?" I asked, amazed by such a request.

"Stand up for me, they listen to you in the village. It's a nuisance, it's not my turn. Vaska's son hasn't gone once yet. It's Vaska's son's turn to go to school this year, but Vaska argues, he says, 'My oldest son's serving in the army, I myself was in the militia, why should I carry the burden of service for three people!' So what if one's in the army! Vaska's got four sons, and I have one. Mine went to school last winter, this year they're calling him again—is this the law? Do something, find out, ask someone what the law is."

In fact, when the muzhik has no grain in the winter, when almost all of the children are going after crusts of bread, as it was the first winter I spent in the countryside, and the whole family lives off these crusts, it is understandable that the muzhik considers "service in school" a heavy obligation. But after I looked into it, I quickly found out that even in years of good harvest it was not all as "gratifying and so forth" as they described it in the *News*.

However, it has gotten easier in regard to schools nowadays; it's not that schools are being destroyed but that they are somehow fading away. Right after the Emancipation, the peasants applied themselves seriously to the schools, so that even now among the twenty- to twenty-five-year-olds there are rather many who are literate, that is, who know how to read and write some. But then things eased up with the schools and there are already very few literate boys in the village. The prosperous ones, however, even now teach their children, but in "their own," not in "compulsory," schools. Several men in the village agree to hire some kind of soldier for the winter, and he will teach.

After the schools came orphanages. Orphanages were set up everywhere and there are accounts of them given, but now the orphanages are also giving way.

Now resolutions about contributions to the society for the care of the wounded are more in fashion, and most recently, resolutions to destroy taverns and cut down on drunkenness have priority. You only have to spend a little time reading the newspapers and you can recite by heart whatever correspondence you choose . . . "The peasants of X communal assembly resolved, with the goal of cutting down on drunkenness, to destroy two of the four taverns in the village," and then, "it is gratifying that the consciousness is awakening among the peasants . . . ," and so on and so forth.

[Engelgardt describes his conversation with the other gentlemen and discusses the inaccuracy of Petersburg perceptions of rural life and of most newspaper accounts of developments in the village.]

What an amazing contrast! The soft seat in the compartment, the mirrored glass, the fine table trimming, the elegant netting on the beautiful wrought iron arms, the elegant stations with beautiful buffets and laid tables, servants in frock coats, but you go a half a verst from the station—gray izbas, gray jerkins, gray cabbage soup, gray people . . .

It was dark by the time we arrived in the provincial capital. Sidor and I hired a cab and went to the hotel. The driver took us to the best hotel, an enormous stone building with a broad stairway, with a public hall and buffet below with tables fully laid with hors d'oeuvres and clear tables; we took a suite of two rooms: the larger one with upholstered furniture and mirrors for receiving guests, the smaller one with a bed, washstand, and similar necessities. The maid arrived—a lady! She addressed Sidor in the formal you form!

It is hard to convey the impression that the train station, the ride in the train, the city, the hotel in European style made after I had lived without a break in the countryside for more than two years. And it's not far, it would seem, but compare a village road and a ride in a cart with a ride on the railroad; a country inn, where there is nothing but vodka, real raw vodka and military issue herring at three kopeks apiece, a place where they do not know of handkerchiefs or napkins or table linen, with a splendid hotel!

After I had changed I set out to see my relative.[. . .]

I met landowners who, it turned out, had brought cattle to the exhibition; we began to chat. It turned out that many more were expected, that only a very few had already been sent. We set out for the club. What splendor! An enormous reading room, lamps with shades, a large table covered with newspapers and journals, several gentlemen buried in their reading.[. . .] Here several parties were busy at green tables and at one of them was the source of all the "gratifying" reports, the one who wants to build schools, who wants to cut down on the number of taverns, who wants to contribute to the construction of a Russian pomological garden, in a word, the peace mediator, deftly playing the king of spades. We went through all of the rooms, we chatted with a zemstvo delegate who explained the project of some kind of special bank to us, we passed on into the dining room and sat down to eat. I returned to the hotel after midnight. Sidor was sleeping on the sofa in the first room, which I had given to him for his use at night, warning him ahead of time to take off his dirty boots when he lay down.[. . .]

After I had lain down in bed I could not get to sleep for a long time, I kept thinking how many changes there had been in two years and what a radical change! Three years ago I lived in St. Petersburg, I worked as a professor, I received a salary of almost three thousand rubles, I did research on isothermic cresols and diphenols, I wore thin boots and trousers over my boots, I lived in such a warm building that I could go barefoot inside, I rode in carriages, I ate oysters at Erber's, I was carried away by Liadovaia in "The Beautiful Elena," I believed what was written in the newspapers about the activity of the zemstvos, agricultural conferences, about the striving of the people for education, and so on. I was unacquainted with current rural life, although I was raised in the country until I was sixteen. But that was still before the Emancipation, when even not very wealthy gentry lived in mansions, ate various fines herbes, wore city clothes, had carriages and teams of six. Of course, I knew nothing at that time about the daily life of the muzhik and of those minor folk who made way for us when we children with our nurse, preceded by two coachmen, entered our village church. After that, I lived for twenty-three years in St. Petersburg, which I only occasionally left to visit my relatives in the summer for vacation. In general, I was acquainted with the village from novellas, and from novellas describing village life before the Emancipation at that, I learned about the peasantry only from newspaper reports, concluding with "it is gratifying," and so forth. I believed that we had made great progress in the last decade, that the people were becoming enlightened, that burning activity was taking place everywhere: roads were being built, schools and hospitals were being built, improvements in agriculture were being introduced. I believed everything, even in agricultural conferences, in agricultural societies, I myself am a member of several.

But now I live in the country, in the real country, which it is sometimes impossible to leave in the autumn and spring. I have no position, I earn no salary, I have forgotten about cresols and diphenols, I farm, I plant flax and clover, I raise calves and piglets, I wear tall boots with my trousers tucked into the tops, I live in the kind of house in which it is not only impossible to go barefoot on the floor, but in which you can't always stay seated in felt boots, and my health is fine. I ride in a wagon or on runners, I not only drive the horse myself, but sometimes I even harness him myself, I eat cabbage soup with salted beef, borshch with ham. For several months at a time I don't see fresh beef and I am pleased if fresh mutton turns up, I am carried away by the songs the babas "cry out," and I dance to the song of the dove, I don't believe what is written in the newspapers about the activity of the zemstvos, the various conferences, commissions, I know how all of those "gratifying phenomena" which fill the newspapers happen, and so on. What an amazing difference! Imagine a man not believing anything written in the newspapers, or it is better to say, knowing that all of it does not happen at all as it is described, and at the same time who sees that others believe everything, everyone accepts it at face value, regards it all in the most serious manner![. . .]

Farming always interested me; the theoretical side of agriculture did not satisfy me because I wanted to apply theory to practice; it is clear that it is one thing to study strategy in an office and another to apply it in war. I myself had thought I would go to the country when I had earned my pension. Fate, however, decided it would be otherwise. I had to leave service before my term was complete. I had two choices in this situation: I could either move into the house of my wealthy relative in the country, where I would have had complete city comforts and where I, set up splendidly in the material sense, could have buried myself in books and, cut off from life, could have become a parlor scholar, or I could have gone to my own estate, which had been neglected terribly, which did not offer any conveniences whatsoever for daily life, and take up farming there. I chose the latter.

I decided to go to my estate and to take up farming. Once I had resigned myself to this idea, I left St. Petersburg, happy, full of hope, with a desire for new activity and work. I left in January. You recall what a terrible winter there was in 1871. I left St. Petersburg dressed very warmly, but not practically at all: a city coat, tall felt boots, a heavy warm fur coat, a long scarf.[. . .]

The cold in the train compartment was unbelievable. At the beginning it was all right, but in the middle of the night I could stand it no longer. Although I was dressed in a warm fur coat, tall felt boots, wrapped in a scarf, in a word, so wrapped up that I could hardly move, still, after I had gone through several stations in the unheated and nearly empty car—besides me there was only one passenger, I could not stand it any longer. It was impossible to breathe such cold air, my throat seized up immediately. I could not stand it, I paid extra and sat in the heated car of first class. Look what an activist I am! I thought, what am I going to do in the country, how am I going to farm if I cannot stand even a few hours in the cold? This saddened me very much and I was consoled only by the fact that the other passenger who had alone sat with me in the compartment, a Jew, also could not bear it—and everyone knows how fiercely a Jew will hold onto a kopek—and moved into the heated car at the same time that I did.[. . .]

I was very taken aback by the first encounter with my new life. The minus thirty degrees temperature tired me out so much that I absolutely could not breathe the cold air, my throat began to hurt, and I began to shake with fever. The heavy fur coat and tall felt boots which I could not take off at the stations interfered with my walking, and I had to sit immobile the whole time like a statue. And just look out the compartment window at where I was to live and work—snow, snow, and more snow! Everything was covered with snow, everything was frozen, and if it were not for the smoke coming out of the snow-covered izbas which flashed by along the sides of the track, it would have been possible to think you were riding through uninhabited tundra. I looked at these little izbas and I wondered how they could live there, how I was going to live, what I was going to do, how I would farm, if from the first day I already felt that I did not have the strength to endure this terrible cold. I was so upset that I became utterly depressed and I felt that the energy with which I had left Petersburg was abandoning me . . .

Now, having lived three years in the country, I have adapted to everything, and most important, I have adapted my dress, because clothing is the heart of the matter.

Nowadays, anyone who wants to take up farming himself, who wants to grasp both the technical and the commercial side of the farm, who cannot maintain a multitude of servants for his own service, must change everything, from his dress to the layout of the buildings on the demesne, because everything in Russia was set up for a noble life with a multitude of servants.[. . .]

I'll talk about dress. Noble dress is so different from the muzhik's, which has been adapted to the life-style of the country's entire population, that a man who wears noble dress of necessity must carry with him the entire setup that goes along with this dress. Even on the railway, even in provincial and district towns where St. Petersburg city life continues to a certain extent, one already senses the uselessness of noble dress; in the country it is absolutely unthinkable.

I left St. Petersburg dressed in city clothes: a starched shirt, a jacket, thin chamber boots, and on top, a heavy fur coat, a fur hat, felt boots to my knees. The impracticality of this outfit was manifest already during the train journey. On the second day after my departure from Petersburg I began to sense what Goethe wrote about in his "Italian Journey."

Torbole den 12 september 1786.

In der Abendkuhle ging ich spazieren, und befinde mich nun wirklich in einem neuen Lande, in einer ganz fremden Umbegung. Die Menschen leben ein nachlassiges Schlaraffenleben: erstlich haben die Thuren keine Schlosser; der Wirth aber versicherte mich, ich konnte ganze ruhig sein, und wenn alles was ich bei mir hatte aus Diamanten bestande; zweitens sind die Fenster mit Oelpapier statt Glasscheiben geschlossen; drittens fehlt eine hochst nothige Bequemlichkeit, so das man dem Naturzustande hier ziemlich nahe kommt. Als ich den Hausknecht nach einer gewissen Gelegenheit fragte, deutete er in den Hof hinunter: "quiabasso puo servirsi" (You can take care of your needs there!); ich fragte: "dove?" (where?)—"da per tutto dove vuol!" (why, wherever you want) antwortete er freundlich. Durchaus zeigt sich die groste Sorglosigkeit, doch Leben und Geschaftigkeit genug . . .[7]

Armed with Goethe as my authority, I will continue.

"Where?" I asked the watchman.

"There in the booth."

Of course, as you see, we have advanced far ahead of the Italy of Goethe's time and the watchman of the station does not say, as the Italian house servant did, "Wherever you like," but pointed to a booth. I went to the booth in my fur coat, of course, because it was two hundred yards from the station to the booth, and it was thirty degrees below zero. I walked in. The booth was made of planks, everything was covered with ice. What was I to do there?

Arriving in the provincial capital, I stopped in the best German hotel. The hotel was absolutely German: the manager was German, the lackeys were German, the maids were Germans, it was just as if I were in Königsberg or Düsseldorf. After spending the night I asked the next morning, "Where?" They pointed upstairs. In only a jacket I went up the cold staircase and after a long search I found a small room with the sign Retirade [Restroom], I walked in—everything was covered with ice, you could have ice-skated there. How could one not catch cold in such conditions?

And that was even on the railway, a provincial capital! After all, here there are at least booths, here there are Jewish trading stalls, here there are Germans who love cleanliness and who consider you "Russian swine," while in the country . . . Even in posting inns there are rarely any kinds of facilities at all, and in peasant households there is evidently nothing. Clearly one can travel in a city outfit under such conditions only if you have brought a "Petrushka"[8] with you. In the past, a lord always had a Petrushka with him or two Petrushkas, and carried all of his crockery with him. Then, of course, you could dress however you pleased.

But now! Someday they will introduce various conveniences at posting inns, like those a civilized people have! But as long as these do not exist, one must either go out into the cold in a jacket or change one's dress. Generally a gentleman dressed in city clothes and a fur coat literally cannot take a step without a servant. To say nothing, for example, about tying up the horse, even driving a horse, looking after it at the posting inn, taking it to the water trough, he cannot do anything. And there is no Petrushka and no Selifan![9] One must change one's outfit, one must have one which will be warm, light, will not hamper movement, so that one can sit in it in an izba where there is a draft from the windows and the doors, and go outside to look after the horses. A warm jacket, a fur jacket, none of this will do; in the end you must come to the point that you find that the most comfortable outfit in the winter is a sheepskin coat.

But it makes no sense to put a sheepskin coat over city clothes. A sheepskin coat should replace a jacket. The muzhik wears a sheepskin coat as indoor dress and takes it off only at lunch and dinner; he sits in his sheepskin coat in the izba, goes outdoors in it, works in it still. Having put on his sheepskin coat in the morning, he does not take it off until evening except for lunch, because he works in his sheepskin outside, gives the cattle their feed, carries and chops wood in it. The master finds himself in the same situation: even if does not work himself, but only manages workers, he must still be outside the entire day. Setting out on the road, the muzhik puts on either fur over the sheepskin for terribly cold weather, or a heavy quilted coat in wet weather. Throwing off the fur in cold weather and staying in the sheepskin, he can do any kind of work; after he comes into a posting inn and takes off his fur, a muzhik stays in the sheepskin, which he does not take off in the izba until he sits down at the table, and he goes out in the same sheepskin to look after the horses. The sheepskin coat is the most comfortable winter dress for us when we put it on directly over a waistcoat or a wool shirt in the Garibaldi style. That kind of shirt is also very appropriate dress and corresponds to the muzhik's cloth homespun coat. It is warm in a sheepskin coat and one's mobility is not restricted at all; its cut is very rational: the arms are long, wide at the elbows and narrow at the wrists—loose, but wind cannot penetrate; there is a double layer of fur on the chest, the skirts are long and one goes behind the other, the waist is long. As soon as you put on a sheepskin coat you will need a belt like the muzhik's or one like those that house servants used to wear so that you can pull the coat in at the waist. Then a wool scarf around your neck, mittens, wool stockings, a warm felt hat, long hair to cover the ears, and a hood. Hoods have become very widespread among petty officials, former house servants, traders, and merchants riding around the district; but you rarely see a hood among the peasants because the peasant generally tries not to buy anything and to get by with his own things, not with purchased items.

Dressed like this, you are comfortable in the winter. If it is cold or wet, you put on a fur coat or a quilted coat. Once it gets warmer, you get rid of the fur coat. If something goes wrong with the harness, if the horse gets caught in a snowdrift, then you get rid of the fur coat, even in freezing weather you can do a repair or help a horse. After you have arrived at a posting inn, you will sit in your felt boots and sheepskin coat, because there are usually drafts from all over in an izba.

You will be comfortable everywhere: at home, on the farm, on the road, in your dealings with peasants, priests, merchants, traders, in general, with people who live, as it is said, in the Russian manner and who do not consider Russian dress improper.[. . .]

But it is not only dress which is not suitable for the new order of things. Everything needs to be changed. To this day, everything still operates according to the old ways and it is these old ways which are some of the main reasons why the gentry cannot manage agriculture. Everything needs to be changed and adapted to the new order because everything, from the structure of one's house to the boot on one's foot, was so constructed under the old ways that it required a multitude of servants. No matter how stingy I was, no matter how much I tried to reduce my staff, I still did not achieve the desired result, even so. Even so, a significant portion of my income goes to maintaining staff. And I still do not have a driver, a lackey, or a cook.[. . .]

After I had been in the provincial capital [during his initial journey to his estate in 1871] several days where the clean-loving Germans live, and after I had recovered a bit from the fever and sore throat, I went on by train to a station fifteen versts from my estate. The steward came alone for me at the station in a sleigh. A white sleigh without springs, a poor, tousled horse; the steward in felt boots, a sheepskin coat, and fur, a muzhik with a cart drawn by an emaciated little horse to carry my trunks, snow, freezing cold . . . So here is real country life! I thought. Since I had already lived through it and had begun to get accustomed to the climate and had begun to get used to the cold, my previous mood passed. My energy and thirst for new activity reappeared, my spirit became somehow gay and light. I liked everything: the sleigh, the horse, and the fact that I myself would be driving. As I got in the sleigh, I noticed a rifle in it.

"Why the rifle?" I asked the steward.

"Just in case; maybe we'll happen on a grouse."

Later I saw that almost everyone here drives armed in the winter "just in case." The wealthier gentry, for the most part, carry revolvers. The petty gentry, low officials, stewards, house servants, and peasants who have rifles ride with their rifles or carry them, while the simple muzhik has either an axe in his belt or a club in his hands: everyone takes something along when he sets out alone in case of some kind of an emergency, especially in winter. Don't think that it is not quiet around here: we haven't heard of murders or robbery or serious theft in our area; horse theft only began to occur recently. But still, everyone has "something just in case" with him, who knows, an animal or an evil man might jump you. Of course, wild animals are feared most of all, but they always have "just in case" in mind, and everyone looks suspiciously at anyone he meets, expecting that he will be, in fact, a robber. I think, however, that a firearm, a rifle or a revolver, for example, is a useless thing, and that a club in strong hands is much better, but a rifle is meant for "fear": even so, he won't move in so much if he sees a gun in your hands or some other kind of weapon. It is rare that one would need to put a revolver to the test because there are no professional thieves around here, there are no people who do this as their work, as real robbers, waiting for passersby on the roads. Of course murders and thefts happen, but they are accidental for the most part, without a premeditated goal, and it is usually drunks who commit them, very often people who are very good in everyday life. "If you don't leave things lying around carelessly, you won't tempt a thief," the proverb says. If something is lying around carelessly, without guard, I'll take it, and there you have theft. A good man, a peasant farmer who has allotment land, a homestead, and family, not some kind of homeless rogue, morally dissipated man, but just simply an ordinary man who works during the summer harvest to the point of exhaustion, who observes all of the fasts, who respects "all the laws," will become a thief just because something is lying about without supervision. Some children slipped into the barn to take a block of lard or an osmina of hemp, the farmer unfortunately woke up, jumped up at the noise, the club in his hand got one of the kids—murder. Some friends were sitting around together, they got drunk, the host's fine watch was shown to one of the guests, a knife got into his hands—murder. Someone was drunk, he had his eye on someone's sheepskin coat, an axe got into his hands, "he" (the devil) made him do it—murder. Some fellows were drinking together, one noticed at the tavern that the other had some money, they left together, etcetera.

All accidents. I repeat that there are no professional murderers or thieves, no real robbers, but everyone always fears an "accident" and is wary of everyone else, even one's own acquaintance. You could meet up with someone in an obscure place—get going, brother, get on your way, be off with you! Who knows you, who knows what you have on your mind, you don't even know yourself what'll come to you. And anyone you meet, seeing that you have something, will be wary. At first I was very much struck by this caution and distrust with which a good muzhik regards everyone he meets, especially if he has money on him. It is fine when Sidor and I ride together; as soon as he notices someone walking along, especially if it is in an obscure, wooded place, he immediately takes up the reins, looking at the passerby askance. As soon as he sees something, he is on the horses. Because, who knows, you can't get inside a person, you don't know what he has in mind. I am used to all of this now, but at first it grated on me somehow when I saw that everyone thought I, I personally, was capable of murder, robbery, theft, deception, swindling, cheating, shortchanging. Of course, in three years, the peasants of the neighboring villages, especially the young ones, have become, bit by bit, more trusting, seeing that I do not cheat them, I don't deceive them, I pay them according to our agreement, I don't put pressure on them.[. . .]

Disturbed by the memories of all that I had lived through, I could not sleep for a long time and I got up late the next day and immediately set out for the exhibition; I hurried because the opening of the exhibition was supposed to take place on this day and I had promised to show Sidor the bishop.

The opening of the exhibition was ceremonious. The Right Reverend [the bishop] himself performed the service. There were few bystanders; only the authorities, the organizers of the exhibition, who were distinguished from the others by large green cockades of silk ribbons—why green? Is it because green is the color of hope, is it because the farmer, in the summer, of course, lives surrounded by green?—were there for the opening. Five or six exhibitors, a few students from the agricultural institute who had been sent to the exhibition, a few ladies who clearly came for the service. Of farmers of the province who had come to the exhibition there were two, that is, Sidor and I: I was the representative of the gentry farmers (I found out that I was the only one in the whole province who had come to the exhibition), Sidor was the representative of the peasant estate. Having glanced at the grain and vegetables exhibited in the main hall, you could think that market gardening was booming, because such pumpkins, corn, artichokes, cabbages were on display—it took one's breath away! Sidor was especially interested in the pumpkins when he found out that you can eat them. He liked the large heads of cabbage very much, because, among the peasantry, cabbages usually only have loose green leaves, and if there is a head, it is no larger than a good apple.

"So market gardeners must have brought these, Aleksandr Nikolaevich?"
"Of course."
"So that's how it is. These market gardeners know what to do."

Market gardening is in extremely bad shape among our peasants, you won't see a white cabbage even at the most prosperous peasant's and for the preparation of sauerkraut, they usually use beets and green cabbage leaves and beet leaves, consequently, the sauerkraut is gray. Our peasants are convinced that the market gardeners who rent gardens at gentry houses, and for whom all kinds of vegetables grow splendidly, grow good vegetables because they "know," that is, they know how to cast a spell, how to practice sorcery.

Having glanced at the grain and vegetables, Sidor and I, while the bishop and officials looked over the main hall, ran to the special place set up for the cattle. We were most interested in the horses and cattle and Sidor was especially interested in the horses, for which every peasant has a weakness. We came to the cattle room: the stalls were constructed as they should be, but they were empty. Our province was exhibiting a total of *one* horse. It was standing "alone, the poor little one, like a recruit in the reserves," and it was covered with a horse cloth, probably to protect the eyes, and it had on a tag on which was written: Ardennes-Russian breed. I asked them to take off the cloth, they took it off and showed the horse: a roan mare, a fine mare! I asked about it: they said that it was bred from a simple mare and an Ardennes stallion from a breeding stable. It was a fine horse, it was born just like the stallion, with a roan color, a broad back, and a good height, a fine chest— from the feed, of course. I thought about buying it, not for work, of course, but for riding on my own. It was not for sale. I asked if there weren't more such horses at their stable for sale? They did not say anything. Thus I did not even get to the talking stage. Thus, our entire province exhibited only *one* horse; our neighboring province did not exhibit any at all.

[Engelgardt describes his examination of the horses at the exhibition.]

There are only five horses at the whole exhibition, our province exhibited only one, and four of them were from the state farm. The state horses won the large silver medal and they were worth it, they were good horses.

The sheep-breeding department came after the horses. As I said earlier, sheep are a very important item for our province, especially for peasants. Landowners keep few sheep here—why? I don't know—but sheep constitute a major business for the peasants because sheep not only pay for their own feed, but even bring in some income, while horned cattle do not bring in income.[10] A sheep requires little feed because it finds grass earlier in the spring and later in the autumn than cattle. Cattle are still starving when a sheep has already eaten its fill. In the summer sheep get enough to eat in pastures where there is nothing for the cattle. Sheep give wool and a pair of lambs which grow up by the fall without any care whatsoever. It was natural to expect that at a local exhibition sheep breeding would be represented in keeping with the importance it has in the local economy. But that wasn't the case. Sheep breeding was represented even less than the peasant farmers, which Sidor, whom I had brought, alone represented as the sole peasant who came to the exhibition to study the items on display. Our province did not exhibit *a single sheep,* the neighboring provinces also did not display any sheep, the state farm put on this department as well, it sent merinos, one pair each of pure Electoral breed, Electoral black sheep, and Electoral bulls and meat sheep of the mixed Flanders-Oxfordshire breed.[. . .]

There were also very few large-horned cattle at the exhibition. There were five exhibitors from three districts from our province; the remaining eight districts did not send anything; the peasants did not send anything, the city dwellers, who have the best local cattle, did not send anything, the well-known cattle breeders who own large herds of excellent cattle also did not send anything.[. . .]

We looked over the cattle, we glanced at the poultry, Sidor liked the small hens very much moreover (because, he said, pet chickens are even better for a peasant's dwelling than doves who fly and make a mess everywhere) we glanced quickly at the exhibition of books on agriculture . . . and meanwhile, music was playing, the restaurant opened, and the crowd grew. I stopped by the restaurant and met the two gentry exhibitors I had met the night before. "So, gentlemen," I said, "did many farmers come to the exhibition?" "No," they said, "no one's here yet; perhaps they'll come." We sat down, had a bite, listened to the music, and went to look at the department of field cultivation and market gardening. There was little of interest: a little sack of wheat, a little sack of rye, a little sack of oats, and again a little sack of wheat, of course, all of the grain in the selection was fine. There were also good collections but mostly various harvest products. In all, there were twenty-three exhibitors from six provinces who presented one hundred eighty-two items. Of course, this includes everything: one sent onions, another teasel, a third wheat, and so on. While we were looking at the technical and field cultivation sections, Sidor looked at the machine department, where eight exhibitors presented fifty-three items, the majority of which were out of storage from a Swedish firm, which has already been shut down, it is said, and items of a local agronomist-inventor who presented a wooden plough, harrows, runners, special rakes. When we entered the machine department, Sidor, who had already seen everything, pulled me aside in a secretive way.

"There's something here, Aleksandr Nikolaevich."

"What?"

"The kind of thing, they say, that will keep hail away."

"What are you saying? Where is it?"

"It's over there."

In fact a local agronomist had presented a "hail driver" consisting of a pole with a copper spike attached on the top end, from which there was a wire that wrapped around the pole in a spiral.

"You should buy that in case there's hail, because you never know, all of our fields were beaten down once."

"But why should we buy it, we can make one ourselves, it's not a very complicated thing."

"If something is not complicated to make, then it won't be of any use; it's clear what we have here, it's been made with a spell. What use can there be from just a pole if there's no spell over it! There are old men who drive hail away, they cast spells also, there's got to be a spell over this pole here too."

"And if it is a simple pole, without a spell?"

"And why should they show a pole without a spell! What use is there in it without a spell! As if hail is afraid of a simple pole?"

"Look, if they give the hail driver a medal, then I'll buy it."

However, they did not give a medal to the hail driver and I didn't buy it; Sidor remained convinced even so that this was no simple pole. It was not the first time that I had heard from Sidor that there were those even among the gentry who know how to cast spells. There is a noblewoman here who cures with homeopathic powders and sometimes she helps—Sidor and all of the peasants are convinced that this noblewoman "sees" and casts spells on the powders. No matter how much I have tried to convince Sidor that there is no spell involved here whatsoever, that it is simple homeopathic medicine which you can buy and dispense when someone gets sick, that everyone uses homeopathy to treat illness because it is not difficult, and requires no special knowledge, he still holds fast to his conviction.

"What kind of medicine can there be in such a little powder? This powder's got no taste, no odor, you hardly put it in your mouth, what kind of medicine is there here! Everybody knows that it's a spell; she casts a spell on these powders. Now the feldsher gives medicine, and now there it's clear that this is medicine, it's either sour or salty or bitter. That's medicine, but these, it's clear, is a spell!"

Having looked at all of the sections we went into the restaurant, sat down, listened to the music, and went back to the cattle-breeding section again. I spent the next morning at the exhibition—there was no place to go, I had no acquaintances. I would wander through the halls, stop by the cattle-breeding department, stand, watch how the cows were chewing their cud, I would sit listening to the music, I would go into the restaurant, drink a shot of vodka, go to have a look again at the cows chewing their cud, listen to the music . . . I went to the exhibition every day, I kept hoping to meet farmers who had come to the exhibition, but I saw no one because no other simpletons like me showed up who would go to a provincial exhibition. You come in, you wander through empty halls, around noon a few visitors would come by to listen to the music or to lunch in the restaurant; if there had been no restaurant or music, the exhibition would had been empty all the time. Empty, dull, it was obvious that this entire exhibition was not needed by anyone except the organizers.[. . .]

Yes, so near, and yet so far.

[Engelgardt describes an equally unsatisfying lecture and luncheon sponsored by the local agricultural society.]

This entire trip cost me twenty-eight rubles fifty kopeks, that is, four sacks of rye or nine sacks of oats. What did I learn for this money? What did I find out that was useful?

That exhibitions and conferences of farmers and agricultural societies are no more than "gratifying phenomena," just like the resolutions about schools, about the destruction of taverns, and so on.

It is a shame to see, however, that there are people like me who believe in exhibitions and conferences and accounts. And what an account was written about our exhibition!

Letter V

✉   In the fifth letter Engelgardt hits his stride as a raconteur and social ana-
lyst.[1] He opens the letter with an evocative and charming description of Old
Lyska, the most beloved dog on the estate. While this account provides more
local color than critical information about post-Emancipation rural Russia, it
conveys the texture of life on Batishchevo and reveals Engelgardt's ability to
delight in the daily life of farming. The remaining sections of the letter are more
clearly analytical and suggest the tensions Engelgardt is beginning to feel as he
farms for profit and depends on peasant labor to meet that end. Whereas he
remains true to his earlier praise of intelligent and skilled male peasants, he
offers a considerably less fond portrait of peasant women as the decisive factor
in his success or failure as an employer of peasant labor. While Engelgardt
eschews that more romantic idealization of the peasantry characteristic of
many of his peers who looked to communal institutions in the village as a sign
of Russia's ability to withstand the ravages of a money economy and capitalism, he reveals that he shares certain key objections to the Western model.
Chief among these are individualism and the urge for profit. In the fifth letter,
unable to attribute individualism and money lust to the male peasant, the good
muzhik, he assigns these undesirable features to the baba.

In describing flax production on his estate, the primary cash crop and thus
the source of his own profit, Engelgardt explains the critical role of the women
who brake flax for him. Admitting that his own success largely depends on their
willingness to work for him, he then launches into a thinly veiled accusation of
the baba for the very qualities that are essential to him as her gentry employer.
He describes her as mercenary, motivated, and as a fierce individualist at the
expense of the collective of the family. The baba is thus the object of
Engelgardt's projection of his own growing distaste for the realities of farming
for profit.

Engelgardt's harsh portrayal of the role of peasant women in the economy
suggests at least two things about the patriarchal culture of post-Emancipation
Russia. First, peasant women were able to carve out their own space and share
of power within that culture. Second, pervasive paternalism ensured that the
women's power would be met by resentment and vitriol not only from peasant

102

men but also from educated members of society, especially if they found, as Engelgardt did, that peasant women might block their access to the village. This section of the fifth letter thus adds both to the portrait of peasant women Engelgardt is developing and to our understanding of the particular frame in which that portrait is placed.

⊠ ⊠ ⊠

Old Lyska

I celebrated my fifth anniversary . . .

Winter this year is just as fierce as in 1870–71. The cold temperatures are horrible—the birds are freezing to death. It is December. It is already dark by five o'clock . . .

I returned from the cattle yard, listened to the steward's accounts, gave orders for tomorrow, recorded the receipts, expenses, yields, and so forth, drank some tea, asked the children[2] for their lessons, and at eight o'clock . . .

"Having drunk a little vodka and eaten supper," I go to bed. My first letter "from the country" also began with this phrase, but my acquaintance whom I asked to deliver the letter to the editors crossed out the words "having drunk a little vodka." That made it awkward, in my opinion, and more important, untrue because who in the country who is wealthy enough always to have vodka in the house would go to sleep without drinking it after dinner? It is clear that my acquaintance crossed out these words because he wanted to keep an eye out for me. It is well known that in Russia, if someone loses his position and finds himself without work, and, moreover, lands in the country, then he cannot find anything to keep him busy, and begins to drink from boredom and becomes a drunk, just as, vice versa, the muzhik usually becomes a drunk if he lands in service where he has no real work. My acquaintance was probably afraid that others would think that I had become a drunk in the country and, looking out for me, crossed out "having drunk a little vodka": usually everyone begins by drinking only at dinner, then they get in the habit of drinking at lunch as well, then, little by little, they get in the habit of having some of the hair of the dog that bit them in the morning, and as soon as a man starts that—it's not for nothing that it is said, "drink, but don't take some of the hair of the dog that bit you"—in the morning, and on an empty stomach, instead of tea, to drink vodka—it's all over. It's all over, of course, for a man who does not work. For a muzhik who is working it is nothing, it is even beneficial to drink a glass of vodka at five o'clock in the morning before breakfast.

Now there is no cause to worry about me, it is not necessary to keep an eye on me because five years have already passed and I have not taken to drink, despite the fact that in St. Petersburg, before my departure, many predicted such an end for me.[. . .] Therefore, wanting to describe my winter day again, having no fear whatsoever, I begin:

. . . Having drunk a little vodka and eaten supper, I go to sleep, having put the children to bed, of whom the youngest sleeps in my room next to me and is under my special supervision at night because I have neither a nanny nor a governess. As I fall asleep, I no longer dream now about clover because my dreams have been fulfilled and clover fields exist on Batishchevo; now my visions go further and I dream about how to build a distillery, and I will build it when the excise question is truly settled so that it is possible to count on something solid. I sleep peacefully, nothing disturbs my peace, I do not even hear the periodic barking of Lyska, who, alas, is no longer with us. Yes, Lyska no longer exists and it is because of me, who brought new things to the peaceful life of the former inhabitants of Batishchevo. No matter how clever, how careful old Lyska was, he still fell into the wolf's teeth and it was all my fault. What kind of connection, you may ask, could there be between me, living in St. Petersburg, and Lyska, living in some kind of remote Batish-chevo? Well it is this. If I had not landed in Batishchevo from St. Petersburg, if I had not expanded my estate, if I had not introduced various innovations, then old Lyska would have lived and would have passed away peacefully between the stacks of firewood behind the barn; of course Lyska is also guilty because if he had lived the way he used to and not become infatuated, he would still be alive and unharmed today; but to be infatuated is not only a dog's trait, but man's also, blessed with higher intelligence. Yes, poor Lyska, you paid heavily for your infatuation in your old age!

Before, when besides me only the steward, the herdsman, and Sidor lived on Batishchevo, when we lived as I described it in my first letter, we had only one dog, old Lyska. Lyska lived then on the porch of "the old woman's" izba, which was well locked at night; for that reason, Lyska, smelling the wolves, could bark, but the wolves could do nothing to him since the doors were locked tight. In the daytime, Lyska did not wander far, only sometimes, if the old woman began to be stingy about throwing him some bread—he would run off in a little trot, carrying his tail like a hook, to the mill to eat the flour dust there, to drink at the stream, and then to return home right away to lie around the izba and bark at passersby. He was amazingly intelligent: he never bit anyone, but he also never let anyone pass; he had only to hear the bell or sound of a cart—which often we had not even heard—and he would start up right away, lying down, to bark sharply.[. . .] Lyska knew his own bell, the sound of his cart, his horses excellently and he never barked at his own, the way that the stupid young dogs who replaced him do, who bark at both strangers and their own people, even at me when I come home late at night. It used to be that we would wait for Sidor to come home from the station, we would hear the bell, Lyska would not bark, that meant certainly, that Sidor was coming, Lyska knew his bell; we would go to meet him to get the letters and newspapers more quickly—that was when I still believed what was writ-ten in the newspapers—and Lyska would already be running ahead and wav-ing his tail happily, just as if he wanted to say: it's Sidor who's come from the station bringing you letters. Lyska even understood when Sidor had letters and when he did not; because when he had some to bring me, then, knowing that it would bring me pleasure and that I was always happy when I received mail, he would drive faster, more gaily, but when there were none, he would go at a snail's pace. I would listen, if there were the bell, if Lyska ran to the gates happily, I would run: surely there were letters or, at the very least, a journal—a journal also always made me especially happy; if Lyska ran limply, in a little trot—then it was not worth hurrying: that meant there were probably only newspapers. And what amazing hearing this Lyska had[. . .]—he would never make a mistake.[. . .] Toward evening, Lyska did not go out anywhere, only in the summer sometimes—Lyska knew very well that there is nothing to fear from wolves in the summer—he would come to the house, ask for some kind of little morsel, would eat it and go to his spot at the old woman's izba; in the winter, on the other hand, Lyska did not even come to the house: from early morning until dusk, he would stay in the old woman's porch and as soon as he heard wolves, he would bark sharply on the porch, not taking his nose off of it. This was the smartest of dogs and he would have lived to a ripe old age if what happened with me had not happened.

I arrived, began to manage the farm, and everything changed. I lived the first winter on Batishchevo in the same conditions that had prevailed before. But, when spring came I made some changes: I replaced the bulls that had been raised on the estate until then with cows; consequently we began to milk and feed cows; I got a pair of horses, sheep, pigs, chickens, ducks, in a word, I began to run a gentry house. The number of people grew, so did the area under cultivation because we began to plant the wastelands in flax, there were innovations everywhere. The herdsman needed a dog; you have to have a dog in the field around the sheep, and around the house when there are horses, cows, and so forth, it is impossible to be without a dog.[. . .] We talked and decided to raise dogs. The herdsman got a female puppy from somewhere. We decided to have a bitch first, in order to have our stable of dogs; and second because it's no good without a bitch in a cattle yard: usually when a cow calves and passes the afterbirth, the herdsman takes the afterbirth to the backyard of his izba, where it is eaten by dogs. If a bitch eats the afterbirth, it is considered an omen that the cow will give birth to a female the next time, but if a male eats the afterbirth, then it will be a male calf. Since everyone wants female calves to be born on his place, you must have a bitch in the cattle yard.

Until this time, Lyska lived the life of a recluse, he never went farther than the mill, and never even ran into the nearest neighboring villages when bitches were in heat. It is true that the local bitches treated Lyska with respect and every one of them, when she went into heat, came to our place, but Lyska, treating his visitors politely, was never carried away, and when a bitch, having mated in our garden, ran farther off, Lyska never went after her but remained at home at his post.

When the herdsman acquired the bitch, Lyska's life was completely changed. Summer passed, autumn arrived, the peasants put the cattle in the stalls, the herdsman's bitch began to hang out around the old woman's izba, where a common dining hall had been built in which the old woman, Ivan, Sidor, Savelich, Avdotia, the soldier's wife, and others ate. It is understandable that it was less profitable for the bitch around the herdsman who was on board and valued his grain than at my dining room where there was plenty of bread. Little by little, the bitch gave up the herdsman's izba entirely, moved to the dining hall, and only went to the cattle yard to sleep in the hay at night. Meanwhile, Lyska began to get used to the bitch and attached himself to her and began to be less careful. If someone drove by, Lyska would hear them while they were still a way off and bark a time or two; the bitch who was playing with the children somewhere in the backyard would run to his assistance like a madwoman at the sound of his bark, would throw herself at the passersby and chase them for almost a verst. Lyska, of course, also got carried away and ran in a trot after the carriage . . . and then the bitch—because she was young, she wanted to play—began to play with Lyska, to jump around him, to take him by the snout, the legs, provoked him to fight and play; Lyska would growl, waving his tail, but would not leave; little by little, the old man himself began to be carried away and we began to hear noise from the dogs behind the barns, and then, you see, someone would drive by—Lyska began to yawn a bit—he needed to bark; the bitch would take off again after the carriage, and the old man would trot after her.

Meanwhile, the cows began to calve toward winter. A cow would calve, she would pass the afterbirth, the herdsman would take the afterbirth to the backyard for the bitch to eat it; if the calf died, the herdsman would skin it and still take it to the backyard to the dogs to eat. And a baby calf, even one that is still wet, is far tastier than the crusts of bread which the old woman gives the dogs in the dining hall. Lyska also got into the habit of going to the cattle yard. He would eat the calf and bury whatever remained in the snow or hay so that the crows would not take it, he would play in the snow and lie down to rest on the hay next to the bitch. Lyska became the bitch's friend, began to go to sleep with her in the hay, it became boring for him to sleep alone on the old woman's porch: as soon as they finished eating supper in the dining hall, just look, the bitch would already be flying to the cattle yard, and running after her in a trot would be Lyska.

The first winter went well; the wolves did not come close even once, although six versts from my place the wolves not only caught the dogs, but one of them, a rabid one, bit people, so that several people died, and only one was saved who, being slightly wounded, ran to us in the village immediately—I saw him and I will never forget the look of terror on his face, and how could he not be terrified, knowing that he would go mad in a few days?—to the old miller Andrian so that he could say an incantation over the wound; but Andrian refused to say an incantation, explaining that he could say them only for the bites of mad dogs, and could not do it for the bite of a rabid wild animal. He told him of another old man, however, who managed to cast a spell in time and the muzhik lived.

In March, the bitch went into heat and, one has to be fair to her, she did not deceive her old friend; all of the suitors who ran over from neighboring villages received a refusal. When the bitch whelped, we all decided to keep one, however, because the litter was fine. We chose the strongest male, the spitting image of old man Lyska. This pup was the source of many misfortunes.

The bitch, of course, fed one pup excellently, then in June, my son came for vacation, and with children, as is well known, the first thing is to play with puppies, and while they are playing, of course, they give whatever they are eating to the puppy. They fed the puppy wonderfully, and, I do not know why, called it Tsurik; at first they called "Tsutsu, Tsutsu," then "Tsutsi," then "Tsurik": thus he came to be called Tsurik. The dog turned out to be enormous, fat, with long hair, strong and intelligent, but lazy in the extreme; at first Tsurik took it into his head to do stupid things: he began to bite on the sly. He would be lying down around the house, near the porch, some stranger would come up, he would not bark, he would let them pass, and as soon as he went up on the porch, he would jump without barking and take them by the hem from behind and pull them down, so that some people fell off the porch because of this unexpected attack. However, Savelich, who is an amazing master at training dogs and cats, soon trained Tsurik not to bite, and he became the most splendid dog. He had only one shortcoming: he was very lazy; he would be lying around the house and as soon as he heard something, and his hearing was no worse than old Lyska's, he would bark once or twice and then howl out of laziness, and so loud and long. I am certain that Tsurik howled out of laziness;[. . .] Ivan, of course, thought otherwise. Ivan did not like this howling of Tsurik's at all and if I had not intervened, he would have shot him for sure. "He's howling at us," Ivan constantly declared. "Akh, how I hate this howling! He's really a fine dog, only we shouldn't keep him."

"But it's out of laziness that he howls."

"No. And what's he howling about: someone's death, or some kind of misfortune, or a fire. And he's always howling, raising his head: not about himself, that means, but someone else."

"That is foolishness, he is howling out of laziness."

"Don't say that, Aleksandr Nikolaevich, there've been cases here. Our old lord hunted with dogs; he had the most splendid setter and what d'ya think? Suddenly he began to howl, he howled all winter, and in the spring the Emancipation Edict came out. The lord also refused to believe it, but as soon as it happened, then he says to me: "You were right, see he was howling at something." Look, and at my place, the bitch was constantly howling before my brother died. I even shot her, but my brother died anyway, and then his wife died."

Once, it was during Holy Week, the hundreder[3] brought me a summons. I read it: Savelich was being called to court to hear the decision of the procurator K. of the district court. I was amazed, what kind of business could Savelich have at the district court? I went out of the kitchen.

"What business do you have, Savelich, at the K. district court?"

Savelich looked at me in bewilderment.

"They've brought a summons, they've called you to the court to hear the announcement of the K. district court's sentence. What kind of business do you have there?"

Savelich became confused and began to rub hard on his bald spot with his hand, which was a sign that he was upset. I began to question him; it turned out that several years ago, when Savelich was collecting for the church, at some posting inn in K. province someone stole his collecting box with the money he had collected, about which he had immediately notified the police. Savelich described in detail how, while he was sleeping, someone had stolen the box in which there were two silver rubles, how he complained to the police, how he had then been called once already to the inspector.

"Why did you complain?" Ivan remarked, who always addressed Savelich with respect in the formal you form.

"I was very angry, because they took it right out from under my hand."

"Ekh, you! And you're even an experienced man, you served a general. But look, you're answering for it now. You can go a year without bread over a little court case."

Savelich was very agitated and for the first time in all the time he worked for me, he asked me for some money, just in case. I gave him some money and tried to explain that he had nothing to fear, that he did not have to answer, that they could call him only as a witness, generally I tried to calm him down. However, even I myself did not know, could they call Savelich, even in the capacity of a witness, to K.? How would he get there? Who would feed him there? Would he have to go there by coach or, somehow feeding himself only by begging in Christ's name? There is no train to K., could Savelich go with the mail? Of course I did not tell Savelich all these doubts so as not to upset the old man, I promised not to abandon him and proposed that when the matter became clear, I would go to the posting inn or, if necessary, to town. Here, and not for the first time living in the country, I regretted that I did not understand even such elementary juridical issues.

It seemed that Savelich quieted down and we decided that he would go to the posting inn the next day because it was a holiday, but this calm was only apparent . . . Savelich did not leave on the first holiday, or the next, or on the Saturday of Holy Week, and the first holiday Savelich lay on the stove all day—he said that his head hurt—he only got off the stove when they brought the "Holy Sacraments." He did not even make me any kind of special cake for the holiday!

I went visiting on the second day of the holiday, and Savelich went to the posting inn without me. Ivan told me that Savelich had left when I got home in the evening.

"I don't know how the old man dragged himself, he's been sleeping these days, you know that he lay on the stove all the time, he didn't eat a thing, he didn't even drink a glass for the first meal after the fast. Today, when it came time to say good-bye, he began to cry. He gave his belongings to me, his coat and bag, he asked me to send them to him in jail if he doesn't come back. He asked me to take care of his dog Shumil. Now we see who it was Tsurik was howling about!" Ivan added.[. . .]

It turned out, however, that, Tsurik was not howling at Savelich. Several days later, Savelich returned home cheerful, happy, healthy, even a little tipsy—they had told him that the case was closed.

Savelich lives with me to this day and he is a very useful person for me: he washes the dishes, sets up the samovar, lights the stoves.[. . .]

Doing his duties thoroughly, Savelich finds time to do something for himself as well, "for his whims," as Avdotia says. Sometimes he makes soap: he collects tallow when he is cleaning the candlesticks, various candle ends, and suet from the pots, and makes soap.[. . .]

Savelich's favorite thing is to make candy and to invent new sweets from the kind of ingredients that could never be used, it would seem, to make candy, for example, raw green beans. As soon as Savelich has a little money he buys sugar or powered sugar, which Avdotia cannot tolerate.

"The old dreamer bought a lot of sugar; he doesn't have any shirts but he buys sugar. Don't give him any money, Aleksandr Nikolaevich, it would be better to buy some cloth and ask Khima to make him some shirts."

Having bought sugar, Savelich begins to make candy: fruit drops, almond cookies in which he puts ground green beans instead of almonds, this is Savelich's invention, filled cookies made of corn, cranberry juice, left over from the preparation of cranberry *kisel*[4] or punch made from berries which were used for brewing brandy, candied lemon peel, carefully taken by him out of the punch I sometimes drink after lunch when there are rum and lemons, and so on. There are always all kinds of things soaking and marinating in jars in Savelich's quarters, which he will turn into candy later. Having made his goods, Savelich sets out to the village market and sells them there. He buys sugar again with the money he makes, makes candy again, and sells it at the next market; and so it goes on until he has used up all his money. In the end, this trade of Savelich's is always a loss: he buys sugar for a ruble, he makes candies and sells them for sixty kopeks; he then buys sugar for sixty kopeks, makes candies and sells it for thirty kopeks, and so on until he has only ten kopeks for tobacco. All of this happens not because Savelich does not know how to keep track; on the contrary, he keeps track splendidly, he knows how much went for the sugar—he always weighs all the ingredients in all of his candy making, how much the candy cost to make, how much he must sell the candy for in order to receive one ruble profit for every ruble spent, and, setting out for the market, he is utterly convinced that he has wares worth two rubles and that he will earn a ruble for his labor, but, he comes back with only sixty kopeks. This lack of profit happens because Savelich, in his goodness, gives out the majority of his confections to his innumerable acquaintances who all love him very much. Be that as it may, this making and selling of confections constitutes the greatest pleasure for Savelich, which is why Avdotia calls it his whim.[. . .]

In the summer Tsurik did not howl and was rarely at home, he was constantly with the workers in the field and in the meadow that I rented on the Dnieper, about seven versts from my estate. When autumn arrived, Tsurik began to howl again and this time howled too much. My farm was expanding at this time, and one can judge how much it had expanded from the following figures.

In 1871, 1,562 rubles went into the cash box and 1,453 rubles were withdrawn; there was a turnover of 3,015 rubles in all.

In 1874, 6,047 went in and 5,839 were withdrawn, a turnover of 11,886 rubles in all.

Since only an insignificant portion of the expenses goes for buying tea, sugar, tobacco, and similar necessities in town—this sum changed little from 1871 to 1874—the majority of money spent is spent here on the estate for labor. It is understandable that the estate has livened up and that there are more people on Batishchevo. Sometimes it happens that on Sundays I do not leave the books from morning to night—I am either paying for something or receiving payment: this one came to buy some rye, another brought oil cake, a third came to ask for a loan of money in exchange for labor or to offer himself as a hired hand, and so forth. The number of people in the house has grown— now, even in the winter, rarely do fewer than twenty-five people sit down at the table in the dining hall—there are more people and it is noisier. It would seem that there should be less danger from wild animals, but it turned out to be the opposite: the wolves, probably, are not afraid of daytime noise, but at night, even though there are a lot of people, even so, a deathly silence reigns, because I do not allow drunkenness and debauchery at night on the estate, and hoping for a big catch, they try to get into the very place where they smell more dogs, poultry, and all kinds of livestock. Other predators which abound on Batishchevo, for example, owls—the first year, owls lived even in the attic of the house—vultures, skunks, wild cats who lived in the barns and storehouses and so forth have moved; but still a multitude of crows turned up and after them even the wolves also have begun to trot right around the house.

The first one to be caught was old Lyska, cautious, sharp Lyska; the wolves caught him no further than fifteen feet from the dining hall in the evening before everyone had gone to sleep, at the time when he, after they had finished in the dining hall, went to sleep in the hay. Several days later, Tsurik was also caught; the wolves got this one when the workers had not yet finished in the dining hall and everyone was gathered together; having heard the row and guessed that the wolves had come after a dog, the hired hands jumped out of the izba—the courage of the Russian is well known; in such instances everyone runs to the assistance of the dogs with bare hands, without any kind of weapon unless someone lays his lands on a log of firewood; consequently, if a rabid wolf turns up, a lot of people are wounded, which is frequently reported in the newspapers. Having heard the noise, the wolves took fright and ran off, the peasants ran after them in the direction more wolves ran and did not notice that the inexperienced Tsurik ran after one wolf who took off on the road into the village. Seeing that there were no people after him, the wolf, in the middle of the street in the village, attacked Tsurik;

they fought for a long time, all of this was seen by an old landless woman; the fight took place opposite her izba. Tsurik did not give in and was even getting the best of the wolf, it was probably a young pup, but its comrades arrived in time and tore Tsurik to pieces.

Only the sly bitch, who had also learned from her comrades' destruction, escaped. Ivan quieted down and was constantly claiming: so this is what Tsurik was howling about, and you thought that he was howling out of laziness.

[Engelgardt continues to describe other antics with the dogs on the estate.]

We simply cannot get by without dogs in the country, although sometimes there is unpleasantness because of the dogs, who bark at all passersby indiscriminately, not distinguishing the authorities from mere mortals.

Once, it was in the spring, in the height of the thaw, I was coming from the cattle yard, dressed in my usual farm outfit—a sheepskin coat licked clean by the cows. Suddenly I heard a bell; my heart even skipped a beat; who, if not the authorities, and then even on the most urgent business, would drive at such a time when the river is flooding?

Having heard the bell, I stopped; the dogs surrounded the passing wagon with a loud bark; the tormented horses, which could hardly pull the wagon along the melting snowdrifts which had been swept around the estate's fences in the winter, had stopped completely.

"Hey, come here!" the bureaucrat sitting in the wagon shouted, obviously having taken me for the steward.

I had already discerned from the uniform frock coat with a cockade that this was not a real official, but some kind of civil servant passing by . . .

"Hey, come here! Did you hear me, or what?" the civil servant continued to shout, having been driven mad by the horrible road in the spring thaw.

I walked up.

"What kind of dogs do you have? How dare you keep such dogs who stop passersby?" the civil servant shouted wildly. "And you even dare to stand there without taking your hat off. Who do you think you are, I'll see to you!" he leaned over me, addressing me in the familiar.

"Permit me, sir," I said, "if the dogs caused you harm, you can complain to the justice of the peace, but please do not shout here."

"What! Akh, you son of a . . ."

"And if you do not calm down and stop swearing, I will call the laborers and we will see how you . . ."

"And whose estate is this?" the perplexed civil servant asked.

"Mine."

"And who are you?" he asked in a completely different tone, shifting to the formal you form.

I gave my name.

"But still, you must agree, how is it possible to keep such wild dogs?"

"It's part of the cost of farming," I answered, laughing.

"What kind of use can there be in this?"

"If you please, how could it be otherwise? In order to protect such a spread-out estate as mine, built, of course, during serfdom, it would be necessary to have instead of the dogs, two more good watchmen; it costs one hundred rubles to support a watchman, two hundred for two watchmen, one thousand rubles in five years. No matter how wild the dogs are, a simple mutt only barks and rarely bites, furthermore, the dogs cannot bite someone riding in a carriage and pedestrians always carry planks, especially approaching an estate—just look how they have pilfered from the paling around the garden during the winter; but let us assume that the dogs bite someone; the largest fine that the justice of the peace can levy is one hundred rubles; there is little likelihood that this could happen more than once in five years. Consequently . . ."

The civil servant began to laugh.

"If you please, but, really, that's Asiatic."

"And you thought that this is Europe?"[. . .]

The civil servant stayed for the night; we talked the entire evening and he turned out to be a most sweet boy. Of course, there was no mention at all of the first minutes of our encounter. In Russia, of course, everyone who has a position, who wears a cockade, considers himself in charge. What is the head of the railway station—he has no cockade, only a red cap—and even he considers himself the authority over all of the passengers in arriving trains. But some kind of a general from St. Petersburg, he considers everyone his subordinate and if need be will report the head of the station for holding up the train. It would seem that it would be hard even to live in the presence of such an innumerable multitude of all kinds of officials, but it is possible to live if you figure out what the trick is: you need do nothing else besides become an official yourself for a while. If the head of the station or a postal employee shouts at you, you say to him immediately, "And what are you doing!" He will step back without fail and think that you are yourself the chief authority. This approach is good even with a general.[5]

The Role of Peasant Women in the Rural Economy

I sleep peacefully, I do not dream at all, but I always wake up early at the horrible barking which the dogs raise at one o'clock in the morning when the babas go to brake the flax. The babas have driven Ivan completely mad over the flax: the first roosters in the village have not risen before the women get up and run, literally run, to our place to brake the flax, each one trying to be ahead of the next, to get here earlier in order to get the best spot, closest to the animal barn, and begin to work faster before the women from distant villages arrive. [. . .] When enough babas have gathered, the most daring of them walks up and knocks for Ivan on the window, and the others have already set out for the barn to the man in charge of threshing so that he will distribute the warm flax faster; the hotter the flax, the easier it is to brake it. Meanwhile, Ivan has been awake ever since the first bark of the dogs, gotten dressed, he lights a lantern and goes out to the barn. The braking begins.

The first time that I introduced flax—and without flax our agriculture cannot produce a good income, as I am now convinced—I had some difficulty finding workers; but now that the babas understand that flax gives them a good salary, now that they are convinced that I will give the money they have earned directly to the women, that I will under no circumstances give it to the muzhik who is the head of their household, that I do not even withhold anything toward a debt if someone of the heads of household is in debt to me, everything goes excellently; there are no difficulties whatsoever in finding workers—just give me work. And this is understandable; a quick baba can earn as much as 70 kopeks in a day when the flax is being broken. But, if she stays at home, in the same day, a baba can earn at the very most fifteen kopeks if she gathers berries or mushrooms on a holiday. The flax is gathered on my place on holidays for the most part—I will explain why below—or on Fridays, on which the women consider it a sin to gather their own flax and do some other kind of work; it is not a sin for them to work on my place, because the sin falls on the master or, it is better to say, on his field, which can be beaten down with hail and so forth for this, which I, the master, do not fear, however, because I can transfer the sin to the company which provides insurance against hail and fire, that is, on their shareholders. Braking flax, a quick, strong, and fat baba—the fatter and heavier the better—can earn up to forty-five kopeks in a night, while at home, if she cards wool, she earns four kopeks a day. It is understandable that the women come themselves to brake the flax and leave the wool to be carded on a wool carder by the man who travels from village to village doing this. Knowing how unproductive, in comparison with work done on a machine, all the work done by babas in the winter is, I am sure that if the women found good local work on the side, they would stop spinning wool and flax in the winter and weaving canvas and cloth, and would buy factory-made items. That is why there is no reason whatsoever to fear that, as many think, with the development of flax production there will not be enough working hands to be found—there are always enough hands if the job is profitable and the master does not want to rake everything into his own paws. It is much more profitable for me to pay fifty kopeks for working a stack of flax in a workday and to receive fifty rubles pure profit per desiatina than to pay fifteen kopeks a workday for cultivating rye and oats and receive zero income or a loss, as I observe on several neighboring estates; it is more profitable for me to pay a milkmaid three rubles a month when she milks a vedro[6] of milk a day than to pay one and a half rubles when she milks two glasses at most. This is all so elementary that it fails to be understood only among you in St. Petersburg where farmers, running their affairs in the parquet halls of the assembly of societies, bemoan not the fact that our farmers still do not know how to put their farms in order, but the fact that working hands are expensive, that is, the fact that the peasants want to eat pure bread, and not adulterated bread.

At first I had some difficulty introducing flax; the peasants assured me that this undertaking would not succeed and that I would not find anyone who wanted to work the flax, which the rich bigwig of the neighboring village was especially insistent about—every village has its big wig—for whom my estate really went against the grain. Now the peasants, seeing that the business is going well, say, "Why not go? Everything goes well with money—money will even chisel a stone, and even you have fit in, Leksandra!" they add.

"You" in the informal, "Leksandra"—I was at the height of bliss when I heard such expressions for the first time because they serve as an indubitable expression of respect for this farm.[. . .]

Now I will describe how I "fit in" with the flax, as the peasants say.

Having arrived in the country and having nothing whatsoever to do on the farm at first since the farm had to go on as usual until spring, I tried to become familiar with my own and other local estates and made a plan for new farming.[. . .] According to the plan I drew up, flax production should be introduced into the system of farming. The first year, I gave out the cultivation of flax by the desiatina for twenty-five rubles a desiatina: the peasants of the neighboring village took on two desiatinas of flax to work for twenty-five rubles each with the provision that I gave them half the money as an advance. The whole village took on the work together and in terms of the speed of work, it went well; flax requires many hands at once, for example, for the gathering and braking, which must be finished as soon as possible, for the scutching, and for that reason, the business goes well when the entire village works and sends many hands at once.

The work was done, but the entire time they were working, the babas were swearing unmercifully—as only babas know how to swear—and were constantly cursing the muzhiks (husbands—here the baba says "my muzhik," "her muzhik") for having taken on this work: "Look they took on this work to make our life hell, the devils," "Work for them now so, may their guts be torn out," and so on and so forth, without stopping, for days on end. The muzhiks laughed it off, "You're not working for us, but for your own gut—you know you stuffed yourself with grain this winter." "Yes, I stuffed myself," a baba would growl, "so that this bread would stick in your throat—while you're off getting drunk, I'm here killing myself." "So, so, work," the muzhik answers, "I know you, you have only to sit and the bread ferments on your . . . , you lazy stick." At work and leaving work, and at home, the babas ground away at the muzhiks incessantly. The latter defended themselves, brushed them off, but the babas, however, got the upper hand—the babas always get the best of the muzhiks in all matters where their interest is at stake, and anyone who would introduce some new business, in order to succeed, must pay attention before all else to how much the babas' interest will be involved because *the babas have all the power.* This is understandable to anyone who, knowing the women's position in the village, takes into account that (1) the baba does not pay taxes and (2) you cannot beat a baba. It is true that even a muzhik cannot be beaten without going to court, but, of course, it does not cost anything to arrange a court session. The next year this village did not take on flax production for me.

Peasant Individualism in Labor

In essence, cultivating flax for twenty-five rubles per desiatina is more profitable for the peasant, I think, than cultivating one *krug,* that is, one desiatina of rye, one desiatina of winter wheat, and one desiatina of meadow, but the point is that with flax cultivation, the babas have to do most of the work; furthermore, part of the work must be done at the time—after the last day of the fast—when babas in the village are no longer working for the master, nor for the muzhik, but for *themselves;* besides, with flax cultivation, it is not easy to divide all of the work and much has to be done together. In order to make all of this clear, I will describe how the work is done.

The muzhiks needed money to pay taxes, especially the poor peasants, but, since even the rich peasants answer for the poor ones through the system of mutual obligation,[7] they keep an eye out for the poor peasants and often take on work in order to make the poor peasants take it on with them. They see that a new lord has arrived who wants to amuse himself with flax, but the lord is a neighbor. One must, therefore, indulge him, because you may need a friend: you may need a watering hole, a birch grove, since there is nowhere else except on his place to chop wood, your livestock might also cause damage by trespassing, and then there are the mushrooms. And Ivan, who tries to please the lord and seeing as there is no getting out of planting flax for the lord, had already notified the appropriate village and *made the proposition,* of course he talked with the *bigwig,* and, maybe, treated him to a little vodka. The bigwig, for his part, having taken into consideration that there are people who are behind in their taxes, that a pasture is needed, that trespassing will be tolerated, and he, the bigwig, has eight horses, passed on the proposition to the peasants. The muzhiks got together, groused a bit, and decided that the whole village would take on the cultivation of two desiatinas of flax on the Batishchevo lord's place, they concluded a contract, they received half of the money in advance and immediately divided the money among the households: one took on a half desiatina, a quarter desiatina, a third took on an eighth desiatina, depending upon his capabilities and his need for money. They drank a little vodka to set the deal, which you can't do without, which I provided, and went home happy. "Look how you slobber all over each other," the women reproached them. "As soon as you brake the flax, the lord'll give you some vodka too," the muzhiks tried to win the babas over. "Devils," the babas answered, "you would be glad to give our souls to the devil, if only you could stuff yourselves with vodka." "Ekh, you women, fools, and *you* aren't going to pay the taxes? Just wait until the constable comes, you won't be singing this song while he does an inventory of your underclothes." "So I'm to answer for you, what's this, as if you gave me my petticoat? I brought my own petticoat, I made it before I was married." "We know what you were doing before you were married." "Whatever I did, the petticoat's mine." "Shut up or I'll hit you with a plank." "You're so smart, I'll never shut up . . ."

Spring comes, we need to go plough the meadow; the steward has already called the peasants out twice. If there were soft soil to be put under cultivation for rye or spring wheat the peasants would come primarily to divide the land into half desiatinas, quarter desiatinas, or eighths, corresponding to who borrowed how much money.[. . .] There is the most horrible shouting and cursing during this division, it seems as if a brawl is about to break out any minute, it is impossible to understand anything, but as soon as the division is finished, everyone gets quiet and you will see how accurately all of the shares are cut. Having divided the land, they cast lots to see who gets which piece—they cast lots because although the shares are equal, the land is not and its position is not the same—and each one begins to plough the share which has fallen to him.

That is the way it would be if the land were soft, but for flax you have to turn over an empty field, that is, a meadow, the master won't allow you to divide the desiatina into rows because the ploughing will turn out poorly, there will be a lot of ploughing and dumping—and the contract says that "one must obey the orders of the master"—and it requires that the entire artel plough the desiatinas all together. You have to provide eight horses per desiatina—four with harrows and four with wooden ploughs, and plough together one after the other. This is already the first source of dissatisfaction.

Peasants usually take on work in common either as a whole village or as several partners who have come to an agreement. However, this has recently already begun to disappear and they are beginning to hire themselves out separately for many jobs, alone, usually under the leadership of the local bigwig who already has taken the name "boss" and who often takes a cut of up to ten percent of the money earned as so-called bast-shoe money. Having taken on a job together, the peasants divide it up: each one does his share separately from the others and receives a corresponding share of the money earned. Under serfdom, peasants did a lot of jobs together because joint labor was often more profitable. That is why in the first years after the Emancipation, the peasants, out of old habit, still did several jobs together and did not find such jobs oppressive. But now, one cannot hire for joint labor except with special conditions through the boss in charge, who has roughly the same relation to the artel as a master has to hired hands with the sole difference that he not only may verbally abuse an artel member who has slacked off, but will even box him on the ear or send him off without pay, which a master cannot do because a master is under the justice of the peace, while the local boss answers only to *his own,* in a special sense, court of judgment . . .[8] And so, everyone must plough the meadow together. They have agreed to begin at a certain time. They go out in the morning; six have already arrived but two have not—one overslept, he was drunk yesterday, the harness was broken. Those who have arrived stand on the desiatina, they wait for those who are late, they have slipped the horses a bit of hay, they smoke pipes and swear. But here come the others too—who should go first? An argument breaks out; at last they have established the order. They plough. If someone's wooden plough has broken, everyone stops. He has fixed it, they continue: one horse has a better harness, another has the worst one possible. Dissatisfaction.

"If I'd ploughed by myself, I'd've been out before daylight but this way you wait in the village until the others get up, then you wait here," one says.

"I'd've finished long ago on my own horses, but here you wait, oh Lord, that flax!" another says.

They have ploughed, harrowed, planted, and covered the rows. The women harrow and cover. Of course, they curse, but this is still not anything because in the summer, from April fifteenth to November fifteenth, the baba *must work for the head of her household and it is all the same* to her where she works: on her own field or the master's. Of course it will be more demanding on the lord's land, you can't finish off the land any which way, the way you would at home, because the steward will make you do it over, but, essentially, it's all the same: you have to work from sunup to sundown either here or there, and the lord, maybe, if he is satisfied with the work, will give each one a glass "to the planting."

The time has come to gather the flax: the women have been called, thirty of them have come at once, they harvest it quickly. Of course, in this case, they do it together, there is no way they will form an artel to do the harvesting, instead they divide the desiatina according to the number of women, into thirty parcels, and each woman harvests her parcel separately. The allocation is done very simply, although, of course, you can't get by without swearing. The women stand in a line, they link arms or a rope and walk along the desiatina, dragging their feet, they drag so that they will leave a mark, then each one works on her parcel. If there are several women, girls of marriage-able age in the household, that is, if the household is made up of several families and is still controlled by the old people together in one household, the women of one family will divide the field at home in precisely the same way, so that one won't have to work more than another, so that the work goes faster. Otherwise they would do much less since each one would fear that she was doing more than her share. Since pulling flax can be divided up, since the work is done at a time when the women are obliged to work for the master, there is no great dissatisfaction yet: they curse, of course, they curse since the work is hard and extremely unpleasant because flax cuts the hands, but, even so, it's still nothing: all of this is a mere blossom, but the berries are yet to come. Then comes braking—here again they divide the work: each baba does her share and spreads out a certain number of sheaves, while the men stack and bind it together and, already thoroughly cursed by the women, work silently. But then it is time to do the braking; this is when the women have finally lost their temper because the work is done at a time when the women work in the village *for themselves.* They broke the flax as an artel and there was no end to the recriminations because each baba tried to work as little as possible. Thirty women, each one working for herself, will brake, for exam-ple, thirty puds of flax in a given time; but these same thirty women in the same time, working as an artel, and furthermore, if the work is done by the desiatina, will brake no more than fifteen puds. And that's not all; if the babas work for themselves and brake flax as piecework for a certain pay per pud, then a desiatina will yield, for example, thirty-five puds of flax. If they work by the desiatina, then that same desiatina will yield no more than twenty-five or thirty puds, and five to ten puds of flax will remain in the bark, will be wasted uselessly. And the master will suffer from ten to twenty rubles loss because it is all the same to the baba how much flax turns out. She will even try to throw more flax in the bark in order to have less work and so that it will be easier to carry the bundle of flax into the storehouse.

Thus there are two aspects of this method of cultivating flax, which can explain the lack of working hands: (1) first, that the work is done jointly, in common, and not through assignment to each worker separately, and (2) that the work is done at a time when the baba, by custom, works at home for herself and here she has to work for her own household's master. But one has simply to change the order of work and the hands will be found right away, especially if you raise the pay, which a farmer can do without losing his shirt . . .[9] I said that the baba has to work as a hired hand for the household in the summer for the household head, whether she be his wife, sister, or daughter-in-law. For the most part, especially in extended households, the women's attitude toward this work is that of hired hands: "Don't wear yourself out on the boss's work." In the winter, the baba works for herself and her chief occupation is spinning wool and flax, and weaving; beyond that, everything that the baba earns in the winter on the side becomes her own property. The man gives the woman nothing for buying clothes, she dresses at her own expense; furthermore, the baba must dress her husband and children. The wool from sheep is given over to the women to distribute and divide; they divide the flax in exactly the same way.[10] This is what a baba receives as her share of the household and then only as long as her husband is alive; if her husband dies and the baba does not have any children of the male sex, then she does not receive anything, not even the woman's portion, and she is not an heir to her husband's property. A baba receives raw, unprocessed wool and flax; she must card the wool, brake and hackle the flax, spin and weave the canvas, cloth, material for skirts. The baba must dress her husband, that is, make his shirts and trousers; she must dress herself and the children, anything that is left over—money gained from the sale of carded wool, extra canvas, thread, and so forth constitutes her inalienable property, to which neither her husband, nor the head of the household, nor anyone has any right. Everything that she brought to her marriage, collected during her wedding, all of the kopeks which she earned gathering berries and mushrooms in the summer, and so forth are also precisely the same kind of property for the baba.

The baba is always mercenary and greedy for money; she always values money, always tries to earn some. Among the muzhiks you can still meet the kind who work only when there is no grain, and if there is grain, they spend their time idly, hanging about from corner to corner. Among the babas— never. The baba is motivated, she goes to work willingly if she sees some profit for herself in it because there is no end to the baba's desires and no matter how wealthy the household, no matter how wealthy the baba, she will not refuse the few kopeks which fall to her lot when they are given to the participants at a wedding, honoring the young people and guests. The baba is always saving; even as a young girl she runs for berries and mushrooms if there is someone to sell them to, and saves the money she earns for luxuries, for scarves, and beads. As she grows up she saves money, cloth, thread, and knitting for her dowry. When she marries, the baba saves for clothing for herself, her children and husband. It is worth nothing that the baba considers it her duty to dress her husband and to clean his clothes *only so long as he is faithful to her;* as soon as he is unfaithful to her, has sex with another woman, the first thing that a baba does is to refuse to dress him: "You are sleeping with her, let her dress you as well; I'll find someone for myself."[11] This threat is usually very effective. In her old age, the baba saves for herself in the event of death: for the grave, the funeral, for prayers for her soul.

There is no money in the household for paying taxes, there is no grain, but the baba has money and fabric, and luxuries, but all of this is her property which the head of the household does not dare to touch. The household head should get money and bread from wherever he pleases, but don't dare touch the baba's property: the baba's trunk is her inviolable property just as the property of *our* wives is and if the household head, even her husband, takes something from the trunk, then this will be theft for which the court will even punish him.[12] Now a husband, when there is extreme need, can borrow from his wife, especially if they live separately in their own household, but if the head of the household is not her husband—never. This would cause a riot of the entire village and all of the women would rise up, because no one guards their rights as jealously as babas do. Upon the husband's death, his property goes to his sons; upon the baba's death—primarily to the daughters.[. . .]

Since the baba's labor belongs to the head of the household in the summer, if he puts her out as a hired hand in the summer, all of the pay coming to her goes to him; but if the baba is put out as a hired hand in the winter, she gets the money, and the household head profits by the fact that the baba is not at home. However, the woman receives the wool and flax which is her due in any event because this is her pay for her summer labor. Therefore, hiring female day laborers presents many more difficulties than hiring male workers. For the most part, single women without farmsteads, widows, childless soldiers' wives, spinsters, married women who are not living with their husbands, and so forth hire themselves out as day laborers. Women who are living in house-holds hire themselves out rarely and only for a high salary—such a baba does not count her meals for anything because the household head is obligated to feed her all the same—and then only when they are certain that their winter pay will go into their hands and they have a store of fabric to dress their husband. However, the success of hiring female workers will depend on how many and what kind of men hire themselves out; female hired hands or permanent day laborers are found for all free men with a job and for male hands; no one lives alone and one way or another, he will find a baba for himself.

I will give another example of the extent to which all farm matters depend on these relations. I give out some of my land to the peasants to cultivate by the *krug* [the cycle of three fields for the entire season, using the peasant's horse and plough] because otherwise it would be difficult for me to handle the rye harvest. Until now, the peasants took on cultivating *krug*s with threshing included, but I saw long ago that threshing oppresses them and they would work the *krug*s much more willingly without the threshing; although the peasants offered various explanations for their unwillingness to take on fields with the threshing included, it was clear to me that the main reason here consisted of the fact that first of all, threshing is done jointly and secondly, that threshing is done in the winter, at the time when babas are working for themselves. The babas have been eating away at the muzhiks for a long time and finally they got what they wanted: this year, peasants took on the fields on my place without the threshing. What happened? Both I and the peasants came out ahead, although I paid much more for the threshing than it cost when done as part of the contract for a *krug*.

Before, sixteen people, eight men and eight women, came to do the threshing. They would stake out on the average no more than nine hundred sheaves and would thresh this quantity the entire day. The threshing usually lasted almost until Lent. They would thresh badly and there was nothing to be done to prevent it.

I had my workers rethresh some of the grain this year, the oats, to be exact. But the majority, the rye, I gave out to be threshed though piecework, fifty kopeks per sack,[13] on condition that as they threshed they would cut off all of the tailings for the livestock's feed. The threshing was taken on by a boss who gathered seven men, so that the artel consisted of eight fine fellows under the command of an able, strong, and intelligent chap who would not allow anyone to slack off and took the lead himself in all of the work. They staked out, on the average, eleven hundred sheaves and the eight men managed to thresh them in a day. They threshed superbly, not a single grain could remain in the straw because they cut off all of the tailings with the ears, the tailings cut off for the feed were beaten until fine, it was to the threshers' advantage to thresh well because they were being paid by the sack and, furthermore, only when all the threshing was done; there was twice the yield of chaff as before. They finished the threshing by Christmas.

The peasants' pay was good. Each thresher had a clear profit, excluding meals, of six rubles fifty kopeks per month, which one must consider good pay for dead months like November and December.

I also made a profit and if you calculate everything, then the threshing, in comparison with being included in an agreement to cultivate a field was, one can see, free. The threshing was finished earlier, therefore there were savings on the upkeep of the thresher; they burned up less firewood; they threshed more cleanly and this, in my calculation, increased the yield by one sack per desiatina, which itself paid for the threshing.[. . .]

People will now ask: why in the world do peasants, working by the *krug*, threshing as an artel, spend, obviously at a loss to themselves, twice as much time threshing as the same kind of artel separately? And the answer is because here (1) there is a boss and (2) the artel members are of equal strength; the other way there is no boss; my steward is the only supervisor in both cases and the artel members are of all kinds; therefore, they all work at the level of the very weakest in order that no one will do more than any other, everyone calculates his labor; it is nothing for a strong peasant, for example, to carry a sack to the granary, but a weak peasant will struggle and struggle while he lifts it and while he carries it; having done his task, the strong one will stand around all this time, waiting until the weak one has carried his, and only then will he take up another sack. And it is this way in everything.

The peasant commune, the peasant artel is not a beehive in which each bee, *not taking anyone else into account,* works diligently to the extent of his strength for the common good. If peasants were to make a beehive out of their commune they would hardly be walking around in bast shoes!

[Engelgardt goes into a long discussion about his success with flax cultivation and how his manner of setting wages contributed to his success.]

Not only poor babas come to pull and brake the flax, but also rich ones; one can even say that the rich ones do the majority of the work and take in the majority of the money given out for harvesting and threshing. In wealthy households, all of the babas are strong, tall, healthy, well-fed, clever; a wealthy peasant will not marry some kind of weakling, and if he somehow ends up with a bad baba—you cannot imagine a more horrible situation than that of such a poor baba in a rich household where there is a multitude of strong brides—then he will whip her, beat her, drive her to her grave, and then marry another. A well-fed rich baba will brake up to one and a half puds of flax, at the same time that the poor, short, skinny, weak ones will brake thirty pounds each. It is understandable, therefore, that it is not worth it for the wealthy ones to work jointly with the poor peasants; but even in piece-work, the poor peasants must stay behind, in the shadow. These days, it seems to me, there is a natural selection among landowners and among peasants. The landowning farmer, especially an average farmer, can support himself and manage his farm only thanks to knowledge and capital and, in addition, by using his own labor, that is, by being personally involved in his farm and living in the country. As far as I am concerned, one's own labor and knowledge mean more even than capital if capital is applied, for example, to the farm according to the old system. Everyone who does not want to work himself, who does not have knowledge and energy or who does not have enormous capital and a large amount of land should step inside and, having abandoned the farm, having sold the estate, look for a means to support himself in civil service. On the other hand, even among the peasantry there are clever people, diligent, strong, and capable of work, quick, in a word, good farmers, and prosperous besides—although in the peasant mentality, strength and hard work carry more weight than capital—they are the best at everything, they own land, they prosper; while the unintelligent ones, the weak, poor ones leave the village, abandon the land, find easy pay following someone else's orders, go to town to work there for those who themselves live by service, also following someone else's orders. In the final analysis, I think that, since nothing is given out for free here, since no one here as a household head will live under someone else's command, there will remain only hardworking, energetic people who prefer working independence over servile security. Of course, it may be that all of this just seems so to me; but as much as I have been able to observe in five years, everything is moving in that direction . . .

Peasants as Skilled Laborers

Bit by bit, clear empty fields that were not overgrown with bushes and birch seedlings were cleared, and I set to cultivating flax on empty fields which had been overgrown by seedlings with trunks two vershoks thick [about 3½ inches]. We had to uproot the seedlings, which increased the cost of cultivation; furthermore, it is also difficult to plough fields from under such seedlings with wooden ploughs and I had to buy steel ploughs. Now all of the fields are ploughed with Swedish steel. [. . .] People usually say that it is difficult to introduce steel ploughs where the peasants are used to ploughing with wooden ploughs. Not at all. The ploughs were a success on my place right away. When I decided to plough with steel ploughs, I began to look into who had steel ploughs and whether they were any good. All of the steel ploughs seemed inappropriate to me; at last, by chance, having visited a landowner in a different district, I saw a plough I liked. I decided to try this plough and I asked the owner to allow me to send a worker to learn how to use it.

"Yes, send him," he said, "I'll show him."

When I got home, I called Sidor after a bit.

"Listen, Sidor, I am thinking of ploughing the meadows for flax this fall with a steel plough. You know, the steel one like our wooden one, the one we saw at the exhibition."

"Okay."

"I saw them ploughing with steel ploughs at a lord's place in D. district—it was good."

"So we can do it too, if it's good."

"So, this is the thing; here are some money and a letter for you; go to the station today, take a ticket as far as Iartseva, there you will come out and walk along a big road, it will be twenty versts, to the village of K.; ask for Kh. there. That is the same lord who has the ploughs, he is not far from the village. Go to the lord, give him the letter, look at the plough, see how they plough, try it yourself, and when you have learned how, go back to Iartsevo, buy a ticket to Smolensk, buy that kind of plough—find out from the lord from which store, and bring it here. We'll plough the meadows."

"Fine."

"By the way, buy Mikhei some nankeen for shirts and some ticking for pants, and change these notes in the bank, they are called coupons."

"Fine."

"Maybe they will accept these coupons in the store. If not, ask Trofim where the bank is, he will show you. Each note costs two and a half rubles."

"Okay."

"So, God be with you."

"So, good-bye."

Sidor went to the station, reached Iartseva by train, went on foot to Kh.'s, looked at the plough, watched how they ploughed, how they set it up, learned from the workers how to get it to work, tried out ploughing himself, and the next day announced to Kh. that he understood it; the latter examined him, made him, it seems, put the plough together, and sent him on his way. Sidor went again on foot to Iartseva, took the train to Smolensk, found a store, bought the plough I had requested—along the way, he got an good chain for a bull because our Kholmogor bull Pashka, whom Sidor had brought from Moscow and raised, had already begun to be up to tricks and break the feed troughs—and, having done all of his errands, returned home.

"Well, and so?"

"I brought it."

"Did you learn how to plough?"

"I did."

"But how can you be so fast; after all, you were on the road only a total of three days?"

"And what was I to do there? There was nothing tricky about it. The workers showed me and the lord himself also showed me how to put it together. You know yourself, Aleksandr Nikolaevich, that I can set up the wooden plough, and repair it besides, and there is nothing to fixing this one— the only thing is that it has its own moldboard."

"And does it plough well?"

"Splendidly, Aleksandr Nikolaevich, especially for new land. It does it so well that it couldn't be any better. How could you do it that well with a wooden plough! And it's easier for the ploughman, and you don't need a special ploughman. It'll clear any new soil right away, and there's no need to talk about it breaking down, you'd have to bungle it."[. . .]

"When are you thinking of starting?"

"Tomorrow. I'll put on the harness today and tomorrow I'll try it on the broken soil. Only let me take Mikheika—he'll need to lead the horses until they get used to it."

The next day Sidor began to plough the turned soil, that is, the land on which the flax had been planted in the freshly turned beds. He ploughed a desiatina beautifully and finished it in four days—the desiatinas were good and full, despite the fact that it was muddy and the horses were very lazy and not quick. After the turned soil, he moved to a new field, which he also ploughed in four days. Then Sidor taught one of the workers to plough with the steel plough, who then ploughed the meadows and turned soil the entire autumn. The plough worked superbly.[. . .] This in no way fits with what our agronomist Dmitriev writes in our "Advice for Smolensk Farmers," who is convinced on the basis of his experience, managing a state farm, that it is impossible to use improved tools because of the "carelessness" and "ignorance" of the Russian peasant!

I then bought two steel ploughs and now—it has already been three years—the peasants do not prepare the new meadows and turned soil for flax any other way except with the ploughs; and what meadows, besides, the kind that were covered with birch trees at least fifteen years old, the kind on which you could not go a step without coming across a root, so that you could not break up a desiatina in less than eleven days. And the ploughs have been working three years already; of course, the blades and ploughshares had to be changed—and there have been no "breakages," no "loss of various parts," as happened to the agronomist who blamed the workers even for the fact that the "horses were extremely thin," as if it were possible to blame the workers for this. If the horses were thin, and extremely so to boot, this is because they were not fed; and what is remarkable about the fact that the workers "did not complete their jobs" on such horses? A horse is led not by the knout but by oats.[. . .]

And who was it who did the ploughing? The ignorant, careless Russian peasants—the "Russian swine," as some German would say, a director of an old school or some professor of an institution where "agronomists" used to study, called from abroad to introduce agronomy to us.[. . .]

The peasants came to look at the steel plough, they were amazed by the cleverness of the foreigners, and they gave their approval of the ploughing.

One of my workers, Stepa, decided to have a contest with the steel plough using a wooden plough and said that he would plough the turned soil and turn over the meadow with the wooden plough in the same amount of time as Sidor ploughed with the steel one, and that he would do it no worse. In fact, he ploughed a desiatina of broken soil in the same amount of time, but he fell behind on the meadow although he worked so hard that he smoked his pipe on the move, and refused to compete any further.

The worker Stepa—he is no longer with me, he has bought a farm himself—was the most superior ploughman with a wooden plough, the kind you rarely meet, who loved to plough, who showed off his work, the condition of his wooden plough, and the horse he selected, just as a fine German boot maker loves his work, who, having made some fine boots, it seems, is sorry to part with them. When Stepa came to my place and chose his workhorse I knew immediately that this was a master because you can judge a worker by the horse he selects, by the way he cares for it, by the bridle. And once Stepa took the plough in his hands, his position among the workers was already clear.

The majority of workers prefer lively horses, showy ones with a good trot, the kind of horses on which they could show off, drive past a baba jauntily during haymaking when each worker takes a baba with him (if there are not enough female hired hands, then a day laborer), to load the hay in the wagon more easily; while all the babas show up to rake and haul the hay in their best finery, covered with ribbons and beads.

I do not tell anyone which horse he must take; the workers themselves choose horses according to their taste and then they work constantly, always on the same horses. The strongest, most adept worker, the first in the artel, the driver, chooses the very best, liveliest horse, the kind who, if need be, can even wear you out; the second worker takes the second most swanky horse; the third the third and so forth.[. . .] Stepa, when they were choosing horses, although he was second in the artel, chose a horse which everyone avoided, not showy, a skewbald, lazy, but steady, without a trot, but with a good pace. The horse, which had been purchased late in the fall and had therefore not worked in the field yet, turned out to be the best plough horse and knew how to be ahead of the other horses in all of the jobs, through strength and intelligence.[. . .] When he saw the steel plough, Stepa announced with a grin that this was something totally unnecessary, that he would do no worse and just as fast on the skewbald with the wooden plough. And in fact, he did: Stepa's ploughing was model, extraordinary for a wooden plough, but, even so, not as good as that done with the steel plough. Although Stepa even agreed that the ploughing done with the steel plough was more precise, he still insisted that the flax on his desiatina would not be any worse than on the one done by the steel plough. In response to my remark that if only a few workers could plough with the wooden plough the way he, Stepa, did, then how well everyone would plough with the steel plough, Stepa said, "And anyone who does not know how to plough should not work on the land." Stepa, as a true ploughman, a specialist at his job, who loved its art, apparently feared that the art of ploughing with the wooden plough would be lost with the introduction of the steel plough, just as our tailor, the old man Mikhail Ivanovich, hates the sewing machine. "What kind of thing is that, stitched by a machine," says Mikhail Ivanovich. "But just try to stitch it by hand."

"Yes, but why do it by hand when you can do it on a machine?" I remark.

"What kind of tailor is it who doesn't know how to sew by hand? No, you stitch, but on the machine! People have gone soft!"

[Engelgardt discusses the potential for land reclamation in Smolensk Province and describes his success on his estate.]

Intelligence of the Russian Peasant

. . . The babas have gone out to the barn to start the braking; the dogs have quieted down, everything has become peaceful; I fall asleep again and sleep an unbroken sleep.

I wake up early and begin to cough: doctors say that this is some kind of catarrh, but the village inhabitants assure me that it is a cough from my stomach, a characteristic of farmers who, having spent a day in the open air, lie down to sleep "having drunk a little vodka and eaten supper." Savelich, woken up by my cough, begins to bustle about behind the wall: he is setting up the samovars, for which he has had everything ready since last evening already—both the water and the coal. Having smoked a few cigarettes—even after five years of farming I have not become so prosperous that I smoke cigars, I don't want to waste the money: a hundred cigars, the very worst ones, cost five rubles and for five rubles I can clear a meadow, and a hundred cigars hardly bring as much satisfaction as one extra desiatina of flax or clover—and after I finish coughing, I get dressed and set to the accounts and various calculations or to writing articles. Savelich brings in the samovar and looks at the thermometer while he is at it.

"So, Savelich, what's happening outside?"

"Not much."

"Is it feeezing cold?"

"Not so bad."

"But still?"

"It's pretty cold, but there's no wind."

I drink tea and work until the children wake up and the farming business of the day begins. Avdotia comes in.

"What shall I cook?" she asks.

"What is there to cook?"

Silence.

"Sometimes at least you should decide for yourself what to cook: you know better than I do what we have."

"How am I to know what you want? We have everything: salted beef, ham, veal, tongue, kidneys . . ."

"Well, spendid, make some soup with kidneys."

"And what else?"

"What else?"

"The children, you know, never eat soup: we need something else for them."

"What else is there to cook?"

Silence.

"Well, then make some pork cutlets: you know, you said that there is some pork."

Avdotia leaves.

"And should I put garlic in the cutlets?" she returns.

"Put some in."

She goes out.

"And should I make some potatoes to go with the cutlets?"

"Of course, make some: you know that children love potatoes."

"But you are always afraid that they are going to get sick."

I drink tea and work on the accounts.

Matrena arrives and begins to open the inside shutters.

"So, has it gotten light?"

"Not yet, it's only getting light now."

"Where is Sidor?"

"He went to the cattle yard."

"Has everyone had breakfast?"

"No, they're just getting together now. Mishka is watering the horses."

"And is it cold outside?"

"Not so bad."

"Is it freezing?"

"Not terribly."

Matrena, having opened the shutters, leaves.

The light is just breaking; it is impossible to work without a candle; the samovar is already beginning to go out and is giving off some kind of sad, hoarse sounds.

Sidor comes in and greets me.

"Hello. Well, so?"

"Everything's fine, thank God; we gave 'em clover."

"Did they eat well?"

"Beautifully."

"No new calves? No new kittens?"

"No, only Darka had a baby."

"Boy or girl?"

"A son."

"How long ago?"

"Oh, just now, We had just put out the clover and she gave birth."

"Did everything turn out well?"

"What would be wrong with her?"

"Who looked after her?"

"The old woman."

Silence.

"Darka is asking for a half bottle of vodka."

"Well, tell Ivan to give it to her."

Silence.

"And when will they christen him?"

"Today."

"And who will do it?"

"They want to ask Ivan Pavlovich to do it."

"And will they be through braking the flax soon?"

"There's a little left."

"And so, will you be hauling firewood?"

"Yes, as soon as we've finished breakfast we'll harness the horses."

"Well, go on."

Sidor leaves.

It has already gotten light. The children are beginning to move about, the samovar has gone out entirely; Savelich is disciplining the kittens and little Milton in the dining room for their nighttime tricks.

I drink tea and work on the accounts.

"Are you coming to water the cows?" Avdotia asks.

"I don't know: it depends on how the women do on the flax."

"Shall we water without you?"

"Yes, but see that they don't give more than a tankard to each calf."

"I know, I know."

"Even if they are tearing things up, don't give more than a tankard."

"I know. But we need to let 'Whitey' out—as you wish."

"It's still early."

"She's giving almost no milk at all."

"It's fine, you just continue to milk her."

"I milk her, but she doesn't give much."

"It's fine. I'll say when we should let her out."

It's not even fully light but the babas have already finished braking my flax. I need to get dressed and go to the barn to weigh the flax.

Since the women brake the flax each one for herself with pay by the pud, I have to weigh each baba's flax separately. Even sisters, to say nothing of sisters-in-law, brake the flax separately, each one for herself, and they will not agree to put the flax in one sack and weigh it together, and divide the pay equally because their strength and skill are uneven, and they will not work so hard, and working together, they will brake less than each one working separately. Only a mother and daughter will sometimes weigh together; but even this is only when the mother works for the daughter and all of the money goes to the daughter.[. . .]

Usually, I myself am present when the flax is weighed and record it because Ivan is illiterate—of the twenty people currently living on Batishchevo, only Savelich is literate, and he is barely so. "He writes very quietly," says Ivan, "he thinks and thinks and then suddenly he writes, and if he didn't write it right, he erases it and gets going again—it's trying." But if I am not home or for some reason I cannot come to the barn, Ivan himself notes who broke how much. Ivan is not literate, he does not know how to write, but even so, he manages the barn, he receives and distributes grain, flax, lard, butter, corn, oil cake, he counts the hay in the summer, manure, stacks, and so forth and so on. Accounting on my place is in good order; the income and expenses for everything and the progress of all jobs are recorded down to the smallest detail and I manage all of this through Ivan, who daily gives an account on most matters and gives an accounting on a few at the end of the month. Ivan marked all of his calculations, before, he cut them on a stick, that is, on four-sided stakes which he had separately for each item, but now he writes with a pencil on narrrow pieces of thick paper—for this he uses boxes from cigarette cases—using special figures, crosses, lines, circles, and symbols only he understands. In the evening, as he gives the report, Ivan takes out the paper, looks at it for a long time, and, leading with his thumb over it, begins: in the dining hall—two puds of flour, three pounds of barley, one pound of lard, sixteen pounds of salted beef, and so on. At the end of the month, Ivan comes in with an entire bundle of stakes and gives an account, dictating, for example, from the stake on oats:

"Five measures to the poultry, one sack to the horses, to Mishka in town, four garnets,[14] to you in town—one measure, to the driver who brought that dark-haired lord from Petersburg, for Petr Ivanovich's horses, four garnets, and so on. Six sacks in all."[. . .]

Aleksandr Nikolaevich Engelgardt in 1871.

Two peasant men in the typical dress described by Engelgardt in letters I and IV. Note the sheepskin coat and leather boots of the man on the left and the loose-fitting shirt and trousers of the man on the right. (*Library of Congress, Carpenter Collection*)

Peasant children. The boys' caps were typical of peasant dress by the end of the nineteenth century. The child on the right displays the cheerful intelligence that so impressed Engelgardt in his relations with peasant boys and girls. (*Library of Congress, Carpenter Collection*)

An old peasant woman of about the age of Engelgardt's "Old Woman" who supervised the dining hall and cared for sick animals on his estate. (*Library of Congress, Carpenter Collection*)

One alternative form of transportation during the mud seasons. The expressions of the peasants on the sled and those standing above on the hill suggest that this was a staged photograph and a source of great amusement for them. Note the various styles of coats and headgear. (*Library of Congress, Carpenter Collection*)

A troika with driver of the type Engelgardt describes as necessary for any gentry landowner who is keeping up appearances and hopes to make use of doctors in neighboring towns. The bells would signal the troika's arrival. (*Library of Congress, Foreign Geographic File*)

A peasant on the road. He may be a pilgrim, a wanderer, or simply a peasant who has gone out to collect crusts of bread in his pack. (*Library of Congress, Carpenter Collection*)

Two peasant men wearing the types of clothing described by Engelgardt in letter IV. Note the tattered sheepskin coat on the left and the lined cloth coat on the right, and also the loose shirt and trousers. (*Library of Congress, Carpenter Collection*)

A church beggar. Recall that Engelgardt describes how Savelich once collected for the church. A slot box, used to collect coins, hangs from the man's neck. (*Library of Congress, Carpenter Collection*)

Engelgardt describes the development of the lumber industry in Russia and peasant employment in related occupations, such as hauling. Here we see a peasant, probably of the late nineteenth century, pushing firewood on a wheelbarrow. (*Library of Congress, Carpenter Collection*)

Peasant woman braking flax. This is clearly a staged photograph because the woman is dressed in fine clothes and is posing. The photograph's main value is to offer a visual image of the tools for braking flax. (*Library of Congress, Stereographic Collection*)

This frosted landscape suggests the cold monotony of the scene Engelgardt watched from his train window as he left St. Petersburg for Batishchevo. (*Library of Congress, Prokudin-Gorskii Collection*)

Women gathering hay during the harvest. The prominence of women in this scene confirms Engelgardt's statement that they played a decisive role in the rural economy, especially during the harvest. (*Library of Congress, Stereographic Collection*)

Ploughing with a wooden plough. Although this photograph comes from the early twentieth century, it offers an image of the traditional ploughing methods that Engelgardt replaced with his imported, steel ploughs. (*Library of Congress, Stereographic Collection*)

When he receives the flax from the babas, if I am not there, Ivan notes in his own way how much each baba has broken, and giving the report at night, he dictates to me from his paper:

"Darochka thirty-three pounds, Akulina one pud, eight pounds, Semenikha Deminskaia thirty-nine pounds, Kozlikha with her daugher one pud twenty-two pounds, Nemaia twenty-seven pounds, Semenikha Antsyperovskaia one pud, Katka thirty pounds, Katka the soldier's wife one pud, Khvorosia twenty-three pounds, Fruza twenty-nine pounds, Matrena one pud twenty pounds, and so on."

Thirty to forty babas brake flax and there is never a mistake of any kind, and any mistake here will be noticed immediately because each baba remembers excellently how much she has broken and when and, at the final settling of accounts, knows quite well how much she has broken in all and how much money she should receive.

"How much did you brake, Katka?" I ask at the end.

"You can see better in your book, Aleksandr Nikolaevich."

"How much by your reckoning?"

"Three puds, twenty-two pounds."

"Just so."

"And how much money do you have coming?"

"You know better."

"How much?"

"One ruble and six kopeks, and a half kopek."

"Take a ruble and seven kopeks; use the extra half kopek to light a candle."

If, when we are settling accounts, I have to pay a little extra, the extra is given for a candle to God so that the other babas will not be insulted that someone got extra. The baba will use it for this and, the first time she goes to mass, as she gives a one-kopek candle,[15] if she received a half kopek, "she will take it into her head," as Ivan puts it, that half of the candle is for her and half is for me. "God will remember you for this," Ivan says.

When he records the income and expenses on his papers, Ivan records with his figures only the quantity disbursed and received, but to whom it is disbursed, from whom received, all of this he *remembers*. In general, peasant traders and such have a memory for everything they do and an ability to measure with their eyes and by touch that is incredibly developed and, besides, all of the peasants count amazingly accurately.

Every peasant boy, every girl knows how to count up to a certain number. "Petka knows how to count to ten," "Akulina knows how to count to thirty," "Mikhei knows how to count to a hundred." "Knows how to count to ten" does not mean at all that Petka knows how to count one, two, three, and so forth to ten; "knows how to count to ten" *means that he knows how to do all arithmetical equations with the numbers up to ten*. Several boys bring, for example, crayfish to sell, one hundred or one hundred fifty. They know how much money they should receive for all of the crayfish, and having received the money, they divide it absolutely accurately among themselves according to the number of crayfish caught by each one.

When teaching peasant boys arithmetic, the teacher should always keep this in mind and he has only to develop counting with material which has application and, having understood how the boy counts, show that "it is possible to count to infinity." Peasant boys count much better than city children; their quickness, memory, measuring by sight, hearing, and smell are developed immeasurably more highly than among our children so that seeing our child, especially the city child, among peasant children, it is possible to think that he has no ears, eyes, legs, or hands.

The peasants, around here at least, are extremely ignorant in religious, political, economic, and juridical questions. You will see that here on the day celebrating the Renovation of Tsargrad, the peasant will pray to "the Tsar of Hail (grad)," that the grain will not be beaten down by hail; you will see that girls were seriously frightened and believed after the marriage of our Grand Princess to the English prince, the rumor circulating that the most beautiful girls would be gathered and if they were virgins, sent to England because the Tsar had given them as a dowry to his daughter so that there in England they would marry Englishmen and convert them to our faith—not only the girls believed this, but even serious, older peasants, even veterans. Here you will hear the peasants' opinion that the Germans are much poorer than we are because they buy grain from us and that if the lords were forbidden to sell grain in Riga, the Germans would die of hunger; that when they succeed in making enough paper rubles, they will not collect taxes. And so on. And as for knowledge of their rights and obligations, despite the existence for ten years of a public court, the institutions of the justices of the peace, no one has any concept whatsoever of his rights. In all of these matters the peasants, even the traders and merchants are ignorant in the extreme; even the priests, to say nothing of the other church people, among whom one can still meet people who are more or less educated, although rarely—that is, all the men of the cloth, deacons, [. . .] various of their old men and relatives, in a word, all of the people who have lived in villages without working at anything, drunkards, shaggy-headed men in cassocks and leather belts, who have not gone much beyond the peasants in their understanding of religious, political, and juridical questions.

But as for knowing how to count, to produce the most scrupulous accounts, peasants are masters of the first rank at this. In order to be convinced of this one has only to watch how the peasants divide the land, how they settle accounts returning from hauling. Of course, you will understand nothing here if you do not know the method of counting; you will hear only cries and shouting and will think, "How stupid they are," well, just as in Uspenskii's story "Caravan"! Uspenskii grasped only the external aspect of the question; but his story fails in that the reader who is unfamiliar with the peasants carries away the impression of the complete nonsense and stupidity of the peasant haulers depicted in the story.[16] But wait until they are through and you will see how the accounting is done and you will see to what result these senseless shouts and arguments have led—the land will turn out to be divided so accurately that even a surveyor could do it no better.[. . .]

But what is most striking for me is the peasant's unusual memory. An illiterate village elder remembers who has what arrears, how much and from whom, and when he received money and so forth. The peddler who trades in women's articles—scarves, beads, and various trifles—gives out his wares in a territory of one hundred versts on credit and remembers where and how much each baba owes him and precisely what she bought. Finally, even in hauling: the time comes to go out hauling; the peasants get together in the village. Someone from the village, of course the head bigwig, goes to the town to find jobs. Having found work in town, he makes a deal, for example, to carry hemp from D. to S., he bargains with a merchant, comes to an agreement on the price and amount of the load. Severals days later, the peasants of the entire village set out for town to do the loading, one on a team of four, one on a team of three, one on a team of two. They do the loading. They put a different weighed amount of hemp on each horse, according to the horse's strength. All of this is done in the presence of the foreman, who receives an advance and deposit from the merchant. The foreman must remember how much hemp was loaded for each household head and consequently, how much money each one has coming to him in the final accounting.[. . .] They settle accounts at home: they calculate how much hemp each one has taken and how much money each one has coming, how much shortfall anyone had, how much each one spent along the road, how much in town and how much remains for each one to receive.

The muzhik understands counting splendidly, he understands all financial calculations splendidly: he is in no way a ninny. Of course, not all muzhiks are intelligent; of course there are also idiots, fools, and ninnies among them, who are not capable of running a farm; but since fools, in the peasant milieu, will inevitably perish from poverty because they cannot farm, it is understandable that one rarely meets a fool among the peasants in the country, and anyone who has had dealings with the plain folk carries away the impression of their indubitable quickness and cleverness.

All of the peasants who work at special professions are extremely interesting examples of quick, intelligent people who possess an unusual memory. One of the most curious types of this sort are the itinerant horse doctors, our homegrown veterinarians. There are practically no local horse doctors in our province and those who do exist—primarily former serfs who studied when each prosperous landlord tried to have everything of his own—do not enjoy a good reputation. Meanwhile, no farm can get by without a horse doctor because at a certain time of year, for example, in the early spring, it is essential on every farm to castrate some kinds of animals: piglets, calves, bulls, colts. Therefore, no one can get by without a horse doctor, because otherwise, one would have to slaughter all of the uncastrated animals before putting the stock out to pasture. So necessity has created people, horse doctor specialists, who castrate the stock and treat them a bit, to the extent that this is possible for these itinerant veterinarians. Horse doctors come here from far away. Somewhere there are entire villages, in Tver Province it seems, where peasants study horse doctoring especially, learning this trade primarily from each other. Two times a year—in the spring and the fall—horse doctors set out from their villages to work, they work in the spring and return home for the harvest; then they set out again for the autumn and return home for the winter. Every horse doctor goes along a set route, from year to year always along one and the same, going to the villages and gentry houses that lie along his way; consequently, every horse doctor has his own permanent practice, and vice versa—every village, every landlord, has his own horse doctor who comes to his place four times a year; two times in the spring—going and coming—and two times in the fall.

The horse doctor goes to each household and castrates all the animals that need it; it is understandable that he knows all of *his own* villages and in the villages all of the farmers *by name*. Usually, coming ahead in the spring, the horse doctor only works, but he does not receive pay for his work, from the peasants at least, because if the operation was not a success, no pay is due. Having worked the entire spring and returning home, the horse doctor, on his return route, goes again by everyone's place where he has done work and collects the pay which is due him. It often happens that the horse doctor does not receive money on his return route from the poor peasants, who rarely have money in the spring; then he waits until fall, when the muzhik will have his new harest, when he will be rich, and receives spring debts on his second run, furthermore he receives not only money, but also grain, lard, and eggs, for which he usually has his horse with him. Going hundreds of versts, going by thousands of peasant households, having castrated an incalculable number of calves, piglets, and bulls, the horse doctor remembers where, how much, and what he did and how much each farmer for whom he worked owes him. Horse doctors serve as the most interesting example of how necessity creates the requisite workers. The castration of domestic animals is the kind of need which not a single farm can do without and here this need has created an entire class of workers who have achieved a remarkable skill in this area and have established it unusually pragmatically, simply, suitably.

The horse doctors have achieved great skill in the procedure of castration itself, which is completely understandable in view of the enormous practice they have. The horse doctor who comes to my place, Ivan Andreevich—horse doctors enjoy great respect among the peasants and they are usually called by their patronymic—has castrated a multitude of different animals in the course of five years, and there has not been a single mishap: all the animals recovered easily and quickly after the operation. In just the same way, I have not heard from a single of the neighboring peasants that the horse doctor at some time did an unsuccessful operation so that an animal died as a result of the operation. And this is understandable: since the horse doctor values his reputation, having looked the animals over before the operation and having noticed that one of them is unhealthy, he warns the farmer about this and points out the illness so that the latter will not think later that the animal fell ill because of the operation. Besides, there is no reason for the farmer to fear because, if he wishes, he can *insure* his animal with the horse doctor himself. The horse doctor does not take much for his work: for castrating a calf—five kopeks, for a hog—five kopeks, for a young bull—ten kopeks, and besides, if there is a lot of work, the horse doctor receives a half bottle of vodka and a piece of lard in which he, at the conclusion of the job, cooks the organs he gets through the operation, for a treat; moreover, the horse doctor does not drink the vodka and eat the organs he has cooked alone, but along with the workers who assisted him in the job, who caught and held the bulls that were operated on. What veterinarian would agree to castrate animals for such prices!

Of course, the horse doctor receives such insignificant pay only for ordinary work. If, however, he needs to castrate old bulls, hogs, horses, then the pay to the horse doctor goes up: he receives a ruble, five, ten, twenty-five rubles, depending on the difficulty of the operation and according to the value of the animal and so on.[. . .] Any boy horse doctor can castrate calves and piglets, having studied with his father or brother [. . .] to castrate young bulls is already more difficult, colts even more difficult; and most difficult of all is to castrate old animals. Here the horse doctor acts more carefully, studies the animal with care, calls other horse doctors in for consultation who are working on parallel routes and whose location he always knows because, no doubt, there are points at which the horse doctors going on different routes meet. It often happens that even after the consultation, the horse doctors explain that it is impossible to castrate the animal because they, valuing their reputation, are generally very circumspect in their work and value their practice and routes, to which they have become accustomed. Horse doctors also treat animals a bit; but their importance in this area is insignificant, because they work only at certain times of the year. But the most valuable thing is that, giving your animal to the horse doctor, you can *insure* yourself with the horse doctor himself; if you do not want to take a chance, if you value the animal greatly, if you do not trust the horse doctor, then you appraise your animal and the horse doctor gives you the appointed sum on deposit and does the operations: if the animal dies, the money the horse doctor has given you remains at your disposal. It is understandable that with insurance, the pay for the operation is much higher and the higher it is, the greater the deposit you demand of the horse doctor. Once the horse doctor acknowledges that it is possible to do the operation, he will also always insure the animal if you want to because even if he does not have money himself, he will find other horse doctors and collect the requested sum.[. . .]

. . . Having weighed the flax, I go by the house to have a bite and then I set out for the cattle yard. I wanted to describe my winter day; the day is only beginning and I have already filled a whole notebook. This no longer resembles our short winter day in any way. Would it not be better to conclude on this note?

Letter VI

✉   When the sixth letter appeared in *Notes of the Fatherland* in 1878, it offered Engelgardt's impressions of the impact on the countryside of Russia's involvement in the Balkans.[1] He described developments from 1877 and 1878 first, then returned to the account he had written in 1876, which was not published then because of problems with the censors.

The events Engelgardt alludes to were part of Russia's long involvement in Balkan affairs, which heated up in the second half of the nineteenth century when the Ottoman Empire was in decline and the Hapsburg Empire and the Russian Empire were vying for influence over the subject populations in the area. Russia's interest was both ideological and geopolitical. As a Slavic and Orthodox empire, Russia assumed the role of protector over all Slavic and Orthodox peoples in the Balkans. This aspect of Imperial Russia's self-image became increasingly prominent as the Pan-Slav movement grew in Moscow. It geopolitics, Russia intended to figure as a Great Power in European politics, and therefore was unwilling to concede territory or influence to Austria-Hungary. Furthermore, Russia's historical determination to gain and maintain access to the warm waters of the Black Sea ensured that Russia would be actively involved in Balkan conflicts.

The specific events that form the background of Engelgardt's sixth letter began with revolts in Bosnia and Herzegovina in 1875 of Christian and Slavic peasants who eventually called for self-rule within the Ottoman Empire. A series of revolts followed in Bulgaria in May 1876, and these were met by swift and brutal repression by the Ottoman Empire's troops, including massacres of the civilian Christian population. In July 1876, Serbia and Montenegro followed the Bulgarian lead by going to war against the Ottoman Empire, and volunteers from Russia, mobilized by Pan-Slavs, headed to the area. The participation of a prominent Russian general, Michael Grigorevich Cherniaev, added to the glory of the cause. These accelerating developments culminated in the outbreak of the Russo-Turkish War in April 1877. The Russian victory at Plevna signaled the end of the conflict, and an armistice was signed in January 1878.

✉   ✉   ✉

Rural Responses to the Russo-Turkish War

Several years ago I wrote you in my first letter from the country, "You want me to write you about our rural way of life. I am fulfilling your request, but I warn you that I absolutely cannot think, speak, or write about anything else except farming. All of my interests, all of the interests of the people I see daily are focused on firewood, grain, livestock, manure . . . Nothing else matters to us."

Seven years ago, that is the way it was: we followed our usual routine, we did what was required, and nothing else mattered to us. But now, even in our backwoods, a different current of air has begun to come through and gradually to budge us . . .

The peddler Mikhaila, who formerly offered scarves with pictures of roosters, doves, and various unknown beasts and flowers, suddenly is offering scarves with pictures of "the leaders and heroes of the Serbian uprising in Bosnia and Herzegovina who fought for the Christian faith and the liberation of the fatherland from the barbarians." Well, how could you not buy one! For twenty kopeks you receive a scarf with a title and twelve portraits and even the signatures: here we have "General M. G. Cherniaev" and "Lazar Sochitsa," and "the Serbian Prince Milan" . . .

A gentlewoman from Petersburg has arrived wearing a tricolor, blue-red-and-white tie . . .[2] The assistant to the head of the railroad station has become a volunteer and left for Serbia to die for the Christian faith . . . The so-called "Hungarian" who trades in various small wares offers tri-colored, blue-red-and-white, Slavonic-Russian pencils . . .

Once I happened to go by the neighboring tavern; I walked in and heard, "Cherniaev! Now that's a hero! Do you understand? Isn't that so, your honor, what I'm saying?" Fomin, a permanently discharged cavalry sergeant, surrounded by a crowd of peasants to whom he was explaining the Serbian question, turned to me.

This evening the soldiers on unlimited furlough were summoned, including my thresher Fedoseich as well.[3] He had only just let down the last of the warm flax when they galloped up with an order from the volost authorities. The steward woke me up too; it was an emergency, an order with "a quill," the tuft of a goose quill was glued to the sealing wax, which means, get going and fast! . . . I had to settle our accounts in the night, pay Fedoseich the salary he had earned, raise a glass of vodka for the road, wake up a new thresher. We bid farewell, cried, the driver hurried in order to make it to town by dawn; "the order is absolutely to be there by dawn." Fedoseich also hurried, he needed to go by the village to change his shirt, get boots and a coat, and say good-bye to his wife and children.

"So, farewell, Fedoseich."

"May you remain happy, your honor."

"Have another glass, and you, too, driver, have a drink."

"We thank you most heartily, your honor."

"Farewell, Ivan Pavlych, farewell, Andreianych, farewell, Prokhorovna, may you remain happy, your honor. As for my son, your honor, I only ask that you hire him as a herdsman for the summer."

"Fine, fine. Farewell, Fedoseich."

"May you remain happy, your honor."

Again they wake us up at night; an order from the volost—they are demanding horses tomorrow, all of the horses must be there by dawn without fail . . .

Fedoseich returned happy and beaming from town.

"Well, and so, they did not take you?"

"They didn't take me, your honor."

"How's that? So are you going to heat the barn again?"

"I'm going to heat it up again, your honor," rejoices Fedoseich.

"Well, get going, fire it up. Put Akenia in the cattle yard again and let Foka out."

"I understand, your honor. I thank you heartily that you're taking me back."

"Why should I not take on a good man?"

"They aren't taking people back in other places. They say you have trouble at night with your people on indefinite leave. You're worth it today, but tomorrow they'll call for you; it's nothing but trouble. So they don't take people back."

"And did they let a lot go?"

"A lot. They just took a very few."

"And did they summon everyone?"

"Everyone, they summoned everyone to town."

They are collecting strips of material for the wounded. The babas were stubborn, they did not want to contribute, but the muzhiks made them . . .

The village elder has arrived. I go out. He takes something out of his chest, unwraps a rag—it is a small book with a red cross.

"No, brother, I have my own!" I go into my office and ceremoniously take out the very same little book with a red cross.

"Have you collected a lot?"

"Only a bit! What kind of money does the muzhik have now in the spring, many of them don't have any grain."

"I also have collected little; the gentry aren't giving much either."

"There are a lot of people collecting."

Again they call for horses.

It is harvest time. The day is hot. The peasants are dragging the clover. The mowers have sat down to rest and smoke their pipes. Dust appears on the road, someone is galloping . . . The steward, Ivan, on a young horse.

"He's probably coming for me," says Mitrofan.

Mitrofan is a noncommissioned officer on indefinite leave from the local district militia.

"For you! Have the merchants broken out in rebellion against the city?" one of the mowers asks, laughing. "Why would they take you! You don't know any kind of service, you've only escorted prisoners."

"They've called for Mitrofan," Ivan announces, jumping down from his horse.

We go back to the house: I need to settle our account. Mitrofan has a wife and two children, one of whom is still at the breast. And an old blind woman, his wife's mother. He has his little izba in the village, his little shack, as the old woman says, a cow, and a little garden. Mitrofan feeds his family with the earnings he makes hiring himself out in the winter to cut firewood, and in the summer as a hired hand. According to the record, Mitrofan has a total of one ruble forty kopeks coming because he took all of his salary in flour and buckwheat to feed his family. If they take Mitrofan, his family will be left without any means of subsistence whatsoever and probably will be fed by the commune if they do not get some assistance.[. . .] They were detained for a few days in town, Fedoseich and Frolchenok were sent back, but they took Mitrofan.[. . .]

"They have beaten the Suleiman," the steward Ivan reports.

"What are you saying!"

"I came back on purpose to tell you. I met Osip Ilich at the crossroads, he was coming from town, he was so happy. "What's up?" I asked him. "They beat the Turks," he says. "They've raised the flags in town, everyone's reading newspapers in all the shops. They've beaten the sultan, it says." And I say to him that it must be the Suleiman . . . "Right," he says, "right, he's their Tsar."

"Mikhei! Go to the station as fast as you can for the newspapers."[. . .]

Mitrofan's wife came by.

"What can I do for you, Mitrofanikha?"

"A letter from my husband, I came to read . . ."

"Fine. Give it to me, I'll read it."

"To my dear, sweet, and trembling mother Arina Filipevna from your son Mitrofan, in the first lines of my letter I send you my respect in my absence and a low bow from my face right down to the moist earth and in my absence, I ask you for your parental blessing and beseech you, oh mother of mine, to pray to God about me so that the Lord will spare me. Your maternal prayer will be a great help. And to my dear and beloved brother" and so on greetings followed to all the relatives. And then: "And I inform you my family that I was present at a place four hundred versts from the Caucasus, that I am now standing in the camps near Kartsee in Turkey and I see my death at twenty versts and it is only my fate that I do not know, I hear the Turkish bombs and see the smoke and I wait from hour to hour to enter the battle" . . . Then greetings to his wife, children, mother-in-law again, and finally, "Write me about how you are doing and about the flax harvest, have you had any problems, did the lord pay you the money that was due me or did he take it out for food, and tell me how you are doing with the assistance for the children."

Mitrofan had already taken an advance of money in the winter for harvesting the rye and for gathering flax for a neighboring landowner. His wife, left with a blind old mother and two children without any means of subsistence because her husband fed her with his earnings, still had to fulfill the obligations which he had taken on. And she did.

"They've taken Plevna!"

We received an order to dry one vedro of cabbage per soul.[. . .]

The peddler Mikhaila brought war pictures: "The Marvelous Dinner of General Skobelev under Unfriendly Fire," and "The Storming of Kars," "The Taking of Plevna." Mikhaila knows all the pictures in detail, and just as he previously explained the merits of his cottons and scarves, so he now describes his pictures.

"Here you have," he explains to the babas and day laborers who have gathered around him in the dining room, "here you have Skobelev, the general, he took Plevna. Here's the same Skobelev standing and pointing to the soldiers with his finger so that they'll run faster to take the gates to Plevna. Here, you see, are the gates, here are our soldiers running. Here they're taking the Osman pasha by their hands—look how he's hunched over! Here our soldiers are taking Kars; do you see how our soldier has seized the Turkish flag?" Mikhaila points to a soldier who has erected a two-eagled flag on the walls of the fortress.

"That is the Russian flag, not the Turkish one," I remark.

"No, it's the Turkish flag. You see, there's an eagle drawn on it, and there'd be a cross on the Russian one."[4]

"Here you have Skobelev dining . . ."[. . .]

Mitrofanikha came by again. Another letter from Mitrofan.

After the usual greetings, requests about "blessings," and so on, he wrote, "We have suffered in the war, we were hungry and cold at the city of Kars. We attacked it during the night from the fifth to the sixth of November. As soon as the Turks began to shoot at us with heavy artillery, we, even so, went right into their fire, went up to the fortress, lost our commander and colonel, and they killed the commander of the brigade. But our soldiers didn't lose heart and drove out all of the Turks from the fortress with our bayonets. The battle was so bad that many of our brothers fell, but we beat the Turks all the same and dragged them into the forest like branches, the night was cold, the wounded suffered very much from the cold." And further, "And my dear wife, tell me how you and the children are doing and are you all alive and well, and write me about the cow, did you sell her or not; if you still have her, then I ask you not to sell her, try to avoid this somehow, and maybe God will grant that I return home in the spring. But if it gets hard to live, then sell the sleigh, don't die of hunger."

"Well, Mitrofanikha, do we need to write an answer?"

"You write it, Aleksandr Nikolaevich, you know better what to write."

"And you have been so afraid that they would kill Mitrofan, while he, thank God, is alive. Let us drink a little vodka to rejoice."

Mitrofanikha smiles.

"Mikhei, bring Mitrofanikha a little of the red vodka. Well, and how are you doing?"

"We get by somehow. But getting firewood is hard: we gathered branches in the forest in the fall; look, 'We dragged the Turks into the forest like branches!' Mitrofanikha began to laugh, remembering the letter, "but now the snow has covered them."

"And as for assistance, did you make a request to the elder?"

"I did."

"And what did he say?"

"He got mad. He swore, you know yourself what a foulmouth he is: you should be put in jail, he said. What are you thinking of! . . . A request! You should get it into your head to go to town with your request. And this is what I'll do to you!"

"But he took your request?"

"He took it. The clerk read it. Ikh, he says, it's well written, and what white paper! Go home and wait, when the authorities send down an order we'll call you. You wrote about your blind mother also. Why? This is your mother, not the soldier's. The soldier's mother lives with another son."

"But you know that the soldier's mother goes after crusts of bread, too."

"You're just wasting our time with that talk."

The situation of many soldiers' wives, left behind when the men on indefinite leave were called to war, is, in fact, quite pitiable. More than a year has already passed and the village soldiers' wives—urban soldiers' wives have received assistance—have received no assistance up to now, not from the volost, not from the zemstvo, not from the parish charities which exist, for the most part, only on paper. Private charity takes the form only of crusts of bread. They sold whatever they had and have eaten these funds up, it remains to feed themselves in the commune, to go after crusts of bread. A childless soldier's wife can still hire herself out somewhere as a worker, although this winter it is difficult to find work even as a day laborer, or she can move in with someone—but then the soldier will file suit because she bore a child—or, finally, she can go to the commune, feed herself with crusts of bread, although even the commune is giving out little this year. But what is a soldier's wife with small children who has nothing except "her little izba" to do? No one will even take her on as a day laborer for food. If she goes for crusts of bread, with whom will she leave the children? There is only one solution. Having left the children in her "little izba" that she has nothing to heat with, because the branches in the forest are covered with snow, she goes begging around her own village. And, do the peasants in the village give out a lot? It is fine if the village is large.

Here they are, long-suffering mothers![. . .]

Mikhei brought news from the station that the Suleiman—this time he got it right, the Suleiman—had been defeated. There is nothing in the newspapers yet, but there is always a rumor.[. . .]

Today there is a blizzard, a snowstorm, it is really blowing. Mitrofan's mother, his own mother, the one whom he asked in the letter to pray to God about him, because a mother's prayer helps a great deal, begging in the commune, came by our place also: we, as is customary, are also giving out crusts of bread.

Communal assistance through crusts of bread truly is excellent assistance. Here at least no one asks who, what, what for, why as they ask in the charitable committees. They give to everyone, silently, asking nothing, without creeping into your soul. If someone has put on a canvas bag, then it means that he is begging in the commune. The woman of the house cuts a crust of bread and gives it. If there were no communal assistance through crusts of bread, *many soldiers' wives would have starved to death long ago.* Who knows when assistance will turn up again, and one has to eat.

Mitrofan's mother, having found out from Ivan the steward that a letter from Mitrofan had been received, that he is alive, began to cry, to rejoice, "I didn't know whether to pray for his health or his soul," she said. And she said she wanted to send a ruble to her son, only she didn't have one, and it was a long way to go ten versts in the blizzard now. Ivan reassured her and promised to send a ruble of his own.

Ivan brought me the ruble in the evening and asked me to send it to Mitrofan from his mother. A week later, Mitrofan's mother came by again for crusts of bread and brought Ivan her debt, the ruble: in order to get this ruble she had sold a piece of canvas.[. . .]

Today Mikhei brought the newspapers! Peace! We immediately raised the flag.

Everyone asks, what does the flag mean?—Peace!—So, praise to You, oh Lord! everyone says, crossing himself. And have our boys taken Kostipol? No. An expression of perplexity. And have our boys taken much Turkish land? A lot. Have they taken a third of it? More. Well, praise be to You, oh Lord! says everyone, crossing himself.

We drank a toast to Skobelev's[5] health. The priest will not accept it: "Say his name," he says.

"Mikhail. Mikhail Dmitrievich."

A rumor has spread that landless peasants will be resettled on the Turkish soil. Two fellows work for me: Mikhei and Matvei. Both are landless, illegitimate.[6] Matvei does heavy work; in the winter he cleans up the cattle yard, in the summer he works in the field. Mikhei works in the house. When the rumor spread that landless peasants would be resettled on Turkish land, I said to Mikhei, "So, Mikhei, they are going to set you up on some land and you know neither how to mow nor plough. Matvei does know how, but you do not." "No matter," he says, "even there in Turkey there'll be masters and they'll need house servants too."

There you have the practical Russian mind!

Mikhei is not afraid of being resettled as a landless peasant on Turkish soil because there also "There'll be masters"; but Matvei is frightened, he does not want to, because on Turkish soil, "they plough with oxen" . . .

Peace!

I have been intending to write you for a long time. The following, for the most part, was already written in the fall of last year, 1876, but I could not quite make up my mind to send it. The time was not right. But now, please accept it, and if I skipped something or did not explain something thoroughly, please do not curse me.

December 1876 . . . Of course we are even now working on all the same things as before: we thresh grain, brake flax, feed the animals, but even so it is not quite the same. "It's all the same, it's all the same," our Smolensk muzhik says as he scratches himself, "but not really!" Before it would be that the Kholmogor calf, which I raised with special care, was interesting in and of itself; I was glad that she was healthy, that she ate well, that she was growing well, I admired how she chewed her cud and raised her tail. But now, what is the calf to me! I still care for her, feed her with grain, but at the same moment that I scratch behind the ear on her beautiful white head that is turned toward me, my thoughts are far away.

It used to be that, in the morning, having received the flax that had been broken overnight, I would go to the house, have a bite, and then go to see how the babas were putting out a new barnload of flax, then I would go the cattle yard, then eat lunch and rest. But now it is not that way at all.

You come home after inspecting the flax. How are you to have a bite, much less go to the cattle yard! No. You don't have the heart for it.

"And so, Kolka, shouldn't we go for a ride?" I ask my young son.

Kolka begins to squeal and jump for joy.

"Let's go. Today the weather is fine and the old stallion needs a ride."

A few minutes later, the horse is ready, we are headed off for our ride and each time we must stop by the neighboring tavern. Kolka and I both love this tavern very much: Kolka because they sell rolls and candy in the tavern, and I because one can always hear the freshest political news in the tavern, really, the freshest political news, although the tavern does not subscribe to any newspapers. Unfortunately, this tavern closed this year. And again the reason was the war, which so disrupted our life that until then had been quiet and monotonous with its exclusively agricultural interests.

The tavern was located on the land of a neighboring landowner, a noble-man on whose ninety desiatinas of land there was nothing but this tavern. The landowner himself served on the railway as a senior repairman, the land had gone to waste, and the tavern was run by a cavalry major on indefinite leave who lived and ran the business there with his wife. The major, just like my thresher Fedoseich, was called several times to serve, kept overnight, taken to town, but he was always sent back because he was not needed. Although the major finally stayed at home, having held the license until the end of the year, he had to close his business because it was impossible to take a license under such circumstances, and there was no credit to be had, which was essential for the business. Having closed the tavern, he settled in the village with relatives and lived, like Frolchenok, from day to day, waiting for them to take him today or tomorrow and send him somewhere near Kars or Plevna.

The tavern was located in a little old, half-rotted-out izba which leaned to one side, the kind that you cannot find even at a poor peasant's. The entire premises of the tavern were eight arshins in length and the same in width;[7] most of this space was taken up by the stove, the owners' quarters, the bar, the shelves on which the dishes, clean bottles, and balsam (a pleasant and useful drink) were set up—and every kind of junk. There remained a space three arshins long and four wide for the customers, in which there were benches around the walls and a small table. In the tavern it was dirty, dark, filled with tobacco smoke, cold, damp, close, and always full—as the proverb says: "It's not the corners that make an izba beautiful, but the meat pies." But it is not the meat pies, but the hospitality of the owners. The meat pies were like all meat pies in taverns, it is well known what they are like: the vodka was a simple vodka, a green, licensed vodka of an illegal strength, in fact it was not even vodka, but "bittersweet" vodka, as the label glued to the barrel says; there were herring, rolls, filled cookies, candies for twenty kopeks per pound. But the owners, the major and his wife Sasha, attracted everyone with their hospitality, honesty, and absence of the tavern keeper's characteristic greed for profit. Both the major and his wife Sasha were intelligent people, they were not kulaks, they had God's faith, as the muzhiks say. The important thing was that it was always possible to find out the most exciting news in the tavern. The owner himself, a major, obviously, was greedy for news as a man who had a close interest in the business, as a man who today or tomorrow could be taken and sent off. As a former muzhik who had not broken his ties with the muzhik's way of life, who even now lived in a muzhik milieu, he understood the essence of muzhik speech, the meaning of the muzhiks' rumors; as a soldier he also understood the soldier; as a major, clearly not a stupid man, an intelligent, civilized man, he was interested in newspaper accounts, appointments, and so forth. He spoke splendidly, energetically, especially when he spoke about Cherniaev, about cavalry maneuvers, dashing crossings, and so on.

The well-proportioned figure of this white-skinned soldier with sparkling eyes and energetic gestures in a rose cotton shirt stands as if alive before my eyes even now. "Cherniaev—now that's a hero!" I hear.

I already said in my letters that we who aren't accustomed to peasants' speech, manners, and ways of expressing themselves and mimicking do not understand anything when we observe some kind of division of land or some kind of accounting among the peasants. Hearing the broken, disconnected exclamations, the endless arguments with the repetition of some one word, hearing this apparently senseless din of a crowd shouting, counting, or measuring, we think that they will never settle accounts, they will never come to any kind of solution. But, wait until the end and you will see that the division is accomplished with mathematical precision—both the measurement and the quality of the soil, and the direction of the field and the distance from the house, all are taken into account, you will see that the accounting is done accurately and, most important, each one of those present with an interest in the business is convinced of the accuracy of the division or the settlement. The shouting, the noise of the din will not cease as long as there is *even one* person who is not satisfied.

It is the same thing with the discussion by the commune of any kind of question. There are no speeches, no debates, no voting; they shout, make noise, swear, it seems they are about to break out into a fight, they make a din in apparently the most senseless fashion. Another one will remain silent, remain silent, and then suddenly throw in a word, only one word, an exclamation, and with this word, with this exclamation, he will turn everything upside down. Finally, you will see, the most splendid decision will be reached and again, most important, a decision that is unanimous.

It is even most difficult for us understand the logic of political rumors that circulate among the peasants and which illuminate their outlook on current events.

Knowing how ignorant the peasants are, knowing that they do not possess even the most elementary geographic, historical, and political knowledge, knowing that the peasants celebrate May eleventh by praying to the Tsar of Hail, so that hail will not ruin the fields, knowing that not every priest can explain what the "Renewal of Tsargrad," that is written in the calendar on May eleventh, is, knowing that even the deacon who sings the "Hallelujah" during prayers and "rejoices" is also convinced that they are praying for the Tsar of Hail and diligently bows in prayer so that his rye also will not be ruined by hail, it is true that you cannot imagine that these people could have any kind of comprehension of current political events.

It seems unlikely that one would be interested in something one does not know, that one could sympathize with the war, understand its significance when one does not know what Tsargrad is.[8]

But on the other hand, can the muzhik remain indifferent to all of this as he carries the entire burden of the war, which he cannot not feel as he hears discussion everywhere about victories, about losses, finding himself, through letters, in close contact with those of his children and brothers who have fallen at Plevna and Kars? We take his inertia and apathy to be indifference toward the cause—but is not this indifference only apparent?

Think about it! Is it possible that these immobile, gray masses don't have any notions at all about something that touches their immediate interests so closely? Is it possible that everything would be done as it is done if there were no sympathy toward the cause, or, to put it better, a consciousness of the need to do something?

As if every separate individual were completely indifferent, completely apathetic, did not have any kind of idea whatsoever about the cause, were moved only by the order to bring money, dry cabbage, bring her son or husband to town . . .

However, Sidor, for example, having heard the story about how the Turks seized a Bulgarian with his wife and child, hacked the child to pieces, burned him and made the father eat him, in no way, apparently, moved by such horrible bestiality, neither oohing nor aahing, completely tranquilly, remarked, "So why did he eat him?"[. . .]

If you listen to the discussions of different folk, you will not understand anything. They come out with the most apparently senseless, even laughable things: China is rising up for us. The Tsar does not believe China, he is afraid China will deceive him, he says, you, China, guard your bank of the Black Sea and I, he says, will guard mine. *She* built an underground railroad from her to Plevna, she sent weapons and food to the Turk on it, while *he*, Cherniaev, immediately saw the Englishwoman's road and ordered that it be filled in. So, now they have just taken Plevna, and so on.

But the masses, as a whole, have completely definite convictions.

They are sick unto death of the Turk: everything is happening because of his rioting. But the attitude toward the Turk is somehow forgiving, as toward a child: it means he is an unreliable person, he's always rioting. He needs to be pacified; he has a rest, begins to make trouble again, there will be a war again, again they will call for horses, hauling, fabric, they'll start collecting cabbage again. You need to be done with him once and for all. At the same moment that some newspapers are talking about the need for peace and others quietly announce the need to move on Tsargrad, some kind of peasant peddler, explaining that this is the Turkish flag because it has an eagle on it, while there would be a cross on the Russian flag, with full conviction says that it is time to put an end to it. He says, "God will grant something, but we need to get to Kostipol." "And we'll get there," he says, "as long as someone is not trapped. But if she is caught, hit her on the tail; then if only China would hold on. But the Tsar does not believe China." They have no hatred for the Turk, all of their hatred is directed at her, the British woman.[9] They simply ignore the Turk and feel sorry for the Turkish prisoners, *they give them wheat bread*. Who does? The muzhiks. But the merchants, they mock them—not all of them, of course, and would be ready to beat them, if there were no police. It is strange that in regard to the Turkish prisoners the gentlewomen and the muzhiks on one side agree, while on the other the merchants, traders, and liberal bureaucrats agree.[. . .]

Let me return to my tavern. I said that it is always possible to find out the most important news there. Indeed, despite the fact that I subscribe to two newspapers, I always find out something new at the tavern. In the first place, the peasants' rumors, which always outstrip the news in the papers and spread with incalculable speed, come to the tavern; in the second place, I subscribe to only two papers but in the tavern people bring news from all the papers received at the station and, finally, news reaches the tavern earlier. Usually I send for the newspapers two times a week and I only sent for them daily during the very height of the action in Serbia. But news comes to the tavern every day and, furthermore, early in the morning. The train that brings the papers arrives at the station during the night, those who work at the station, of course, read the papers immediately. News passes from the higher-ups to the lower workers and, spreading with incalculable speed along the line, reaches the guards, repairmen, stokers, and haulers, who then convey it to the villages, not passing by the tavern, of course. All of this news is transmitted in a completely original fashion, and, besides, not only facts, but also editorials and proposals are presented in a specific way so that with a little practice it is possible to distinguish where the news came from: *Voice, Moscow News,* or

The Market News. I did not know anything about the overthrow of the sultan yet, but they already knew about it in the tavern, and the first word that I heard when I went by there was, "Have you heard, Aleksandr Nikolaevich, that the ministers have slaughtered the sultan?"

"No, I have not heard that."

"It's true. Now there's a big uprising going on. Now, probably, they'll summon everybody on indefinite leave."

It is remarkable that this news about the overthrow of the sultan took such strong root that, despite the fact that a new sultan was put in place immediately, until now, according to the general opinion, the sultan does not exist, the very title of sultan, so to speak, has been destroyed, so that it is absolutely necessary that *the sultan be chosen by us.*

Mobilization began: they requisitioned horses, they called for those on indefinite leave; our regiment came out, traffic in trade along the railroad ceased, the movement of troops began. There were bonfires scattered around the stations; a crowd of babas who were waiting for one or another train in order to look at their son or husband for the last time, to give him a ruble, some kind of shirt, to give him a glass of vodka.

"They took mine also tonight," Sasha said, and began to cry.

"Perhaps, God willing, he will return. Look, Fedoseich returned."

"I heard. Only, they say they're taking the cavalrymen, and mine was in the cavalry regiment."

"But maybe there still won't be a war."

"May God grant it. Only no, it won't turn out that way."

"But maybe it will pass."

"That'd be good. They're saying China's rising with us against the English-woman, only the Tsar doesn't trust him: he's afraid that he'll deceive him and then overthrow us afterward. And what do they write in the papers about China?"

"I have not read anything about China."

"They say that China is rising with us. May God grant it."

"And how are you going to get by, Sasha, if they take Filipp?"

"I'll hold the license until the New Year, I'll collect my debts."

"And then what?"

"I'll move to my husband's brother's place in the village. I can't run the tavern by myself. But then, God willing, if my husband returns from the war, we'll rent your mill. He still had a little time left to serve."

I get the urge to go to the tavern and find out if there is anything new, but you will sit and talk there in the tavern right up to lunch; after lunch, when you go to the farm, you think, "Mikhei went to the station, he'll bring the papers back by evening, I'll nap for an hour or so, so that I'll be fresher in the evening." You wake up, Mikhei is still not back, you go to the cattle yard, you watch them feed the animals, and still you think, "How soon will Mikhei be back from the station?" They water the cows, usually I am personally present at the watering, but here comes Mikhei, you forget about the watering.

"You water them, Avdotia, without me, and I'm going to read the news-papers."

"Fine, fine, go on."[. . .]

I run to the house, attack the newspapers: of course, first of all you look at the telegrams, the market news, then you read the correspondence, the politi-cal news, you skip the provincial correspondence which once took up whole pages in the newspapers, but now is located, in my newspaper at least, some-where in the back and takes up two, at the most three columns.

[Engelgardt discusses his changing attitude about news from beyond Batish-chevo over his years on the estate and also describes the speculation about how the war would affect the prices of agricultural products.]

The newspaper was most important. You begin to drink tea, Ivan comes in to record the threshing, the expenses, and his first words are, "What's new in the papers? What do they say about Skobelev, Gurko?" And Fedoseich is waiting in the kitchen there: He came to find out "which side is winning." You give the newspaper over. They read it loudly in the kitchen. Ivan, Avdotia, Mikhei listen with the greatest interest to the correspondence about Skobelev and they always ask beforehand if there is anything from the person who "writes about Skobelev." Fedoseich explains what a lozhement is, a trench, a division, an artillery company. Yes, because of this war, there has been a great distur-bance on the farm. Of course, it did not all happen at once.

They were already talking about the war a long time ago, three, four years ago. Various rumors circulated in which the "Englishwoman" figured most prominently.[10]

Then they began to say that there would be a gathering of unmarried girls, that the Tsar was going to give these girls as a dowry for his daughter who was moving into the Englishwoman's house. They rumored that the girls would be married to Englishmen so that our girls would convert them to our faith.

The delivery of the Smolensk icon of the Virgin Mother to the Duke of Edinburgh gave much fuel to the talk and rumors, which all led to the same notion; we are trying to convert the Englishwoman to our faith.

In the fall of 1875 I happened to be at the wedding of a certain peasant. At lunch, one of the relatives of the bride, an old soldier, who was seated by the head of the household beside me in order to entertain me as an honored guest, turned to me with the question, what had I heard about the war?

"I have heard nothing."

"But the rumor's going around among us, sir, that we'll be at war with the Englishwoman."

"I do not know. And why precisely with the Englishwoman?"

"She didn't accept . . ." almost mysteriously having lowered his voice, the soldier said, glancing at me meaningfully.

This interested me.

"So," I said, having also lowered my voice.

"She's not converting to our faith . . ."

At this moment, the host interrupted our conversation, offering vodka. The long process of drinking the first glass of vodka, blowing into the glass, bows to all sides, saying "To your health," with remarks about how the vodka is not quite right, that it is weedy, began. The young couple kissed at this, or better to say, the young girl kissed her husband, who was sitting like a statue, and she stood up, took him in her hands by the head, turned him, and loudly kissed him on the lips: the young girl should express love toward her husband, while he only accepts her caresses; if the girl likes the husband, and she kisses him willingly, then this produces quite an effect.

"Yes," I turned to the soldier, wishing to renew the interrupted conversation, "something will happen."

"That's what they say!"

"Only there is nothing in the papers."

"The peasants are talking."

"Yes."

"They brought the icon," he whispered, again having lowered his voice. "Well!"

"He didn't accept it . . . he got angry!" he whispered in my ear.

"What are you saying? It cannot be!"

"I myself don't believe it, because, if that was true . . . wouldn't she, the Tsar's heavenly mother, and the saints explode right then and there?"

"So it would seem!"

"The peasants are talking; the muzhiks' rumors, sir! They say that there'll be a war. Look, they've gotten terribly strict orders in the volosts about the men on indefinite leave. Every elder's supposed to know where everyone is; the cart drivers have to be equipped and so forth."

Our host interrupted again. Again there were bows, wishes for the good health of our host, the young couple, and remarks that the vodka is weedy. Again the princess kissed her young prince.

"And don't we have Krynka rifles now, sir?"

"Yes."

"And they say that new ones, Berdan rifles, have turned up."[11]

"Yes, but only the riflemen have them; but where did you serve?"

"In the Old Ingermanland regiment."

"So, it seems, you are retired?"

"Yes, completely, thank God! I always keep this with me!" and he slapped his pocket with his hand.

"How's that! You carry it with you?"

"With me, have a look!" and he showed me a fine wooden, cylindrical pencil box in which he kept his discharge notice.

"Why?"

"Well, so that it doesn't get lost somehow, it's safer to keep it on you."

The rumors about the war held on stubbornly among the peasants—about war with the Englishwoman. No matter how absurd these rumors and stories, their general idea was that the heart of the matter had to do with the Englishwoman. Something happened, and we had to ally with the Englishwoman, but in order to do so, we had to convert her to our faith. If we don't succeed in converting the Englishwoman to our faith, there will be war.

The spring of 1876 arrived. Rumors circulated about the fact that the Turks were rioting against the Greeks.

"It's not against the Greek," the deacon, who had gone for a meal after prayers to a peasant's izba, remarked, "but against . . . what's-his-name, they've already collected money for him, that's it, against the Serb. Isn't that so, Aleksandr Nikolaevich?"

The sultan was murdered. The peddlers began to bring scarves with portraits of Lazar Sochitsa and others. Cherniaev showed up . . .

But none of this was real. All of this was considered a trifle. So what does the Englishwoman matter, how about China?[. . .]

But then the mobilization began.

There was a rumor that they would be taking the horses. Of course, no one knew what the horse levy would consist of. Not only the mass of the population, the peasants, but even we landowners, even the horse authority himself, did not know anything about what and how it would be. It was said that they would be collecting horses for the troops and that was it.

At first we thought that there would simply be a levy of horses like the levy for troops.

Everyone was lost in conjecture about how this would happen. It was said that the horses would be taken from those who had at least four, and if that was not enough, then from those who had three. Then they said that it would be simply stated how many horses the volost should supply and then you could do it as you wished: you could supply your own, or you could buy some to supply, or you could contribute money, and divide up the order as you knew how. Only one thing was unclear, what about the gentry's horses?[. . .]

The news came that they would come to select horses. Some guard or policeman brought the news at night, he did not explain anything further, he was in a great hurry, he said only, "They're coming to pick horses, they're coming, everyone should be at home." The elder, however, did not wake me up in the night and reported it only when I got up.

"Why did you not ask for more details, when are they coming?"

"He says they're coming."

"Yes, but when? What am I to do now?"

"He was in a great hurry, he had to run to Fedorovshchina, he said."

"But who is it who is coming?"

"The constable, he says, an officer, all of the authorities."

"So where is the constable?"

"At Madame Semenovskaia's estate."

"Well, that is nearby; that means that it will be soon. They can look things over in one day. There is no need to harness the horses for work, the authorities will not go into the forest to look at horses. Bring the sleigh to get ready; surely they will take a ride."

"And what do you want the hired hands to do?"

"Have them chop wood."

"And go after water?"

"Of course."

Outside there was snow, a blizzard. We did not have to wait long. They arrived early in the morning: the constable, an artillery officer, the horse authority. I, of course, as was proper, offered them a bite to eat. They refused, they did not have time, they said. Have your best horses brought here quickly.

"One by one?"

"No, all at once, only as quickly as possible."

I sent the orders. The constable asked how many horses I had, how many stallions, mares, geldings—and he recorded everything in a book. Meanwhile, the peasants brought the horses. We went out on the porch, the blizzard was blowing so that it was blinding; the constable stayed on the porch, but the officer took a ruler—they had that kind of black ruler that indicated that they were horse authorities, as an elder has a medal, the hundreder a nameplate, the land surveyer an astrolabe, the muzhiks carried this ruler *with special respect*—and began to measure the horses, shouting out something as he did it, and the constable put it down in the book. With that the entire examination was complete, they did not look at anything else, they were in a terrible hurry, they even refused to have a bite, they did not show any respect; and everything was already prepared in the dining room. Avdotia was insulted: she wanted the officer to try our ham.

"Why should they eat ours," she remarked, taking away an untouched plate, "they're used to city ham. Only, say what you will, Aleksandr Nikolaevich, but even city ham's no better than ours: I tried the ham that costs sixty kopeks; Georgii Danilych brought some from Petersburg, I know!"

And I learned nothing from the commission. They did not say anything, which horse was suitable, which was not suitable, which one they were taking, which one they were not taking.

"And can we harness them all for work?"

"You may, you may."

"And may I sell them?"

"You may."

"Which ones are you taking?"

They do not say. Ah, I think, they are probably afraid that I will feed the ones that they admired worse, that I will not give them any oats. They were in a terrible hurry. They took off for Fedorovshchina, and from there to the volost where all of the peasants' horses had been driven. They examined all of them in one day, and there are not a few horses in the volost. Thank you that it was done quickly; but, even so, you can still figure forty kopeks per horse [. . .]

Later we found out that the commission was only collecting data, that they were supposed only to count how many horses of what height there were in the district. The officer was sent, we came to understand, so that the constable got the numbers right, and the horse authority came so that the commission would have three members. They collected the data, and with that the business was finished. What happened further with it, we do not know. The commission did not explain anything to us, and probably did not know themselves what it was all about. They said that still another commission would be coming with a different officer who really knew about horses.

There was nothing, however. And then suddenly they called for the horses.

One night, an order came from the volost offices to bring all of the peasants' horses to the volost early in the morning, with the exception of the stallions, and to bring food and fodder along for three days.

"They're going to drive them to town," the policeman explained, "bring food and fodder for three days, they're going to drive them to town to be looked over."

We landowners did not receive any order of any kind in regard to horses. The next day, early in the morning, I went to the volost offices to find out what was going on and to see how they were going to choose horses. All of the peasants' horses were already gathered. The square was filled with loads of hay and horses. The tavern, situated at the required distance from the volost, was full, the trade in vodka and herring was going fast and furious. There were a lot of people in the other side of the tavern also, primarily forest wardens because all forest work, hauling firewood and so on had ceased, since all of the horses and people had been called to the volost.

They measured the horses again on the square, but this time it was no longer the constable with the officer, but the volost elder. They sent the horses that did not meet the necessary height home. I asked the elder, what is going on and how: how many horses are required, how will they pay for the horses?

"I don't know anything in detail," the elder answered. "The guy in charge of the horse bureau received a document from town and immediately told us to get all the peasants' horses together in the volost today, early in the morning."

"And where is the head of the horse bureau?"

"They themselves, as soon as they received the document, last evening already, left for town to find out what's going on and what they need to do, but they ordered me to measure the horses; any that don't meet the height requirement, send home, and the others are to wait until they get back themselves from town."

"And when is he going to be back?"

"He promised to be back at ten o'clock."

"So, and as for our horses: when are they going to be examined?"

"I don't know. There's nothing about the gentry's horses. The order was only to gather the peasants'."

"And where will the horses be received?"

"In town."

"And how many horses do they need?"

"I don't know anything. I heard that they want six horses, but I don't know for sure."

I walked around the square and looked at the remaining horses. In fact, all of the horses of the right height were left: old ones, lame ones, broken-down ones. It was clear that something was not right; it was impossible to suppose that such horses would be taken not only into the artillery, but even for pulling carts. We heard that the prices that had been set for the horses were large; so they will not be such fools, really, the inspectors and authorities, that they will choose any kind of trash or old things. At least half of the remaining horses were unsuitable. There is something wrong, it occurred to me, it cannot be that there, where they made the regulations about receiving the horses, that they do not understand what kind of losses there are for a farmer if he uselessly brings his workhorses to town and loses several days. I expressed my doubts to the elder.

"It is required that all the horses, all the horses come to town."

"But what is this old bag good for?" I pointed to an old white jade which was standing dejectedly, with its ribs sticking out. "She must be thirty years old, she doesn't even have any teeth."

"They're calling for all of 'em, all of 'em. The bureau chief said: 'The more horses that we bring to town, the better.' "

"Look, her ribs are sticking out." I thumped the horse on the side. "She doesn't want to face the Turk in her old age."

The muzhiks burst out laughing. The elder looked at them sternly.

"The authorities know what it's all about."

We waited for the bureau chief, and we waited. He did not show up. And did this all happen nearby? It is thirty-five versts to town. And outside it was freezing, there was a cold north wind, everyone froze standing on the square. Well, how could you not go by Borisych's in the tavern to warm up? A mass of people gathered in the drinking side and the other side of the tavern. Borisych was simply rubbing his hands, and prayed to God in his very soul that the chief did not come for a bit longer. He was still not there, still not there, so that one, then another ran in and knocked back a glass.

Evening began to fall, and the chief was still not there. It grew dark, I went home, and without even having found out anything.

That night I received the order—and *this all has to be at night!*—to bring horses to the volost in the morning. It was a strict order. In the order the prices were indicated which would be paid for the horses; the prices set were very high, not one of my horses was appropriate. For the very best of my horses I paid sixty rubles about six years ago, the rest, thirty to forty; there were several horses, bought for six rubles fifty kopeks, all old horses with flaws, which were suitable only for agricultural work. It was clear that my horses were not even suitable for pulling wagons, and why would the state pay sixty to ninety rubles for a horse they could buy for twenty? However, in fulfillment of the instructions, I sent all of the horses to the volost with my steward, having left only one for hauling water to the livestock: was I to leave the livestock without water? and I set out myself after them with a team of three.

At the volost I found my horses and the horses from the estates of landowners who are *not wealthy,* who themselves do not live in the country; and several priests' horses. There were no horses from *wealthy* landowners. The volost elder had already measured my horses and ordered that all those which met the measurement requirement should be taken to town as quickly as possible, but my steward had waited for me to get there: for *us* the volost elder is not an authority, we have our own authority. At that point, neither I, nor the steward, nor the *volost elder himself,* knew that the volost elder was the bureau chief's assistant and therefore he, although he was not an authority over us as a volost elder, was *an authority as the chief's assistant.*

Again, the volost elder could not explain anything. He only kept saying the same thing.

"It is ordered that all horses which pass the measurement be sent to town. Yesterday they drove the peasants' horses, today the gentry horses are ordered."

"Yes, but judge for yourself, surely you understand horses yourself, so, look, the dun one, what is he good for? He is twenty years old."

"I see. It is ordered."

"But, look at the bay—he's broken-down."

"Of course, I see."

"And these: the light brown one with the black mane and tail, and that brown one—they are broken-down."

"It is ordered . . ."

"That it is ordered, yes it is ordered—you keep saying the same thing! Surely you know yourself what kind of prices they have set for the horses; so, for what reason will the state pay money for this kind of horse? What, am I to take such horses to town in vain? You say bring ten horses now—but why should I waste my time? You know that this will cost me at least twenty rubles."

"It is ordered."

"Write a document, then I will take them. Go to the clerk, show me the regulations, you should have written regulations."

"We don't have any regulations; the bureau chief has the regulations, but he didn't leave us any."

We went to the volost offices. The clerk also did not know anything or acted as if he did not know anything.

"May I see the order?"

"We don't have it."

"And where is the bureau chief?"

"At home. And we also need to go examine the horses right away in P., F., O. . . ."

"Why? Are they not going to bring those horses here?"

The volost elder fell silent.

"We're going to look those over at home."

So that's how it is! I thought. They are going to examine the horses of the wealthy, powerful landowners at home, but we had to bring ours to the volost. No, brother, stop there, something is not quite right!

"And why is that?" I ask.

"It is ordered."

"The horses are working on B.'s estate now, but I had to bring all of the horses, my workers are idle. You know that this all is a dead loss. You know that the stallions on B. are not for breeding, but are the same kind of workhorses."

The elder exchanged glances with the clerk.

"I told'ya it'd be like this," the clerk remarked.

"Ask the sexton Borisych to draw up a document. Then I will send the horses to town."

"No, it's better if I send for the chief."

They sent for the chief. I remained to wait for the chief. Others also stayed behind: the manager of a neighboring estate, the deacon, and so on. No one, of course, wanted to take horses to town for no use. We went to Borisych's to have a drink and a bite to eat. After a while, the bureau chief arrived and began to apologize that he had disturbed me by mistake, that he had wanted to examine my horses also at home, that he had even gone by, but I had already left, and so on.

I asked him to let me read the written order. The chief, while I read it, went to look over my horses. Having run through the order, I immediately saw that everything had not been done as the order instructed.

But meanwhile, the chief, having rejected several, ordered that the rest be taken to town. Coming out again onto the square, I pointed out to him that there were horses with defects among the ones he had selected and that in general not a single horse was worth more than half the price that had been set. He kept stating, "The more horses they take to town, the better," and did not pay any attention whatsoever to my remarks that it was a loss for the farmer to take the horse in vain, that it was a loss for the government, that it was ruining the producers and the taxpayers on whom the entire burden of the war was falling, that there was no economic rationale and it was not in the government's interests. He just kept repeating his, "the more horses they take, the better." I asked how many horses were required, how many horses had been presented voluntarily, I tried to explain that he was not handling the business correctly, not as ordered, I said that I would not present such horses in vain as some kind of joke, but if he wanted to and had the right to take them, then let him take them, and we will write a document to that effect. I became convinced from my conversation with him that either he had not read the order or that he did not understand it, it is more likely that he had not read it. Our argument got more and more heated, but I, even so, defended the horses, I did not send them to town, and I even took a receipt that said that I had done all that was required.

Everyone envied me afterward. It turned out, of course, they had taken their horses for no reason and had only wasted their money. It is difficult, of course, to calculate all of the expenses which the peasants, primarily, carried. But the expenses were not small, if you take into account the time that the horses and people were idle. For the tavern keepers, both in the volost and in town, there was income, of course.

They took horses for pulling wagons. They said that they took even a lot of useless ones, but I myself did not see, I only heard it from the peasants and dealers who got rid of cheap and old horses. This horse levy was very profitable for many people because horses were very cheap last fall. They said later that when these horses that had been collected but not broken in were harnessed to military vehicles that they had terrible trouble with them: one wouldn't go, another kicked, which, they said, killed some people . . . Again, I did not see anything, but passing soldiers described it.[12]

The regulation about the horse levy was designed well. It was clear that those who prepared it aimed, as far as possible, to make the execution of the horse levy easier. They set good prices for the horses, and if you keep in mind that they paid little attention to appearance, gait, even to age, then one can consider the prices high, for our locality at least. Furthermore, anyone who presented his horses voluntarily then received 20 percent above the set price; they were to call for stallions only if there was no one willing to present his horses voluntarily. The whole business was supposed to be done publicly, openly. Attention was given to the effort not to drive the horses in vain, not to hold them uselessly; it was even written that the official, when examining the horses, had to have the order with him. Those who had written the regulation, obviously, understood that one should not uselessly ruin people up front on whom the entire burden of the war is falling. But those who executed the order, the nearest authorities, the elders and stewards, did not think anything about this and knew only, "Drive them, it is ordered."

All of this is entirely understandable: the illiterate elder, who does not know any laws whatsoever, who does not have any notion of legality, who is almost always drunk, knows only one thing—it is an order from the authorities and the muzhik only must fulfill his, the elder's, orders, without fail.

Currently, all of our rural authorities are disciplined in the most excellent manner, and whatever they are ordered to do, they will do without any discussion at all: Take this person and bring him to town—they will bring him; take this person and flog him—they will flog him. The elder and steward do not think about anything else, they do not concern themselves with anything else except the unconditional execution of the authorities' orders. Discipline has reached perfection. "Drive, it is ordered!"

The levy of noncommissioned officers, the levy of the militia—all of this was utterly splendid. Everything was orderly, disciplined, and I think that in no country could the mobilization be done so quickly, so precisely as in Russia. Everything was prepared ahead of time, everything was explained to the elders in advance, it was explained accurately, in detail, firmly, in Russian, almost as if the elders were shown future "medals" in advance. The elders, in turn, disciplined the village elders, and the local militia explained everything to them accurately: an order is coming, "take, drive, do it quickly, and if not . . ." And the elder has a healthy fist. Everything was prepared: a guard was always on duty at the volost offices who was to distribute the orders to the nearest villages. The village elders knew all of the noncommissioned officers and men in the militia in their volost and where they were located; it was forbidden to go far away for wage labor: feed yourself right here in the region, and they watched after them closely. The local militia in the villages were also trained: horses and drivers were equipped everywhere. The order came, couriers flew around the villages, drivers harnessed the horses in a minute, they galloped as if to a fire, took the noncommissioned men and quickly took them to town in the allotted time. No one asked, "Why, what for?" It was ordered: get them, bring them, drive them.

The rural authorities fulfilled their task irreproachably, there were few mistakes on their part; only once, having received an order about retired soldiers—and this was not foreseen, and the retired soldiers began to shout. "We are completely retired," they said, "we have served our time, no matter what they order, we are not going!" The elder decided that if they were calling for retired soldiers it meant, "Our Tsar has had a loss," then he should drive the retirees in all the more and he sent those on indefinite leave. They got a dressing-down for this: don't make decisions. It was lucky even that the retired soldiers, out of joy over being released, did not decide to sue the elder for losses. However, after several days, these retired soldiers were called for as well, so that there was no time to file suit. It was all the same. There was nothing to sue for. For this was also—the authorities.[. . .]

Yes, all of this was set up excellently. There was only one thing they did not know how to do: help the soldiers' wives, children, and mothers in a timely fashion.

Mitrofanikha came by, her nursing infant died. Everything was easier: now she could hire herself out as a day laborer, and her daughter will take the blind grandmother around the commune. It is all easier . . .

Today, returning from the village, I met Mitrofan's mother on the dam: she was begging around the commune with another daughter-in-law, the wife of Mitrofan's brother.

"Greetings, sir."

"Greetings. Where are you coming from?"

"I've been going for crusts of bread. I was at my daughter-in-law's. Her son died."

"I know, I heard."

"He died. How many times did I tell her: 'Look, don't swear at him! I know it's hard on you, only don't curse, you never know, you don't know when your time will come!' She said, 'Little mother, I never curse him: let him live, God be with him!' He died. Well, and so it is better, everything is easier."

"Everything is easier . . ."

Letter VII

✉   The seventh letter was undoubtedly the most important in the series as Engelgardt's apotheosis of Populist principles.[1] It appeared in two segments in January and February 1879. The central issues Engelgardt addresses in this letter are collectivism, individualism, and exploitation as competing tendencies in the peasant mentality and as competing trends in village culture.

He opens with an admiring description of a group of rural specialists, diggers. Working together in a labor collective called an artel, these diggers display both a collectivist mentality and efficient, skilled labor, the perfect combination in Engelgardt's view. As an anecdotal account of how the artel functions, this sketch is useful for historians and students. As a statement on labor relations, it reveals the depth of Engelgardt's desire for an escape from the mechanistic, individualistic, contractual, and exploitative arrangements he considers to be the alternative to the artel.

Shifting from the artel, Engelgardt examines the extended patriarchal peasant household as another example of the virtues of collective enterprise. His discussion of the advantages of large households, made up of several generations working and living together as one economic unit, was consistent with the opinion held by most educated Russians that large families prospered, while small families almost inevitably fell into financial ruin. While lacking the type of statistical analysis that would dominate the discussion of this issue in the press, Engelgardt's explication was one of the best in exploring the personal concerns of the various actors, and also thoroughly typical in identifying the culprits in the divisions. As did his peers, Engelgardt points his finger straight at the women, at the babas, and picks up where he left off in the fifth letter in investing them with pernicious, selfish, even stupid individualism.

Engelgardt concludes the first half of the seventh letter with a vignette that illustrates the peasants' ability to undermine the state's tutelage as well as their narrow comprehension of formal law by describing the peasants' response to the order that they plant birch trees along the village street as a fire-prevention measure. First he explains the idiocy of the measure, then how the peasants, who understand the futility of the exercise of planting seedlings, simply break off branches from trees elsewhere, sharpen the ends, and stick them in the ground for the benefit of the local official who comes by to inspect the execution of the order. Engelgardt clearly considers the peasants the brighter of the actors in this episode. That view is confirmed by the report of the local agent who explained to his superiors that "by no means do all the birches planted in the villages survive, although they are planted everywhere—their withering results for the most part from [the peasants'] ignorance of planting methods. . . ."[2]

The second half of the seventh letter marks Engelgardt's shift of focus, his determination to find a way out of the implications of his deepening realization that individualism and the urge to exploit are present among the peasantry and thus are not the peculiar sins of the Westernized gentry. Returning to the beloved model of the artel, he urges his St. Petersburg and Moscow readers to take up the task of farming. In an effort both to retain the virtues of the manual labor of the muzhik, and to place his hopes on enlightened educated youth, rather than on mercenary "parasite-leeches" in the form of peasant renters and kulaks, he proposes a new form of farming in Russia: collectives of educated people who learn to work like muzhiks and join together to rent and cultivate the abandoned estates of gentry landowners. This letter was written at the height of activity on Engelgardt's estate as a school for young people who came to live and work like muzhiks. Clearly excited by the possibilities before his eyes, Engelgardt exuberantly declares that two years of study on such a farm can provide the educated young man or woman all he or she needs to be a good working hand in farming

⊠ ⊠ ⊠

The Diggers' Artel as a Model of Collective Labor

Once in the autumn, and this was soon after I arrived on the estate, I happened to go look at some digging work. That autumn the diggers worked for me by the day and were clearing meadows overgrown with willow bushes.

The diggers were sitting around the fire and eating lunch.

"Bread and salt!"[3]

"Welcome!"

"Thank you."

[Engelgardt here writes a twenty-page discussion of the peasant diet and stresses its rationale for the laboring man, while contrasting it with accepted notions of diet and nutrition among educated Russians.]

I confess that I passionately love these diggers, or it is better to say, the diggers' artels. There is something special, noble, honorable, rational in them and this *something* is commonly true of them, distinctive to them, only as *artel* diggers. A man can be a swindler, a drunkard, a villain, a kulak, a scoundrel as a man in and of himself, but as an artel digger he is honest, sober, and conscientious when he is in the artel.

Not far from me on the other side of the Dnieper there are several volosts where diggers live, diggers of long standing, from time immemorial, who were already working at this trade during serfdom. The diggers' specialty is earth-work: digging ditches, ponds, graves, clearing dams, digging up meadows, digging up peat, tilling gardens, trimming parks, in a word, all jobs done with a spade and a wheelbarrow. But if need be, the diggers' artels will do any other kind of farm work: they will dig up stumps, woods, bushes, they will mow, plough, thresh, in a word, they will do everything that needs to be done on a farm. Diggers do all farm jobs well because they are themselves farmers and work at farming at home while the diggers' trade serves them only as a supplement.

Diggers of long standing from time immemorial who have worked at dig-ging from generation to generation have reached the highest degree of perfec-tion in farm work. One should see how a digger cuts the land, cutting out, for example, a pond—how much dirt he puts in a wheelbarrow, how he hauls the wheelbarrow! One should see how he handles pieces of sod with a shovel! To what perfection, to what elegance the work is taken! A digger seems to work slowly: he carefully looks over the layout of the job, as if to orient himself better. He carefully selects the type of shovel he needs, digs the earth slowly, accurately so that there will not be a single crumb left, not a single crumb falls from the spade, he knows that this will all be wasted work, that all of these crumbs will have to be lifted again to the same height from which they fell. It is impossible not to admire diggers' work all the more since you do not see that the digger has made any special effort, that he has suffered over the work, that he has exerted his muscles in any special way. There is none of this. He works as if he were playing, as if it were very easy: he digs out the sod, the blocks of dirt of a pud's weight each and takes it out to the wheelbarrow just as if he were cutting slices of cheese. This is all done so easily that it seems as if you could do it yourself.

You will only understand how difficult this diggers' work is, how much knowledge it requires, when you see a young man who is just beginning, who has entered the artel recently, working side by side with an old experienced digger. The old one will have already dug out his share of dirt and sat down to smoke his pipe—he has finished his share, while the young one is still working on his share: his blocks of dirt are not the same, and the dirt crumbles and he has a lot of cleaning up to do, and he turns the wheelbarrow over without having brought it to the end of the planks, he has to clean up. The old ones have done their share, have rested, it is already time to start on a new section, but for the young one there is no time to rest because he needs to do as much as the other members of the artel. Let us suppose that each member in the artel receives his pay for the number of cubic meters of dirt he has carried away, but still they eat together, it would be shameful to lag behind the artel. And so, having sucked on his pipe nervously, and rested for a total of some minute or so, the young digger again takes up the shovel and hurries onto his section. The diggers' skill at farm work stands out even more clearly if you look at the same work as it is done by ordinary peasants who are not diggers. I have only to look at the spot from which they have taken the dirt to determine unerringly who did the work: diggers or ordinary peasants. Where it was not diggers who took the dirt it is immediately obvious that people did an enormous amount of unproductive labor, that they wasted their strength uselessly. Peasants, however, almost never take on real digging work now and if a ditch or pond needs to be dug in the village, they hire diggers.[. . .]

I don't know whether it is because of the comparative prosperity, resulting from high earnings, or the peculiarities of diggers' work which requires skill, but the diggers are very intelligent and clever. To say nothing about the fact that a real digger splendidly figures out how to construct a ditch in order to dry out a meadow, to drain the water excellently; he makes dams and drains to repair the worst spot on the road in the cheapest manner—the constable himself with all of his "chicken stealers"[4] could do it no better—he calculates the volume of a dug-up pond (there is always a special, intelligent man in the artel for this), he puts up markers to survey a spot. It is also remarkable that diggers possess great taste, they love to do everything so that it is pretty and elegant. For work in parks and gardens, cleaning out wastelands, if someone wants to combine the useful with the pleasant, the diggers are simply a treasure. Even German gardeners who scorn the "Russian swine, the muzhik," value diggers. In fact, one has only to tell a digger to build such and such a path, lay out the sod, dig up the flower bed, make an embankment, a drainage ditch, and he will immediately understand what needs to be done and he will do everything so well, with such taste, with such accuracy that even a German will be amazed.[. . .]

Diggers, in sum, are among the prosperous peasants of our region. After the Emancipation several villages managed to purchase large gentry houses next to their villages. They pay cash rent for water meadows for the most part.[5] At home, diggers farm, but in the winter, many villages work at calcining lime, and breaking off and mining limestone. The wages from digging constitute a great financial supplement for them. The most important thing for the diggers is to have earnings as close to home as possible. Diggers, reliable farmers at least, do not go for distant work, on the railroad, only some kind of impoverished single men do, men who have abandoned the land.

Diggers mainly look for work nearby on the estates of neighboring landowners. Now that gentry farms have begun to decline, there has been less work, diggers have joined together in small artels of five to ten men and they value work at landowners' highly, especially for young landowners, zealous ones, novices who settle on the farm with money, who know little about the business, who love to dig ditches in fields, to dig little ponds, which is why they quickly squander their bit of money on digging jobs which are often completely useless for the farm.

[Engelgardt digresses to discuss the peasants' attitude toward "mental labor."]

Diggers never hire themselves to work for the entire summer, but only at the spring shift, from April twenty-fifth to July first and for the fall shift, from

August twenty-fifth to October twenty-second. During the summer itself, from July first to August twenty-fifth, the time for hay making and the grain harvest, consequently, they work at home.

In the spring, as soon as the snow is gone, the diggers' foremen set out to gentry they know to look for work. Having looked around and considered the job, the foreman will determine how large the artel should be, he will negotiate the wages—how much per day, cubic meter, sazhen of ditch, and then he will go home. When the time to work arrives, the foreman appears with his artel, in which he works alongside the others if the artel is not too large and if everyone is working in one place.

As for housing, diggers, like all Russian people, from the rich merchant to the poorest shepherd boy, are not demanding—as long as there is a stove where he can dry out his wet socks and cook his meals. Diggers usually hire themselves out, providing their own meals, and if the artel is large, they keep a cook; if the artel is not large, one of the diggers prepares the meals, which he manages to do before breakfast.

The foreman, as I have already said, works equally with the other diggers, eats the same food that the others do. The foreman mediates between the employer and the artel. The employer does not know the members of the artel, he does not interfere in its internal affairs, he does not set their tasks, he has no direct accounting with them. The employer knows only the foreman, who manages everything, answers for the work, receives the money, takes in the food, handles the accounts with the employer. The foreman's significance is completely different in diggers' artels than in carpenters' artels, where the foreman usually is a manager who takes on work at his own risk, who takes all the profit from it and carries all its losses, and the members of the artel are simple hired hands who are hired by the manager-boss for a set pay per month and meals at his, the boss's, expense.

In the diggers' artels, all of the members are equal, they eat together and they pay for the food out of the total amount they earn, from which each one then receives as much as he has earned according to the number of cubic meters he has hauled away, the number of sazhens he has dug, and so on. The work, although it is taken on in common by the entire artel, is divided: when they dig a ditch, they measure it off into sections of equal length (usually ten sazhens each), they cast lots to see who digs what section because the earth is not the same everywhere, and each one, including the foreman along with everyone else, digs his section; if they are clearing away bushes or digging up small stumps, they also divide the desiatina into sections (plots) and again each one receives his section through casting lots. In a word, all of the work *is divided up,* if this is possible of course, and *each one is paid according to the amount he has done.* In this regard the foreman has the sole advantage over the other members of the artel that, in addition to the money he earns with his own hands, he receives so-called bast-shoe money, that is, a certain percent, five or ten kopeks per ruble, from the joint earnings. The foreman receives this money for his trouble: going out to find work, which is why it is called bast-shoe money, choosing food, settling accounts with the employer, conversations with him regarding the work, during which the foreman loses work time, and has extra expenses for clothes and so forth. But, chiefly, the foreman receives this percentage for the fact that he found work with a familiar employer. This is clear from the fact that now that there is less work, this percentage has risen because the foreman, especially if he got good work, in putting the artel together, tries to squeeze a bit and negotiate a high percentage for himself.[. . .]

The diggers always have excellent behavior in the artel; there is no drunkenness, no noise, no fighting, no stealing, no swindling. The artel not only keeps an eye on its members, but protecting its good name from any kind of suspicion, it also observes everything that is done on the estate, to make sure that there is no kind of stealing over which suspicion could fall on the diggers. All of the diggers are happy to drink vodka, love to drink, and when they are idle at home, they drink a lot, in the Russian manner, several days without a break, but there are neither drunkards nor is there drunkenness in the artel. No one in the artel drinks alone, and if they drink, they drink when everyone agrees to, everyone together, during their free time, when it does not interfere with work. When they begin work, for example, they drink a glass "for showing up." When they finish a job, they drink one "for taking off," and on this occasion they drink a lot; during the work itself, they drink a little, when it is cold, damp, and if the work is especially difficult.[6] All of this, just as with any change in the meals, is done through mutual consent. In general, the accord in the artel is remarkable and only the work is divided up, and then no one helps anyone else, even if someone is killing himself on the job.

During the spring shift, the diggers work only until the first of July. After St. Peter's Day, there is no way to keep them—just deduct what you want from their pay. No one will remain, they abandon everything and leave. The foreman is to settle everything as best he knows how. After they have returned home, the artel members settle accounts. First of all a certain percentage is taken out of the earnings, through mutual consent, for the local church for the icon of the Holy Mother of Kazan, who is especially revered by the diggers, since both the spring and fall shifts end with the holiday of the Virgin of Kazan; then the bast-shoe money for the boss is taken out, the cost of the food is calculated, and the rest is divided among the members of the artel according to each one's earnings. After they have caroused for several days and celebrated the summer day of the Virgin of Kazan, July eighth, the diggers take up mowing and work excessively hard the entire harvest season so that they even visibly lose weight; at the end of August they go again on diggers' jobs on the fall shift and return home by the winter day of the Virgin of Kazan, October twenty-second. After they have celebrated the day of the Virgin of Kazan, and made merry at weddings, they settle in on their winter jobs.

Currently there are neither drunkards nor swindlers in the real diggers' artels, that is, they, if you please, exist, but they are restrained by the artel because they are not yet total alcoholics. But of course, even among the diggers there are total drunkards, there are also thieves, who are capable of stealing even from their fellow diggers, there are also brawlers, swindlers, shrews, people who are not capable of getting along anywhere, not artel people, as the muzhiks say. Not a single artel will accept such people. Finally there are those who are not very strong, old people, dull-witted people, people who have failed at farming, who do not want to hire themselves out as day laborers, who do not want to abandon their farms, who cannot even enter the artel because they cannot obligate themselves for the entire shift. All such people do not stay in artels or the artels do not keep them. Usually such diggers work alone, they hire themselves out to landowners where there is a small amount of work that is not enough for an artel. The best of them, who have suffered a decline due to a breakup of their households or from a misfortune, look for work with nearby landowners they know where they worked previously in artels; the worst ones, the ones who have gone to drink and the old men, hire themselves out in the villages to dig ditches, ponds, and so forth for peasants. Sometimes alcoholic men working on their own will join the artel, the cleverest of them are even picked as foremen and they find work somewhere. But such irregular artels often end a job dishonorably: they will take on a job that they do not have the manpower to do, they drink up, they eat up, they take the money in advance, but they do not finish the job and leave when harvest time arrives, leaving, for example, an unfinished pond so that the village will be left without a watering hole in the hot weather. The victims of such artels are novice landowners, and even more, good-hearted and trusting peasants in the commune who sometimes hire an artel of diggers to clean ponds and so forth with the entire village paying. For this reason experienced farmers hold onto foremen with whom they have had good relations before and artels which they know.

I said earlier that diggers generally live comfortably, but in essence, all of them could also live well and even prosperously.[. . .] Spring and autumn earnings give the diggers a clear profit of up to thirty-five rubles per person, and sometimes even more, depending on the kind of work that falls their way, and what kind of weather there is; it is possible to pay taxes out of these earnings and rent a water meadow which brings in a good profit even if they sell the hay and don't use it to feed the horses on their own farm. Finally, in the villages which calcine lime, there are also good winter earnings.

How could anyone not live well, it would seem, in such circumstances? But even so, although in general (counting the wealthy ones as well) the well-being of diggers' villages is higher than the well-being of the majority of simple peasant villages, still, even so, even in diggers' villages, side by side with the rich ones there are a multitude of naked poor peasants who have abandoned the land and hired themselves out as hired hands. What is the cause, the root of this phenomenon? The reason for this lies in the fact that even diggers who organize their workers' artels so well, *work individually, separately, on their own farms,* they cannot, they do not try, they do not even think about organizing farming collectives to carry out farming together.

In my letters I have already indicated many times the strong development of individualism among the peasants, their isolation in action, their inability, it is better to say lack of desire, to join together in farming for a common task. Other investigators of peasant daily life also have pointed to this. Some even suggest that it is contrary to the spirit of the peasantry to do anything together. I disagree with this completely. The entire matter consists in how one looks at a common task. In fact it *is* contrary to the peasants to do something together, wholesale, as the peasants say, to do it so that it is impossible to calculate the work of each one separately. They will not enter this kind of joint effort on a job, given the current level of their development, at least. Although it does happen even now, that when necessary,[7] when it cannot be done otherwise, peasants will work together, even now. Collectives that hire themselves out to thresh, to haul manure, to mow serve as an example of this. But peasants join together extremely easily and willingly for jobs on the *artel principle,* like that of the diggers' artel, where the work is divided and each one receives pay for his own work.[. . .]

But, one wonders, why is it impossible then to farm on the artel principle? Below in this same letter, I will return to this important question again.

Extended Peasant Households, Collective Labor, and Prosperity

The best example of the significance of *doing work together* in farming, united in joint living quarters, is the prosperity of large peasant households and their impoverishment when they break up.

The peasant household is prosperous as long as the family is large and consists of a sizable number of workers, as long as there exists any kind of family union, as long as the land is not divided and the jobs are done together. Usually this union is preserved only as long as the elder is alive and falls apart upon his death. The stricter the elder, the more despotic, the more forceful morally, the greater is the respect he receives from the commune, the more *economic* order there is in the household, the more prosperous the household is. Only a forceful character can be a strict despot-manager, one who knows how to hold the reins of control by the force of his mind. And that kind of intelligent, forceful man is without fail, along with that, also a good manager who can, as the muzhiks put it, plan everything well; on the farm itself a good plan is the first concern because with a good plan the work will both go faster and turn out well.

But, no matter how important the head of the household's plan is, even so, the fundamental cause of prosperity and relative well-being of large, undivided families lies in the fact that the land is not divided, the work is done together, the whole family eats out of one bowl. The proof of this lies in the fact that large families live well, even with a weak old man, a bad manager who does not know how to keep the household in order.

I know of one household which consists of the old man, his wife, and five married brothers. The old man is no good at all, old, feeble, not a leader, works on the farm only around the house and does not enter into general management. One of the brothers is considered to be the head of the household. All of the brothers, although they are splendid workers, are not very bright and lively people, they are meek, slow, as the peasants say, even dense, completely under the control of their wives. But the babas are, as though through natural selection, from one splendid one to the next, intelligent—of course in their own, baba's way—they are healthy, strong, all of them know how to work splendidly and in fact do work splendidly when they are working *not for the household, but for themselves,* for example, when in the winter they brake flax for me and receive money for *their own use.*

Farming in this household is in complete disorder: the women do not obey the household head or their husbands, they go to work late, whoever goes out earlier waits for the others, they work badly in a slipshod manner, considerably worse than hired hands; every baba watches so as not to over-work, not to do any more than another one. All of the inside, women's, domestic work is divided up. Thus, rather than make one of the women the mistress who would prepare the meals and bake the bread, all of the women are mistresses in turn and bake bread weekly—one woman one week, another the next; all of the women go for water and watch to see that no one has to bring back an extra bucket of water, even the pregnant women, or those who have just given birth, even the young girl who has not come into her full strength—the daughter of the oldest brother—has to bring her fair share of water. In just the same way they milk the cows; every baba washes her husband's and children's laundry separately; each one gives her husband a separate towel to dry his hands before lunch; each one washes *her little section* of the table where they eat.

It happened in this household that three women had nursing children at the same time whom they needed to feed kasha made with milk, whereas there was only one cow in the winter, who had calved early, so that all of the milk had to go to the nursing children. It would seem that it would be easier for the mistress to milk the cow daily and cook a common pot of kasha with milk for all of the children. No, every day, one of the nursing women, in turn, milked the cow, divided the milk into three equal portions, and every baba separately cooked kasha for her child; finally, even this was not enough—probably they feared that the one who did the milking could hide some milk—they began to do it this way: the babas milked the cow in turn, and she who milked received all the milk for her child, that is, today one sister-in-law milked the cow and received all the milk for herself and then cooked her child's kasha with this milk for three days; tomorrow another sister-in-law milked the cow and received all the milk for herself; day after tomorrow, the third . . .

Even in fieldwork, the babas of this household are eternally keeping track; everyone mows a separate plot and, if she leaves high stubble, then all of the others will leave just the same. In a word, they work worse than hired hands. The babas of this household even carry out separate money-making operations independent of the household: one of the women, for example, rents a few plots of land from peasants, independent of the household, with her own money, plants barley and flax for her own use; another feeds hogs at her own expense and sells them for her profit.

However, even given this kind of disorder, *even so, the household remains prosperous:* there are no arrears, there is plenty of grain, there are seven horses and eight cows, good tack, the women have fancy clothes, the men have boots, red shirts, and blue coats, there is extra money. And the home is called a household of "rich people." And why is that? Because *the land is not divided* into small plots, because *the plots are large,* the work is done *together,* they thresh in *one* barn, they put their hay in *one* larder, they feed their livestock in *one* courtyard, they live in *one* house, they heat up *one* stove, they eat out of *one* bowl.[. . .] Such an extended family household, even with a weak head of household, although it may not be so rich, even so, will live without want; and there will be no arrears, and there will be enough grain, they will not be forced to work as rural hired hands, and as for having to go begging for "crusts of bread," there is not even any suggestion of that.

But suddenly the old man dies. The sons of some of the brothers have begun to grow up—they could be made shepherds. One brother has no children, another has only daughters. The babas begin to eat away at their husbands, "It's slavery to work for someone else's children," "Look, Senka left the land, hired himself out to the lord as a herdsman, he receives seventy-five rubles with meals and he set his wife up in a little house. She doesn't reap, she doesn't plough, she sits like a lady and does spinning just for herself," and so on and so forth. The force which united the family and held it together in one household has cracked. And so, despite the fact that "one man is no warrior in the field," that "for one person there's no fighting over kasha," that "company in distress makes the trouble less," the household begins to break up.

Instead of one household there are, for example, three. The fields are divided into narrow little plots, which it is impossible even to cultivate well, because it is impossible not only to plough, but even to harrow: the baba wanders around with the harrow, circles, and it's still no use. Everyone works separately on his own plot. They thresh in three barns, and that is even good, if having divided they gather the forces to build three barns. But usually, the barn remains the common barn for three and each one threshes his grain there in turn separately, so how can they manage to thresh for seeds in time and keep the grain clean? One has pure rye, the other threshed yesterday for seeds and has straw in his. No one takes care of the barn, there is no master for it, no one repairs it on time. Each one gathers his hay separately on his plots and, if something turns out well because each works for himself, and not for the household, then it is lost as a result of the fact that one person can't take advantage of good weather, the way an artel will. They put hay in three separate larders. They feed the livestock in three separate yards and, for their care, for laying feed it takes three people, where it used to take only one to do this. Three women tend to watering the cattle, where before one did. Three heads of household go to the mill to thresh. Three stoves are heated up, three mistresses bake bread, they eat out of three bowls. All of the essential "spoons" and "dishes" seem like trifles to anyone who does not know the reality, but just try and acquire everything. If a large trough in which they fed six pigs in a wealthy household costs a ruble, then three little troughs cost no longer a ruble, but approximately, maybe two.

Calculate everything, calculate the work, and you will see what kind of enormous loss of energy occurs, when out of one household there are made three, or even much worse than that—five.

The inevitable result of a household division must be poverty. Almost everything gained in a division goes to the construction of new izbas, new yards, new larders, new barns, fences, for the purchase of new washtubs, pots, bowls, "spoons and things." "Wealthy peasants" have divided and here one household of "wealthy peasants" usually turns into three poor households. Of course, it does happen that even with a division the households remain prosperous. This happens in those cases when the "old man" had a lot of money saved up, when he had an entire village, when, except for him, "the wealthy one," all of the rest were utterly poor, when all the rest of the peasants in the village owed him money. Then, out of the divided household of the "rich man" three households of "rich people" are formed, for whom all the rest of the village poor work as hired hands. But this happens rarely;[. . .] they divided, and from one "rich man's" household three poor ones are made. Everyone knows this, everyone understands this, and, still, even so, they divide, because each one wants to live independently, in his own little house, according to his own will, every baba wants to be the "head woman."[8]

People say that babas cause all household divisions. Talk with anyone you want. Even the priest will tell you that divisions are the greatest evil and that babas cause them. And the priest will say this, agreeing out of habit, he will confirm this, because there is no reason for the priest to be against divisions since they are profitable for him: one household—one service; two households—two services; at most five rubles go for the sacraments from a rich household (five services), but from five poor, divided households, it would be a low estimate to say two rubles come out of it for two services.[. . .]

And every muzhik says that divisions are an evil, ruin, that all divisions come from the babas because the peasants are "weak" now, and women have been given a lot of leeway, because the Tsaritsa gave the babas a manifesto that said they could not be beaten.[. . .]

Individualism of the Peasant Woman

In this way everything, it is said, results from babas, all of the divisions are because of babas, all of the scenes are because of babas, babas are very strong in the village now.

In fact, as far as I have been able to observe, individualism is more highly developed among babas than among muzhiks; babas are still more egotistical, even less capable of a joint task—unless this task is ganging up to curse someone—less humane, more heartless. The muzhik, on his own, if he is away from the house, away from the influence of babas, can still do something in common; he does not keep track so much in common work, he is less egotistical, more capable of working for the general good of the household, artel, commune, of living jointly, and most important, a muzhik does not gossip, does not spread rumors, does not bear a grudge. A muzhik relies on his mind, his strength, his ability to work. A baba does not rely on either her mind or her strength or her ability to work; a baba places all of her hopes on her beauty, on her femininity, and if she once succeeds in sensing her beauty, that is the end.

I have decidedly observed that those villages where babas rule, where babas have mastered the men, live more poorly, work worse, do not farm as well as those where the men are the masters. In such babas' villages, the men are more idealistic, less forceful, more likely to submit to the kulak in their village who has become powerful and gathered the babas in his hands. It is just the same in separate households where the babas have mastered the men, there is none of that unity of spirit, order in farming, quickness to work. However, I must say that if the babas have become the masters in one or two households in some village then this spreads to all of the households in the village. And if the babas in the village gain control once, then every new one who comes to the village through marriage immediately falls into the general spirit. There is a remarkable natural selection in this regard: where the babas are the masters, there, of course, the babas are splendid, rare is the one who cannot carry an osmina of rye, they are strong, healthy, excellent workers in their ability to do everything, they are excellent musicians; when the men are in control, the babas are worse, beaten, unattractive, worn-out. When she marries, a girl looks to see what kind of village she is entering: a splendid one will go to the first village, the worse one will go to the second, because the babas beat her down in the first one. And the babas also watch to see who comes to them and they cultivate the new arrival in their own fashion.

One can explain the men's greater capacity to do joint labor by the fact that they are freer, more experienced, have seen more of the world, have lived more in artels, have been imbued with the artel spirit, have become, as the muzhiks put it, artel people, that is, more humane people, capable of restraining their egotistical instincts, of yielding to others, of yielding to the common will, common needs, common well-being.

But still the babas have more highly developed initiative than the men. Babas will more quickly take up a new task as long as it is personally profitable for them, the babas. The babas are somehow more greedy for money, for small change, without any accounting for the future, as long as they receive more money right away. You can do everything with money with babas more quickly than you can with the men. This is to the kulaks' advantage and they always try to bridle the babas, and as soon as this is done, the household or village is in the hands of the village kulak who then has control of everything. The muzhik has a certain decorum, a certain understanding of the honor of his village; therefore, there are many things he will not do in order not to ruin the dignity of the village. With the babas, first and foremost is money. A baba will sell any young girl in the village for money, a sister, even a daughter, to say nothing of herself. "It's not soap, you don't use it up," "It's not a puddle, something will be left for the husband too," the baba reckons. But the muzhik, a real muzhik, who has not been corrupted by gentry wiles, who is not under a baba's command, will not sell her for anything. And once a girl is sold, they will sell all of the girls in the village, or make it possible, even for free, it is better to say, *so that all of them will be equal.* Those looking for village virgins know this very well and always make use of it. The morals of village babas are incredibly simple: money, some kind of shawl, in certain circumstances, as long as no one knows, as long as there are no comebacks, make anything possible. Well, and judge for yourself; a day laborer on her own meals gets from fifteen to twenty kopeks, thirty kopeks for braking flax—they brake flax at night and in a night only the best baba will brake a pud; for a day of braking, twenty kopeks. What does a five-ruble note, even a twenty-five, even a hundred-ruble note in rare cases mean for a gentleman arriving from Petersburg? Judge for yourself. A hundred-ruble note for something that "you don't use up," and fifteen kopeks for a day's labor. Placed in such circumstances, would many bureaucrats' wives stand firm? As for *real feelings,* love, then the baba does not fall short of the bureaucrat's wife in any way, and even surpasses her. I think that anyone who does not know how a village baba can love, ready to sacrifice everything for her beloved, does not know in general how a woman can love.

Babas in the village are indeed an ulcer for the authorities. The men are more willing patiently to endure the despotism of the head of the household, the despotism of the village commune, the despotism of the volost elder, and of the authorities: the district policeman, the village constable, and so on. But as for the babas—no—if the business touches their personal babas' interests directly. The authorities once tried to do an inventory of the babas' undergarments for their arrears and the babas raised such an uproar that it was terrifying—"We'll go to the Tsaritsa to complain," they said. And they would have. The authorities came out ahead on this occasion, however: the babas ate away at the men, they even slept separately, until they put the money together and paid the arrears—they took on various summer jobs. However, after this, the authorities did not touch the babas' undergarments.

I say all of this, however, not because any kind of measures are needed to strengthen the family union or to prevent divisions. I am an opponent of any kind of bureaucratic measures which touch domestic life.[9]

Divisions are harmful, divisions are the cause of the impoverishment of households. If peasants operated on the farm jointly, if the villages consisted of a small number of undivided households, which jointly cultivated the land, which jointly farmed, if, even better, entire villages farmed together, then, without a doubt, the peasants would live prosperously and, one way or another, they would gather all of the land in their hands. Divisions are harmful, but I repeat: any kind of measures for strengthening the family union would be absurd.[. . .]

The Futility of Legislation for the Village

All such measures will never lead to anything, they will always be avoided easily and they will only bring harm to the peasants, they will restrict them and, in the opinion of the muzhiks, only make a laughingstock of them. It is just the same as saying "walk with your feet in the air." And we walk, that is, we do not walk, but we act as if we were walking. If you walk in the usual way, you will meet an official, "Why are you not walking upside down?" "But, your honor, just now I turned over for a rest." And you act as if you want to stand with your feet in the air. The official knows himself that it is impossible to walk that way, but satisfied with what he has heard, smiles kindly and goes on further. By the way, I will take the most futile example—birches, which were ordered to be planted in the villages along the road.

The officials there in town came up with the idea, out of having nothing to do, that it was necessary to plant birches along the village road. It will be pretty, that is the first thing. In the event of a fire, the birches will serve as a defense, that is the second thing. How is it that birches planted along a narrow village road can protect against fire? But that's what the authorities thought up. They thought about it, they wrote an order, immediately you have the strictest command in the volosts, the volost officials sent an order to the village elders, and they—to the militia in the villages. The muzhiks planted birches, they wondered, why? It happened that the Archbishop passed by that summer, they thought that it was for his passing, so it would be more pleasant for him. Of course, all of the birches that were planted dried up over the summer. Anyone who knows the structure of the village and village life will immediately understand that no kind of trees can grow on a village road. On the very narrow road, the mud is usually up to your knees, the peasants drive the cattle along it, who scratch themselves on the planted trees, loads of manure are carted along the road, loads of hay, firewood, someone else will catch on to one of the planted birches. The birches will not survive and they will only dry up. The bureaucrat comes in the spring, some kind of a fire agent (there is such a title and it even has a little star) or the "agel," as the peasants call him. Where are the birches, he asks. They dried up. They dried up! And here I am, and he lets fly. He made a great noise, he shouted, he ordered them to plant again, and if not, he said, he would take a five-ruble fine for each birch. The muzhiks were frightened; they planted a second time, they dried up again. The third spring they sent out the order again: plant! And so the muzhiks came up with the idea, why pull up the birch from the root, just cut away a small seedling: they sharpened the end and stuck it in the ground for the arrival of the agent—it stays green for a long time. And in the winter it would go for kindling because it would dry up excellently in the wind over the summer. The bureaucrat will not lie down to see if it is planted from the root; well, and if one turns up who does, then they'll say, "the root rotted" how is he to know that the birch was simply cut off?

But here is the question: where are the peasants to get the birches? For there are none on their allotment land. Cut it off the lord's land? The warden will not allow them. So, they stole them at night.

Truly, what a queer thing! First, on Whitsunday, they do not allow the peasants to "plant May trees around the izba because many birches are destroyed this way,"[10] and then they order them to plant birches every year on the road![. . .] Suppose that we even now avoid all orders and do everything only for show. What does that cost? I spent a day planting birches, this day cost me at least thirty kopeks. Would it not be better for me to pay fifteen kopeks in order not to plant birches? Indeed, it would be better to give away thirty kopeks than to bury them uselessly in the land with the same result!

LETTER VII (CONCLUSION)

The Peasant Economy in Post-Emancipation Russia[11]

But why is it that a household becomes poor after it has broken up? Can a couple, a husband and wife, live prosperously on the labor of their own hands?

Let us take, for example, a couple, a husband and wife, who are equipped with everything they need for their farm: they have a homestead, livestock, tools, and as much land as they can cultivate on their own as a couple.

What determines the level of productivity of this couple's farm?

In the non–Black Earth Region, the size of the crops is determined by the amount of manure that one can gather; the amount of manure is itself determined by the amount of feed; the amount of feed is determined by the quantity of hay which the couple can prepare, having enough meadow, in the time between St. Peter's Day and St. Semen's Day. This quantity, thus, determines the entire course of farming here: the number of livestock depends on it, the amount of bran, grain, meat, lard, and milk that our couple can use. The ability to gather the grain that has been produced in the short time available for this harvest also serves as another measure for determining the amount of arable land.

I suggest that I will not be far from the truth if I say that the couple can harvest as much grain as it is possible for them to plant according to the amount of hay which this same couple can prepare.

During the harvest (when the grain is reaped and gathered), this couple must work at full strength. The entire existence of the farm depends on the amount of grain processed during this harvest. Every farmer, every muzhik understands this. During the harvest season, the muzhik loses weight, grows dark from the sun, and it reaches the point that if there is good weather for a long time, during which they do not sleep more than six hours a day during *their* reaping, that the muzhik, exhausted, will sometimes quietly ask God for some rain, so that it would be possible to rest, if only for a bit. No matter how exhausted, he will not rest during good weather. That would be shameful.

During the harvest, no one thinks about anything else except reaping, no one does anything else. At this time there are no craftsmen in the village, no village officials, no priests, and if they do fulfill their duties, their demands, they do it all as quickly as possible, looking at the field and thinking, "Ekh! We should be raking the hay now!" During the harvest even the church service is special, done rapidly, as it is at the war front. Everyone reaps, everyone understands that there is no way to be compensated for what is lost at this time. A city dweller might think that everyone has gone out of his mind in the village during the harvest. But it is essential, however, that city dwellers also understand that everything that they eat and drink is provided precisely by this harvest.

But, excluding the *harvest* season, our couple will have a lot of free time during the rest of the year. In the spring, from April 25 through July 1, and in the autumn, from September 1 through November 1, our couple will not only manage to complete all of the fieldwork on their arable land easily, they will also have free time which they can use for work off their farm, if they are able to leave it. In the winter, from November 1 through April 25, our couple will have even more free time which they could also use for work off their farm.

But what can this couple do on the side when they must, willy-nilly, sit idly on their farm? And thus, remaining alone and working on their farm, they live from hand to mouth, as it's said.

If several such couples were to join together, even if it were as the diggers unite in artels, for joint farming, then something else would result.

I will turn again to the diggers to illustrate, through an example from real life, the significance that couples uniting for joint labor has. I take the diggers as my example from real life because these are artel people, industrious and able workers.

I knew a very prosperous family of diggers which consisted of three married brothers, consequently, of six workers. From such a family, in the spring and autumn, two brothers leave for work as diggers in artels, and one brother stays home with the three wives and manages to complete all of the fieldwork and domestic economy associated with farming, while serving as the village elder at the same time. Around here, women plough, thresh, and in some villages, even reap.[. . .]

The two brothers who have been off digging return home by July 1 and remain there until September 1. At this time, all six work in the most intensive fashion on their farm, especially during the reaping, for which they also save themselves during the spring shift.[. . .] The diggers, just like the other peasants, have very few or no water meadows. There are no good meadows even on the land bought by some villages after the Emancipation.

Therefore, prosperous diggers rent good meadows, paying from 12 to 15 rubles per desiatina for water meadows. They do this because they understand very well that it is not enough to use all the time from July 1 through September 1 on the meadow, but that it is essential also that the meadow be good, because the better the grass, the more feed that can be prepared in the time available.[. . .]

Having worked at home during the harvest season, having prepared the hay, gathered the grain, and planted the winter wheat, two brothers again go off for digging work, while one brother stays home with three women and manages to harvest the spring crops and the garden produce, to thresh the grain, process the flax, and so on. Thus, again in the autumn, one third of the people in the household go off for work on the side.

In the winter, there is no digging work, and that is why diggers do other jobs: calcining and hauling lime and slab, cutting and hauling firewood, threshing grain for gentry households; while the babas spin and weave fabric. In the winter, the household could release two thirds or one third, at least, of the people in it for work on the side, or to do nonagricultural labor at home.

Anyone who understands the *essence* of our agriculture will understand how important it is for agriculturalists to gather together for farming together and what enormous wealth could then be realized. Only through *joint* farming is it possible to plant feed grasses, which makes it possible to mow earlier and to make more profitable use of the harvest season. Only with joint farming is it possible to purchase the most important farm machinery, namely machinery that *speeds up* the harvesting of hay and grain; only with joint farming is it possible to release a significant number of people for work elsewhere. Given the rapidity of railroad transportation, these people could go to the south, where the harvest season starts sooner, and, having done their work there, they could return home to their own harvest. On the other hand, it becomes clear how important it is to suspend any other production which takes hands away from the fieldwork during the harvest season. All factories should shut down their operations during this time. Again, the enormous number of free hands points to the necessity of developing small-scale domestic production. We do not need factories or mills, but *small* village distilleries, dairies, tanneries, weaving mills, and so on, whose refuse can also be used profitably in farming.

The division of land into small plots for individual use, the settlement of separate farmers on these plots, living in their own households and cultivating their plots separately, is senseless in agricultural terms. Only agronomists who have been "translated from German" can defend this manner of farming by individual farmers on separate small pieces of land. Farming can *truly advance only when the land is under joint use and cultivation.*[. . .] I said above that several diggers' villages purchased land as their collective property after the Emancipation. I need to clarify this a bit, because some might think that purchase of land by peasants may be more and more widespread among the peasants. But this is not the case at all.

In fact, there was a period soon after the Emancipation, when many peasants went on redemption, when it was easy for them to purchase land as property. A special kind of legal agent even appeared who arranged these deals. At this time, many estates were released from their mortgages and the gentry made use of the opportunity to sell separate small bits of their estates: wastelands, separate homesteads, cutoff lands. In addition, most of the redemption payments went for the payment of old debts on mortgages, and whatever the gentry received, right away they spent, they lived and farmed on it.[. . .]

Of course, such lands were most often purchased by wealthy muzhiks who had old money saved up. They say that there were cases where very significant sums were paid in coin rubles and gold ones.

Sometimes prosperous peasants with large families settled on the purchased land, if it had been an individual farm, and they got by by practicing small trade and crooked dealing at the same time. With time, villages are formed from such households of peasant property owners because the children leave the communal land after they hive off and build separate houses, and they use the land in strips. Such individual farms were bought predominantly by former volost elders, former bailiffs on gentry estates, and similar people in whom the liberal mediators and landowners were able to inculcate the concept of private property in land, at least to the extent that the muzhik talked about private property in land with *gentlemen*. I say "talked with *gentlemen*" because the muzhiks, even those who have been most civilized by the mediators, will still have somewhere in their brain a secret spot (it is very easy to recognize that he is a Russian because of this secret spot) from which, no matter what, springs the muzhiks' view *that land can only be collective property.* That a village, that is, the entire community, can buy land *in perpetuity,* that every muzhik understands, and that no one can give that land to another village; but that land bought by some peasant Igor, when a "New Emancipation" comes out about the land, could not be given back to the village, this not a single muzhik can understand. No matter how civilized a muzhik may be, I think, even if he were the most wealthy railroad boss, as long as he is a Russian muzhik—of course even a muzhik can be given champagne so that he looks like a German and delivers German speeches—he will still have this "secret spot" in his brain. One needs only to reveal this secret spot.

The muzhik considers *his* plot that he planted after the division of the common field to be his property, just like the plot he rents, until he gathers the harvest from it. It seems to me that the muzhik considers only his labor to be his property and he sees the product of his labor only in money and moveable property in general.[. . .]

Peasants who have bought land as property, in most cases, remain in the village and do not move onto their own land; furthermore, if these lands abut the village, it often happens that this land that has been bought as private property will become the collective property of the village over time—truly, however, I do not know—his fellow villagers probably gradually pay the buyer back the sum he spent.

Finally, whole villages purchased land as collective property in another way. A landowner would return to the old system of farming—giving the land out to the peasants by the *krug*—after having tried agronomy, equipment, feed grasses, the cultivation of various fruits, livestock breeding, hiring hands, having spent what money he had. And if the landowner had a lot of arable land, but not enough money, and there was extra land, then it would be arranged so that some homestead or other, cutoff lands, wasteland would be handed over to the peasants as private property, and the peasants were obligated to cultivate the land on the landowner's estate for a certain number of years in exchange.

Now this no longer happens; now it has become much more difficult to purchase land in this fashion. First of all, the landowners have recognized what the *cutoff lands* are, that is, the lands that were taken away from the peasants who had more land under serfdom than they had the right to receive according to the Emancipation. Now the landowners understood very well that through these cutoff lands, which constitute a necessity for the peasants, they can always put pressure on them and force them to work by the *krug* in exchange for these cutoff lands. Therefore, it is very difficult for the peasants to buy cutoff land, especially in exchange for labor: the landowner knows that even without this, the peasants will work as many *krug*s as they are able to cultivate in exchange for the right to use the cutoff lands.

Also, with the introduction of the railroads, the forests have come into demand and a source of income has appeared such as no one dreamed of. The value of forests went up, so did the value of land: the great forests began to be cut down and the small seedlings to be protected.

Finally, the banks appeared, which began to give money in exchange for mortgages on estates and in this way made it more difficult for the peasants to purchase land, because estates are handed over to the banks in entirety including all of the cutoff and wastelands. The peasants are not able to buy entire estates, and it is not easy, and besides, even if a landowner wanted to sell some wasteland or other or piece of cutoff land because he needed some money, he could not. He could not because it is mortgaged as part of the entire estate. Of coures, in time, it might be arranged so that banks can sell land to peasants in separate parcels.[. . .]

The diggers' household, consisting of three brothers, lives prosperously. But then arguments have broken out, the babas have begun to eat away at their husbands. One brother has a lot of sons, another has no children, the third has only two daughters. The brother who has no children has brought his spring earnings from digging and given it over to the head of the household, he cannot hide it, his business is public, in the artel, it is not as if he went somewhere to Moscow to earn money where it would not be known how much he earned, and he could give his wife some of it. The baba begins to harp: "Look how many shirts you ruined working this spring—it's impossible to make enough for you, and I don't have any time to weave: the old woman sits at home, always at me, 'You, you go first after water, then to feed the animals.' " She does nothing but harp, she cannot restrain herself: "We are slaves to someone else's children, look, the lord in Bardino would happily give you 100 rubles a year to dig for him! Leave the land—nobody can do anything to you if you do; why work so much, it's better to have enough to live on." And she harps and harps and harps. It is said that the baba loves a half-kopek piece, it even smells good to her. So the arguments and reproaches begin.

The business ends with the diggers' household breaking up, it is good if it is into two, but even into three new households. There is no doubt whatsoever that the result will be poverty, especially if there is no money saved up in the household, if the village does not have any land other than that received as allotment land. In addition to all of the disadvantages of the division that I mentioned above—three plots, three izbas, three services on holidays, three bowls—there is also the fact that on his own, even the digger, who knows a special trade, *cannot* leave to earn money elsewhere, cannot profitably make use of the time he has free of agricultural tasks. Formerly, the household sent out two men for spring and autumn out-labor, and now three households cannot send out a single one.[. . .]

In the spring and autumn there is nothing, or practically nothing, to earn on the side, because it is impossible to be away from the farm. He has to work half of the most intensive season for someone else. Poverty is unavoidable. There is no grain, there is nothing to pay the taxes with. And on top of this, there are small children, some kind of misfortune happens: one of the animals dies, a horse is stolen.

Finally, *the land gets the best of the muzhik,* as the peasants say, and once the land is the master—it's all over. And here there is a temptation besides: Peter there goes to work for the lord as a coachman, he gets ten rubles a month, he wears silk shirts; Vanka came to visit from Moscow—in an overcoat, with a watch and so on . . .

Thus broken, the muzhik decides to abandon the land. If the land is good and the village values land, the muzhik will give the land to the commune which will pay the taxes on it; if the land is poor, so that it is not worth it to pay for it, and the commune does not agree to take it on, then the muzhik rents it for virtually nothing to some rich peasant for a year or two as long as it is possible to get something out of it, and then he leaves it empty, not using it, pays taxes on it out of his earnings.[. . .] Having abandoned the land, having sold all of his extra buildings, cattle, tools and kept for himself only the garden and izba his wife lives in, usually working as a day laborer, the muzhik hires himself out as a hired hand or goes to Moscow for wage labor. If he doesn't have any luck, he returns home, but since he does not have anything to cultivate the land with and his farm is ruined, he, having settled in his little shack, works as a day laborer; then he tries again to be a hired hand, again he comes back, and more often than not, becomes a drunk, a ruined man.

But if he succeeds in finding a position with a lord, his position will bind him and he will prefer secure dependency as a lackey to insecure independence. Such a peasant, who *has gotten on track* by having abandoned the land, by leaving the village and taking up a position, will no longer return to the village, and will try to send for his wife and children. Having gotten on track, he will usually despise the peasant's dirty labor, he will prefer the easier work of a lackey, he will dress like a German, he will wear a watch, he will try very hard to have all kinds of clothes; his wife will act like a gentlewoman and will envy such and such a trader's wife who left the village earlier to go to Moscow to live with a merchant and has six servants; or she will envy someone else who has a good position and has seventeen dresses. She will raise her children like *little lords,* and even though she beats them, she will feed them sugar and teach them how to *curtsy.* The children will no longer know what peasant labor is; when they grow up, their parents will try to find them good positions serving bureaucrats where their chief qualification will consist of their ability to curtsy. The husband and wife and children will already be ashamed of their rural relatives and will call them *uneducated muzhiks,* while the latter will pay them back by calling them *hired hands.* And "hired hand" is such an abusive term that there is nothing lower, and it will enrage even the most polished curtsier—he still has that secret spot of the Russian muzhik in his brain!

To get on track!—for this it is not necessary to do anything, but only *to know how* to humor an official or lord, to get on track—this is the secret dream. *To learn how to please!*—this is the goal of all one's strivings and for which one does not disdain any means, for example, marrying for the lord! This is typical of a muzhik who has abandoned the land. Having abandoned the land, he loses everything, as it were, turning himself into a lackey!

In these muzhiks who have gotten on track, who have become little bureaucrats, who are called "a man," you will no longer see the sense of one's own self-worth that you see in the muzhik-farmer-agriculturalist. Look at a real muzhik-agriculturalist. What a frank, honest, fully self-confident individual! Compare him to a curtsying lackey! The muzhik, if he "is not guilty before either the lord or the Tsar,"[12] does not fear anything. A muzhik, even if he is poor, as long as he holds onto some land—Mother Earth is an amazing force—utterly despises those who have gotten on track and become rich through serving a lord. "And what a fine salary these birds get—250 rubles, some get even more—they take a ruble from one person, three rubles from another!" one muzhik said to me, a true, passionate farmer of immeasurable strength, who enjoyed great health, intellect, and farming skills.

"And would you take such a job?"

"Me!?"

"Why, yes, you."

"God save me! Me? Become someone's hired hand!"

Some muzhiks once came to buy some rye from me for bread.

"Why don't you buy it from your own lord?" I asked.

"What grain does our lord have, our lord himself's working as someone's hired hand!"

What contempt there was in these words! In fact, he was one of the poorer lords and he worked as a manager for a neighboring landowner.

Of course, even now, the muzhik, out of old habit, takes his hat off in front of a lord, the constable, the volost elder—the volost elder is even stricter, just try not to take your hat off in front of him! He is also one of those who curtsy before any official; but you will see in this muzhik that he is an independent man. A muzhik stands without his hat, but he senses his independence, he recognizes that he does not have to waste his time serving and pleasing. But this is not so with the muzhik when he has not mastered the land, abandons it, and goes into service among the gentry where he will also try to please, serve, and get on track. Then the sense of his own self-worth, his self-confidence and faith in himself is lost and the man in him fades. Bit by bit he begins to feel that his entire well-being depends on how well he knows how to please and to serve. Once he has bitten into a pie and had a taste of mead, he no longer wants black bread, gray cabbage, manual labor, or a coarse caftan. Such peasants who have abandoned the land, have gotten on track, and have a good position usually do not return to the village and the land. And if they still have land and the village does not take it on because of the burden of paying taxes on it, then, once they get rich, they pay off their redemption for their allotment and then either leave the land empty, or give it to a relative to use, or, finally, sell it as private property to some other person who then uses it, however, in strips, in rows.

I should note, however, that muzhiks who get on track through service are undoubtably capable people in a certain sense, who usually do not love agriculture and farming, and for the most part, are not able farmers. But are there many such fortunates who get on track, especially now when there are a mass of young soldiers on indefinite leave, who rarely return to the land and who disdain the uneducated muzhik and his muzhik labor? Therefore, most peasants who leave the land do not get onto any track whatsoever and are ruined working as hired hands and day laborers. What will become of their children?

[Engelgardt becomes repetitive here and continues the theme of the harm of individual farming and the virtue of collective agriculture.]

There is still one more very important circumstance which has enormous significance, which is often the cause for the failure of individual farms—that is *the inability to work, the inability to farm,* an inability which is simply the result of insufficient mental skill in a certain turn of mind. This circumstance is extremely important and confirms even more the necessity and importance of artel farming.

Some people think that it is enough to be born a muzhik, and to learn muzhik labor from early childhood to be a good farmer and a good worker. This is not the case at all. There are very few good farmers because a great deal is required of a good farmer. "Running a farm is not just shaking your trousers; a farmer," the muzhiks say, "when he's figuring out one job should see the second and third." And there are many among the peasants who not only cannot be good farmers, who not only cannot work except by following someone else's orders, but who do not even know how to work well.[. . .]

Who has not had the experience of seeing so-called *fools* in the country? I am not talking about the kind of fools, holy fools, holy people who go around the commune and gather kopeks, but about those fools who live with their families, in households, and work to the extent of their abilities.

I have known one fool since he was born who cannot learn how to chop firewood. He goes when they send him, and sometimes he thinks about chopping, but how? Sometimes he even does a good job, but most of the time he cannot chop a three-arshin log at all—he is probably thinking about something else at the time—into three equal-sized logs: either he cuts off a half-arshin log, or one that is three vershoks; or into two arshins—he ruins all of the firewood.

I also know a fool who weaves bast shoes excellently, who chops excellently, who ploughs excellently, but he does all of this only when he is reminded to, and if he is obstinate, then nothing in the world can make him work. He ploughs excellently, but he ploughs through all the strips in a row, both his and other people's—he would be a wonderful ploughman in collective farming!

I know a girl in the village here—you can tell she is crazy just by looking at her face—who works excellently, but completely mechanically, not knowing what she is doing or why.[. . .] We have one house servant here, Filat, who is very handy at any craft, although he does not know any one very well—he is an invaluable man for the village because he knows how to make frames, and how to put in glass, and how to put up wallpaper, if need be, how to build a stove, and he can tin-plate, in a word, he is a master at everything. Filat, as a former house servant, does not have land and does not farm, but he does keep a cow and a sheep, and he prepares their hay himself. Every year he sharecrops a small meadow from me and I have been marveling at his gathering of hay for eight years already; he cannot figure it out at all, there can be a week or two of such clear weather that any fool would gather his hay. But as soon as the weather becomes changeable, which usually happens here—just watch, Filat will have steamed his hay. On the very same meadow, right next to Filat, others harvest splendid hay, but not him, no, his is spoiled. Either he does not spread it out in time, or he rakes it up wet, he hurries, but he cannot get any kind of rhythm. And it is not enough that the hay is a mess—in every pud of Filat's hay, there is at least two times the labor expended as there is in the others'.

If you take on one hand a fool who cannot chop hay, and on the other a splendid muzhik-farmer for whom everything succeeds, who can organize the work of an enormous artel, then there are innumerable gradations in between these two extremes. If complete fools are rare on the one hand, then especially remarkable farmers are even rarer. Average people predominate, and in their number, the largest contingent is made up of people who have learned mechanically, as a result of constant repetition from childhood, to work more or less well, who are not capable of independent farming on their own, but are capable of working only according to someone else's plan, under someone else's direction. As long as the family has not divided, then everyone does his work well according to the plan of a good master or according to *the collective plan of everyone in joint labor,* the work succeeds and even a fool, if he is not a complete idiot, makes his contribution. But if the family had divided—and stupid babas are even quicker to work for a division—people who are not capable farmers become heads of households. Of course, if he knows how to work, such a farmer will do everything according to the village's plan—if everyone else is ploughing, then he ploughs, if everyone else is planting, then he plants. But in the details, the business, there is no one with any imagination for farming, there is no one to do the planning. He can be healthy, and strong, and know how to work, but it still does not work; he works a lot, but it turns out the way it does with Filat, for whom every pud of hay costs twice what it does for other people. This lack of skill in farming is the reason that even in prosperous villages which have particularly propitious conditions you always encounter one or two poor peasants whose farms are strikingly different from the others'. And this is so even when they all live in one village, own the land collectively, practice the same kind of farming, and much is done according to a general plan—the time to plant, for example, is always set in a joint council—and they work on rows that are not far from each other. And what would happen if you settled these people on separate plots of land where each one would run an independent farm? One can state positively that the village and communal ownership of the land saves many people who are ill equipped for farming from total ruin.

[Engelgardt continues on this theme and offers an example of a muzhik who is not in tune with the demands of farming.]

Nowadays, the question of peasant land, of peasant allotments, has become the question of the day. All the research, as is well known, concludes that peasant allotments are too small and burdened with excessive taxes. The enormous arrears, frequent famines, the rapid rise in the number of landless peasants who abandon the land, having destroyed their farm, sold their home-steads, leaving the villages, only nominally consider themselves members of the commune, when in fact these same landless peasants, like those also who did not receive allotment lands, who are also recorded as landless, clearly prove that all is not well. Finally, the very rumors circulating among the peasants that a "New Edict" will soon come out point to the difficult position of the peasantry. The question is obviously ripening.[. . .]

Both I, a country farmer, and the constable who beats out arrears, and commissions investigating the causes for the bankruptcy of the peasants, can-not fail to see that the peasants were alloted an inadequate amount of land, so that even a reduction of taxes will be only a palliative measure.

The first thing that hits you in the face is that in many villages the peasants received in their allotment *less* land than they had the use of under serfdom. All land that was beyond the established allotment was cut off and given to the landowner and comprised so-called *cutoffs, catches, or catch-lands.*[. . .] These cutoffs, which often are worth nothing in their composition, are ap-praised not by the quality of land, not by their productivity, but only by the degree to which they are *essential* to the peasants, the degree to which they *crowd* them, by how much one can *squeeze out of* the peasants in exchange for these cutoffs. It is clear that everything depends on a multitude of various factors.

It would still be fine if these cutoffs were let to the peasants in exchange for rent paid in money, but no—without fail, it is in exchange for labor.[. . .]

I tried to clarify above the significance of the harvest season from July 1 to

September 1 for the farmer, and how it is important for him to work *for himself* at this time, because this harvest prepares him for the entire year. But here, the muzhik must work for the lord in exchange for cutoffs during the most valuable time. For prosperous peasants in extended families, who have many workers (men and women) in their households, many horses, and the right tack, it is still nothing to cultivate a *krug* or a half *krug,* but for the single poor peasants, who have few horses, the cultivation of *krugs*[13] is pure ruin.[. . .] The position of peasants who received the land they owned[14] under serfdom in their allotment, who therefore did not lose cutoffs, is a different matter, probably better, but even here there's a snag of its own kind.

The kind of peasants who had the use of less land under serfdom were usually peasants of petty gentry, and their villages' fields abutted the landowner's arable. Of course there are villages whose land was particularly good, who had good water meadows, excellent gardens, and so on, as a result of which the landowner could give the peasants less land; but there are villages where there was nothing of the kind, and the peasants still had only a small amount of land under serfdom. Such villages—make note of this—always abut the gentry fields with their fields. Under serfdom, peasants in such villages, in addition to *their* land, *also had the use of gentry fields:* during the work season, they were given gentry meadows to feed their horses for the spring crop, when they hauled manure, they were also given meadows, during the mowing, the muzhiks' horses were fed on the mown meadows, and furthermore, every shepherd boy could, albeit under fear of punishment, take away an armful of hay for his horses. After the meadows and fields were cleared, the peasants' horses and cattle grazed in the gentry meadows and wastelands. Finally, in extreme cases, the landowner gave feed for the horses, or used his horses to help in the work on the gentry fields, especially for harrowing and hauling.

Now the following order of things has been established: to make up for their lack of meadows, peasants sharecrop hay fields for gentry landowners; to make up for their lack of pastures and free spaces, they take on the cultivation of *krug*s for a set pay, in order to have the right to pasture their animals. The situation is a bit better than in those villages which must work gentry land for cutoffs, because they still get some money for their labor, and the landowner cannot crowd them so tightly, since, if the fields are contiguous, it is possible that the landowner's cattle will get on the peasants' land. But even so, they have to work their most valuable time on someone else's field.

No matter what, it is clear that the muzhik does not have enough land.

[Engelgardt here discusses the poor condition of gentry farming.]

And so, on the one hand you have the "muzhik" whose farm cannot be improved because of the land shortage, and *most important,* because of the lack of unity in the farming activities of the members of the commune; on the other hand, a "lord" who understands nothing about the land, on whose farm the muzhik futilely works his land because he is crowded for pasture.[. . .]

There can be no doubt whatsoever that if the peasants were allotted land in sufficient quantities, productivity would increase enormously, the state would become very rich. But I will say, even so, that if the peasants do not move over to an artel system of farming, and instead continue to farm each household by itself, there will also be landless peasants and hired hands even given an abundance of land for the farming peasants. I will go further: I suggest that the difference in the conditions of the peasants will be even more significant than now. Despite communal ownership of the land, alongside "rich peasants" there will be many landless, real hired hands—what is it to me and my children that I have a right to the land when I do not have any capital or tools to work it—it is all the same as giving the land to a blind person—you can eat it!

[Engelgardt discusses the possibilities for peasants renting abandoned gentry estates as farming artels.]

Of course, such a form of artel farming is far from ideal, but I assign even this enormous significance, because it is a step forward.

For peasants, renting estates this way through artels is also profitable because it provides income nearby, without having to go elsewhere, not taking them away from their own farming, which for the peasant living on his own is, furthermore, impossible. Besides, once peasants come together for renting estates as an artel, then it becomes much more likely that, seeing in practice the good of artel cultivation of the land in common, of maintaining livestock together, and so on, they would more quickly shift to artel cultivation on their own allotments, to communal farming; that division, those egotistical relations which exist in villages would be more quickly destroyed.[. . .]

Of course, there are very few of these, as the muzhiks call them, *union* villages. But what enormous good could educated people, wanting to farm, settling in villages, and forming such artels bring!

Having learned how to work, and without this nothing will come of it, they could form their own artels for renting estates, and what excellent examples these artel farms of civilized people would serve as for the peasants.

But to do this, one must know how to work, one must know how to work the way a farmer-muzhik knows how to work. One must develop in oneself the kind of qualities which would make it possible to live without the muzhik, one must acquire muzhik legs, hands, eyes, and ears. One must develop oneself to the point that a farming *muzhik would hire you as a hired hand and would consider you as valuable as a hired hand who is a muzhik.* It is possible to achieve this. You don't need to go to America. You need to learn from the muzhik, working among muzhiks, side by side with them and in the same conditions to the extent possible. Educated people bear military service equally with the muzhik, and they should. No one coddles them in the trenches at Plevna! In my opinion, there is no smaller a percentage of people suitable for farm labor among the educated than there are among the muzhiks. I am convinced—I have been convinced of this through experience—that with the sincere desire to become a farmer, with unstinting labor, a healthy, strong, able, intellegent man of the educated class can in *two years* acquire the skills of *an average* muzhik worker, even, probably, he can become, if he is especially assiduous, capable of getting by without the muzhik, that is, he will know how to make himself an axe handle, rakes, how to repair a sickle, a wooden plough, to make a harrow, he will know how to slaughter and butcher cattle, to ride a horse, even how to build a little izba. If he cannot attain the skills of the average hired hand in *two years,* through constant labor, that means that something is missing, that he is something like what the peasants call a "man of God." Many may think that the term of *two years* that I have indicated is too small, given the fact that one needs thirteen years to get a master's degree in chemistry or the title of physician, but I have in mind that desire alone will play a role here, and also, that given the upbringing of educated people, they, *even so,* acquire some physical agility, activity: games, boxing, and so on; in this regard, seminarians will have an advantage over cadets, and cadets over gymnasium students. Of course, in order to become a *master farmer,* the kind who become *real* muzhik-farmers, you would also need thirteen years, you would also have to study from an early age.

[Engelgardt discusses various aspects of gentry leasing of their estates.]

I especially insist on the fact that renting estates to peasant communes for artel cultivation is profitable for owners and offers the only way out of their— I don't know how to put it—strange position. Landowners constantly complain about the unprofitability of farming, about the high cost of workers, just as if they wanted to return to serfdom, or to some kind of system of mandatory labor for hired hands at low pay. Neither is possible and never will be. They are delivering their sentence of their method of farming with their whining. It is obvious that the only thing left for them is the service, as long as there are jobs, and to turn to those who know how to get by on the land to find methods of exploiting the land.

I will say it again: I did not come to the views I have outlined in this article through theory. Real life in the countryside, the life with which I have acquainted you in my letters, observations of the position of the peasants and landowners led me to this. I think that anyone who penetrates this life will come to the same conclusions.[. . .]

There is no other way out than artel farming on jointly held lands!

Rational agronomists may ask: yes, but will there be progress in farming when it passes into the hands of the ignorant muzhiks? Everything that has been worked out by the science of agronomy will be unknown to an ignorant muzhik commune, which will keep simple livestock in cold stalls, will feed it not according to the norms worked out by science, will plough with simple wooden ploughs, and so on and so forth.

I will answer this question with a question. And where is there progress in farming now? To whom is scientific knowledge familiar and by whom is it applied? Where except in inflated, deceptive reports does this notorious rational farming exist? What has come from all of these schools in which peasant boys were subjected to agronomy? What has come from those experimental homesteads where agronomists who run institutes go? What did they teach? And finally, where do these agronomists go who are graduated from these institutes? Some become bureaucrats for the state, others become the same kind of bureaucrats in private employ where they apply their agronomic knowledge to exploiting peasants through cutoffs and pasture rights.

Believe me, it will be no worse, because it cannot be any worse than current farming.[. . .]

Have no fear! Peasant communes cultivating the land as artels will introduce grasses, if it is profitable, and mowing machines, threshing machines, and Simentalskii cattle. And whatever they introduce will be solid. Just look at cattle breeding on monasteries. If there are itinerant horse doctors, carders, drillers, tailors, and so on, then why won't there be itinerant teachers, doctors, agronomists? Last year the famous agronomist and cattle breeder Bazhanov came here to enlighten our farmers and zemstvo. There will be everything: if the peasants now have *their own* unofficial schools, *their own* midwives, *their own* bonesetters, seers, healers, then there is no doubt that communes that have prospered under the new system will not remain in the same situation they are in now: they will introduce literacy schools, trade and agricultural schools, conservatories, gymnasiums, universities.

Truly useful science will penetrate even communes. But until then! until then the masses are ignorant . . .

Are there not a few educated people who, having finished their studies, do not want to follow the usual path—do not want to become bureaucrats? People who have gone through the university are running to America and becoming simple workers for American plantation owners. Why not think that people will be found who, having learned to work like a muzhik, will join in communes, rent estates, and cultivate them with their own hands with the help that knowledge and science give them?

Such communes of educated farmers will serve as the very best models for peasant communes. Such farms will serve as much better models than any kind of model state farm or model gentry estate. If knowledge and science can bring good to farming, then it will be here, in these communes, that its full meaning will be displayed.

Finally, why can't educated people who have learned how to work unite with peasants to rent and cultivate land jointly? Why can't educated people enter peasant communes as teachers, midwives, doctors, and agronomists as stewards?

Just demonstrate that you are not playing around, but are a truly intelligent man who knows how to work and the commune will adopt you, will take you as their own, will listen to you and your learning.

Nowadays there are rumors about building agricultural schools for the peasants. It would be no less important, in my opinion, to build practical schools of *labor* not far from university towns where those wishing to could learn agricultural labor, that it, could learn how to mow, plough, and generally learn to work like a muzhik.

Letter VIII

✉   The eighth letter provides one of the most amusing and instructive descriptions of local officials and the bureaucratic mentality to appear in Russia since Nikolai Gogol's *The Inspector General*.[1] Engelgardt's central message in criticizing would-be reformers, specialists, and lawmakers throughout the letters is that the gap is enormous between the intent of reform and the execution of reform in the village. His letters in a sense are one long indictment of the system of tutelage over the peasant population in Russia, of the attitude that the peasants are incapable of caring for themselves, and that state and society must, therefore, take measures to protect them from self-destruction. That tutelage was indeed extensive. One of Engelgardt's peers in the public debate over the peasant, the writer Nikolai Nikolaevich Zlatovratskii, once calculated the number of officials in the countryside who could order the peasants to do any number of things. His list included forty individuals to whom the peaseant was obligated to answer for everything from how he dressed to how often he opened his windows to where he kept troughs of water to when he paid his taxes to whether he took out an insurance policy for his izba.[2] The hierarchy of the officials Engelgardt mentions throughout the letters would be as follows, with the lowest officials listed first: tenners, hundreders, volost court judge, the petty police officers described in this letter (the *uriadnik*), the chief of police or constable, the justice of the peace, zemstvo officials, representatives of the governor, and the governor himself. This is a rough hierarchy, which, of course, does not include the thirty or so other petty officials roaming the countryside to monitor and supervise the life of the peasantry. Engelgardt's wry accounts in this letter of the newly introduced *uriadniki* and of measures to prevent the plague demonstrate that he had little faith indeed in bureaucratic measures for reform.

In the closing section of the eighth letter, Engelgardt reveals to his readers just how corrosive the various pressures he feels have become for him. Here he describes his decline into alcoholism, a rather frank and unusual public confession for the time. He frames his disease in the context of the petty surveillance he has had to endure as a political exile. Local archives confirm that the surveillance was indeed constant and petty.[3] It is surely fair to assume, however, that not only the irritation and even fear of petty tyrants drove Engelgardt to drink. He was also battling his own demons, his own discomfort as a highly intelligent man in the throes of what Richard Wortman has called the "crisis of Russian populism," the realization that the future of Russia did not lie in the village in the hands of noble muzhiks, that exploitation and individualism were universal human conditions, and that he, personally, could no longer tolerate his ambiguous position as a gentry farmer solely occupied in farming.

⊠   ⊠   ⊠

New District Officials

[Engelgardt opens this letter by describing the scene at the local railroad station during the mobilization of soldiers during the Russo-Turkish War.]

In the summer there was already a rumor that still more officials would be introduced to assist the existing officials.[4] Many were happy about this, especially those tearful ladies who were sitting in their boring estates, who were eternally afraid of robbers, arsonists, thieves, about which we have heard nothing in our woods. The ladies thought that the new officials would ride around their estates on horseback and keep an eye on everything, in the manner of St. Petersburg policemen or, even better, the famous London constables. Then you could ride wherever you wanted without fear: there would be nothing to fear, neither blizzards, nor wolves, nor robbers. If you got caught in a blizzard, the officer riding around your district would lead you back to the road; if wolves attacked, the officer would fly to your assistance and tear all the wolves apart with his saber, there is nothing even to be said about robbers: the officer would catch all of the robbers, thieves, horse thieves and put them in the bug-infested jail where volost elders are put for arrears. No less than the ladies, those landowners who are constantly going to court with the peasants were happy about the new officials. In fact there are such unfortunates who do nothing but go to court, with the result that they do not have any time to work on their farm; they are constantly going to court, to the volost court, to the justice of the peace, to various authorities. Either their workers do not last since they don't make firm contacts, just look, they will stay a week or two and run off; or the peasants do not finish their work; they will take on, for example, a meadow to clear, mow, rake, set up stacks, everything as it ought to be, but then, you look, they set up the stacks which stand and stand, and snow has already fallen, but the stacks still stand in the meadow; either trespassing, or poaching wood; no one will come for day work, no one comes to sell berries or mushrooms, no one will be hired as a shepherd, there is no one to drive the cattle into the field. The lord rides around to the various courts and it is senseless; the manure remains, not taken away, almost until August: other people have already mowed and carried everything away, but on his place, they still have not begun to mow. Such gentlemen placed great hopes on the new official: *he* will make the muzhik knuckle under; *he* will make all the sluggards work; *he* will keep a hold on all the workers who do not stay because they are paid poorly; *he* will eliminate trespassing and wood poaching; *he* will even make them work by the day, *he* will order them to sell berries and mushrooms, *he* will eliminate all kinds of stealing because his first concern will be to protect property.

Sinner that I am, I doubted that the new officials would succeed in preventing blizzards, wolves, fires, and horse thieves.[. . .] Hearing that new officials would be introduced, I must confess, I thought that they would be not for governing, but, for "formality" in and of itself, in order to give a crust of bread to the men who have served in the war. Were not a few people ruined in this war, why not reward them for their service, by giving them positions to go along with a nice title?[. . .]

But it turned out not to be that way at all. They did not even allow the men who had served in the war to sniff the new positions; they put *noble* bureaucratic people in the new positions. People from Tashkent of the very lowest rank. Everyone who could not find any outlet for himself, everyone who could not attach himself to any kind of position, all these people wound up as the new authorities. And what was to be expected from this noble horde under whose command the muzhik has been placed? The most superficial acquaintance with these people is enough to predict *how* they will rule. Consider only that if he consumes a half bottle a day—and what is a half bottle to him!—then seventy-two rubles a year are required.[5] Well, and how is the "noble" man to live here on some kind of two hundred rubles!

It is well known how much has changed since the Emancipation. There were peace mediators, then justices of the peace arrived. The peasants began to lose the habit of being flogged, of being punched in the mouth, in the courts even, they began to address the muzhik in the formal you form. The police, even this has changed a lot. The former dentists[6] have disappeared or have been quietened down under the new order. But of course, if something happens, the official begins to shout, gets angry, begins to curse, but as for flogging or a punch in the face—there is neither. I well remember the old days before the Emancipation; I still remember that era when the district police officer did not eat with gentlemen in fine homes, but if he did dine with them, it was somewhere at the end of a table; I remember when even the superintendent, when he rode up to a gentleman's house, tied up his bell. There was a completely different order then. Without vodka, flogging, punches to the face, one could not even imagine the police among the muzhiks. After the Emancipation, much changed. The superintendent became an important person, he rarely leaves town; he does not go crawling to anyone, it is not polite; he does not come into direct contact with the muzhik. The superintendent now has become as important as the governor was before; district ladies, if he is young, call him "notre chef."[. . .] In these twenty or so years, everything has been ennobled, has been turned away from physical justice, even the district police officers have become different, many do not drink vodka, they are accepted in gentlemen's homes, they dine with gentlemen, they ride right up to the formal entrance with their bells, so that the old servants who grew accustomed to the old order are simply amazed, "Gentlemen are not what they used to be!!"

Formerly, the muzhik knew only his volost elder, his village elder, his hundreder, his clerk (by the way, it is said that the volost clerks also will be bureaucrats, will be on state service through appointment by the authorities). It was rare that the district police officer rode by, or the fire agent, or some revenue agent—the latter paid some attention to the miller, the butter maker, or trade. Yes and the authorities only rode along main roads, from volost to volost, or to the homes of gentlemen who had arrears, but he did not even glance at the villages which lay out of the way. But now it is not like that: *this one* darts about everywhere; he knows that he is more likely to find disorder in an isolated village and take a fine. And what did the muzhik do that a "noble" horde has descended on him for no reason whatsoever? And they have descended *precisely on the muzhik*.[. . .] Furthermore, *he* is a useful man for those landowners who constantly have quarrels with the peasants about wood poaching, trespassing, failure to do work. And so, he will arrive, shout at the muzhik, make him afraid, and the muzhik is terribly afraid of shouting, he will immediately become meek and feel that he is guilty, just as we do at the appearance of a gendarme.

In a word, these new officials are nothing to the gentry, the bureaucrats, they cannot even understand what there is to fear here.

The muzhik is a completely different matter . . .

A landowner can set up a night guard on his estate or not—it is nobody's business, but in the village, even if it consists of two households, it is ordered that there be a watchman. Whether it is bitterly cold, or there is a blizzard, the guard must not sleep, he must always be there in person, he must knock on the door and interrogate passersby. A man begins to fall asleep, he goes into the izba to warm up, to smoke a pipe . . . suddenly, "he" flies up!

A landowner can set himself up however he wishes; even if it is in the middle of the hay barn—it is no one's business; a landowner can plant around his buildings with trees or not, he can have tubs of water or not, he can have fire-fighting equipment or not. But in the village it is not so: one must set oneself up according to a plan, as the authorities require, without establishing whether there is enough land or not, whether it is convenient for you or not. Even though the barn is placed near a steep slope, and, in order that there be the distance required, you have to go a verst for water. If it is ordered that birches be planted along the street, you plant them, although this is completely useless, inconvenient, and even impossible. Troughs so that there will be water everywhere, cardings must not be dried out in the stoves, equipment so that everyone is supplied, so that there is a little plank over every house with the design of the equipment with which the household head should go to a fire.[7] *He* has flown up; here a pen was built for the geese without permission, there a little storehouse is not in its right place, this man's birches dried up, that one does not have a fire sign . . .

A landowner can open or not open his little window [*fortochka*][8] into the room to clean the air; he can change or not change his shirt—whose business is this? But it is strict in regard to the muzhik: it is ordered that the izbas be "cooled," as the peasants say, that is, the doors of the izbas must be opened several times a day to clear the air; it was ordered that one's shirt be changed two times a week for cleanliness.

"He" is quiet when he is with the landowner; he arrives sober, he *requests* that the road be repaired in the morning, and apologizes besides, justifying himself with the fact that the authorities are leaning on him, you see, not long ago some senator or other rode by with a team of four, there was a dressing-down from the authorities because his horse fell on one little bridge. But in the village he is *ferocious,* he curses, you can hear him from a verst away, he stamps his feet, he gets right up in your snout.

One should see what kind of alarm there is when *he,* all irritated, flies unexpectedly into an izba: the children cry with fright, have hidden themselves in the corner, the muzhik stands dumbstruck, but *he* yells and stomps. "How dare you! How dare you! . . ." Bang, his fist is not enough, he uses a saber, in its sheath, of course. I once described such a scene to a high official. "Not really with a saber?" he asks. "Yes, with a saber." "Unsheathed?" "No." The official was relieved.[. . .]

So again I say, that if the new officials are essential for "formality," for decorum, then they would have drawn them from troops who served in the war, since these were more splendid, formal, and decorous than the current "noble men."

Suppose that honorable soldiers would not have been of any use, it would have still been easier for the muzhik. A soldier is more simple, closer to the muzhik, and therefore, would have been satisfied with less. He also does not have any "noble" requirements, he has no lordly whims, but, most important, an official who is a former soldier does not know the laws.

Suppose that even the muzhik who has just been made "an official," for example, a volost elder, quickly makes himself into an official, he is civilized by the clerks and higher officials who order him to make the muzhik knuckle under. Suppose that he also demands that they take off their hats in front of him, that they show him every respect, suppose that he also tries to extort, still, he is simpler, he is their brother-muzhik, with muzhik concepts, and, most important, he does not know the laws. In just the same way will some kind of noncommissioned officer carry himself like an official, will demand respect, will consider the muzhik to be below him, will also extort given the chance, but even so, he is simpler, his brother, and he does not know the laws. Yes, and he will not make difficulties for the muzhik as does the noble one who knows only how to do one thing, to show his official power.

Spring has arrived; joyful, we welcome her with songs, special spring, Trinity songs. The gray folk, who have sat for seven winter months in gray izbas, in gray homespun coats, eating gray cabbage soup, rejoice at the first green growths of spring. On the first spring holiday, on Trinity Sunday, the muzhik decorates his gray izba with May trees,[9] the women set out for the light May woods to decorate the birches with ribbons, they gossip, they sing songs, they dance, they entertain with vodka, pies, cabbage. On the last day before the fast they go to the same woods, cut down birch trees, garland them on the top, dress up with scarves, beads, crosses, put crowns of birch twigs on their heads, and go with songs to "drown May" in the river. "The Passion" has begun.[10]

"Stop!" the official who has flown up shouts. "You are cutting down birches again for 'May'! Don't you know that it is forbidden to cut birches for May. A fine!"

"Have mercy, your honor, we did not know, there was no order this year."

"You did not know, you did not know. Look how many people have gathered—disperse!"

"Have mercy, your honor!"

"Disperse to your homes, I tell you. You, what are you doing standing there, you scatterbrain, in your cap?" He falls on a little one who was gaping and had forgotten to take his cap off in front of the official.

It has happened more than once—it has even been reported in the newspapers—that they have broken up round dancing, parties in the evening, games, young people's gatherings, weddings; the Minister of Internal Affairs even had to publish *a special circular* on October 23, 1879, about this, in which he explained that games and similar entertainments of the peasants were not a disturbance of the peace. But if he had to make such a clarification to the governors, then how are we to know what is allowed and what is not? Who knows all of the laws, orders, decrees? And will *he* suddenly forbid work bees for hauling manure? For this is also "a gathering," and it is also noisy, because it is accompanied by drinking, and also everyone has pitchforks. If it could occur to him to break up round dances, young people's gatherings, wedding feasts, then why could it not occur to him to break up work bees and other joint labors?[. . .] Maybe he is right, and if he is not right, how can you not obey an official who is fulfilling the duties of his position? What does this smell of? No, it is still better to part on good terms.

"Come along, folks, let's entertain him," someone observes.

Your honor, won't you have a bit of vodka? Women, give his honor a bit of cabbage. Please, your honor, have a bite!"

The heart is not a stone, indeed even *he* is a man. He has a drink, a bite, he softens. Look, he lightens up, he listens to the songs, he winks at the women, he dances a bit, and is happy, with a crown on his cap, he goes to drown May.[11] Isn't he a man after all? Can he really not rejoice at Trinity? Thus it is better to part on good terms . . .

And, it would seem, why spare the birches? We are overgrown in birches even without this order. There are neither fields nor meadows, all are simply overgrown with birches. No grain, no grasses, no livestock, everything is vines and birches, birches and vines. And will you go far on birch kasha alone?[. . .]

It is a hot June day. The shepherd is driving the herd; it is eleven o'clock, it is hot, it is time to take a rest. Pine woods. They have stopped the herd, the cows have lain down and are peacefully chewing; only the bull is standing sullenly, just as if he were guarding his brides. The shepherd has sat down under a little pine and is smoking a pipe.

Suddenly . . .

"What's that you are doing there? Don't you know that it is forbidden to smoke tobacco in a coniferous forest in the dry season?"

"But I, your honor, am not smoking tobacco, but cheap tobacco," says the shepherd, thinking to joke.

"Cheap tobacco! And you want to chat about it! Just look what I'll do to you!"

"Laika" and "Bosonozhka," seeing that their master is being cursed, jump up with a bark to protect him. The bull, fearing that a strange man will take away one of his cows, threatens: he bellows, breathes heavily, tears at the dirt.

"Go, go," one of the herdsboys urges the dogs on.

"Run, run!" the shepherd shouts, seeing that the bull is getting ferocious. "Run, he'll kill you!"

"How, how, wh-wh-where!" the herdsboy quavers from behind a bush.

"Run," the shepherd shouts, "the bull!"

The official hides.

"Look how you gave a fright to the bull!" says the shepherd, scratching. "However, it has become strict now. O-ho-ho-ho! . . ." he rouses the herd, starting to smoke his pipe again.

And he, the official, can interfere in everything because he does everything according to the law. You don't even think, you don't even guess, and look, it's not allowed by law. You can never know whether you are right or not. Well, and so a man is afraid.[. . .]

Of course, all of these laws and orders were issued even before because the concern about the muzhik has always constituted and still constitutes the main sympathy of educated people. Who lives for himself? Everyone lives for the muzhik! We all, members of the intelligentsia, know and feel that we live on the muzhik, that he provides our food and drink. We are ashamed and so we try to be useful to our younger brother, we try to pay him back for his labors with our mental labor . . .

The muzhik is stupid, he cannot arrange things for himself. If no one takes care of him, he will burn all of the forest, he will kill all of the birds, he will catch all of the fish, he will ruin the land and die off himself.[. . .]

I repeat: there were also many laws before, but still it was easier, because the authorities were far away. An order would come out, they would give out an order in the volosts—well, and they would carry it out in the villages which were on major highways. And that would be the end of it. No one would begin to carry it out without a new order; everyone would think that it was ordered only for "that time." If an order came out not to cut birches for "May trees" wherever the order reached "properly," there they did not cut trees in that year. The next year, there is no order, everywhere, they put up "May trees." If a "strict" order came to plant birches along the streets, they planted. The birch trees dried up; there is no order the next year, no one would plant new ones, and even the volost authorities forgot about the order. Furthermore, the volost elder, hundreder, as muzhiks, also think as muzhiks do, that an order is made only for this one time.[. . .] It would seem that it was already absolutely necessary to put up landmarks in the winter along the roads—you get lost yourself without landmarks at night—however, without an order, no one puts up landmarks because they have gotten in the habit of waiting for orders. It is now time to pay taxes. Everyone could know from experience that one should pay taxes on time, that they will not be waived; but even so, without a special order, and a strict one besides, no one, not a single "wealthy peasant" will begin to pay: maybe it can be avoided, maybe they won't demand them.

And I repeat again: there were always a lot of laws, but it was easier before. If the highest official, the district policeman, or Sir Superintendent himself were to ride up, how was he to remember everything? He only remembers what it is that he has come about, that should be "due" at that time. The plague broke out,[12] they insisted on cleanliness: air the izbas, change shirts, don't eat rotten fish. We were tired of cleanliness; we already were afraid that they might somehow forbid us to shovel manure in the yards. We are happy when we have a lot of manure, we love it, its odor is pleasant to us, but the authorities do not know that "you put down shit, but you get gold." After the plague, it became easier in regard to cleanliness: they do not give orders to air the izbas, or forbid eating rotten fish. Fires became the rage. Birches, tubs, fire-fighting equipment, buildings according to plans arrived, tear down storehouses, don't smoke pipes, put barns fifty sazhens away, (the peasants have so much land, so what do fifty sazhens mean here?). Subversive people appeared, again there was alarm: they ask for passports and passes, they look each one over. It is impossible to go to town without being under view, people going on visits have even begun to carry passes with them because if you go without a pass, just watch, you will wind up in jail.[. . .]

The plague passed, and cleanliness passed; the fires passed and storehouses stand on their former spots; subversive people will pass, and passes will also pass away. But since the authorities will not want to sit idly, something else will turn up. For example, that birds' nests not be ruined and that peasants treat animals gently.

Thus everything gallops along. It is understandable that it is difficult for the highest official, the head of the district police, for example, to know and remember everything. He must be an architect, and a chemist and a doctor, and an engineer, and a zoologist, and a politician and a historian. He rides by and sees that a boy is sitting in a tree and is destroying a bird's nest. This is forbidden, but there is an exception for this: it is permitted to destroy the nests of birds of prey. The question is, whose nest is he destroying: carrion crows or doves, sparrows or wagtails? How is the official to know all the birds, what kind of bird has what kind of nest and what kind of eggs? Fortunately the following comes to his rescue: destroying animals of prey in forbidden times is allowed only with the previous notification, each time, of the district police.

"Hey! Petrov," he turns to a lower official who is galloping beside the carriage, "did he inform you that he was going to destroy the nest of some birds of prey?"

"Not at all."

"Hey, you, boy!" . . .

But here again, one is reminded that this regulation does not include landowners and their hunters, who can destroy birds of prey in their own country houses at any time and without informing the police.

"Hey, boy!"

"What?"

"What village are you from?"

"What?"

"What village are you from?"

"From Poderevo," the boy answers as he slides down from the tree.

"Are you people under temporary obligation?"

"What?"

"Don't you understand, are you temporarily obligated peasants?"

The boy, God granting him legs, takes off into the forest. "Whoa-o-o-o!" is suddenly heard resonating from the forest.

[Engelgardt here describes the kind of petty surveillance he was subjected to and the interrogation of the peasants in his area about his behavior and the activities on his estate.]

The establishment of village constables was marked by the fact that night watchmen were introduced in the villages. I do not know whether this was required before or if the new officials introduced them, only it was very strict last fall in regard to watchmen.

The establishment of village constables was marked by the fact that night watchmen were introduced in the villages.[. . .] Everywhere in the villages boards were hung up on which the watchmen were supposed to knock at night.[13] And in fact they did knock; if you came out on the porch in the autumn, you would hear a rumbling from all of the surrounding villages. They stop all passersby and question them. In one village they stopped a liquor licensing agent—just you try and catch the diversion of liquor—they took him for a subversive and wanted to put him in jail, but fortunately someone identified him.

But *he* flies like an eagle from tavern to tavern and wherever there is no guard on the street—a fine. In one village the peasants told how a peasant woman had to be the night watchman in the winter: it was their household's time and her husband was not there. So she—everyone knows that a baba is a fool—went back into the izba to breast-feed her child, you see she was a gentle one, she could not feed and change the baby on the road. And to her misfortune, the official turns up. "What's this? Where is the guard?" He shouted out, the noise filled the entire village, he gave the woman a five-ruble fine. Five rubles! Around here a woman earns fifteen kopeks for a day's labor, for twenty kopeks she will brake flax all night long. Five rubles! And her husband will beat her besides. The woman became afraid, she began to beg hin to have mercy, she dragged on his feet, but he stood firm, with his arms akimbo, he laughed, he was cheerful!

And why are there these watchmen in the villages? And who is it they are to catch? Horse thieves, robbers? As if a horse thief with horses is going to go right past a guard! As if you are going to catch a thief—it is not written on his forehead that he is a robber! "Who's passing?" "Our people." The watchmen see that it is really a muzhik, one of ours, so, go with God. As if a robber is going to begin to dress like a nobleman, in German dress so that the guards will stop him. The guards have also not been any help against fires: there have never been as many fires as there were last year, when they introduced the guards. The muzhiks explain that the guards were introduced "for the sake of strictness," that means, so that it would be "strict." But what do these guards cost the muzhik! To say nothing of the fines, of the missing teeth, if you put a price only on the time spent by the muzhiks on the guarding, putting thirty kopeks a night for two men, the enormous sum of one hundred rubles a year for each village accumulates. One hundred rubles for each village! And for this money you could buy off all of the robbers and horse thieves. On my estate I long ago got to the point that I eliminated watchmen and guards because, in general, this was more costly than the theft of horses.[. . .]

Persecution of Local Jews

They [the officials] pestered the muzhiks, to say nothing of how they perse-cuted the Jews, so much so that it is amazing how the Jews even survive. A Jew must always be afraid, it is always possible to irritate him, it is always possible to insult him, to extort from him, for even he knows himself that it is impossi-ble to do without this, he can only accept his own "groveling." And this was somehow put on them, the Jews, it was self-determined; a new breed of officials appeared, "groveling" appeared for them also.

Formerly Jews were not allowed to live here, now only craftsmen are allowed to live here.[14] Meanwhile, there are Jews whose fathers lived here, who themselves were born here and gave birth to a pack of children. Of course, they were all dyers and distillers and so on. It is impossible, of course, to live by a craft in the village, and this is not in the Jew's character, and that is why the Jews who live here keep mills, taverns, practice trade and various things. All of this is forbidden, but one way or another, they get away with it. The Jews are profitable for the landowners because they pay well and are capable of doing anything. The Jews hang out primarily around the rich land-owners who have influence, especially around those who have liquor distiller-ies. No matter that everything is done according to the law, the official can still find fault and the Jew must feel this and does feel it. Finally, if the Jew himself lives according to the law, and all of his "passes" are in order, it can still turn out that some relative lives with him illegally, some kind of teacher for the children or simply various illegal Jews who have come for a holiday, wedding, or the Sabbath.

They do not keep an eye on the Jews constantly, but sporadically, in certain years. Sometimes they do not touch them at all, and, having done their "groveling," the Jews live in peace. There is no order from above, and without a special order each time, no regulations, orders, decrees, all that is called the law here, will be executed and will not be required. That is the only reason why it is possible to live, for "if one always lived according to the laws, the Sir Chief of the District Police himself could not live," says a Jew I know. Sometimes Jews live for a long time in peace without any artisan's licenses whatsoever—and nothing happens. In locations that are suitable in such peaceful times, close to roads that are being built, close to liquor distilleries, large lumbering operations, in general where an enterprising, intelligent Jewish man can equip himself and earn money, a great number of Jews multiply. When I arrived in the country, there was just such a peaceful period for the Jews around here, when they were not persecuted or driven away; furthermore, before that the railroad had been built and there was every kind of speculation: they built trackmen's huts, cut rails, hauled stones, provided bread for the workers—to say nothing of the vodka. Of course, the muzhik also cuts rails, and the muzhik breaks stones, and the muzhik drinks vodka; but without smart Jews he will not do any of this. There were a lot of Jews here then; Jews were at almost all, even the smallest, mills, they managed taverns and were involved in all kinds of speculation, they had completely beaten the small merchants out because how was some kind of small merchant to stand up to the Jew?

Suddenly they began to persecute Jews. They did not allow those who did not have trading licenses to live here, and there was not a single such person. So, the Jews said nothing, did nothing—it did not help! They persecuted them, they sent order after order to the hundreder: escort them out of the district! They gave the hundreder liquor once, they did it again, they slipped him something . . . again, order after order! The Jews started to go headlong to get documents and to ask "their elders" to help, to intervene; some succeeded, others did not, and at the same time that "their people" were hustling higher up, orders and more orders kept coming. You can't do anything; they began to remove Jews from district to district. It was impossible to stay in one place, a Jew would hire a wagon, gather all his goods, feather beds, cattle, poultry, women, and children, move to a neighboring district, settle there and live until they drove them out of there as well. Then he, depending upon the circumstances, would go to a third district or return to the former one. Of course, such upheavals could not be long-term. The Jews began to disappear, but those who remained lived rather peacefully, and bit by bit, new ones also began to appear again.

And then the new officials appeared. These soon found out where the crayfish winter;[15] there was no living for the Jews: no kind of "groveling" satisfied the new officials.

One day, as I was walking around the fields, I met a Jewish woman who was trading in various small wares.

"Sir, oh Sir, where does the road here go closer to the town?" she stopped me. I pointed to the road.

"And who are the gentlemen on this road?"

"Well, right beyond that little wood an official lives, he is of the 'nobility,' he lives with his family, maybe they will buy something."

"An official! Akh, dear sir, isn't there another road, isn't it possible somehow to get around the official?"

"It's possible. But is something not in order with you?"

"No, everything's in order."

"So what are you afraid of? He is nothing."

"Dear lord! It doesn't take much to insult a poor Jewish woman!"

Of course, I showed her another road.

And then a rumor spread somehow that *they* [the officials] were being eliminated.

A Jew I know came by who had been born here illegally at a time when Jews were not allowed to live here at all; he also grew up outside the law, and outside the law he also had children.

I immediately guessed that the Jew, riding past, could not resist coming by to share some fresh news.

"They are going to be eliminated! They are going to be eliminated!"

"Well, and thank God!" I crossed myself.

The Jew almost crossed himself by mistake.

"And all of our people made a great fuss," the Jew boasted. "That's why nothing was enough for them. So take your 'groveling' and money too, and flour, and corn, and roosters. Isn't that enough?"[. . .]

Bureaucratic Measures to Prevent Plague

The plague appeared. This plague caused such terror that our gentrywomen wanted to flee. However, they did not flee; they felt remorse about leaving their husbands, who were staying "at their posts." But they were terribly afraid even so.[. . .]

An order came about the plague. They are not going to allow the plague to spread. They have established an office to prevent the plague. In one of our district zemstva, they proposed appointing two constables, paid for by the zemstvo, whose sole responsibility would be "not to allow infection" within the boundaries of the district. They turned to doctors; in this same zemstvo, the doctors unanimously supported the need for strict surveillance over passports of all people who have recently arrived. And the doctors could not think up anything else. Constables and passports, passports and constables.

They are not allowing the plague to spread!

The doctors' proposal about passports was especially successful. They insisted so intensely on passports and tickets that even now they will not let you off. Formerly it was simple in regard to passports; you could go not only to your neighbor's, not only to the district town, but even to the provincial capital without a pass, but now, no, don't try that with me! The hundreders, tenners, elders, and guards have been made so strict that you cannot slip past. "And who are you?" "May I ask for your pass?"

The muzhiks are most strict in regard to passes for those in the upper class whom they suspect of being noblemen who oppose the Tsar "because he wants to give the peasants the land." The muzhiks do not stop their own brother, the Russian man, the muzhik, the priest, the trader, the merchant; the muzhiks are also afraid to stop a real lord who is riding on his own horses with "a man," who has a noble demeanor, real noble ways. However, even so, the rule holds: "If you keep a good reserve you won't live in misery and you won't beg for bread," one must always have a pass "in reserve," if you don't want to go to jail or even worse. Especially if you are caught on Nikola, the Feast of the Holy Virgin, or of the Savior, when the villages are making merry, when even the chief avoids the merrymakers.

But *he,* he leaned more heavily on the muzhik about the passports because here he would get more to drink as a bribe.

"Who are you?" he asks a muzhik who is coming from a neighboring district, is looking for work, or is visiting his relatives.

The muzhik quails.

"You are not from here?"

"From Podkalinovka, sir, I'm not from here."

"Do you have a pass?"

The muzhik totally loses control.

"A fine! Come with me. You are loafing around here without a passport . . . just see what I will do with you! Come, come with me."

"Let me off, sir."

"A fine. Three rubles."

And the newspapermen were all saying that they are going to eliminate passports entirely? And we believed it, we thought that the people there in St. Petersburg know everything! Know-it-alls! Then the business of "cleanliness" appeared. They found out that the plague does not like "cleanliness" and they began to get strict. Kolenov, a columnist at the *Smolensk Herald,* described how there was an order throughout the volosts to "cool" the izbas three times a day, that is, to open the doors to clean the air, and to change underwear two times a week. And this for the muzhik who often has no more than two shirts—to change his underclothes twice a week! To ventilate, three times a day, a little izba full of holes in which it is practically impossible to retain heat. Of course, it is true that the air is not very good in an izba where there are children, swine, cows, and sheep; but first, rather than order the ventilation of izbas, the zemstvo would have done better to take care that the muzhik had enough forest for building and for firewood. Why "cool" here when many have nothing to heat with? We were afraid that they would order us to carry the manure away from the yards and burn it in the name of "cleanliness." How is it that they did not order the muzhiks to eat well every day, to eat beef, and wheat bread? It is said that during the infectious season, this is essential.

How is it that the zemstvo did not issue such an order?[. . .] During the plague we also found out that one needs to use fresh supplies in food. We always ate smoked salted beef, and fish that had gone bad, and rotted Astrakhan herring. We ate all of this before and suddenly it turned out that this was all poison. Doctors were ordered to inspect the fish and if they noticed even the smallest amount of plague in it, the police were supposed to destroy the infected fish. It was a little difficult to accept this; it happened, and more than once, that the burned fish, which had been identified as harmful and rotten, or fish which had been buried in the earth and covered as a precaution with filth taken from latrines were still taken from the fires or dug up from the ground and cooked. It happened that they even sold the stolen fish, having washed off the filth well!

Then came disinfection; they said that we needed to disinfect the fish. But how does one disinfect fish? With carbolic acid? With chlorine? With sulphur? It would be curious to know what kind of taste chlorinated sturgeon, caviar with carbolic acid, sulphuric sturgeon has. But it did not reach that point yet. But what about the herring, the herring, the Astrakhan herring which the muzhik eats with vodka in all the taverns, posting inns, fairs, and markets? How much of this herring is brought to each town, and in each herring, perhaps, there is plague, every herring can contain unhygienic conditions and every herring you look inside of, you sniff. Who is to execute all of this? Who is going to be these protectors of the herring? Doctors? Constables? Or some new ranks will be introduced in uniform, with a little copper herring head on his cap: Sanitary man, they say, a disinfector. Yes and disinfect every herring, and however you disinfect it with carbolic acid, it may still be that one cannot eat it. Furthermore, carbolic acid also grabs your insides.

And how are the doctors to recognize which rotten thing can be eaten, and which cannot? He will smell it and recognize it! Of course, each one of them studied at least twelve years in various institutions and should know everything. But even so there is something strange; is there something about their noses that distinguishes them? I was so seized by this doubt that whenever I happen to be in town I look at the nose of every doctor I meet to see if I notice something special.[. . .]

Everything passes. They have eaten and eat rotten fish and rotten salted beef. It tastes fine.[. . .]

A neighboring gentlewoman strictly forbade "the folk" to eat simple herring, but we ate it and did not get sick, did not die. Yes, and "the folk" also ate it because the gentlewoman, having forbidden Astrakhan herring, did not buy good Dutch herring for "the folk."

Simple people, Russian people, muzhiks, traders, did not recognize plague, they did not believe in the plague, they considered this all to be an invention of the lords. "Who knows whether the lords dreamed up this plague?"

"You may as well give up trade completely," the merchant said, "he comes into the store, sniffs, sniffs, just as if he knew what the plague smells like. Ruin; they have rejected so much fish; they bury it in the ground, but then they will dig it up and eat it! They are seeking cleanliness everywhere, don't cut your calf in your own courtyard."

This year in our province, worms which were terribly alarming for farmers attacked the flax. The first one to be alarmed was the landowner Sharapov from Viazma and he immediately called the police superintendent. Having received the despairing telegram, the superintendent was frightened: what kind of worms are these? He galloped up with the district police officer and two cans of carbolic acid (*Smolensk Herald* 1879, nos. 56 and 57). But the worms were not afraid of either the carbolic acid or the district police officer, or Sir Superintendent himself; they are eating the flax up, and that's that, no respect for the authorities. Articles about the worm from the quick hand of Mr. Sharapov and from various districts of the Smolensk Province poured in. All of the correspondents reporting about the worm write one and the same thing: they are eating the flax and the authorities aren't keeping an eye on it. The peasants, not knowing any other means, turn only to prayers and holy processions, but the authorities do nothing, neither the zemstvo, nor the administration turns to any measures whatsoever!

In fact this is really terrible! A worm is eating our flax and the authorities watch, and don't take any kind of measures whatsoever. Akh! Sir liberals, sir liberals! You can't do anything yourselves, you keep running to the authorities. And what is there for the authorities to do? Is it not enough for you that Sir Superintendent himself galloped up after receiving the telegram, and with the district police officer and two cans of carbolic acid to boot? What else do you want? Not really for the governor himself to come? How is the administration to blame for the fact that the carbolic acid did not work, that the worm was not afraid of even the district police officer! The worm is really no match for students, look in what bunches they crawl. The superintendent remembers the carbolic acid from the plague, and so he brings it. What else do you want? Not that new authorities to deal with the worms be introduced, not that they think up special passports!

My Descent into Alcoholism

I wrote you that when I left St. Petersburg, at the station, among the other relatives and friends, one of my close relatives came to see me off, a gentry woman who is not young, who had lived and farmed for a long time in the country, but who had long ago come to St. Petersburg to do other things.

"I don't know," she said, "may God grant that you have luck with farming; perhaps it will turn out with you; only I don't know . . . I fear only that you will turn to drink in the countryside."

"Why?"

"Because there have been many who have gone to the country, full of strength, hungry to do something, but who turned to drink there."

"Yes, but why?"

"Just think about the fact that you will always be alone; just imagine the winter, winter evenings! If only several people were gathered in one place . . ."

"I won't turn to drink."

Since I drank vodka before, I continued to drink in the country. I drank after lunch and then I slept; I drank after dinner and then I slept. Moreover, talking as the muzhiks do, I even "made merry" upon occasion. Weddings, Nikola, mowing, threshing, planting, farewell parties, welcome home parties, the forming of artels, and so on and so forth, all of this is accompanied with drinking, in which I also took part. There was occasion "to make merry" in a big way, in true fashion. However, all of this was fine. And now eight years have passed, and in the ninth one, the prediction of my relative came to pass. I turned to drink. Now this is already a thing of the past, but I turned to drink, I got sick, I began to have hallucinations . . .

How did this happen? Well, listen . . .

I must tell you that I had a terrible fear of any kind of official, I was irrationally afraid, nervous, the way others fear mice, frogs, and spiders. I could in no way get used to the little bells, especially in the evening, at night, when you can't look out to see who is riding past. As soon as I hear a little bell, I break out in a nervous shiver, my heart races, I have a certain uneasiness; I could only save myself with vodka; I would toss back a wine glass immediately. They passed by. So, thank God, my heart lightened. And if they turned into the yard, I would take the bottle and drink straight from it . . . Thus the constable never saw me other than drunk.

Formerly our constable was a terribly penetrating man, he would notice right away. And I must thank him, he was a tactful man, he rarely came himself, he sent everything through the hundreder, and I was not afraid of the hundreder: perhaps because he was a muzhik, not in uniform. But whenever it was necessary for the constable to come himself, his first words were, "Don't worry, it is nothing special." The constable was wonderful, I was under his authority for six years, living as Christ lived in the wilderness. He was a tactful man. Then a different constable arrived, he was also a splendid man, and he came by rarely. Well, and I always behaved properly so that there would be no reason to come to see me: the taxes were paid on time, the roads were all in good order, and if I knew that the higher authorities would be riding past, I would order that the dirt along the sides of good roads be dug, as if they were under repair, so that it would be clear to the official that we had taken care about his passage, that we had showed respect. If they came to collect for some good cause, I was also in good order; if they were collecting for cruisers, for a cross, for the lottery, I would hand over a three-ruble note right away . . .

Finally, the new official also arrived, and it was also fine; he did not even give me a glance, because everything was in order.

But since last winter, it has suddenly become different. The official rides up sometime in the morning; of course, I, as soon as I heard the bell, I grabbed the bottle right away; having looked through the window, I see the official's horses, I grab it again. I felt better. I thought it was about some collection—no. No, only empty papers; he sits down for a chat, he looks startled somehow, he asks who comes to my place, he asks about outsiders who come to learn about farming.

I found out later that there was someone in the village as well, he asked, and mostly among the women, about who comes to my place, what they do, how I live, what kind of behavior I have, "that is, how you are with women," the muzhiks explained to me.

After several days, a lower official, one of the new ones, came by. The priest dropped in, I see that he is acting strange somehow, he beats around the bush, he makes hints, just as if he were justifying himself for something.

An "opinion" about me began to gather, and that was already the last straw; the muzhiks say that "slanders" come most of all from "an opinion." I began to drink more and more.

It continued, I drank more. I saw them coming and that was it. And every time I would drink and drink and always at different times; sometimes in the afternoon, sometimes in the evening, sometimes in the morning. If you have to, you drink on an empty stomach. In order not to have to run after the vodka, I put a bottle in my room on my writing table. In anticipation of visits, I began to have a drink even without the bell.

I heard rumors even among the muzhiks, they began to put them up to it. "You will have to answer along with your lord," they say. "What is going on at his place? What kind of people go there? Is it right for the gentry to work themselves?"

I need to point out that I recognize only one science in farming for educated people who want to settle on the land—learn to work, work as the muzhiks do, yes, even in the muzhik's skin. I say to the person who wants to learn how to farm, "become a worker, work, plough, mow, thresh, work like a muzhik, live a bit with the workers, be in their skin." The Russian educated person is lacking precisely the *ability to work,* and there is nowhere for him to learn this unless he learns it by having been a worker-muzhik. I value an educated person who wants to be a farmer only to the extent that he is a muzhik. I am convinced that more than anything else we need educated muzhiks, villages of educated people, that our future depends on this. If only 1,000 young people of the educated class who had received an education, every year, instead of becoming bureaucrats, became muzhiks, settled on the land, we would soon receive results that would amaze the world. I believe that this is the calling of Russia's educated youth. And people have been found who agreed with my system of teaching farming, who came as workers, who worked like muzhiks, and *worked honorably.*

Of course, it was strange for the muzhiks that suddenly gentry sons were working, working like muzhiks, that they did not "take it easy," but really worked. But the muzhiks understand that this is a real "business," although they look at it with mistrust, even suspiciously, supposing that a noble's son can never reach the muzhik's level of work. The muzhiks are afraid precisely that if the gentry sons learn how to work, then the muzhik will lose his entire meaning, all of his greatness. Here the pride of the muzhik suffers: look, he's of the nobility, and he has learned how to work, "Only what can he do, he has a long way yet to catch the muzhik! How is he to be a farmer![. . .]" the muzhik says, as if to console himself. The muzhik begins to laugh when he sees someone of the educated class beginning to work. He is as funny to him as a monkey imitating a man is to us; he regards him scornfully, but not with malice. The half nobility regards it completely differently, all of these people who play the noble, the village and settlement people, who dress "like the lords" and wear "frock coats," who mistrust the uneducated muzhik and his work. Here the attitude is completely malicious. What! How can the son of a priest, a literate, educated person who could have been a sexton, who could have entered the service, who could have earned a rank, suddenly be working, and really working, side by side with peasants, with uneducated peasants! It is disgraceful. Well, and it was these who did most of the talking, who badgered the muzhiks, who wrote denunciations. Although even the muzhiks said, "What's this! They're not hiding, they're working with the peasants, there's no trickery, there's no empty business! You go and plough—there's nothing tricky here!" However, they had an influence also on the muzhiks, it seemed to me in the end. Or maybe it was that the "opinion" had overwhelmed me, only I will say: if you give a muzhik money, he will turn the paper, turn it and look it over. Aha! I think, does he suspect that counterfeit money is being made on my estate! In the spring, the officials began to come even more often, they asked for everyone's passes, they recorded, looked around, looked over outsiders, they wrote down their features. "It was ordered to know everyone by face," they said. My children arrived; I saw that the little gymnasium student had a pass also, which had not happened before; he was even happy because now he has a passport like *a grown-up*. The official came by, I presented the children's passes to him to record.

"Your children's? No, forgive me, that is not necessary."

"Yes, but you said yourself that all of the arrivals must be collected to be recorded. And if he goes to the village to play with the children, and the tenner[16] will say to him, 'Where is your pass?' No, it is better to register them."

The longer it went on, the more often the officials began to come by. And it seems to me that they are interrogating, they are working on the muzhiks, turning them against me. I began to drink seriously, without a break. I got sick, I couldn't walk, I was terribly short of breath, I had pressure in my chest, my heart was beating fast, my hands trembled; you drink up, it is as if you are better for a minute, but then it is even worse. I fell off work, a terrible irritability set in, any trifle irritated, upset me . . . You go out into the field, you don't have the strength to go, you break out in sweat; you go back to the house, you pick up a newspaper, you shake even more, the letters merge in some kind of cloud and suddenly through the cloud the face of the official in his cap appears . . . I myself understood that I had already drunk myself to the point of seeing demons; I myself knew that I should not drink this poison, but I couldn't give it up, I didn't have the willpower.

Once, toward evening, *he* came by my place, he was drunk; as soon as he came by, he began to make merry, and came to call. We drank together; *he* left, and I went to see him off, we came out from the porch, we walked around the yard, suddenly *he,* I still don't know why, became conciliatory somehow, shook me by the shoulder, "You are a splendid fellow, Aleksandr Nilolaevich, a splendid fellow!" he said. "A Napoleon! A real Napoleon! . . ."

Several days later, my brother arrived and he was horrified. My nephews arrived and with them, a doctor I knew well. The doctor advised me not to drink and to be out in the air more. I obeyed him, I was frightened of death, and I gave it up.

Now I am healthy, and I am not afraid.

That is how it happens.

Letter IX

✉   The following excerpt consists of Engelgardt's clear and concise exposition of the factors shaping the economics of seasonal labor.[1] This phenomenon was a source of great concern for observers inside the government, agronomists, gentry landowners in need of hired labor, and radicals who hoped to capitalize on the emergence of a peasant proletariat to destabilize the Imperial regime. In the wake of the Emancipation, gentry landowners needed to adjust to their loss of subsidized free labor in the form of their serfs. Many were long in becoming reconciled to the fact that peasant labor henceforth would be compensated labor. Peasants, meanwhile, needed to develop a system for meeting their new cash obligations, securing access to pasture and forestland, and providing a subsistence on their allotment lands, which too frequently were inadequate in either quantity or quality or both.

Engelgardt explains in the ninth letter that the goals of most gentry landowners are the very opposite of those of peasant farmers. He identifies the central tension inherent in farming for profit using wage laborers who are themselves farmers: gentry employers aim to compensate the peasants as little as possible for the greatest amount of work during the farming season, while peasants strive to avoid as much as possible being forced into doing any kind of work for gentry landowners during the planting and harvest. "The landowner wants to get hold of the peasant, to harness him, to tie him to the shaft, while the muzhik will not give in, he breaks free, he tries not to be harnessed."

Peasants continue to be harnessed, Engelgardt explains, because of the gentry's clever, farsighted, and ultimately exploitative success in cutting off pasture and forestlands from the peasants' allotments in Emancipation land settlements. In a pattern that has been repeated in other land reforms (Mexico is a particularly appropriate comparison), landowners continue to be able to force labor out of their former serfs after the Emancipation in exchange for access to these cutoff lands. In addition to this primary factor, Engelgardt also discusses the impact of grain prices on the gentry and the peasantry, and the peasants' approach to winter wage labor as opposed to summer wage labor for the local gentry. This excerpt serves as the background for the following three letters in which Engelgardt will explain the causes for the increasing prosperity, even in the face of these pressures, of several villages in the area around his estate.

✉   ✉   ✉

[Engelgardt begins this letter with a discussion of the complexities of farming and a critical description of bureaucratic measures that tried to impose "scientific" ideas about agriculture on the peasants.]

The Economics of Seasonal Labor for the Peasant

The muzhik who does not obligate himself to do work in the summer, who works for himself in the summer, prospers; the muzhik who obligates himself to do summer work becomes poor. How many times have I had to hear the muzhik accused of laziness, of having no desire to work, when gentry farms offer so much seasonal work. "So what if grain is expensive," people say, "take on some work on gentry estates, then you will have grain." But one must really look into the kind of wages these are that the muzhik avoids, which he is ready to flee from even to the kulak. The muzhik is impoverished by these wages, he is ruined; this is the kind of wages these are.

The muzhik who has his own land, his own farm, must not go to do summer harvest work for someone else for any kind of money, because, working for someone else in the summer, he will inevitably neglect his own farm. You cannot put a price on a horse you haven't had to sell, and happy is he who has such a horse. You cannot put a price on labor you haven't had to sell, and happy is he who has such labor. But hunger will force one to sell one's beloved horse, hunger will force one to sell even labor during the harvest.

If you have ever lived in the summer as a guest at a landowner's, then you have undoubtedly seen how the farmer will be disturbed, how he will be upset in the summer when rain, for example, hinders the gathering of hay or grain, you have seen how the landowner, the steward, even the workers become upset at the sight of passing clouds. So just imagine the moral state of the muzhik-farmer when he must abandon his own hay which is being beaten down in the meadow by rain, who had just barely before the rain managed to put it into stacks, and must leave it to go gather someone else's hay. Imagine the situation of the farmer who must leave his grain in the rain in order to go haul someone else's sheaves. One needs to be a farmer oneself to understand fully that terrible moral state a man is in in such instances and one cannot be surprised by the indifference with which the muzhik, having left his own field, goes to the gentry's. Only many years of slavery, of serf labor for the lord could develop such coolness. "Ours must wait only so that yours, the lord's, is gathered," the muzhik will say to the lord even now, still, out of old habit, repeating what he was accustomed to saying when he was a serf.

But this indifference is only apparent, one must see what is happening inside, in the soul of the farmer, how he curses fate, how he swears never to take on harvest work again. This is visible on the outside only among the young, those who were not worn down by the habits of serfdom, and among the babas. The hired hand, the landless peasant who does not have his own farm does not experience anything like this, but as a result, he develops a certain dullness.

Working on a gentry estate in the summer, during harvesttime, ruins the muzhik; and that is why he goes to such work only out of extreme need, trying to avoid such work as much as possible.[. . .]

I am talking not about hired hands but about muzhiks, agriculturalist-farmers, people who are capable, as long as there is something with which and on which to work, of following their own plan. For such people, piecework during the harvest on gentry estates is a calamity, ruin. The muzhik flees work for the landowner during the harvest. He will struggle to the bitter end and take on harvest work only when there is no possibility whatsoever of avoiding it, when there is no grain, when he has to sell his cattle for his arrears. If there is any way at all of getting money, even at a high rate of interest, the muzhik prefers to borrow as long as he is not obligated to do summer work, especially constant work for the entire summer, for example, cultivating land for the full cycle on gentry estates, which consists of the peasant, for a certain pay, obligating himself for the duration of the summer with his horse and tools, to do the complete cultivation of the land on three fields for the landowner, just as this was done during serfdom.

Winter work is a completely different matter. The muzhik takes on winter work willingly and cheaply, and if there is no profitable work, he will take on even the kind which brings only grain and manure, that is, he earns only enough to feed himself and his horse. The whole crux of the matter for the muzhik consists of profitable winter earnings, because winter earnings give him the chance to work in the summer for himself, of not obligating himself to do summer harvest jobs for others. It is more profitable for the farmer who has his own land to work for twenty-five kopeks a day in the winter than for three rubles during the harvest. Meanwhile, it is precisely in the winter that gentry estates do not offer jobs or offer only very few, but they require summer labor. The interests of the peasants and the landowners, in the existing order, are completely contradictory. The constant dream of the muzhik is to free himself from summer work for the landowner; the constant dream of the landowner is to force the muzhik to work for him in the summer.[. . .]

The existence of gentry estates *is made possible* precisely by *the very existence of such dependents,* poor peasants who have no real grain, but only *weak grain and even that is dropping off the stalk,* while the muzhik does jobs for which he obligated himself in the winter, whose "mouth is wide." The prosperous peasants do not hire themselves out for any kind of money. Consequently, *in order for there to be someone to work on gentry estates, it is necessary that there be needy, poor people.* Does this constitute a system?[. . .]

Even now, the foundation of gentry farms has not changed from what it was during serfdom. Of course, gentry farms, in our localities at least, have declined, have become smaller, but the essence, the foundation of the system remains the same as it was before 1861.

Formerly, during serfdom, gentry fields were cultivated by peasants who went out to these fields with their tools and horses; gentry fields are cultivated now as well in just the same way by the very same peasants with their horses and tools, with the sole difference that these are not *serfs* doing the work, but people who are already indebted during the winter.[. . .]

And thus, on the one hand—it is ruin for the muzhik if he has to work in the summer for someone else; on the other hand—the landowner cannot run his farm without the summer labor of the muzhik-farmer. Therefore, there is a constant contest between the landowner and the neighboring muzhik-farmers. The landowner wants to get hold of the peasant, to harness him, to tie him to the shaft, while the muzhik will not give in, he breaks free, he tries not to be harnessed.[. . .] And you see that wherever the muzhik succeeds in avoiding work on gentry land, wherever he works for himself in the summer, the peasants grow rich and do well. On the other hand, wherever the landowner has harnessed the peasants, he has collared them, there the peasants have a lower standard of living, there there is poverty and drunkenness. The very first, the most important means, the strongest harness for keeping the peasants bound to the shaft are *cutoff lands* and *pasture rights*.[. . .]

The need for pasture is now the most important thing for peasants. If the peasants have enough of their own grain, if there is enough grain to last until the "new harvest," if they also have winter earnings, then nothing, except the need for pasture, can make them take on the cultivation of gentry land. No amount of money can seduce the peasant farmer who works the land. Peasants can rent meadows for money or as sharecroppers even at a distance from the village; they can buy firewood and forestland elsewhere; they can also rent land; it is only pasture that they absolutely must rent near the village from the neighboring landowner. That is why we hear this kind of praise for estates: "The peasants cannot not work for me because my land goes right up to the village, there is nowhere for the muzhik to let his chickens go," or "He has a splendid estate, the cutoffs make a narrow strip for fourteen versts and take in seven villages, they cultivate all of his land for these cutoffs!" In a word, in assessing an estate, people look not at the quality of the land, not at the arable land, but at how the land is distributed in relation to the neighboring villages, whether it abuts them, whether it is essential for the peasants, whether they can get by without it or not. For that reason now, given the existing system of farming, an estate even without meadows, with bad land, produces a big income because it is laid out propitiously for the landowner in relation to the villages, and most important, it includes "cutoffs," without which the peasants cannot get by, which mark the border between their lands and the land of other landowners, so that it is not even profitable for the peasants to have competition between landowners, each of whom wishes to attract the peasants to work for him.

The most profitable case for the peasants is if they can rent the cutoffs or pastures for money or get the use of them in exchange for some kind of winter work—chopping or hauling firewood, loading wagons, and so on, as happens in those instances when some kind of merchant, or timber merchant who does not do farming buys the estate. In that case, the peasants immediately do well, become rich, because, having paid with winter work for the pastures or cutoffs they need, they then work all summer for themselves, they store up a lot of hay, they rent land to put under flax and grain. Fodder, which they buy from other people's arable, is eaten by their livestock in their own courtyards and they get manure which goes for fertilizing their own peasant allotment land. But if the landowner himself is farming, then he will give out neither pasture nor cutoff lands for money, but will require that the peasants cultivate his land in exchange for pasture and cutoffs. The entire design of the gentry farmer consists in making those peasants who need cutoffs work as much land as possible; all of the efforts of the peasants are directed to working as little as possible, and it is even better not to work by the *krug* at all and pay for the cutoff and pastures with money.

Thus, there is a constant struggle between the gentry and the peasants, and when the peasants win, their well-being increases and the gentry farms, often *to the profit of the landowners,* are crowded out. Yes, *it is profitable,* because instead of running an unprofitable farm, the landowner then *rents out his lands to the peasants* and receives more from them than he received when he ran a farm whose income was eaten up by maintaining the stewards and administration.

But wherever a landowner runs a farm, he forces the peasants to work on this farm. And the muzhik, pressed by pasturelands, by not having enough land, at a loss to himself, works for the landowner. And they both lose out: one receives little for his land, the other receives little for his labor.

The muzhik is oppressed, he is impoverished, the muzhik cannot pull himself up as he would if he did not have to work in vain on the stupid, useless, unprofitable gentry estate and could rent, or, even better, buy the same land that he *uselessly works* for the landowner. On the other hand, the landowner also does not get any income from his farm—all landowners justly complain about the unprofitability of farms—because the income the muzhik brings goes to the maintenance of the administrative staff, the horde of people who do not work and who are even suspicious of work and the muzhik, the parasites who, when they survive, become kulaks, oppressing the folk. For whom is there any profit? No one, except the future kulaks.[. . .]

I said that in our region most of the landowners farm without equipment and working stock, putting their land out to be cultivated entirely by the peasants. But there are farms on which there is equipment, and working stock, and the work is done by hired hands. However, even these farms cannot get by with hired hands alone and must hire peasants during harvesttime, especially for mowing. It is possible with hired hands only to cultivate the land, haul the winter manure, gather a part of the meadows, but for joint tasks, for mowing, gathering, hauling, generally during the harvest, extra hands are needed. The most important is mowing.

The first to hire themselves out for mowing are the landless babas, babas who live on their small plots, but who do not have land; for them mowing is the most important work which ensures their survival in the winter. Since the single woman does not plant grain, she has no mowing at home, she willingly hires herself out for this work, and for her it is important that there be as little competition as possible, that is, that there be fewer women who have their own grain, their own mowing, and who have taken on mowing for the gentry in the winter out of need. Consequently, it is important for the landless babas that the harvest be good, that grain be cheap, the muzhik expensive, that there be less need in the winter. But for the landowner, the landless babas alone are not enough, it is necessary that women from households also, who have their own mowing, abandon it, and go to mow on the gentry fields. But as soon as mowing has begun, as soon as the grain has ripened and it is possible, if not to bake bread, then to make rye kasha, not a single baba from a household will leave her plot, her mowing, and go to mow on someone else's field for any kind of money. In order for a baba to leave the grain on her plot to dry up and crumble and go to mow on someone else's field, this baba has to have obligated herself in advance during the winter. As soon as the mowing season has begun, it is impossible to hire anyone except the landless babas until the babas from households have reaped their own grain. Therefore, in order not to be left at the mowing with only single women, one needs to have enslaved the women in the winter already, and that is possible only when the muzhik does not have grain. There is no other way.

It is clear that the landowner needs grain to be expensive, and not only because he produces grain for sale, but also because *if grain is expensive and the muzhik is cheap,* it is possible to harness the muzhik. On the other hand, the muzhik needs grain to be cheap because the muzhik does not sell grain, but buys it for the most part; if the muzhik even has a little extra grain, he does not sell it, but wishes that there be enough grain until the new season so that it will be possible to live on his own grain for another year in the event that God sends hail. If a muzhik sells his grain in the autumn for small change, then he is either a drunkard who sells it for drink, or a poor peasant who does not have anything with which to buy salt, and tar, and nothing with which to pay the priest for prayers on holidays. A real peasant farmer of the land will not sell grain, even if he has a surplus, and even more so will not sell it in the autumn. Why sell grain—*grain is the same thing as money,* the muzhik says, and if, having sold hemp, flax, seeds, and hempseed oil, he can pay taxes, he will not sell grain, although he has enough for two years: he will feed his swine and cattle.

Which is why the muzhik sincerely prays to God for a good harvest, so that grain will be cheap.

Given the existing system of agriculture, given existing relations, it is profitable for everyone who produces grain for sale that grain be expensive. No one will say, of course, "This year, praise God, there is a bad harvest," but how can they not rejoice when there is a failed harvest abroad, when the demand for grain is great, when prices for grain are high? "This year the

German had a bad harvest, he needs grain, the demand is great, the prices are going up," everyone exults.[. . .] Herein lies the entire difference. The lord wants grain to be expensive, the muzhik wants grain to be cheap. A muzhik, even a rich one, will never rejoice over the high cost of grain. This need of the mass of the peasants for grain, this necessity that grain be cheap, is reflected in the fact that not a single peasant would ever say, "Praise God, grain is expensive." To say, "Praise God, grain is expensive"—this is more than impolite, it is more than shameful, it is an outrage, it is a sin, a great sin which God will punish.

[Engelgardt launches into a lengthy criticism of the policies on grain pricing and exports, and discusses their harmful effects for the peasant population.]

And is it not a mistake for us to rejoice when grain is expensive and the muzhik is cheap? Do we not mistakenly hope to raise our unfortunate ruble by putting the muzhik on potatoes? Yes, and is it really good that the cultured man lives well, although meat and the muzhik are cheap? Is this well-being not illusory? Should we not envy the American? The American eats well, he drinks well, he works with a machine, he has enough leisure; for without leisure you will not think up a machine; he is rich, he does not begrudge himself, and he gives others grain. But in Russia we have a bad harvest, poverty . . . Is it that we do not have enough land, that our land is not good?

There is plenty of land. Go wherever you wish, everywhere you see only empty lands, empty lands. Is the land bad? Not this either—plant wherever you wish, flax and grain and grass will come up splendidly. But dig deeper into it, plough well, test it the way the German tests it, and you will not be able to gather all the grain. One needs to fertilize land, and there is a wealth of substances for this, lime, peat, phosphorites, so much wealth that the Germans have not even dreamed of it.

There is a wealth of untouched land—there is room to expand.

We plough a total of some two vershoks and if this layer is destroyed, there is no need even to say it, there is still someplace to expand in the backwoods.

But still there is crop failure, famine, poverty. Why is this so?

I cannot believe that it is possible to acquire wealth by having put the muzhik on corn and potatoes. Something else is needed, but what? I am not educated enough to answer such questions, let those who have been schooled in all kinds of science answer, but I, for my part, will limit myself to describing in the next letter one "Happy Little Corner" where the peasants live well, where the well-being of the peasants has improved over the last ten years, where even this year, despite the high cost of grain, there is no great need. It is interesting, in my opinion, to point out the causes for the well-being of the agriculturalists of this "Happy Little Corner."

Letter X

✉   The tenth letter picks up where the ninth letter left off in laying out the economics of seasonal labor for the Russian peasant.[1] Here Engelgardt is able to develop a full analysis of developments in neighboring villages on the basis of the meticulous records he has kept over his ten years on Batishchevo. Among his many writing projects, he maintained a daily journal in which he recorded the weather; any grain, livestock, or equipment sales and purchases; labor agreements made with local peasants; and his consultations with Ivan and Avdotia. Drawing on these materials, he charts the course of peasant purchases of grain and labor agreements for a decade, and offers his analysis of the reasons for improved conditions in his area. He returns to the themes that have appeared throughout his discussion of peasant farming in Russia: seasonal labor, the significance of cutoff lands, fertilization, and peasant attitudes toward innovation.

In addition to this economic analysis, Engelgardt also devotes the final section of the letter to a social analysis of the kulak. Engelgardt's examination of this figure and his activities was a fundamental contribution to contemporary debate over the peasant mentality and a valuable essay on the subject for the historian of village culture and politics. Like most of his peers, Engelgardt identifies three chief features of the kulak's character: "individualism, egoism, and the striving for exploitation." In a private letter written at this time, he bemoaned the fact that the phenomenon of the kulak was growing "not by the day, but by the hour" in rural Russia.[2]

While Engelgardt attributes the urge to exploit to every peasant, he narrows his definition of the kulak to those peasants who not only exploit the need of others but themselves scorn work and pride themselves on their fat bellies and full moneybags. The kulak is thus the antithesis of both of Engelgardt's sacred principles of love of work and communal loyalties. By admitting that every peasant admires and hopes to emulate the kulak, he concedes that individualism was the sin of everyman, of even the good muzhik.

✉   ✉   ✉

Prospering Peasants in the "Happy Little Corner"

In my last letter I promised to describe one "Happy Little Corner" where the peasants live well, where the condition of the peasants has improved greatly over the last ten years, where even in this disastrous year of famine, when the price of rye rose to fourteen rubles a chetvert[3] even before Nikola, the peasants are not suffering and will not suffer. The majority of these peasants live on "their own" grain until the new grain comes in, and those who do not have enough of "their own" grain find money to purchase grain without enslaving themselves for summer work. This "Happy Little Corner" consists of several villages around the settlement of Batishchevo from which I have been writing my letters to you for ten years already.

Until now I have said very little about the condition of the local peasants, but even so, from my previous letters you could see that this condition was not enviable. But now ten years have passed and the condition of the peasants in the "Happy Little Corner" has noticeably changed for the better, and if some kind of special circumstances do not interfere, one can hope that it will continue to improve. The region of the "Happy Little Corner" is not large, it is some eight, ten villages. But you do not have to go far—about ten versts—to encounter villages where the condition of the muzhik is completely different, where the muzhik is poor, sells himself for summer labor early in the winter, abandons the land, hires himself as a hired hand, goes to work elsewhere.[. . .]

Having lived in the "Happy Little Corner" for ten years, and furthermore not simply as an outsider, but as someone who is personally running his affairs as a farmer, who must inevitably enter into close relations with the neighboring peasants, I have studied their condition in this specific spot and can say not only whether this condition has improved or worsened over the years, but I can also say precisely *why this happened*. In my opinion, what is really interesting is *elucidating the causes* which influence this change in condition because such causes should have influence in other areas as well.

I will say straightaway that in the "Happy Little Corner" *the condition of the peasants has improved* over the last ten years, it has improved greatly, *it has improved immeasurably*. But first of all, we will talk a bit about what I mean by the expression "improved" and how this improvement is measured.

If someone who is unfamiliar with the muzhik and the village is suddenly transplanted from St. Petersburg into the izba of a peasant of the "Happy Little Corner" and, not only in the izba of an average peasant, but even the izba of a "rich peasant," he will be shaken by the entire scene and will be horrified by the poor condition of this "rich peasant." A dark izba with blackened walls (because it is lit with a torch). Heavy air because the stove is closed early and the food sits in it: gray cabbage soup with lard and groats, or potatoes. In the alcoves by the stove there are a calf, a lamb, a piglet which smell. The children are in dirty shirts, they are bare-legged without pants, there is a stinking cradle, and a complete absence of any of the comforts which are typical even of the poorest educated man. All of this will shock a man who is unfamiliar with the village, especially someone from St. Petersburg, but he will be no less amazed by the fact that when he goes into the izba to hire horses to the nearest railroad stop, which is only six versts away, he will hear from the muzhik, "Nope, I won't go, look what kind of thaw there is, it's wet out, ask in another household, maybe somebody'll go, but not me."

The poor setup of the muzhik's izba and this unwillingness to go six versts in bad weather is usually very amazing for people who are unfamiliar with the village. One absolutely cannot judge the situation and wealth of a landed muzhik, even of a merchant who lives in the Russian style and trades Russian wares, by his decor, especially if *you take as your measure the decor in which educated people live.* Of course, it is possible to judge the prosperity of a muzhik by his possessions, but only those of the farm, or better to say, by his setup in the sense of those tools that are used in farming and for its expansion. Just as it is possible to judge the prosperity of the muzhik-kulak who works at moneylending by the quantity of money he puts in circulation, so it is possible to judge the prosperity of the landed muzhik who works with the land, at farming, by the number and quality of the horses and cattle he has, by the quantity of grain he has in storage, by the state of repair of his gear and tools. But the most important, most sure means for determining the condition of landed peasants in a given locality is to know *how much the peasants obligate themselves to do other people's work,* for example, for a landowner during the summer season, the most important one for farming.[. . .] If I say that the well-being of the peasants of the "Happy Little Corner" for the last ten years has improved it is precisely because I see a decrease in their need to obligate themselves for summer work for the gentry.

Around here a peasant is considered rich when he has enough of *his own* grain to last to the new harvest. Such a peasant *no longer needs to sell his summer labor* to a landowner, he can *work all summer for himself,* and consequently, he will prosper, and soon he will have enough grain to last not only to the new harvest, but even beyond. And then he will not only not sell his own summer labor, he will even buy the labor of the poor muzhik, of which there are a multitude not far from the "Happy Little Corner." If a peasant has enough of his own grain to last until the new harvest and he does not have to buy any, he is well provided for, because he pays his taxes through the sale of hemp, flax, flax and hemp seeds, extra animals, and winter earnings; if he also has the possibility of renting land from a landowner for planting flax or grain, the peasant will prosper quickly.

Furthermore, the degree of prosperity is really determined by the time when the peasant begins to buy grain: before Christmas, before Shrove Tuesday, after Easter, just before the new grain harvest. The later he begins to buy grain, the greater is his prosperity, the more quickly he can get by on the money he earns elsewhere in the winter, fall, and spring, the less he obligates himself to do summer work for a landowner. The earlier a muzhik eats up his own grain, the earlier he *is finished,* in the expression of the elders and the stewards, the easier it is to *harness* him for summer harvest work, the easier it is *to collar him, to bind him to the shaft.*

During the ten years I have farmed, I have only once sold my rye in bulk to a distillery; usually I sell all the rye on the spot to local peasants. Since my rye is of excellent quality, it is processed well, it is clean and thick, the peasants buy rye from me first and only go to town to buy rye when mine is all sold. As I sold my rye in small amounts to the peasants over ten years, I accurately recorded how much rye I sold, to whom and when, so that by this ten-year record, I can judge when and who of the local peasants began to buy grain, how much he bought, at what price, whether he bought it for money or took it *in exchange for labor* and precisely what kind of work, winter or summer. Since there is no reason for the local peasants to take grain anywhere except from me, my records represent an expense record of the neighboring peasants and provide splendid material for judging the situation of these peasants for the last ten years, which is enhanced by my personal acquaintance with these buyers of my grain, and along with this, with its producers, since work on the estate is also done for the most part by neighboring peasants.[4]

Ten years ago, in the villages of the "Happy Little Corner" I am describing, there were very few "rich peasants," that is, those peasants who had enough of their own grain to last until the new harvest, no more than one "rich peasant" per village, and moreover, even the rich peasants had enough grain only in years of good harvest; during a bad year, even the rich peasants bought. I should also mention, furthermore, that the rich peasants then were all kulaks who had money from way back or acquired in some unclean manner. With the exception of these rich kulaks, all of the rest of the peasants bought grain, and moreover, only a few of them began to buy grain just before the new harvest, most bought it beginning with Lent, there were many who bought beginning at Christmas, finally, there were many who sent their children after crusts of bread all winter long. I described this lack of grain among the local peasants and crusts of bread rather fully in my first letters "From the Country."

Now, it is a completely different situation. In one of the villages, *everyone has been rich* for the last two years already, that is, no one bought grain, everyone had enough grain to last until the new harvest, they have enough even this year. In this village, there are even several households which this year used last year's old grain long after the new harvest, who have not yet eaten the new grain, consequently, they can sell a portion of this year's grain or give it out in exchange for labor. In the other villages, almost half of the peasants are rich, they make it to the next harvest on their own grain, and the remaining ones begin to buy grain only just before the new harvest and have enough money for this from winter earnings, so that they will not have to enslave themselves for summer work *because of grain.* Of course, even now there are several poor peasants in these villages who must buy grain beginning at Christmas—I am not talking about landless peasants—and given the current high cost of grain they will be forced to send their children after crusts of bread in the winter, but even here there will be a difference from previous years in that these children will not go far, but will beg in their own village and, at most, will go to neighboring villages. There are now very few of this kind of poor household in the "Happy Little Corner," in all there are very few of them, just as there used to be very few households of rich peasants. These households are poor either because the master is not in control, he is bad, he is not an enterprising man, a poor, unsuccessful farmer, or because of some kind of accidental special circumstances, for example, because the head of the household is the only worker, but has many little children; because there are few working hands, but many mouths; because the household head is no good: his oldest, intelligent son has become a soldier, and the younger son who has stayed at home is no good.

There has not been the kind of need for grain that there was formerly, ten years ago, there has not been that need for money when it was time to pay taxes, because the opportunity arose to use the earnings from the sale of hemp, flax, and cattle which formerly went for the purchase of grain, for the payment of taxes. In the "Happy Little Corner" the taxes do not hang heavy, there are no arrears, one hears nothing about floggings or the sale of cattle for taxes, while in the other part of the same volost—I repeat: the "Happy Little Corner" is a small region of eight, ten villages—there are constant arrears, livestock sales and so on.[. . .]

Ten years ago, even in the "Happy Little Corner," despite the fact that there were still many landowners who were farming—it is better to say, precisely because there were many landowners—despite the fact that peasant summer labor was in demand everywhere, the peasants worked land in *krug*s for twenty-five rubles. That is, a peasant cultivated a landowner's plot of three agricultural desiatinas (3,200 square sazhens) for twenty-five rubles—fallow, the spring crop, rye, and did all the work on them, including the threshing. That meant planting and pouring the grain into the bin for twenty-five rubles a plot. For twenty-eight rubles they would work a plot of four desiatinas—fallow, spring, rye, and a desiatina of meadow. Labor was dirt cheap. Receiving twenty-five rubles per *krug,* the peasant received no more than fifteen kopeks for a day's labor, providing his own food and tools. What, if not extreme need for money to buy grain and to pay taxes, can move one to sell one's summer labor for such insignificant pay! The very same reason that cattle are being sold now for a pittance also influences the cheapness of labor: money is needed in order not to die of hunger, and because, no matter what you sell, as long as you sell something, you get money and buy grain. Formerly peasants took on the working of *krug*s not only in order to have pasture for the livestock—that is already a different matter, even rich peasants have to do this—but precisely *for money,* in order to receive some money in advance in the winter. Then it was possible to put out land for cultivation not only wholesale, a certain number of *krug*s to a neighboring village, but even separately by the *krug* to peasants of distant villages. Not having any money in the winter for grain, the peasant went from pillar to post, took on a plot for one landowner, took on some from another, and then was everywhere at once doing work there, here, all summer, without having a chance to cultivate his own plot on time. I described this long ago, by the way, in one of my letters.

Over the last ten years, bit by bit, all of this has changed in the "Happy

Little Corner." It has become harder and harder every year to put out *krug*s, and now there are no longer peasants who would take on *krug*s for money; if a few villages work *krug*s for landowners, then it is only in order to have pasture, if they cannot rent this pasture for money.

The price per *krug* has risen in recent years; peasants take on land without the threshing and reaping, but most important, they *take it unwillingly*. Every village tries to take on as few *krug*s as possible and do so only to get pasture; every head of household also tries to have as small a share as possible.

Before, when the peasants took on *krug*s for money, the rich peasants worked less, while poor peasants who needed money were the largest group to work. But now, when the peasants take on *krug*s only for pasture, and no one is tempted by pay—if pasture were not needed, they would not work for twice the wage, they would not work for any kind of wage—they have begun to divide the work according to the number of horses and livestock, so that a rich man who has a lot of animals is overloaded with work also.

The same has become the rule in regard to all kinds of harvest summer labor as in regard to the *krug*s. Peasants go willingly to any kind of winter work, to many spring and autumn jobs, but for summer harvest work— no.[. . .]

It is the same in regard to hired hands, and female day laborers. It used to be that around "Aldakei" (March 1, the day of Evdokia), when taxes came due, every day you would hear one and the same:

"A muzhik from D. has arrived."

"What can I do for you?"

"I have no grain, I need to eat, don't you have some kind of work?"

"No, there is no work."

But now, these days, some kind of dejected, worn-out Filimon comes to ask for money in exchange for clearing a desiatina of meadow. Whereas formerly there was farming on all of the gentry estates in the area, many working hands were needed everywhere, female day laborers, mowers, and reapers were needed, there was a vast quantity of work and all of this work was done by peasants in the region and they received money. And, despite the mass of work provided by the gentry farms, the peasants were poor, they were constantly in need, although grain was cheap (eight rubles for a chetvert was a high price then, but now it is fourteen rubles), there were a lot of arrears. *A bit of gentry money, probably, did not make them rich.*

But now, many gentry farms are completely shut down, consequently, jobs are not needed, and they are not needed by anyone, no one of the peasants is looking for these jobs, no one needs them. And still the peasants have gotten richer: where there were formerly twenty horses in a village, now there are fifty, where there were forty cows, now there are sixty. Whoever does not have enough of his own grain, without any difficulty, will buy it for fourteen rubles for a chetvert and will pay his taxes as he should.

Formerly peasants worked on the gentry estates and lived in poverty, they were constantly looking for work, money, and grain. Now they work on their own farms, they rent land from the landowners and prosper. The muzhik's proverb speaks the truth: "God loves work," "God will give more than the rich man will."

Formerly, despite the fact that there was farming on all of the estates, and consequently, labor was in demand, there was no way to turn away those who wanted to sell their summer labor, and at the same time, many young people went to Moscow for work. The young people from many households lived in Moscow then doing wage labor from year to year, winter and summer, they sent money from Moscow as they should have, but the yards were still empty, there were neither cattle nor horses. The farmers who stayed at home were constantly in debt, they were always drunk. Now no one goes to Moscow for long. "Why go to Moscow," the muzhiks say, "we have Moscow here now, just work and don't be lazy! You'll make even more money than in Moscow."[. . .]

Drunkenness has also decreased noticeably in the "Happy Little Corner," despite the fact that, because there are fewer taverns due to the increase in the prices of licenses, the secret sale of vodka, which takes place in all of the villages, has spread considerably. Of course, even now, peasants make merry at weddings, on communal holidays, they celebrate with a vengeance, they drink a lot, more, maybe, than before, but once the holidays have passed, the merrymaking is over, and there is no drunkenness, no drunkenness. Where has the passion for drinking gone! The drunkards have become sober muzhiks, many have even stopped drinking completely. You will not meet a drunken muzhik on a wedding day, or a communal holiday, to say nothing of on workdays, and even on Sunday it is an unusual rarity. One can meet a drunken priest, deacon, or policeman rather more often than a drunken muzhik.

Along with the decrease in drunkenness, a passion for hunting has developed strongly among the peasants. Almost all of the young people are hunters, almost all of them have guns, and sometimes it is possible even to see a hound. On Sunday, or a holiday, the young people set out to hunt for hazel grouse, black grouse, and rabbits.

The striving for education, for literacy has also noticeably increased. When the spread of literacy was in fashion just after the Emancipation, even here there was a school in the volost, but it was necessary to gather the children by force in the school, the fathers did not want to release their children for school, they considered school attendance a burden. Fathers unwillingly released their children for school, the children also went unwillingly, and what use was school when the children went for crusts of bread in the winter?[. . .] But in recent years, the striving for literacy has begun to increase considerably; not only do the fathers want their children to study, but the children themselves want to study. In the winter, the children themselves ask that they be taught how to read and write, and not only children, but also grown young people: they work in the day, and at night they study how to read and write. *Even their own* schools have begun to appear among the peasants in the villages. The heads of household get some kind of literate teacher, they rent an izba from a landless woman, and there you have a school.[5] Classes begin in December and last until Easter. The teacher is a former soldier, a part-time deacon, former house servant, or other such literate person, he receives a ruble for each student and room and board. The parents have a system of room and board for the teacher; in a household in which there is one student the teacher will live, for example, three days, where there are two students, six days, and so on, just as the village shepherd does. The izba for the school is rented by the parents together, the firewood for heating it is provided in turns; the schoolbooks, paper, blackboards are bought by the parents.

These muzhik schools serve as an example of the fact that if something is needed, the people will know how to arrange what they need; literacy came into demand, and so the muzhiks established *their own* schools, they got *their own* teachers, just as they have *their own* horse doctors, *their own* midwives, *their own* doctors, *their own* tailors, wool beaters, carders, night watchmen, painters, singers, and so on.

Of course these schools are bad, the teachers are bad, the children will not soon learn how to read and write even badly, but it is important that these are *their own* muzhik schools. The important thing is that this school is close by, that it is right there in the village, that it is their own, that the teacher is one of their own kind, that he is not someone afraid of hard work, that he is not a lord, that he is not there on a whim, that he eats the same thing that the muzhik does, and he sleeps the way a muzhik does.

[Engelgardt describes official objections to peasant-organized schools and issues a summons to educated young people to come to the country to serve the people.]

And so: the increase in grain harvests, the decrease in the need to sell their summer labor, the increase of working in the summer for themselves, the decrease of leaving for wage labor, the strengthening of the desire to farm, for land, the decrease of the urge to abandon the land and become a hired hand, the decrease of drunkenness, the desire for literacy—this is what proves that the condition of the peasants in the "Happy Little Corner" has improved over the last ten years. Let us now consider what this improvement depends on.

The first general cause is the *increase in grain harvests on the peasant allotment lands because of the increase of the use of manure and the improvement that is produced by this fertilization: the enrichment of allotment land.*

[Engelgardt discusses the peasants' practice of taking all the produce they can from rented gentry lands without replenishing them, which, he explains, adds to the depletion of gentry holdings and the decline in Russian agriculture.]

Over the last ten years, peasant allotments have noticeably improved before my eyes and harvests have increased. Every year the peasants take hay, straw, flax, grain, and firewood from neighboring gentry estates to their farmsteads; all of this is turned into fertilizer in the villages and is then put on peasant fields. The amount of manure taken out to peasant allotments each year has noticeably increased over the last ten years. The peasant hemp fields and fields fertilized at the expense of gentry lands have become unrecognizable. In the future, there, where the peasants have done well, their allotments will become rich market gardens on which peasants will practice intensive farming; these allotments will be oases among the deserted gentry lands which will be extensively exploited by these same peasants.

[Engelgardt explains how the peasants in the area have used wage labor off their farms solely as a supplement to their agricultural income and how that has increased their well-being.]

For a better clarification of how it happened that the muzhik has done so well in the "Happy Little Corner" over ten years that he is not suffering even in this year, I will describe the condition of several villages in detail.

Here we have the village D. The village is built around a foul, swampy pool which is good only for watering the livestock. The peasants bring water for drinking and cooking over two versts from another village. There are no meadows in the allotment lands, no forests, the land in the fields is bad, *the cutoffs,* which went to the lord, cut right into the peasants' allotments, the landowner's forest abuts the allotment lands and in places cuts into them. There is no place to let the animals run, except their own fallow land, and you have to keep a close watch or they will immediately be on the lord's cutoffs or on the wastelands of neighboring gentry. The railroad passes by not far away, about five versts from the village, and there is a small station from which lumber and firewood are sent off.

Under serfdom, the village D. was one of the poorest in the region; they say that the landowner was a beast, he served somewhere in the old days as a police superintendent, which means that you can imagine what kind of bird he was—he had the most enormous amount of arable lands, he tormented the people at work, the peasants never had anything else except adulterated bread. After the Emancipation, although it got easier, still, ten years ago when I arrived in the country, the peasants of D. were very poor, *they ate adulterated bread,* they had a lot of arrears, they had few cattle and horses, their buildings were poor, the village was one of the poorest in the "Happy Little Corner." To have plenty of pasture for the cattle, to use the cutoffs, the lord's lands in general which abutted their allotment lands, without touching the forest of course, the peasants of D. worked *krug*s for their landowner on the estate, which stood five or six versts from the village, and mowed the landowner's meadow.

The landowner himself did not live in the country; a steward was the manager. The farm was run in the usual way: the hay was eaten up by the livestock which were kept for manure, they fertilized the fields, but the grain came up badly. Only an insignificant part of the land was ploughed in comparison to what was ploughed during serfdom, the rest was left empty, it turned into a swamp, it was overtaken by forest brush. The landowner had the most insignificant income for all of his expenses and the oppressed peasants simply worked the land in vain. It was difficult for the peasants of D. to improve their lot despite the fact that the railroad passed nearby, which provided jobs when firewood began to be cut in the district, and if they did do better it was not so much because the railroad provided jobs as because they cultivated cleared forestland, they rented the half of the forest that was good for clearing from the *impoverished* landowner in exchange for half the crop, they cut firewood in exchange for half of what they cut, they burned the brush and planted wheat in exchange for half the crop. The peasants began to do well with this cleared forestland and with this wheat, the peasants received their share of wheat in sheaves and brought home seed and straw: they sold the wheat, but the straw and chaff went to the livestock.

Several years ago, the landowner sold his forest for cutting rights over a large number of years with the provision that the buyer could use the forestland during this time. For the peasants, this was a gift. First of all, winter work at home appeared in cutting and hauling firewood right around the village; they could make money hauling firewood to the stations in wagons. But this was not all: the most important thing was that the lumber merchant bought the forest for cutting rights for years with the right to chop down the forest whenever he wanted, and to use the land over the course of the entire period for which the forest was purchased. But what is a lumber merchant going to do with land? Of course, he put it out through sharecropping to the peasants and not in exchange for a share of the crop, but for a set wage and then not in money, but in winter labor, hauling firewood and so on. It was profitable for the lumber merchant, and it was excellent for the peasants, everyone got something.[. . .] Soon after he sold the forest, the landowner rented all of his estate to a lumber merchant. The merchant rented the estate not at all to farm, since he was exclusively involved in the lumber business, but as a central support point for offices, and furthermore he calculated that, since he was not involved in grain production, if he rented out the meadows and fields to the peasants, he still would not lose money. He sold the livestock right away and got some capital which he could constantly have in circulation as long as the rent continued; he began to sell low meadows to those who wanted to mow them; he practically eliminated the cultivation of grain and began to rent fields to the peasants for planting flax and grain; he began to give the peasants the use of the cutoff lands in exchange for a certain payment on their part in *winter work*.

In this way, the peasants of D. became *completely free,* they no longer had to clear the gentry's meadows and cultivate land in exchange for the use of cutoffs. *All summer they work for themselves.* Having the summer free, they plant grain on the cleared forestland, they rent meadows and prepare a lot of hay for their horses and cattle, they rent land to plant flax. In the winter they work in the forest, they haul firewood, they load train cars. After several years, the village became unrecognizable; the peasants built for themselves, they bought more horses and cattle, recently they have even begun to improve the cattle and buy Kholmogor-bred calves from me,[. . .] they began to fertilize the land better. What was happening here? Nothing more than that the peasants *received the possibility of working in the summer for themselves,* now they are not obligated to work the landowner's land in vain, and they have cutoff lands and pasture in exchange for money or winter labor. When the merchant who rented the gentry estate stopped farming, this had a favorable influence not only on the peasants of D., but also on the peasants of other neighboring villages. The merchant rents out the water meadows for mowing; peasants of various villages take on these meadows and carry the hay home, they feed the cattle and horses with the hay, they get manure, with which they fertilize their allotment lands. The merchant rents out fields to the peasants to be planted in flax and grain; the peasants take home flax and grain in sheaves.

At the end of the lease period, the landowner will no longer be able to renew his former farming, in the first place, because the farm will already be empty: he will have to buy cattle afresh, he will have to repair the buildings, and second, *chiefly,* because *it will be impossible to bind the peasants who have done well to the shaft.*

[Engelgardt returns to the theme of the unprofitability of gentry farming and the misplaced notions about agricultural innovation prevalent among educated Russians and offers an account of the improvements in the village S., which were similar to those in village D.]

The third village, A., was one of the most prosperous under serfdom. The landowner never lived on the estate and for that reason, even under serfdom, the peasants were not very oppressed. The peasants in the village A. are special, exceptional in the entire district, tall, healthy, hardworking, quick, and enterprising. The peasants received good allotment land: there are good meadows, there is a good birch grove which the peasants guard and out of which after the Emancipation they did not chop down a single twig; there are splendid hemp fields, superb field land, some of the best in this area. One of my fields abuts the allotment land of the village and this field always produces three to four chetverts of rye more than my other fields. Ten years ago, when I arrived here, the peasants of this village were the most prosperous in the district, they were famous for their good horses and livestock [. . .] and the residents of A. were called rich peasants. Only one household in the village was extremely poor because the head of the household was thoughtless, lazy, negligent, his wife had been thrown out of the house, she hung about with other people, the children were still small; in this household there was terrible poverty: there were arrears, there was not enough grain and fodder, they had to take on summer work in order to get some rubles in the winter. Now that the oldest son has grown up, a healthy, tall child, a hardworking and zealous farmer, even this poor household has begun to recover—proof that the poverty of the household depended not on general circumstances but on personal ones, on the failing of the head of the household himself.

Even ten years ago, the peasants in the village of A. already lived in an orderly fashion, they paid their taxes punctually. Many had enough of their own grain to last until the next harvest, others had to purchase grain, but they easily came around by selling hemp, cattle, and with winter work; they had a lot of horses and livestock. In order to have free pasture and not be constantly fighting like dogs, as they say, with the landowner over trespassing, they worked five *krug*s for money without mowing and threshing for him.

Before I arrived, they say, several men from this village left every year to go to Moscow or to the railroad line, but for the last ten years, no one goes to do wage labor anymore. Only one chap left his father for his wife and lives as a repairman on the railroad line; this chap married a pretty peasant girl of gentle character for love. She was not capable of enduring the hard work in this hardworking village which is greedy for work, she could not endure her harsh father-in-law, who sometimes got drunk and acted beastly when he was drunk. Having lived in the household for several months, the young woman could not endure the harsh, crude life in this village—she was too gentle, spiritual, poetic, if it is possible to say that about a baba—and left to go to her father; her lovestruck husband followed her.[. . .]

At the beginning of the last decade, the peasants of A. did winter wage labor elsewhere, while in the summer, for the most part, they focused on mowing. They mowed every year on the neglected farm of one landowner for a share of the crop, they put away a lot of hay and since no one supervised the mowing on the farm, the landowner's lot was the sexton's share, while the peasants took the priest's share for themselves. Bringing home an enormous amount of hay, the peasants got going with horses—even those who live alone do not have less than a team of three—there are households who have twenty head of cattle—they farmed their arable land, which was excellent to boot, so that in recent years they have not only begun to have enough of their own grain, but many have reserves in advance for the year and surpluses which they give out on credit or for work to peasants of distant villages.

But what especially got the peasants of A. on the right track was the possibility of leasing land at a good price to plant flax and grain. Next door to the village there is a landowner's estate where they lease land. After the Emancipation, the owner of this estate—an old member of the gentry, a zealous serf owner, one of the active opponents of the Emancipation of the serfs not only with land, but even without land—struggled for many years with his farm, but in no way could he get going—he worked by putting out *krug*s, he worked with hired hands, he put pressure on the peasants through passage rights, he was constantly going to court with the peasants. Nothing took, the farm kept declining and declining, no matter how he struggled, the business would not run, no one took on *krug*s, no one would be hired as hired hands. Finally, the landowner abandoned everything: he sold his splendid ancient forest to be cut, he got the money and took off to live in Moscow.

The farm, which had been left to the management of a steward, fell into complete neglect; the fields were left empty, the meadows were overgrown, the cattle died, the horses were stolen, some of the buildings were destroyed, some burned down. The estate stood for several years in complete desolation; finally it came under the management of a bold man who had been a house servant. He came up with the idea of leasing the land to the peasants. The first to take this on were the peasants of the village A., the nearest neighbors, field by field. One tried it, rented a desiatina for eight rubles, planted flax, the flax did well, he brought in one hundred rubles, another took a desiatina and succeeded—the land began to be snatched up to be planted in flax. They tried to plant rye on the broken land after the flax without manure—it produced well, around fifteen stacks per desiatina, and that was threshed. And so it went, more and more, in several years, the peasants of A. ploughed all the fields on the estate, and they cannot boast enough about their profits.[. . .] The peasants of A. got going very well because of this estate, they began to maintain several hired hands, they gave out grain in exchange for work to other villages. Meanwhile other landowners, as well, who had done poorly also began to abandon farming and lease out their lands. The peasants of the village A., and after them, the peasants of other villages of the "Happy Little Corner" also, *finding profit in the land,* began to sniff out everywhere whether they are leasing land somewhere, and not being afraid of distances, began to take lands on lease to plant flax and grain ten to fifteen versts from their own villages, there where the local peasants had not yet gotten on track, or had not reached the point that they had decided to plant flax on leased lands.

Peasants are extraordinarily inert, they will not instantly take up something new, they will give it a long look, but then, if they take it on, the business will succeed. When I came to the country and introduced new farming, began to plant flax, all of the landowners and peasants declared that *I was engaged in a useless enterprise.* The landowners said that flax exhausts the soil, that I was ruining my land with the flax, to which I usually replied, "Let it be exhausted—flax gives a clear profit of at least fifty rubles per desiatina, and you can buy as much land as you want for thirty rubles a desiatina." The peasants said that I was futilely introducing flax, that flax does not grow in our region, that flax is a dangerous grain: sometimes you plant it and the snow carries it off, and it gives no fodder. To this I said, "Just wait, you will begin to plant flax yourselves." It turned out that flax grows well even here, that it provides an enormous income; it turned out that flax does not exhaust the soil and does not dry it up at all as the peasants said it would, of course if it is planted correctly; it turned out that rye grows splendidly after the flax. In just the same way everyone was also opposed to various other innovations I introduced on my farm, planting clover, improving livestock, acquiring ploughs, iron harrows, using flax fiber in bedding, feeding the livestock hemp oil cake, and so on and so forth. All of my innovations did not have any significance for gentry farmers, none of the landowners copy anything from me. But the peasants copied here and there: the ploughs, which they laughed at, saying that I probably wanted to get more of grandfather's manure through deeper ploughing, they now sometimes come to borrow for preparing the soil for flax; many peasants have acquired metal harrows; they have planted high-growing flax everywhere in the region from my seeds; they have begun to clean the rye and are beginning to understand that when you plant straw, you get straw. They buy up my breeding calves, which are born at the same time that the peasants' cows calve, in droves—they cut theirs up, but they use mine for breeding. There is nothing even to be said about clover: everyone is happy to mow the clover for a share of the crop. I describe all of this not for praise, not in order to prove that I have brought good to peasant farming in this locality—they would have reached this point even without me, although perhaps several years later. I understand very well that if it were not for the causes which enabled the improvement of the well-being of the peasants of the "Happy Little Corner," they would still be planting rye with straw, they would not be planting flax, they would be milking their Taskan calves, they would be giving up their oil cake for churning butter, and so on and so forth.

The peasants of the village A. were the first in our region to rent land to put in flax and grain, to acquire good cattle; they chose the best lands on estates nearby and got them at a cheap price; when the best lands were exhausted by them, they left the nearest lands to others and themselves mowed farther away, trying to find new lands in those areas where peasants had not made it yet, had not gotten on the right track. The peasants of A. quickly got rich by skimming the cream everywhere; but one must keep in mind that the peasants of the village A. were also one of the most prosperous in the district earlier, that they received splendid lands as their allotment with excellent hemp fields and meadows, they received all of the land that they had before the Emancipation, and they lost no cutoffs.

The Peasant Exploiter: The Kulak

I will also describe a fourth village, B., which is distinguished from those described above by the fact that there is a peasant kulak there, a real kulak, a usurer.

Every peasant has a bit of the kulak in him; with the exception of those who are stupid, and especially good-hearted people and the "carps" in general. Every muzhik is a kulak, a pike, to a certain extent, who is in the sea so that the carp will not doze.[6] In my letters, I have pointed more than once to the fact that although peasants do not even have any conception of hereditary rights to the land as property—the land is no one's, the land belongs to the Tsar—in regard to moveable property, they have a very strong sense of property. I have stated more than once that individualism, egoism, and the urge to exploit are very much developed among the peasantry. Envy, the mistrust of each other, scheming against each other, the humiliation of the weak before the strong, the arrogance of the strong, the worship of wealth—all of this is highly developed in the peasant milieu. Kulak ideals reign there; everyone is proud of being a pike and tries to eat up the carps. Every peasant, if the circumstances are favorable, will exploit anyone else in the most splendid fashion, it is all the same whether it be a peasant or a lord, he will squeeze the juice out of him, will exploit his need. All of this, however, does not prevent the peasant from being extremely good, patient, in his own way, unusually humane, uniquely, sincerely humane, as a man from the educated class is rarely humane. It is because of this that it is so difficult for the educated man to come together with the muzhik. Watch how humanely a muzhik relates to a child, to a fool, to a madman, to someone of a different faith, to a prisoner, to a criminal—just out of prison, you will not be refused money—in general, to any unfortunate person.

But given all of that, if there is a chance to extort from someone, he will extort. If the cattle from a neighboring village, with which there is no joint pasturing, are caught trespassing by the peasants, they will not give them back for free; if the peasants catch a poacher in their forest, they will give him such a thrashing that he will not let his children go in this forest—which is why there is no poaching of wood in the peasants' forest although there are no guards or wardens there. Everyone knows how they beat robbers and horse thieves.[7] A landowner will more quickly forgive trespassing, poaching of wood, stealing than a peasant; this costs a landowner nothing; he did not get his wealth from the work of his own back. When the peasants of the village A., having exhausted the closest lands, began to take land in distant localities where the peasants are poor, simple, and in great need, they—and not just one, furthermore, but all of them—immediately began to exploit the need of the peasants there, they began to give grain and money to them in exchange for labor.

Every muzhik, given the chance, is a kulak; he is an exploiter, but as long as he is a landed peasant, as long as he labors, works, works the land himself, this is still not a true kulak: he does not think to take everything for himself, he does not think how good it would be if everyone were poor, in need, he does not act in this spirit. Of course, he makes use of another man's need, he makes him work for him, but he does not build his well-being on the need of others, but builds on his own labor. From such a peasant of the land you will hear, "I love the land, I love work, if I go to sleep and my arms and legs don't hurt from work, I am ashamed; it seems like I didn't finish something, like I lived all day for nothing." Such a peasant of the land also has his favorite horse that is not for sale, such a muzhik takes pleasure in his buildings, his livestock, his hemp field, his grain. And not at all just because these provide him with so many rubles. He expands his farm not with the goal of profit alone; he works to the point of exhaustion, he does not get full, he does not eat his fill. Such a peasant of the land never has a big gut the way a real kulak does.

Only in the village of B. is there a real kulak in the entire "Happy Little Corner." This one does not love the land, or farming, or labor; this one loves only money. This one will not say that he is ashamed when his arms and legs don't hurt when he goes to sleep; this one, on the contrary, says, "work loves fools," "a fool works, but a smart man, having put his hands in his pockets, strolls, and runs things with his brains." This one prides himself on his fat gut, he prides himself on the fact that he himself does little work, "People who owe me do all my mowing, threshing and put it in the barn." This kulak works with the land in an offhand way, he does not expand his farm, he does not increase the number of livestock, horses, he does not plough up fields. With this one, everything is built not on the land, not on farming, not on labor, but on capital, in which he deals, which he gives out on loans with interest. His idol is money, and he thinks only about its increase. He inherited his capital, which was acquired in some unknown, but somehow unclean manner, long ago, during serfdom still, it lay hidden, and made its appearance only after the Emancipation. He lends this capital for interest and this is called "running things with his brains."

It is clear that for his business to grow it is important that the peasants be poor, that they be in need, that they have to turn to him for loans. It is profitable for him that the peasants not work on the land so that he can be in control with his money. It is not at all good for this kulak that the daily life of the peasants of the "Happy Little Corner" has improved, because now there is nothing for him to take here and he has to take his activity to large villages. This kulak, like all kulaks, is an important figure; he supports all dreams, all illusions; all sorts of rumors come from him; he consciously or subconsciously, I do not know which, tries to draw the peasant away from the land, from farming, propounding the view that "work loves fools," pointing to the difficulty of work on the land, on the easiness of working for cottage industry, the profitability of working in Moscow. He visibly wishes that the peasants would not work on the land, at farming, there is nothing for a kulak to take from a prosperous landed muzhik, he wishes that they, having abandoned the land, would use farming only as a supplement, basing their life on easy work in town. He visibly wishes that the peasants received a lot of money, but lived from day to day, in an insecure life, "on the market," as it is said. This kind of life for the peasants would be convenient for him because they would more often need to borrow money and would not have the kind of stability that the landed muzhiks have; the young fellows would go away to work in Moscow, they would get used to an insecure life there, to easy jobs, to a careless attitude toward money—why save! we'll earn more!—to calico shirts, harmonicas, tea, they would lose the habit of hard agricultural labor, of the land, of farming, of a solid agricultural existence, of rural interests, of all that is dear to a rural man, which makes his hard labor possible. The young fellows would live in the Moscow way, the old men and women, remaining in the village, would farm however they could, counting on the money sent to them by the young people.

All of this would be fine for the kulak, because it is precisely people with money that he needs, but who live from day to day, who do not save money, who do not take care of their farms. They need to pay taxes—to the kulak. When the children send some from Moscow, we'll pay it back. And the kulak can give the money completely without risk because when they send some from Moscow, he is already right there, "You, brother, have a little debt." They pay interest for an extension, and moreover, out of *respect,* they work a day or two, how can you not respect a man in need who helps out? And he has some land to work on for a bit; he also gives loans to landowners and as interest they give him either a meadow, or wood for an izba, or a desiatina of land in flax, this does not cost the landowner anything, just as it does not cost the muzhik anything to work for a day or two.

I do not know whether the kulak acts consciously or unconsciously, but I repeat, all of his actions are the same. He always supports various dreams, illusions in regard to the land, the freeing of the forests, of some kind of reserves of grain that the Tsar has, of orders to make money to give to the peasant; he is always talking about the hardships and unprofitability of agricultural labor, about the lack of free pastures, forests, fields, about the impossibility of farming under these conditions; he paints the carefree life of the landless peasant who is not tied to anything in bright colors, the ease of wage earnings, and he often seduces young people who listen to him, who abandon farming and the land. Before, the peasants of B. were very poor, almost all of the young people left for work in Moscow, they sent money as they should, but even so, the farmers were constantly in need, they were in debt, they sold their summer labor. Lately, the example of the peasants of D., S., and A. also had an effect on B., they also began to say, "Why go to Moscow, we have Moscow right here"; they began to work more at farming, with the land, and they have visibly done better. This year, already, no one with a family goes to Moscow and only orphans listen to the kulak, those who are adopted,[8] young soldiers who are returning to the village. It has become less profitable for the kulak around the peasants and he is transferring his activity to the landowners around whom, in his words, there is also a good living.

I think that four examples are enough, although I could provide many more of them. But why, it would all be one and the same. The well-being of the muzhik improves where he works on the land for himself, and does not sell his summer labor, where *he works for himself in the summer,* where you do not hear from the muzhik: "No, this year it is bad, this year *you will not get yourself out of it,* you will have to take on threshing for the lord, you will have to take on plots of land, this year you will not get out of it, you'll have to put on the harness."

Here in the "Happy Little Corner" the winter forest work that opened up with the introduction of the railroad gave the peasants a chance to recover enough not to enslave themselves for summer work for the landowners, which also made it possible, because of the constant use of fertilizer at the expense of gentry lands, for the peasants' allotments to improve and to begin to provide better grain harvests. The reduction and the complete cessation of much gentry farming also had a favorable influence on the well-being of the peasants because, having ceased to farm, the landowners began to rent peasants the *cutoff lands and pastures* they needed *for money,* without requiring that they must work at summer labor for the use of these lands which had been absolutely necessary for the peasants. With the shutting down of gentry farms, the opportunity appeared for the peasants to rent lands cheaply to plant flax and grain, which made the increase of their well-being and the development of peasant farms even more possible.

Not far from the "Happy Little Corner" there is a group of villages where the peasants even up until now are impoverished, constantly need grain, have piled up large arrears, and take on a multitude of summer jobs. The conditions in terms of winter earnings are the same for these peasants also, but there is only one thing missing: there the peasants have bad fields, and the *cutoff lands* are enormous. Under serfdom, the peasants had the use of a large amount of land, since it was of poor quality, and now the peasants have to work in the summer for landowners for these cutoff lands which surround their land.

Again I will say, I do not know what the situation is in other areas and why the peasants are impoverished there—and we hear from everywhere that they are impoverished—I am not trained in various sciences to judge such important questions. But I know my little corner, I know it thoroughly, and I know for certain that precisely those causes that I have indicated are at work here.

[Engelgardt concludes this letter with a critique of gentry farming and a summons to educated young people to come to the countryside.]

Letter XI

✉ The following excerpt of Engelgardt's eleventh letter from the countryside focuses on a hot topic of debate in educated society in the post-Emancipation era: the peasants' views of the land as property and their constant hope for a further redistribution in their favor.[1] Like many of his peers, Engelgardt stresses the peasants' desire for a fair and equal redistribution of land in Russia to all those willing and able to cultivate it. The essential element in the peasants' concept of property in land, Engelgardt explains, is that land should go to those who work it. Cultivation justifies possession. Guided by this principle, peasants consider it both logical and inevitable that the Tsar will grant such a wholesale, just redistribution to everyone, peasant and noble alike, who is prepared to farm on it.

Engelgardt goes beyond simply reporting peasant rumors to support the view that the peasants should receive the land. He dismisses the future of gentry farming in Russia according to the principles of scientific agronomy. Gentry farming, he says, is not scientific, not rational for Russia, but rather, baldly exploitative and inefficient. In sum, gentry farming is "a kulak system," and Russia's hope for prosperous agricultural economy rests solely in non-exploitative peasant farming.

✉ ✉ ✉

Peasants' Rumors about the Land

Today I received the newspapers for a whole week and read them all in one sitting. What lucky people you are!

I am overcome with envy even, what bubbling activity: conferences, sessions, commissions; sessions, commissions, conferences . . .

Everything is affected, no stone has been left unturned. How many questions are being worked out, and what questions! Alcoholism, the reduction of redemption payments, regulating resettlement, putting the administration in order, directing self-government![2][. . .]

And all of it is for the good of the muzhik. Now we hear one and the same thing from everyone, "Wait a bit, everything will be settled." The village constable, the district policeman, and the captain, all the officials assert one and the same: "Wait a bit, everything will be settled."

And as for the muzhik, just imagine, somehow he does not even know anything about all of this activity on his behalf. Yes, the muzhik does not think about any of this, moreover, he is not a bit interested in the questions being raised.[. . .] There are no rumors at all or gossip among the muzhiks about this; the muzhiks await *only grace in regard to the land*.[3] They are prepared to pay, and are prepared to endure and indulge the authorities and self-government, as long as a bit of land is added on, so that there will be room to move.

Therefore, you cannot get away from the gossip, rumors, and conversations about the land. Everyone is waiting for grace, everyone is certain— *every muzhik is certain*—that there will be grace in regard to the land, no matter what the gentry do about it. Talk to any boy in the village and he will tell you that there will be grace. Any boy will lay out for you in an orderly fashion, systematically, "properly," and "as he should" the essential points of the muzhik's views about the land, since he imbibed these views with his mother's milk.

There are no doubts at all; everyone is convinced, everyone believes. It is even amazing how people hear and see precisely what they want. However, we know the same from the history of sorcery and magic. People saw gold where it could not be, they talked with the unclean spirit, they believed that there were witches. And is this not the same that we see now at spiritualists?[. . .]

The rumors about the fact that there will be grace "in regard to the land" only gained force this spring, but they had already begun to spread a long time ago. Everyone who, living in the village, is in close contact with the peasants, who, for example, runs his farm himself, surely heard about this as early as 1878, when the gossip and rumors were suddenly aggravated. After Plevna was taken, the peasants talked everywhere openly about "the grace": at village assemblies, at weddings, at work bees. They even turned to the landowners with questions: if they were to buy land in perpetuity, would the money then be returned to those who had bought the land, and so forth, as I described in my earlier letters.[4] Everyone was waiting then for a "new edict"[5] in 1879 in regard to the land. Then every smallest incident gave cause for gossip about a "new edict": if the hundreder took the lord a paper demanding some kind of statistical information about the land, cattle, buildings, and so on, an assembly gathered right away in the village where they talked about the fact that, look, a document came to the lord about the land, that a "new edict" would come out soon, that the land surveyors would come in the spring to allot the land. If the police forbade a landowner, whose estate was mortgaged, to cut timber for sale, they rumored that the prohibition was applied because the forest would soon be taken by the state and then there would be plenty of forest for everyone: pay a ruble and cut as much as you need for your use. If someone mortgaged his estate with the bank, they said that, look, the gentlemen have already woken up to the fact that the land is going to be distributed equally, and so they are hurrying to give the estates to the state in order to lay their hands on some money.[. . .]

I followed all of these rumors and gossip very attentively and came to the conclusion that the idea of equalizing the land circulates among the peasant population persistently, and has done so for a long time, without any kind of propaganda from outside. The very fact that the rumors about this appeared simultaneously at a certain moment (the end of 1877) everywhere, across all of Russia, that the peasants talked everywhere, that they were not timid, they had no fear, that the rural authorities themselves, the hundreders, the elders, supported these rumors, and contributed to their spreading, serves, in my opinion, as indubitable proof that these rumors come from the people themselves, that this idea is endemic to the folk themselves.[. . .]

Here are the sorts of incidents that happened before my very eyes. One morning the hundreder came by and brought a document from headquarters which demanded, I don't know why, that I provide information about the amount of land, the number of buildings on the estate, and so on. It was the most ordinary kind of document I very often receive: the authorities are collecting statistics for some kind of commission. I took the document, immediately put the requested information on the form provided, sealed it, and gave it to the hundreder to take back to the central bureau. I did not say anything to the hundreder, I told my household nothing about the document I had received either, and there was nothing to be said, because there was nothing of interest in it. Even so, very quickly, in a few hours, I found out that they were already talking at the assembly in the village about the fact that the master had received a paper "in regard to the land," that there would soon be a new edict, and that the land surveyors would come in the spring to divide up the land. In the village they could not have found out from anyone else except the hundreder that I had received a document; besides the hundreder, no one could know that any kind of information about the amount of land had been requested from me. It must have been that the person who spread the false rumors was the police hundreder, who simply dropped the spark on a bonfire that had already been laid.

This can be explained very simply: the hundreder heard in the central bureau or in some gentry house where he took the document that they were requesting some kind of information about land, buildings, and so forth from landowners. As a muzhik, and a poor one at that, as a bad farmer who was not capable of work, the hundreder dreams along with everyone about free forest, free land. Having heard that they were requesting information about the land from the landowners in the document, the hundreder took it into his head that this document was "in regard to the land," about "a new edict." Passing through the village, he told the muzhiks that he was carrying a document "about the land" around to the gentry. That was enough. An assembly gathered and the rumors and discussions began. The rumor immediately spread to other villages also where they had already begun to say, "I saw the document myself, a manifesto came to the lord of Batishchevo, the hundreder brought it." What could be simpler? There is no subversive person here at all. And you cannot blame some hundreder Ivan because the hundreder Petr, the hundreder Andrei, any hundreder would have acted in just the same way. If the district police officer and superintendents had tried to convince the hundreders that there was not going to be a redistribution, it would have been even worse: the hundreders would not have understood them, but on the contrary would have thought that now it would happen quickly, "The superintendent himself had said so."

This may seem strange; but here is a fact for you: this summer the babas in the village were saying that the district police officer came and himself said that there would be grace "in regard to the land." Of course, the district police officer said nothing and if he did say something, then it was not that at all. But, I repeat, in a certain mood which has seized everyone, people hear and see only what they themselves want. When strict measures were introduced and it was ordered that everyone's passports be examined, that passersby be stopped, and so on, all of these measures were executed by the muzhiks very zealously because the muzhiks thought that when they caught the members of the gentry who were making trouble, then "grace" would come. It was very strange for an outsider to see how various people understood the matter differently: the upper ranks of the police from the "gentlemen" understood one thing by subversive, and the lower ranks of the police from the "muzhiks" understood something completely different, the opposite. According to one understanding, he who thinks that the land should be distributed equally is a subversive man; according to the other, a subversive man is one who thinks that it is not necessary to distribute the land equally. The confusion of understandings is terrible and sometimes it turns out very comically.

And the volost authorities must also be included in the number of subversive people. In fact, the muzhik wants to buy land from the landowner and in view of the rumors about the redistribution consults his relative, the volost elder. And what happens? The elder advises him not to buy, supposing the money would be lost because soon, at the New Year, "A new edict in regard to the land is coming out."

So the volost elder also is a subversive person. Or, perhaps, some kind of people with evil intentions confused this elder, trying to destroy the public peace? Nothing of the sort. The elder simply, like the hundreder also, and like every muzhik, believes, and out of a sense of family relations, warns his uncle "not to let the money be lost." And the peasant uncle, whom the elder warned, is an itinerant horse doctor. Every summer he goes around thousands of villages in his work in various provinces. And is he really going to keep quiet, after all? As a person who wants to buy good land and who is afraid that the money will be lost, he must inevitably try to find out what has been heard about the land. When he came to work on my place, he even consulted with me and asked me if anything had been heard about the land in government bureaus. In just the same way he will also, without fail, talk with the muzhiks for whom he works, he will make inquiries, he will ask around, he will report his fears, his conversation with the elder. This itinerant horse doctor thus will be, without knowing it himself, the spreader of false rumors. And note that although this horse doctor even now holds his peasant views on the land, this still has not prevented him from buying land. He bought ninety desiatinas of land—the land was being sold very cheaply, it seems, for five rubles a desiatina—and has begun to cultivate it, he dug up and burned part of the brush, he planted rye, and, following my example, he wants to plant clover in the spring after the rye, for which he asked me to order seeds for him.

I am utterly certain that if some simple man bares his soul about taxes, the land, and the gentry over a glass of beer with a gendarme who is bored waiting for a train at the station then the gendarme will also say what all the muzhiks say because he, *as a muzhik,* has the same convictions.

It is useless to caution the rural population about this in the slightest degree. In the same way it is useless to warn soldiers. And no matter how you imitate peasant speech, the document will not be understood or will be understood in entirely the opposite meaning.[. . .]

In the muzhik's view, each man thinks about himself, about his own benefit, each man is an egotist, only the commune and the Tsar think about everyone, only the commune and the Tsar are not egotists. The Tsar wants everyone to have the *same,* because he loves everyone equally, he takes pity on everyone equally. The function of the Tsar is to *make everyone equal.*

The muzhik's understanding of this constantly discussed issue is that after a certain amount of time, after a census, there will be a universal *equal distribution of all the land* across all of Russia, just as now in *every commune,* individually, after a certain amount of time, there occurs a redistribution of the land among the members of the commune, through which each one receives as much land as he can farm. This entirely characteristic, peasant concept flows directly from all the peasants' agrarian relations. A redistribution of the land occurs in the communes after a certain period of time, an *evening out* among the members of the commune; during the universal redistribution, there will be a redistribution of all the land, an *evening out* among communes. Here the question is not the issue of taking land away from the landowners at all, as the correspondents write, but about evening out of *all the land,* both the landowners' and the peasants'. Peasants who have purchased land as property or, as they say, for eternity, also talked about this, just like all the other peasants, and did not doubt at all that these "lands which are bound to them by law" can be taken away from the "legal owners" and given to others. And how can a muzhik doubt this when, in his understanding, all of the land belongs to the Tsar and the Tsar has the power, if a given distribution of the land does not suit him, to distribute it in another way, to *even it out?* And how is one to stand on a point of the law, the right of private property, when the population does not have any concept of the right of private property in land? Have the peasants, who have never owned land, been buying land as property for long!?! Could their age-old views be changed so quickly? And are there many such who have bought lands? Can the single farmers leave the commune so quickly and stand in opposition to them? Having bought the land, has the muzhik really bought along with it an understanding of the right of private property in land as determined by the law? The muzhik does not even know any kind of laws about the possession of land just as he does not know the laws about inheritance.

Moreover, the muzhik even has a confused understanding about the right of property in other items because if the land belongs to the commune, which is made up of certain members, then other items: livestock, horses, and money, belong to households, to families. This horse is ours, that is, of such and such a household. The father, the head of the household, cannot refuse to give a horse to a son who leaves the household. The commune will force him to divide the property of the household fairly. In any case, equal distribution, in the opinion of the muzhik, cannot be unfair or injurious to anyone.

Seeing that the land of the landowners is empty or is not being cultivated as it should be, seeing that enormous expanses of productive land, for example, cleared forestland, remain uncultivated and are being overgrown with all kinds of rubbish, which bring no use to anyone, the muzhik says that such a situation *is a loss for the Tsar*. There is no grain, grain is expensive, and why? Because there are no real farms, the land is abandoned, it is not being cultivated, it is going to waste. *It is better for the Tsar* that the land not be wasted, that it be cultivated, that it be of some use.

According to the muzhik's views the land belongs to the Tsar, of course, not in the meaning that it constitutes the private property of the Tsar, but in that the Tsar is the chief farmer of all the land, the chief master of the land. That's his duty, that's why he's a tsar. If the muzhik says that it's no good for the Tsar when the land is left to waste, that his needs as Tsar require that the land be used, they are not talking about the personal profit of the Tsar at all—the Tsar does not need anything, he has everything—but the good of society. The good of society requires that land not be left empty, that it be cultivated in an efficient fashion, that it produce grain. Social welfare and fairness require that the land be distributed equally, that redistributions take place. The muzhik has a broad view of the question, but not at all as the correspondents report: the land will be taken away from the gentry and given to the peasants. No, it is not this way. The Tsar thinks about social welfare. The Tsar sees that the land is wasted and his Tsar's heart is wounded by such a bad state of affairs. The Tsar sees that some have not enough land, have no place to move, while others have a lot, so that they cannot handle it, and it makes his heart ache.

And the muzhik waits for the Tsar's grace in regard to the land, he waits for a new edict from the Tsar, he waits for the land surveyors in the spring.[. . .]

[In winter], they get together in the evening in someone's izba and there is talk, "The Tsar sees how much of the lords' land is empty—this is no good for the Tsar. The Tsar sees how the muzhik's crowded, he's got no place to go, he doesn't have pasture for his cattle, or meadow, or forest. Look, when spring comes there'll be a new edict, the land surveyors will come. As for the timber there are stricter measures now: don't use it either to heat with or to have a light. But soon there'll be a new edict, the forests'll be free, cut as much as you need for your own use. We'll wait a bit."

And here comes some poor Efer coming home from the evening gathering to his poor hut, he is dreaming about free land, when there will be open spaces everywhere: he has let his mare out untied and no one will take her for trespassing; he is dreaming about free forest when it will not be necessary to hustle to find light and firewood; he goes to the forest, he admires a tree, he chops it down, there you have your firewood and light—you can have heat and light all day long if you want. But in the morning this same Efer will go to the lord to get an osmina of rye, "I'll take on a half desiatina of meadow and I'll cut a desiatina of clover," he calculates.

If you listen to the rumors of the masses, you will only hear complaints, dreams, wishes, and hopes. Events caused an abundance of legends, stories, rumors. "The lords did this, the lords made a deal, they bought them off, they gave them drink, it is ordered to keep an eye on the lords, it is ordered not to hire out to the lords as workers, it is ordered to gather your own grain first; while your own grain is falling, you have to work for the lord! Nothing of the sort! Despite the fact that you have obligated yourself—it is not ordered; it is ordered to smash the Jews" . . .

This is how the masses talk; all rumors are marked by these broken exclamations whose general meaning is understood. Otherwise, the rich ones, the wealthy peasants, the kulaks speak more precisely. Of course, even the rich kulak also does not keep quiet at an evening gathering where they are dreaming about a redistribution, about a new edict, although the rich peasants do not give much significance to these indeterminate dreams and hopes, and stress most of all that the lords are making trouble, that the lords are interfering, and if it were not for the lords . . . The rich kulaks—these are the most liberal people in the village, the most furious opponents of the lords whom they not only hate, but whom they also disdain as people who, in their opinion, are not capable of doing anything, who are not any good for anything. Although the rich kulaks are sometimes even hated in the village, as liberals they always get a hearing, and that is why their significance in the village in this sense is enormous. During all of the talk about the land, a redistribution, about evening out, the rich kulaks talk more than anyone else about the fact that here you have gentry land going to waste and the muzhiks are crowded, that if the land were in peasant hands, it would not go to waste and grain would not be so expensive. But as for the rumors specifically about the "evening out of the land," the rich kulaks, in their soul of souls, consider this to be futile muzhik dreaming, fantasy, illusions. Taking the most lively part in village rumors, pouring oil on the fire, they say elsewhere with a contemptuous smirk that muzhiks are always talking nonsense. "Is it possible," they say, "that they are going to take land away from everyone just like that! You can't do that now anymore because a lot of land has been bought by muzhiks and merchants. It'll just be that those gentry estates that are mortgaged, and only if the lord does not pay on time, will be taken for the state and then given out to the muzhiks!" And what is more, they figure, all of the gentry lands will have taxes put on them, for a half ruble or ruble per desiatina. Will many of the gentry be able to pay such taxes? One, maybe two. Will those who are just managing, who are extorting the peasants through land, really be able to pay? They are the ones whose land will be taken away and given to the peasants, who will take on the obligation to pay. And a lot of rich muzhiks with money will be found: they will bring their money, they will take the land for themselves, and they will make use of the land because the muzhiks need land. It may be, as well, this way: a rich muzhik will be found who will bring his money, the land will go to the commune, but the commune will pay the muzhik. The rich peasant knows how to turn everything to his own good.

There is a lot of talk, a lot of gossip; a lot of different tales go around among the folk. The general conclusion that can be drawn out of all these rumors and talk is that *the land that the muzhik got as allotment land is not enough,* that he *needs more land,* that he *is ready to pay,* and will pay the Tsar *more than anyone else,* as long as he has something with which to pay. The muzhik sees the decline of gentry farms, all of their bankruptcy, the muzhik sees that the majority of these farms are maintained only through extortion, cutoff lands, pastures, and so on, he sees that the mass of gentry land is either left empty or is exhausted wastefully, as a result of bad farming and leasing out to be ploughed. The muzhik says that all of this is a loss for the Tsar, the government, that it is also because of this that grain and everything is expensive, that this is not as it should be. And the muzhik endures, waits, and hopes.

[Engelgardt goes into a lengthy description of his successful projects in land reclamation, introducing a multifield crop rotation, and his use of fertilizer in conjunction with manure.]

The peasants, we know this for certain, are waiting for grace in regard to the land and live by hopes which they, without shame, proclaim loudly. The landowners do not know what to do with their empty, overgrown lands, they are abandoning farming, they are reducing cultivation to such levels that the land is worked by peasants not for money but for use of cutoff lands, they are happily giving their neglected lands to the peasants to cultivate until they are exhausted, they sell off their forest, they are ready to sell the land cheaply as long as someone will buy it.

[Engelgardt continues his polemic with the projects for agricultural reform proposed by the journal *Rus',* continues to criticize exclusive reliance on artificial fertilizers, and describes his own multifield system in great detail.]

In my previous letter (X), I described the "Happy Little Corner" where the peasants have begun to live at the expense of the empty lands. *It is self-evident, of course,* that the muzhik, having rented land on a gentry estate for a year or two, plants flax, rye, and oats on it without fertilizer, exhausts it, takes everything that he can from it, and puts it on his allotment, which he fertilizes in the most careful fashion. The muzhik cannot act in any other way *with someone else's land*. But if this land were his, the muzhik's, then he would treat it just as I do, he would begin to fertilize it, he would introduce a multifield system, planting clover, and so on. "The muzhik may be dull, but the devil has not eaten his brain." The muzhik is in no way as stupid as the newspaper *Rus'* thinks; total condescension toward the muzhik, who does not understand Ville fertilizers and German agronomy, permeates every line of its agricultural ramblings. The muzhik may not have read the popular pamphlets from which you have taken your wisdom, but he understands farming and the land rather more than you do. And that is understandable: the muzhik does not live on a salary, but from Mother Earth.

[Engelgardt continues his detailed description of his system of farming.]

No kind of credit for Ville fertilizers will help, no kind of schools will help, no warehouses, cattle orders, or similar undertakings. The only means to improve our farming, which is a loss for both the landowner and the agriculturalist, is to arrange it so that the land goes to the real farmer, to the muzhik. The muzhik will know how to get use out of it. The peasants see this very well and understand, and from hour to hour they await grace. The peasants are convinced that this grace will be total and they talk everywhere about this *openly*.

It is not out of liberalism that I assert that the only way to improve our agriculture is to increase the peasant allotments and, in general, the transfer of the land into the hands of the agriculturalists. It is not as a "liberal" but as a *farmer* that I say that there will be no economic order in Russia, that our resources will lie wasted until the land belongs to those who work it. Some may ask me, however, why it is that I do not allow for the possibility of improving our agriculture through the development of gentry farms, so-called *grande culture*. To this I say that *"grande culture" is possible only given the existence of a slave*, but there is no such slave in Russia, or very few, and it *is not desirable that there be*. It is impossible to consider the ten or so farms which have blossomed *before their time*, among which I count mine also, and for which there are plenty of workers. But what do these few farms mean among the mass of neglected gentry farms which do not bring income to their owners, which oppress the peasants at no gain for themselves, and which force them to *work the land uselessly?*

Serfdom is gone, gentry farming is gone along with it. Until 1861 a certain system existed. The landowner had a certain number of hands at his disposal on his estate, he had a certain work force at his full disposition which he could direct *as he wished*. Under serfdom, the good gentry farmer usually arranged his relations in this way: the peasants were given a certain amount of land which was usually called peasant land for this reason; the peasants themselves distributed this land, they practiced their farming on it, and for this they provided a certain amount of workers with horses and tools and maintained these workers for work on the landlord's fields. Some of the peasants, *the farmers,* lived in their village, sometimes twenty versts or more away from the gentry house, they ran their farm independently and were independent to a certain extent; the other peasants—*the ones who were forced*—lived on the lord's demesne with their horses and tools and did all of the work on the lord's fields. Besides this, in some cases, during the harvest, when it was necessary at a certain time to increase the number of working hands, there were *round-ups* during which all of the farmers showed up to work. Knowing precisely the number of working hands and their productivity, being the totally powerful owner of these hands, having, furthermore, the possibility of increasing the number of hands at certain times, the landlord could run his farm *entirely correctly.* This was the system, and the more correct the established relations were—and it was so among the good gentry farmers of that time—the better the farming went.

With the elimination of serfdom, this entire system was destroyed and became impossible and the entire economy of the country should have adopted new methods. But it is natural that people who have lived with a certain system wanted this system to continue. They thought that even after the Emancipation of the peasants the same or similar systems would continue, with the only difference being that instead of serfs, freely hired laborers would work.

It seemed that this would all turn out simply. The peasants would receive a small land allotment which would, furthermore, be covered by a high price so that the peasant would not be able to feed himself from the allotment and pay taxes, and therefore part of the people would have to take up work elsewhere. The landowners would receive payment for the land taken for the allotments, their farming would remain the same as before with the only difference that instead of people forced to work there would be freely hired hands; they would be hired for a certain amount of labor which the gentry would get for the land they had lost. This all seemed so simple, and people thought besides that if they began to farm following agronomy, if they bought machines, Alhaus and other cattle, guano, and superphosphates, then farming would go even better than it did formerly during serfdom. In the beginning, many attempts were made to practice farming with hired hands, machines, and agronomy, but all of these attempts did not lead to the desired result. There is no pure farming with hired hands in Russia. *"Grande culture"* with freely hired hands working on the farm turned out to be impossible because it requires a landless worker, the kind of worker who *would sell the farmer his soul,* and no such landless worker turned up, for *every muzhik is himself a farmer.* The number of peasants left without land, who had abandoned farming, was too small to provide a contingent of such workers for the gentry farms and was gobbled up by the factories, mills, towns, by gentry farms as servants, but there was no true *worker, a rural hired hand.* And if there is no such landless worker, then how is it possible for there to be farming with hired hands and any kind of *"grande culture"*?

[Engelgardt launches into yet another lengthy attack on the attempts to improve gentry farming using the principles of agronomy, or "rational farming."]

There can only be one thing: either muzhik farming or "*grande culture.*" Some people think that "*grande culture*" which is organized well according to agricultural science can pay the muzhik more than he gets from his farm, so that the muzhik will abandon the farm in order to go work as a hired hand in "*grande culture,*" just as he sometimes abandons the land in order to become a factory worker, a servant, a member of the intelligentsia. Without even saying anything about the fact that it is completely undesirable that "*grande culture*" make the muzhik landless, I think that this cannot be and will not be. Now we do not see this kind of "*grande culture,*" but we see only incidental, kulak farming which has no future, and an abundance of declining farms whose land is being exploited by overcultivation.

The old gentry system after the Emancipation has been replaced by a kulak system, but this system can only exist temporarily, it has no stability and must fail and move over to some kind of other stable system. If the peasants were to fall in this battle, if they were to lose their land, if they were to be turned into workers, then it would be possible to establish some kind of stable form of farming with hired hands; but this has not happened—on the contrary, gentry farms are failing. More and more farms are closed each year, the cattle are eliminated, and the fields are given out to the peasants on a short lease for cultivation, for planting flax and grain. Gentry farming has failed and no farmers have appeared, and pointless plunder simply occurs—the forests are cut down, the land is exhausted, everyone takes what he can and runs. No kind of technical improvements can help our farming at the present time. Introduce whatever agricultural schools you want, order whatever foreign cattle you want, whatever machines you want, nothing will help, because there is no foundation. I, at least, as a farmer, do not see any possibility of improving our farming as long as the land does not go to the hands of the agriculturalists. It seems that now everyone is beginning to understand this.

Letter XII

✉ Engelgardt's twelfth letter from the countryside returns to the theme of the peasants' approach to purchasing land in his area.[1] He focuses on the acceleration of such purchases through the assistance of the Peasant Land Bank. This institution was established in 1883 to facilitate peasants in buying land. The impetus for the establishment of the Peasant Land Bank was to make more peasants into property holders who would, it was hoped, invest in and improve land they owned rather than rented. Providing peasants with this opportunity to acquire private property would also have the benefit of developing a respect for private property per se as a keystone of their larger respect for a legal system based on its inviolability. Engelgardt's report from Batishchevo suggests that these hopes were well founded. He offers a positive appraisal of developments so far and an optimistic vision of what further peasant land purchases might bring to Russian agriculture, the economy, and society.

The twelfth letter also offers Engelgardt's report on his successful experimentation with phosphate fertilizers. From 1883 forward, experimentation with phosphorite dust had been the focus of his life on Batishchevo. As early as 1884, he confessed to a friend, "The exploitative farm I run on Batishchevo long ago ceased to interest me. . . ."[2] Investigating and experimenting with phosphates became a more compelling and comfortable concern for him. Having accepted the fact that his influence as a progressive farmer was limited, he invested his energies in the distribution of mineral fertilizers across a broad swath of the Russian Empire. Indeed, he judged correctly, for this was his most important legacy for Russian farming.

✉ ✉ ✉

"Dedicated to the memory of K. D. Kavelin"[3]

Peasant Land Purchases and Local Farming

A branch of the Peasant Land Bank has opened here also.[4] In our "Happy Little Corner" the peasants are also buying land with the bank's assistance.

The five villages which border my estate have already purchased a rather large amount of land.

And it is turning out well.

The landowners are happy they can sell the land they don't need, land they don't know what to do with, from which they don't get any income, for which it is difficult to find any buyers other than peasants. For the most part it is cutoff lands that are being sold, land beyond the fields, wastelands, separate abandoned homesteads, and so on.

The peasants are happy they can buy the land they need "for eternity." They can put the land they have purchased "to good use." Purchased land is always absolutely essential for peasants; many of them, for the most part, even before—and others since the Emancipation itself—had made use of them, paying for them with labor for the landowners, usually they worked plots of gentry land in *krug*s. But these jobs were extremely oppressive for the peasants. Only necessity, because there "was no place to move," forces the peasants to work these plots for the use of these lands.[. . .]

Now, thanks to the assistance of the Peasant Land Bank, the question is being resolved splendidly to the satisfaction of both landowners and peasants. The landowners are receiving the money they need, the peasants are acquiring the land they need. Both sides are happy. It is turning out well.

Permit me to describe what I know and see in regard to this question. But I beg you to keep in mind that I am going to talk only about "my spot," about my district, the province at most, and only about that which I observe and know thoroughly.

I am not dealing with the question of the Peasant Land Bank, I have not even read accounts of the activities of the bank. I want simply to describe how the business is going right here, near me, and I also intend to talk about this issue only from the farming, the agronomical point of view. Long ago already, just when I was beginning the second series of my letters "From the Country,"[5] I warned that "I absolutely can neither think, speak, nor write about anything else except the farm. All of my interests, all of the interests of the people I see daily, are focused on firewood, grain, livestock, manure." Now, having lived sixteen years in the country, I am even more buried in the farm . . .

One of the villages that has purchased land with the Peasant Land Bank's assistance, the village B., lies, so to speak, in the middle of my holdings. Its allotment land is divided by a small stream from the portion of my land that I farm. Behind the allotment, in a narrow strip, stretches my wasteland which has been cultivated from cleared forest only for a short time, while I have been here, during the last sixteen years. My wasteland abuts all three of the peasant fields, and only on one side is the peasant allotment land next to the land of the neighboring landowner, which the peasants also bought in 1885 with the bank's assistance.

The peasants' allotment is rather good, both in its location and in the quality of the land. Of course when I say that the land is of good quality that is only relative: it is good in our, Smolensk terms, but it still requires constant fertilization and, without manure, grain grows poorly. The peasants have a rather good meadow along the stream. Most of them do not have enough grain for their own subsistence and they have to purchase grain. Depending upon the harvest, sometimes they have to buy grain at Shrovetide, sometimes at Easter, rarely just before the new harvest. The grain harvests have noticeably improved over the last fifteen years, which is understandable, since the peasants sharecrop several meadows on the side, they maintain a good number of horses and livestock, and fertilize their land satisfactorily. The peasants' allotment is not the maximum—but it falls short only a little of being a full allotment.[6] The peasants received as their allotment what they had the use of during serfdom, and they themselves did not want additional land for a larger allotment, finding that the land that they had had the use of before was enough; but, of course, soon after, there was "crowding on the land," there began to be "nowhere to move." The peasants' meadow is very good, they had enough arable land, but there was not enough pasture for the livestock. Furthermore, after the Emancipation, there was a new order of things.

[Engelgardt discusses the pressures the peasants feel due to their need for pasture for their livestock.]

Well, and now the young people pester the old folks for not having known how to get a bit more allotment land and how to acquire surplus land. Then it was easy. One could often get significant additional empty lands for a very cheap price—to be worked off over the course of several years, as the peasants of several villages did. Land was very cheap then.

"The old folks didn't know how to handle the business, they let the land slip through their fingers, the airheads!"

In the village of B., it is precisely the young people, the new young generation who have come of age after the Emancipation, who have insisted on purchasing land with the bank's assistance. The old folks were always afraid, "You have to pay the 'bank,' you have to work for the landowner (for the supplementary payment), you have to plant the first year on virgin land. And if you don't pay the 'bank' on time, they'll take your land away; this isn't the same thing as being behind paying the state." The old folks would have certainly let the land slip through their fingers again; they would have held on, this way today, that way tomorrow, they say it will be all right, it's not completely impossible, maybe there will be some addition, a new edict from the Tsar will come out, wait and see. They would have wasted time, yes, they would have wasted time. And someone would have bought it, because it was a very good piece of land.

The young people insisted on buying the land. The deed was done. Now everyone, even the old ones, even the babas, is delighted by the fact that they have bought land, they have begun to have enough grain.

The village B. bought, in addition to their allotment, a piece of arable land with a little meadow along the same stream which divides the peasants' allotment from my land. The parcel they purchased abuts one of the peasants' fields.

The purchase was very profitable. About fifty desiatinas were purchased for something close to fifty rubles a desiatina. The bank provided some of the money; the landowner extended the remaining share over six years with the condition that the peasants, as they wished, could pay in money or work it off—"working *krug*s"—for a set, rather good price. Only two households wanted to pay in money, the rest took on working *krug*s. This work is not very burdensome for them and also offers the advantage, that, working for the landowner, the peasants can use his pasture for their cattle, at least, after the grain and grass are harvested.

The land that the peasants of the village B. bought is very good. It is a splendid sloping field of arable land facing the southwest which was once fertilized excellently and has only been left empty over the last five or six years, but is not yet exhausted. Lower, at the foot of the field, there is a small, swampy peat bog with a stream flowing through it.

Formerly, extensive farming was practiced on the estate that the land the village B. bought was a small part of, and the land was fertilized splendidly. The owner himself lived on this estate. Right here, nearby, he had a lot, a great deal of land, something on the order of ten thousand desiatinas, primarily forestland; he had a few homesteads and a multitude of "cutoff lands," which the peasants of various villages worked in *krug*s. There was very intensive farming on the estate where the owner lived. A lot of cattle were kept on the estate, there was dairy farming with splendid Swiss cheese making. There were 150 desiatinas of clover alone. Distillery waste was brought here for the cattle's feed from the distillery located on a different estate, and if need be, feed from other homesteads was brought here, a significant amount of hemp-field oil cake was used; a lot of swine were fed with whey and cheese mixed with grain. The pastures were constantly cleared, new land was cultivated from cleared groves. A lot of manure was stored up, the fields were fertilized excellently, the most superb grain was produced, the kind you can rarely encounter.

When I settled in the country in 1871, farming on this estate was in full flower. Later, however, bit by bit, the owner's affairs began to fall into disarray.[. . .] But since formerly, and for many years at that, the land was fertilized very well, it was not yet exhausted, it had not lost its old strength, but was only neglected, and had gone wild. One has only to take up this land seriously and it will immediately prove itself.

The piece of arable land the peasants bought was formerly part of the field planted for the market, it was heavily fertilized and yielded the most splendid grain harvests.[. . .] Furthermore, the peasants, having bought this plot for fifty rubles a desiatina, along with this, also bought the substance to prepare fertilizer for this land, or, it is better to say, the preparatory substance *for seasoning the land*—namely, the peat from the peat bog, then processed it to be taken out to the fields.[. . .]

When people around here heard about the establishment of a branch of the Peasant Land Bank, the peasants of another village that neighbors my estate, O., were the very first to decide to acquire land with its assistance. In fact these peasants acquired a whole homestead, which I will describe below. And it was this that got the ball rolling.

"They bought land, a whole homestead! . . ."

And, of course, since the peasants dream and keep an eye out to get a bit more land, the fact that land was being bought with the bank's assistance produced a sensation, made others also begin to think about how they too could, like the others, acquire a bit of land. Land is cheap here, there is a lot of empty land, there is an enormous supply of land for sale . . .

Soon word got out that the lord was ready to sell some land to peasants. The rumor spread that he was selling cutoff lands to peasants in the villages D. and Kh., who had already been trying hard to get them for a long time. They found out somewhere that he was not opposed to selling the parcel of land which until now had been sharecropped. [. . .]

"And what a piece—the cream of the crop! Fifty desiatinas in all, from border to border; whether you plant it or leave it in pasture, it's a jewel! There are thirty-six desiatinas of ploughland alone, and what land it is; just suppose, it's empty, but it hasn't lost its strength: it still has the good that was put in it before; and there was a little village here once that the lord took away during serfdom, so that part of the land is good, it was fertilized for many years. And then there's the bog below, the little ravine, a little meadow, although it is not the best, but even so . . . The peat's ready to go. A stream flows down below. It's an excellent piece—who could want any better!"[. . .]

And the peasants can buy: the bank will provide part of the money, and the lord will spread out the other in exchange for labor. The peasants thought seriously about how to acquire this bit of land, but if it had not been for the young people, it is absolutely clear that they would have let the purchase of the land slip away and then they would have been eternally sorry. While the old people thought about it and tried to figure it out, while they were splitting peas, and scratching themselves, someone would have bought it as private property, and wouldn't that have been a holiday! Or the lord, having sold various "cutoffs," would have reconsidered selling this plot. Strike while the iron is hot. The village youth insisted and did everything. However, at first, only a few of the young people wanted to buy the land for themselves, having broken off into a partnership, and even to move onto it. But then the business was handled differently: the whole village bought it. One of the young educated men helped the village in this regard; he explained the whole business to the peasants, pointed out how and what, he persuaded them to buy it as joint property as a whole village. Now that the business is settled and had turned out well—so well, it couldn't be better—the peasants, I have heard, have recorded the name of this young man in the prayers they say before lunch. "And God will reward him!" the peasants say.

"And how God has rewarded him!" one of my acquaintances quipped.

"How is that?"

"You remember, how they arrived with questions and snooping around."

The business was settled by the spring of 1885. Beginning in spring 1885, the landowner gave the peasants the purchased land completely under their management and use on condition that they harvest the rye for him that had been planted by sharecroppers in 1884.

However, you must spoil before you spin. The peasants planted part of the land in spring wheat, but there was a total spring crop failure everywhere here in 1885. All of the spring grains—barley, oats, seeds did not produce well at all, so that in some areas they hardly yielded seed. The grass crop was also very poor. The peasants' rye crop was average, and they had to use this rye to plant the purchased land.

The peasants fertilized the portion of land designated for planting with the peat I mentioned earlier, and they fertilized it carefully; they could not put on manure because they did not have enough of it to fertilize their allotment land fully. In the fall of 1885, the verdure on this field was exceptional, thick, a deep color, better than on the allotment land. Last year, the rye crop was superb so that the peasants would have enough grain from the land they had bought and from their allotment land, without want, until the new harvest, which had never happened before. How could the poor people not include the name "Viktor" in their prayers! After all, if it had not been for him, several wealthier fellows, with a larger family, would have bought the land, but the poor peasants and the ones who live alone would have been left without bread—so buy it then from the partners!

The peasants have not planted spring grain on the purchased land this year, but they ploughed the land for rye next year.[. . .] Last year, however, the peasants did not take peat out to the field because the summer was wet and it was difficult to haul peat out of the bog. Instead, a lot of peasants took manure out to the purchased land, calculating that it would be better to put it on the good, well-situated, newly purchased land than on the poor, low plots of allotment land. The verdure on the purchased land last autumn was very good—the field is visible from my house, so that I can constantly follow it, and it is possible to hope that the peasants will again get a good crop of rye next year. It is interesting that as soon as the land fell into peasant hands, and precisely as property or "for eternity," as the peasants say, the crops became better, although, generally speaking, on the average, the peasants have worse crops, for the most part, than the gentry; but that depends not on the fact that the peasants treat the land worse, that they are too lazy to cultivate it, as some think, but from a multitude of complex causes.

It is true that the peasants are very suspicious of various gentry agronomical ventures and innovations, but one has to admit that there is really no other way to act—how many failures have they already seen, mistakes, and most of all, *thoughtlessness?* What, what has not been tried by the fans of agronomy, and always with the thought of increasing crops immediately or making production cheaper, getting rich quick—but nothing turns out in practice, and gentry farming in general, with a few exceptions, has not gone much beyond the peasants'. And this is understandable: there is no scientific knowledge, and there is also no practical knowledge, which the muzhik, who knows a lot after all, has. And without knowledge, nothing will come of the poorly understood theory of "common sense."

While they view innovations suspiciously, the peasants, however, attentively follow what the neighboring landowner does and if the business really is a success, if it is established securely, then the peasants appraise the profitability of this or that innovation very well and apply it, if this is possible given the conditions of their farm. Thus, here, for example, planting potatoes in fields was introduced long ago by the peasants. Fifteen years ago, when I introduced flax on empty fields, the peasants watched this business very mistrustfully, but now, whenever the opportunity presents itself, they rent empty fields and plant flax. When I began to improve the livestock, the peasants also viewed this business as a gentry enterprise, but now they are constantly buying calves from me and they are breeding excellent cows.

The peasants were also suspicious when I began to plough a future arable field under for the winter, and to trifallow for winter wheat, but they soon saw that this is good. However, they did not plough their field under, despite my repeated arguments, they did not plough under because they need it for pasturing their livestock. No matter how many times I pointed out to the peasants that it was more profitable for them to plough their arable under for the winter and to rent land from me or a neighboring landowner for pasturing their livestock, depending on which would be more suitable for which year, even so they kept to their own ways and did not plough under—probably, they were afraid of becoming too dependent on the "master." But now, as soon as these same peasants have bought land and the opportunity has appeared to plough it under for the winter and to trifallow for winter wheat— now they have done this as well. When the opportunity arose to fertilize the field with peat—they began to haul peat out to the ploughland. The peasants immediately took note even of such a complete innovation as my experiments fertilizing with *phosphorite dust* (see my article "Experiments of Fertilizing with Roslavl Phosphorite," in nos. 40, 41, 42, 43 of the *Agricultural Gazette* for 1886), and two of the villagers of B. have done experiments on their parcels.

The Promise of Phosphorite Fertilizer for Russian Agriculture

In 1885, I did experiments with phosphorite dust prepared by K. V. Miasoedov from phosphorite which I found in the Roslavl District in 1884 (see my article "Smolensk Phosphorites" in the *Agricultural Gazette,* 1884, nos. 39– 40). Phosphorite dust, which I use for fertilizing poor soil after rye, alone, without manure, had a *striking* effect, which *was noticeable to everyone* at a glance. Since the spring of last year, 1886, as soon as the rye began to come up, the plot fertilized with phosphorite dust was immediately sharply different, and this distinction persisted the entire summer so that everyone, from the external appearance of the rye, could always, with complete accuracy, point out the boundary of the plot fertilized with the phosphorite dust. The rye on it was thicker and taller, fluffier, distinguished by a dark verdure, it blossomed earlier, it began to ripen earlier, so that when the rye on the fertilized plot began to turn gold, the rest was still completely green, and for that reason it was possible to see the fertilized plot from far away. By mowing time, the rye on the fertilized plot was much riper, a half-arshin taller, had thicker straw, and was bushier. When they mowed the rye, it was utterly, strikingly obvious on the mown fields which spot had been fertilized with phosphorite dust, so that if the phosphorite dust had left an inscription, then it would have have been possible to read it on the mown fields. The rye on the broken land which was fertilized with phosphorite dust was distinguished like heaven from earth from the rye on the broken land that had not been fertilized with anything and it was just as good as the rye on the broken earth fertilized with manure.

In the spring, on Trinity Sunday, here, by custom, the peasants go to "weave garlands" in the wood, without fail in the rye field. Weaving garlands, and then untwisting the garlands—it is an even gayer holiday when they decorate the May tree and soak the garlands—is, of course, accompanied with songs, wonderful May songs, with their soft, lulling melodies, dancing, a bit of drinking, and eating. In addition to my workers, a lot of peasants gather here from the neighboring villages for this occasion, mostly young people. The desiatina on which the experiment of fertilizing with phosphorite dust was done is located right next to the wood in which they wove the garlands this year. I made use of the occasion and showed the young folks what a striking effect the phosphorite dust which I sprinkled on a part of the desiatina last year had had, which now is so strikingly different in the verdure's appearance; everyone, of course, knew that this desiatina was not fertilized with manure, and that I had sprinkled some kind of dirt I had ordered on it. At this I explained that this phosphorite dust is prepared from a special stone which is turned into dust on a simple mill. This dust, I usually explain to peasants, is almost the same thing as ashes, or better, subsoil, which remains when lye is made from ashes. The peasants understand this kind of explanation because our peasants know very well what excellent fertilizer ashes are; our peasants are well acquainted with the useful effect of ashes as a fertilizer, because they often plant grain on cleared forestland, on burned soil, which is burned after expanses of forest are cleared, also on piles, that is, on burned heaps of twigs. Peasants here also take out the rubbish from the hemp fields, hemp fiber, and so on to the fields and burn them: grain on these spots grows better. Under serfdom, among the various tributes—rams, chickens, dried mushrooms, and so on—here, moreover, *ashes* were also collected, as far as I remember, it seems it was one osmina per *tiaglo*.[7] These ashes were used to fertilize special desiatinas on which seed grains were planted; weeds develop from manure. And that was still when the mineral theory of fertilization was in fashion!

On Trinity Sunday already the rye on the plot fertilized with phosphorite couldn't have been better and it was quite strikingly distinguished from the unfertilized section, which especially hit you in the eye: everyone could immediately determine the boundary of the fertilized plot. The young people were amazed.

Then the rye on the plot fertilized with phosphorite stood out all summer in both its height and its lushness. The peasants took note, and not only the young people, but even the old folks.

At one point this summer, as I was riding around the fields, I went over to the plot fertilized with phosphorite. I rode up, I looked, a middle-aged peasant from a neighboring village, the local rich peasant, was standing near the rye.

"Greetings, Prokop. So, have you come to have a look at the rye?"

"Yes, I was passing by, I'm going to K. for some boots, I came by to have a glance. I saw the oats that you sprinkled that dirt you ordered on: it's good, but the rye's even better. Amazing! And where did this kind of dirt come from?"

"There is a kind of stone, round stones, something like potatoes; come by, I will show you. This stone lies in layers in the sand, as if it were scattered like potatoes. It is collected, washed so that the sand is washed off, and it is ground at the mill."

"At the mill? At an ordinary mill?"

"Yes, at a plain mill."

"But we don't have any of this kind of stone here?"

"No. Wherever this stone is put on the fields, even if it is sandy soil, in a year, without manure, excellent grain will grow."

"But maybe we have some here too?"

"No, we do not have any. Not far from here, in the Roslavl District, there is some."

"Is that where you went year before last?"

"Yes."

"People figured this out! Germans, no doubt, did everything?"

"Of course, Germans. They have enormous factories set up for this. Every year tens of millions of puds of stone are turned into fertilizer and they spread this fertilizer on their fields. Excellent grain grows. But if it were not for this fertilizer, the Germans would never have the kind of grain that grows for them. They would buy even more from us."

"Well, and that's good that they don't buy much. That's probably why, thank God, grain is cheap here. But if this business succeeds, if this dirt you order proves itself, then it will be a big business, a big business."

"Of course, big business. And why should it not succeed, why should it not succeed? In Germany, I'm telling you, tens of millions of puds of fertilizer are made from this stone every year . . . They are not fools, you know. And there is a lot of this stone in Russia, an abundance, lots of it, there are whole towns that are paved with this stone. Why should it not succeed? But, you see yourself that the rye is no worse than with manure. And you yourself know that manure was not put on here, for twenty-five years since the Emancipation, they didn't put manure on it, the land has no 'seasoning,' it was an empty field, it was completely overgrown with grass, year before last there was flax on the plot. So it has just been broken."

"I know it was left plain and they didn't put manure here very often before the Emancipation. Broken ground is broken ground, everyone knows that grain always grows well on land from dried-up felled forest, but even so, you need to use a bit of manure. But here, really, we know, that no manure was put down, and the corner where the German dirt was scattered is excellent. It's as if you cut it out from this side and the other. Amazing! Potapych said to me: come by, he says, have a look: they spread it over twenty sazhens long and ten wide."

"No, it is not ten sazhens wide, but eleven."

"Well, it's the same thing."

"No, it is not the same thing. How is it all the same? No, you come here and measure in steps from the corner to the spot where the rye is excellent."

And I made the muzhik measure in steps the spot where the rye was "excellent." This year I made everyone do this who agreed to ride with me to have a look at the rye on the plot fertilized with phosphorite dust. I would ride up to the plot, ask them to point out where the rye is good, the difference was so great that everyone, every gentlewoman even, could distinguish at a glance where the rye was better, and then I would ask them to measure in steps where the rye stood out.[. . .]

In Russia there is a mass of empty, wild, uncultivated land, wastelands, neglected fields, overgrown with shrubbery, seedlings, and small trees, felled forestland, meadows, cleared forest, and so on; in Dorogobuzhskii District alone there are tens of thousands of desiatinas of such uncultivated, wild land, which, with the aid of phosphorite, could be transformend into cultivated land. With the Peasant Land Bank's assistance, the peasants can buy up such land cheaply. Once they have bought it, they can immediately clear it and raise flax on the field. And the land has been bought. Manure is not needed on the freshly broken ground; I spread only phosphorite dust, and the grain is of the richest sort. Not only will we not have to bring grain from the steppe the way we do now, but we will even begin to sell our own to the Germans . . .

The muzhik stopped.

"Thirty-four."

"No, you have small steps. Look here, I'll measure . . . one, two, three . . . thirty-three."

"Yes, it will be a big business if it succeeds."

"And why should it not succeed? You remember, fifteen years ago, when I arrived here and decided to plant flax on the empty fields, you yourself, specifically you, said to me that flax would not grow here? Remember, you said, 'Nothing will come of it, there has never been flax here and there will not be any!'—do you remember?"

"How could I not remember? I remember."

"And now you plant flax yourself on empty fields. You trade in flax, last year you bought up to 1,200 rubles of flax from me."

"Yes, but we didn't know."

"That's just it, you do not know anything. You are ignoramuses, but you think a lot of yourselves. We can do anything! We are farmers; we know how to get around with the land. Just so, you get around, only you do it without torches. Look, you burned a torch for centuries and you would have burned it for centuries more if you had not been given a pound of kerosene for two kopeks.[8] Just look, you turned down additional land when they were giving out your allotments."

"The people were airheads."

"And now they are not? Ignoramuses? You only think that you know a lot. Remember how the hail agent taught you?"

"I remember."

"But you do not take out insurance?"

"Yes, but who knows . . ."

"So, yes, I know, you pray to the 'Tsar of Hail.'[. . .] "Well, and so? What do you think about phosphorite?"

"I'll need to try this 'prisporite,' as you call it. Only, look, the soldier Akim says that you can ruin the soil with this prisporite. He says that the crops will grow at first, but then they'll stop: prisporite, he says, takes all of the moisture that there is out of the soil."

"But do not forget about manure. Phosphorite cannot ruin the soil, but, on the contrary, it *seasons* it, but all the same, you should not forget manure. One time, put down phosphorite, another, but then, manure. You know that you took peat out to the field, did it work?"

"What do you mean, we hauled it. It works."

"So do you think that you are always going to fertilize just with peat? You know that you have to put down manure too."

"Everyone knows that you need manure too."

"Well, and it's the same thing! And there is even more benefit in phosphorite than in peat, of course, you need to do experiments to find out where it is needed. It is impossible to ruin a plough field with it, but its benefit, you see for yourself, can be great. Look, it will be good if clover is planted after the phosphorite, give the land a year or two to dry out, but then flax, and rye, phosphorite again, and then, manure. Look, you have just bought a fourth field of land, you can put some in clover, the way I do. Clover is food for the horses and the livestock, which makes manure, and grain. If you are going to fertilize with peat, then do not forget phosphorite and manure, put the extra manure on the hemp and barley, that way you will season your fields so that they are marvelous! There will be enough grain 'both for seeds and eating,' and to sell. And then you can buy more land; the bank will help again, if you pay back as you should. Someday, you will buy all of my Batishchevo. Neighbors bought the prince's homestead, after all. They say that this year they got a reserve of grain for two years."

"I need to give it a try . . . Look, Aleksandr Nikolaevich, you order me a little sack of this dirt too. I'll pay whatever it costs. I need to try it."

Yes, one must experiment and experiment, and not judge only on the basis of theory. But this Akim is saying that phosphorite is "trifles," "infatuation";

someone else says that you need to use superphosphate, and that only on good ploughland, and then in no other way except with Chilean saltpeter. But it turned out that phosphorite has a splendid effect on our bad land, and now a third Akim says that it is that way only the first time, that later the phosphorite will ruin the soil, that it will take out all of its moisture, and so on and so forth. Everyone just intellectualizes, sitting in offices, when one must experiment, and experiment sensibly. No small amount of time has already been lost. We continue to wait for the Americans to hit us on the forehead with a hammer.

Later another peasant from the neighboring village asked me to order him a sack of phosphorite dust. Of course, I was in ecstasy because if the muzhiks begin to apply phosphorite dust, the deed is done. At the time I did not have any phosphorite dust because I had already spread all the phosphorite dust that I had received in the spring, some on oats, some on the field ploughed under for the winter for rye. Out of the next order which arrived, I gave the peasants two sacks before I spread it. One of the peasants fertilized a parcel of broken ground with the phosphorite dust, the other, a parcel of fresh soil. In the autumn I went by to see how it turned out. The verdure on the plots fertilized with phosphorite was excellent, very fine.

The peasants who bought land with the bank's assistance, this truly beneficial institution, celebrated this year. The land did excellently. There was plenty of grain. The peasants somehow especially love this purchased land, they talk about it with a special tenderness, if it is possible to put it this way. They constantly think and worry about how to earn money to pay the bank on time. They work superbly for the landowner for the supplemental payment, they always show up all together at work as they should, as a whole village at the first summons.

Other villages as well have managed no worse with this business.

[Engelgardt describes two more villages by way of illustration. He then begins a lengthy discussion of his successful experimentation with phosphate fertilizer.]

The fourth of the villages which abut my land, the village O., which formed a partnership with several people from other villages, bought an entire homestead with the assistance of the bank. And this is not a large village, and neither does it have much land. But the people are bold, hardworking, and prosperous. Even earlier, this little village bought some cleared forestland cheaply at some distance from the village and turned it into meadow. And now, as soon as the branch of the Peasant Land Bank opened here, the village O., the first in our district, bought land with its assistance, and a whole gentry homestead at that. And moreover, there is a tavern in this village, that is, not a tavern—I keep forgetting that there are no taverns in Russia now—but a liquor store, the kind of store in which vodka is sold in stamped crocks and it is not allowed to drink it there, so that the person who has bought the vodka must carry it out of the store and drink it in a special izba, specifically designated for that purpose. I do not know what this izba is called; the muzhiks use the old term for it, that is—tavern—for this entire establishment, the store and the izba where they do the drinking. The muzhiks claim that this was all set up for the comfort of the tavern keepers so that they will not be disturbed by drunkards. Before, vodka was drunk right in the tavern, but, of course, it was a disturbance for the keeper. They get drunk, they make a lot of noise, they make merry, they get rowdy, they sing songs, they argue, they fight, and then someone drinks himself into a stupor—take him away; someone else drinks too much. I have often had occasion to hear complaints from the tavern keepers about these disturbances: "They drink for a ruble, and they swear for ten rubles' worth; I have a daughter here, an educated girl, she studied in the institute, it's no good!" It is a great irritation for the keeper himself and especially for Madame Tavern Keeper. For her, as far as I have observed, the keeper's wife plays the main role because most of the men, the keeper-husbands, are themselves drunkards who are constantly under the influence: they sit by the barrel, well, and they have a bit of the spirits. While the keepers' wives do not drink and they run everything. Of course, great peace—no noise, no swearing—everywhere is gentlemanly, noble. Take your vodka in its stamped crock—they don't give out less than a half bottle—and drink it wherever you want. In the summer, of course, it is possible to drink outdoors, but in the winter this is not too comfortable. Vodka is strong everywhere now, 80 proof—before vodka was weak everywhere in Russia, 54–60 proof, and cheap, 3 rubles 40 kopeks a vedro—the store is not heated and the vodka is almost the same temperature as the air outside, so that in the winter, if you take vodka into a room the bottle will be covered with hoarfrost. And it is this kind of cold vodka, at 15 to 20 degrees below zero, and strong at that, and no less than a half bottle even, that has to be drunk in the cold. Here, in the real cold, your teeth even freeze to the glass. The specialists say, however, that cold vodka is easy to drink, it just dries up the throat, which is why there are so many people in the winter who have gotten hoarse to the point that they cannot speak at all. They say that strong, 80 proof vodka and cold at that, when drunk, does not have an immediate effect, but suddenly grabs you later, so that if you stop en route and drink up one or two half bottles in the cold, you will feel nothing at first, but later, after you have gone a few versts, it will grab you so strongly that you lose consciousness, so that it is possible to freeze or get frostbitten. Everyone says this. No matter how the tavern keepers are attacked for their lack of humanity, they are people even so, they are also Christians; they understood very well that it was impossible, dangerous to drink cold vodka in the cold, out of humanity they built izbas everywhere near the liquor stores where it is possible to drink the vodka that is bought, where there is also a little hook to uncork the bottle, and little glasses and appetizers. One can sit a while, talk a while, drink calmly, without hurrying; if you do not have enough, you can ask for more; anyone who does not like strong vodka can ask for cheaper, diluted vodka.

At first I did not believe that the liquor stores were established for the comfort of the tavern keepers—the peasants are always thinking up something—but later, when the rumors spread that soon state sales of vodka would be introduced, then it occurred to even me that these liquor stores that are peaceful for the keepers were established in order to prepare the people gradually for good behavior in taverns. It is understandable that when state people in uniform are going to be sitting in the taverns, with some kind of badges on, then it will be impossible to make noise and use foul language there; undoubtedly, it will then be required that one remove one's hat upon entering a tavern.[. . .]

So although there is a tavern in the village, still the peasants have not turned to drink, and they have bought an entire homestead. The estate which they have bought belonged at one time to a certain prince, a good master, whose main estate and residence were located about thirty versts from this homestead. Formerly, there was plenty of livestock on the property, clover was planted, and there were good yields of grain. Fifteen years ago I still found good farming on this property, although a lot of land was already being left empty, and they had stopped planting clover. There was a lot of good birch forest on the property. Then, after the owner died, the property was rented out, but the lord who rented it did not himself live there, and the farm was run by a steward. The farm declined even more; they began to plant flax in order to make use of the land left empty after the Emancipation. Finally this homestead, like many similar estates, was bought by a lumber merchant, who eliminated farming, cut down the forest for firewood, and finally sold it to the peasants of the village O. The peasants began to take control of the homestead last year: they are ploughing up the fields, they are using the meadows, and, most important, they have made use of the felled groves for cleared land, they are burning it and planting grain. They say that this year the peasants have gotten so much grain that they have enough for two years. They are working very hard. Since a lot of scrap, twigs, and trees that are not suitable for Moscow firewood were left in the groves cleared by the merchant, the peasant-owners put out the gathering of firewood and everything that could be of any use for a muzhik on the farm to other peasants this year.

Beginning this year, several peasants have already set themselves up on the purchased property and have moved there to live. In this way a new village is growing up, and in the old area, it will become easier in regard to land because of the departure of many people.[. . .]

These peasants live well, they have enough grain, they work in the best possible way both on the old allotment land and on the newly purchased property. They do not neglect appropriate earnings elsewhere, by the way, where appropriate, they now haul planks in the winter with a steam thresher to the railroad station, although the price for hauling this year is not high. They do not let anything slip by—"even if it's a little profit, it still goes into the pouch more often"—they are saving up money to pay the bank. These peasants had never done any work for me, but this year, they took on tying together the harvest of clover in stacks, and they did the work quickly, properly, superbly.

I still have not seen how the peasants divided up the property they bought; next year, if I am alive and well, I hope to persuade them to introduce phosphorites there. These peasants, if they understand, and try it, and it comes out well, then everything will be okay and they will open a storehouse of phosphorite dust for sale.[. . .]

It is interesting and pleasant to observe the peasants' attitude toward the newly purchased land. They love these lands especially, they pour their hopes on them, they look at their acquisitions with pride. It is understandable that, first and foremost, the peasants acquire the land they need most, about which they have dreamed ceaselessly, which they unwillingly rented from the land-owners, paying for them with summer labor which is difficult for the peasants and of little use to the landowners under current circumstances. It was one long, drawn-out process. The bank has untied everyone's hands. The opportunity to purchase land with the bank's assistance has had a healthy effect, eliminating the useless, solely irritating, unfounded dreaming about redistributions, free lands, and so on.

The peasants are very careful about paying the bank back on time, they are afraid to fall behind with their payments; they watch each other carefully in this regard and they have enormous moral influence on each other, making each other earn money and not let opportunities that offer some kind of work slip by. This is especially noticeable for the unstable lazy ones, who are exceptional in the village, who usually did nothing beginning in the autumn as long as there was grain, and never went to do any work elsewhere. This was all especially noticeable to me as a farmer who constantly needs a work force, especially day laborers. I even find that the peasants live a more sober life; formerly they somehow lived more idly. If there were grain, then fine, "If you don't go out, you can lie down"; but now it is not so, everyone is driven out to earn money.

Everyone paid the bank on time and did the work for the supplemental payments well. And this when 1885 was a very hard year, I judge this not only by what I saw in peasant farming but also by what I experienced on my own.

At the time a year before last when the journals were talking about over-production and complaining about the cheapness of grain, the peasants here were simply starving. It is fifteen years already that I have lived in the country, I lived through even those years when rye reached 14 rubles a chetvert, but I had not seen the kind of suffering that I saw in the winter of 1885–86. I do not know what famine means precisely in official language and where the boundary is between a shortage of grain and starvation, but last year, I myself saw starving people who had not eaten for two days. I had not seen such starving people with their special facial expression in a long time. There was no such starvation when rye reached 14 rubles a chetvert here several years ago, there was not such a multitude of people begging for crusts of bread as there was last year. Not only children, old people, and women, but also young girls and boys, who were capable of working, went begging for crusts of bread. Let us assume that of the peasants from the nearest villages which are my neighbors, those who had bought land, few went out after crusts of bread; they were ashamed, they tried to get by somehow, they took on work, they borrowed. But from distant villages, they went out in droves so that in the dining hall, where crusts of bread are given out, there was a noticeable increase in the outlay for flour.[. . .]

Although the rye harvest was good last year, higher than average in our district, all the other economic conditions combined in the most damaging way.

Because of the unusual drought, the grasses came up very badly, and although the weather was good when it came time to harvest, so that the mown hay was gathered early and turned out well, there was still extremely little of it.

The spring grains also came up badly. The barley failed completely, so that many did not even get a return in seed. The oats also failed. Because of the failed spring grain crops, there was also no spring straw, the main feed for the livestock.

Which means, there was neither hay nor spring straw; so that the rye straw had to make up for everything.

The flax and hemp also did not come up well, and this, moreover, is the main item for sale that provides the peasants with money.

Because of the lack of feed, the livestock were not worth anything by autumn, and by the spring, the prices for livestock did not go up.

There were no wage earnings whatsoever. There was even little preparation of firewood for Moscow. The prices for hauling firewood, planks, and so on, which constitute the main earnings of the peasants, went down extraordinarily, despite the high cost of feed and the total lack of oats. Because of this, the prices for all jobs went down, but most important, no one needed workers, even for free, because there was not enough food. In order to get some money, the peasants had to borrow money in advance in exchange for summer labor, for the most part, in greater amounts than they could do. But when they need to eat, they do not think about this. God provides, we'll do the work somehow.

They went in droves after crusts of bread, and even in the commune they gave them out badly.[. . .]

Well, so they got by. They did not have enough to eat. By spring, it was horrible to look at both the people and the animals. The horses were in such a state in the spring that the ploughman could only listen to the larks. He would go one furrow and stop. "Well, little mother! Well, little mother! Well!" and the little mother would only shake her tail. So stand, and listen to how the larks are singing in the sky. It is fine, it is pleasant to listen to the larks, but not behind the plough. However, there was not much ploughing to be done because, due to the lack of spring seed, most of the fields remained unplanted.

When the livestock were let out into the fields, it got easier. There remained only one concern: how to feed oneself until the new harvest. And a lot was still needed because work, the long day, requires a lot of bread. Although it is said, "when spring comes, it warms up and people become kinder," this year no one got kinder in the spring. Everything that could be taken on for work had been taken. They grabbed at any chance. And at the peak of the work season, the muzhik bridles a pair of horses, goes to the steam lumber mill, loads up two loads of boards, and takes them to the railroad station. It is well known what the price is when the muzhik has nothing to eat. He hauls the boards to the station, he feeds the horse along the way, wherever he can let it graze, where the grass is cut in the evening or at night, wherever he can grab with his hands. He delivers the boards, he unloads them—now for the accounting; he buys some flour and lives for a week, but then he goes again for boards. And it was lucky that there was lumber. Hauling planks saved a lot of people. Everyone was delighted with the new harvest. The rye crop was splendid. There was grain, enough for some to last until the next harvest, enough for some to last until Easter, and for the poorest—until Shrovetide. Everyone paid back his debts. Barley, oats, hemp, flax, whoever planted, came up beautifully, it was an unheard of harvest. Rejoice, farmer! There was only one bad thing, again this year there were no wage earnings at all! If there are no wage earnings, there is no money, and they are demanding money everywhere, the authorities know that this was a good harvest. But there is no money . . .

※   ※   ※

Engelgardt's elliptical ending to his twelfth letter from Batishchevo was appropriate for the observations he had offered to the readers of *Herald of Europe*. For, after fifteen years of reporting on developments in the countryside, Engelgardt knew that there was no conclusion, no end of the story, no final point in the evolution of social and economic relations he had been describing. The currents he explored in this final letter testified to the reality of change in the post-Emancipation countryside. Indeed, one might argue that this letter identifies the shift from one stage of land reform to another and the emergence of a second generation of post-Emancipation peasants in Smolensk Province. With this second generation, the Russian peasantry began to enter another stage when the habits of serfdom began to fall away and new possibilities surfaced in the rural world of the agrarian economy. The emphasis on individual enterprise, respect for private property, and willingness to seize the opportunities made available through the Peasant Land Bank contributed to Engelgardt's largely optimistic tone in this letter, and may serve as one explanation for the popularity of his work in Russia in the post-Soviet era. His shift to a more pessimistic recognition of the obstacles to the full development of these tendencies, characteristic of his contradictory appraisals throughout the letters, also rings true, however, to the contemporary Russian reader, and attests to his ability to capture the tensions inherent in patterns of economic and social development in Russia over the last century.

Notes

Preface

1. Zemledelets (S. Sharapov), " 'Schastlivyi ugolok' (po povodu ix i x pisem A. N. Engel'gardta 'Iz derevni')," *Rus'*, no. 18 (March 14, 1881): 11.

2. V. I. Lenin, *Polnoe sobranie sochinenii*, vol. 2 (Moscow, 1958), 521–28.

3. See, for example, Viktor Krivorotov, "Ironiia istorii ili o pol'ze izucheniia diskusii proshlogo," *Znamia*, no. 12 (December 1989): 187–96; the introductory article to the seventh edition of the letters: P. V. Volubuev and V. P. Danilov, "Predislovie," in A. N. Engel'gardt, *Iz derevni. 12 pisem. 1872–1887* (Moscow, 1987), 5–40; I. Tarasulo, ed., *Gorbachev and Glasnost: Viewpoints from the Soviet Press* (Wilmington, Del., 1989), p. 104 (translated article from *Izvestiia* [March 30, 1988]).

Introduction

1. Saltykov-Shchedrin offered as a model an earlier eyewitness account of rural life, *In the Backwoods and in the Capital*, also written by a native of Smolensk—F. P. Elenev—which had appeared serially in the journal in 1867–1869 before it was published as a separate volume in 1870. N. A. Engel'gardt, "Davnie epizody (A. N. Engel'gardt i M. E. Saltykov-Shchedrin), IV," *Istoricheskii vestnik*, vol. 124, 1911, 55–56, and Tsentral'nyi Gosudarstvennyi Arkhiv Literatury i Iskusstva (hereafter TsGALI), fond 572, opis' 1, delo 174, l. 1.

2. Alexander Vucinich, *Science in Russian Culture, 1861–1917* (Stanford, 1970), 74; G. A. Shkol'nik, *Nashi zemliaki-estestvoispytateli (Biograficheskie ocherki o vydaiushchikhsia deiateliakh otechestvennoi nauke)* (Smolensk, 1963), 112.

3. N.a., "A. N. Engel'gardt," *Trudy imperatorskogo vol'nogo ekonomicheskogo obshchestva*, no. 5 (September–October 1895): 66–67.

4. A. Vucinich, *Science in Russian Culture*, 136–37.

5. M. G. Gerchikov, "Pamiati zabytogo khimika," *Priroda*, no. 10 (1932): 951–54.

6. N. N. Sokolov and A. N. Engel'gardt, "Ot redaktsii," *Khimicheskii zhurnal N. Sokolova i A. Engel'gardta*, vol. 1, bk. 1 (1859): iv.

7. Rukopisnyi otdel, Pushkinskii dom, fond 577, opis' 1, delo 15, ll. 4–7.

8. His two most important awards were the St. Petersburg Academy of Sciences' Lomonosov Prize, which he shared with P. A. Lachinov for their joint research on cresols and nitrocompounds, and an honorary doctorate in chemistry, which he received from Kharkov University in 1866. He published frequently in *Zeitschrift für*

Chemie, Biulleten' Peterburgskoi akademii nauk (Bulletin of the St. Petersburg Academy of Sciences), *Zemledel'cheskaia gazeta* (The Agricultural Gazette), and *Zhurnal sel'skogo khoziaistva i lesovodstva* (Journal of Agriculture and Forestry).

9. In 1863 he published an article on Justus Liebig, the great German organic chemist and author of *Organic Chemistry in Its Application to Agriculture and Physiology* (A. N. Engel'gardt, "Liebig v russkom perevode," *Sankt Petersburgskie vedomosti*, no. 272 [December 6, 1863]: 1105–6). Of Liebig's various contributions, his demonstration that plants depleted the soil of major elements and his advocacy of the use of mineral fertilizers had the most obvious impact on Engelgardt. In 1866 Engelgardt was commissioned by the government to explore phosphate deposits in Smolensk, Orel, Kursk, Voronezh, and Tambov provinces. His partner on the expedition was future Minister of Agriculture A. S. Ermolov. See A. S. Ermolov, *Recherches sur les gisements de phosphate de chaux fossiles en Russie avec carte et tableaux analytiques* (St. Petersburg, 1873); and A. N. Engel'gardt, "Nashi vtune lezhaiushchiia bogatstva," *Sankt Petersburgskie vedomosti*, no. 311 (1867): 1.

10. M. Kompaneets, *Uchenie agronomy Rossii. Iz istorii agronomicheskoi nauki* (Moscow, 1971), 99.

11. Later published as a separate volume, A. N. Engel'gardt, *Sbornik obshcheponiatnykh statei po estestvoznaniiu* (A Collection of Popular Articles on the Natural Sciences) (St. Petersburg, 1867).

12. A. I. Faresov, *Semidesiatniki* (St. Petersburg, 1905), 6.

13. P. Ia. Nechuiatov, *Aleksandr Nikolaevich Engel'gardt. Ocherk zhizni i deiatel'nosti* (Smolensk, 1957), 32–33.

14. The student was V. G. Kotel'nikov. See TsGALI, fond 572, opis' 2, delo 29, ll. 1–9.

15. For a study of the emergence of the radical student movement in the 1860s, see Abbott Gleason, *Young Russia: The Genesis of Russian Radicalism in the 1860s* (New York, 1980).

16. N. A. Engel'gardt, "Davnie epizody," *Istoricheskii vestnik* 119 (1910): 549.

17. Ibid., 550.

18. Nechuiatov, *Aleksandr Nikolaevich Engel'gardt*, 37–39.

19. For the history of the design of the legislation and the participation of the gentry in it, see Terrence Emmons, *The Russian Landed Gentry and the Peasant Emancipation of 1861* (Cambridge, 1967); and Daniel Field, *The End of Serfdom: Nobility and Bureaucracy in Russia, 1855–1861* (Cambridge, Mass., 1976).

20. For further discussion of the details of the reform, see Jerome Blum, *Lord and Peasant in Russia from the Ninth to the Nineteenth Century* (Princeton, 1961), 575–600; and Geroid T. Robinson, *Rural Russia under the Old Regime* (New York, 1949), 64–93.

21. Robinson, *Rural Russia under the Old Regime*, 87.

22. A. M. Anfimov, *Krupnoe pomeshchich'e khoziaistvo evropeiskoi Rossii* (Moscow, 1969), 194.

23. N. M. Druzhinin, *Russkaia derevnia na perelome, 1861–1880 gg.* (Moscow, 1978), 134.

24. A. M. Anfimov, *Ekonomicheskoe polozhenie i klassovaia bor'ba krest'ian evropeiskoi Rossii, 1881–1904* (Moscow, 1984), 164.

25. See Arcadius Kahan, *Russian Economic History: The Nineteenth Century,* ed. Roger Weiss (Chicago, 1989), 8–9; and Seymour Becker, *Nobility and Privilege in Late Imperial Russia* (De Kalb, Ill., 1985), 27–32.

26. *Desiatina:* 2.7 acres.

27. Druzhinin, *Russkaia derevnia na perelome*, 116.

28. D. I. Budaev, *Krest'ianskaia reforma 1861 goda v Smolenskoi gubernii* (Smolensk, 1964), 146–54.

29. R. J. Ware, "A Russian Journal and Its Public: *Otechestvennye zapiski*, 1868–1884," *Oxford Slavonic Papers*, n.s., 14 (1981): 130.

30. Jeffrey Brooks, "Readers and Reading at the End of the Tsarist Era," in *Literature and Society in Imperial Russia, 1880–1914*, ed. W. M. Todd (Stanford, 1978), 99.

31. Brooks, "Readers and Reading," 100.

32. Ware, "A Russian Journal," 133.

33. Ibid., 138–42.

34. See Alexander Vucinich, *Social Thought in Tsarist Russia: The Quest for a General Science of Society, 1861–1917* (Chicago, 1976); Alexander Vucinich, *Darwin in Russian Thought* (Berkeley, 1988); Daniel P. Todes, *Darwin without Malthus: The Struggle for Existence in Russian Evolutionary Thought* (Oxford, 1989); and N. F. Utkina, *Positivizm, antropologicheskii materializm i nauka v Rossii* (*Vtoraia polovina xix veka*) (Moscow, 1975).

35. See, for example, Faresov, *Semidesiatniki;* A. P. Mertvago, *Ne po tornomu puti* (St. Petersburg, 1900); P. Metelitsyna, "God v batrachkakh," *Otechestvennye zapiski* 252, no. 9 (1880): 71–112; N. A. Engel'gardt, "A. N. Engel'gardt i ego Batishchevoe delo. . . ." Engelgardt's personal archives also contain numerous letters with prospective and former students of the "Batishchevo school."

36. Much of Engelgardt's correspondence from Batishchevo was with fellow scientists and former students from the Agricultural Institute. See, for example, TsGALI, fond 572, opis' 1, dela 35, 36, 43, 44, 47, 51. See also I. A. Krupenikov, *Pavel Andreevich Kostychev, 1845–1895* (Moscow, 1987), 43 ff.; and I. I. Mochalov, *Vladimir Ivanovich Vernadskii (1863–1945)* (Moscow, 1982), 81.

37. TsGALI, fond 572, opis' 1, delo 142, l. 5.

38. TsGALI, fond 572, opis' 1, delo 174, letters from 1871 through 1883.

39. In the month before Alexander II was assassinated in 1881, Sharapov conveyed his and Ivan Sergeevich Aksakov's urgent desire to have Engelgardt write an article on the peasants' attitude toward the land for *Rus'*, a request Aksakov withdrew following the assassination in March (TsGALI, fond 572, opis' 2, delo 27, ll. 7–9).

40. V. I. Lenin, *Polnoe sobranie sochinenii*, vol. 2 (Moscow, 1958), 521.

41. Zemledelets (Sharapov), "Schastlivyi ugolok," 11.

42. K. D. Kavelin, *Sobranie sochinenii K. D. Kavelina*, vol. 2, *Publitsistika* (St. Petersburg, 1904), 790. This quote comes from a description of rural life published in 1873.

43. This journal can be found in the Central State Archive of Literature and Art in Moscow, TsGALI, fond 572, opis' 2, dela 19, 20.

44. See, for example, D. Golokhvastov, *Pis'ma iz derevni: O pis'makh iz derevni G-na Engel'gardta* (Moscow, 1884), 21–22.

45. A. N. Engel'gardt, *O khoziaistve v severnoi Rossii i primenenii v nem fosforitov: Sbornik sel'sko-khoziaistvennykh statei A. N. Engel'gardta iz Batishcheva 1872–1888* (St. Petersburg, 1888), ii.

46. Ibid., iv.

47. Ibid., 1.

48. TsGALI, fond 572, opis' 1, dela 55, 258.

49. Seven years earlier, Engelgardt had published a synopsis of Darwinian theory

in a popular article, "Po povodu knigi Darvina," *Sankt Peterburgskie vedomosti,* nos. 57, 65, 70 (1864), discussed in L. L. Balashev, "Pervye shagi Darvinizma v Rossii i A. N. Engel'gardt," *Voprosy istorii estestvoznaniia i tekhniki* (Moscow, 1959), 118–19.

50. For a discussion of the institution, and of its importance in the thinking of educated Russians in the post-Emancipation era, see Yoshio Imai, "The *Artel'* and the Beginnings of the Consumer Cooperative Movement in Russia," in *Land Commune and Peasant Community in Russia: Communal Forms in Imperial and Early Soviet Society,* ed. Roger Bartlett (London, 1990), 363–75.

51. For a discussion of the public debate surrounding the fission of peasant households in the post-Emancipation era, see Cathy A. Frierson, "*Razdel:* The Peasant Household Divided," *Russian Review* 46 (1987): 35–52.

52. Students interested in this issue should read Beatrice Brodsky Farnsworth, "The Litigious Daughter-in-Law: Family Relations in Rural Russia in the Second Half of the Nineteenth Century," *Slavic Review* 45, no. 1 (1986): 49–64; Rose Glickman, "Women and the Peasant Commune," in *Land Commune and Peasant Community,* ed. Bartlett, 321–38; and Christine D. Worobec, "Temptress or Virgin? The Precarious Sexual Position of Women in Postemancipation Ukrainian Peasant Society," *Slavic Review* 49, no. 2 (Summer 1990): 227–38.

53. Engelgardt himself served as a zemstvo delegate from 1884 to 1886, and attended all but one of the sessions in the first two years. He did not attend during the final year of his service (*Zhurnaly xix ocherednogo Smolenskogo Gubernskogo Zemskogo Sobraniia. Zasedanie 15 po 26 ianvaria 1884 g.* [Smolensk, 1884], 68; *Zhurnaly xx ocherednogo Smolenskogo Gubernskogo Zemskogo Sobraniia. Zasedanie s 15-ogo po 23-ogo ianvaria 1885 g.* [Smolensk, 1885], 40; *Zhurnaly xxi ocherednogo Smolenskogo Gubernskogo Zemskogo Sobraniia, s 16 po 25 ianvaria 1886 g.* [Smolensk, 1886]).

54. For a discussion of this shift in public opinion, see my work *Peasant Icons: Representations of Rural People in Late Nineteenth Century Russia* (New York, 1993).

55. Rukopisnyi otdel, Pushkinskii dom, fond 577, opis' 1, delo 19, l. 29.

56. Faresov, *Semidesiatniki,* 170–71.

57. S. F. Sharapov, *A. N. Engel'gardt i ego znachenie dlia russkoi kul'turi i nauki* (St. Petersburg, 1893), 60.

Letter I

1. This letter first appeared in the May 1872 issue of *Notes of the Fatherland,* 30–50.

2. *Desiatina:* land measure equivalent to 2.7 acres.

3. *Kholmogor:* a particularly fine breed of dairy cow.

4. Samovar: a large metal urn for boiling water to make tea. The samovar was one of the most important and valuable items in the peasants' store of housewares.

5. *Baba:* a popular and less formal term for a married peasant woman. It could also mean old woman, wife, or simply woman, especially in the peasants' speech. Here, Engelgardt uses the term neutrally, but later, in the eighth letter, the term will take on negative connotations.

6. Felt boots and a sheepskin coat were characteristic winter clothing for the peasantry, not for the gentry.

7. *Izba:* peasant hut or cottage among the Russian peasantry. Typically a one-

story, wooden structure that was the main building on the family's homestead. See Mary Matossian, "The Peasant Way of Life," in *The Peasant in Nineteenth Century Russia,* ed. Wayne S. Vucinich (Stanford, 1968), 4–8.

8. "Starukha" (the old woman) is the nickname Engelgardt has given to this figure on his farm.

9. *Muzhik:* a popular and less formal term for an adult male peasant, much like *baba* for peasant women. Like *baba,* it could carry positive, neutral, or negative connotations. For the most part, Engelgardt uses the term in a neutral manner, following the parlance of the peasant population.

10. *Kopek* (anglicized form of *kopeika*): one one-hundredth of a ruble.

11. Following the Emancipation of the Russian serfs in 1861, many of the middle and poor gentry experienced economic disruption as a result of losing the subsidy of free labor from their peasants. Failing to adapt to the requirements of the new system, a large number who faced financial ruin abandoned agriculture and entered state service. For further study of the gentry during these years, see Terence Emmons, *The Russian Landed Gentry and the Peasant Emancipation of 1861* (Cambridge, 1967); A. P. Korelin, *Dvorianstvo v poreformennoi Rossii, 1861–1905 gg* (Moscow, 1979); Roberta Thompson Manning, *The Crisis of the Old Order in Russia: Gentry and Government* (Princeton, 1982); and Seymour Becker, *Nobility and Privilege in Late Imperial Russia* (De Kalb, Ill., 1985).

12. *Verst:* measure of distance, equivalent to O.66 mile or 1.067 kilometers.

13. *Vedro:* liquid measure, 3.25 gallons or 12.30 liters.

14. As part of the Emancipation legislation, each peasant household received a minimum of so-called allotment land, the amount of which varied according to geographic region. The average for all of European Russia was around 13 acres (5 desiatinas) per male peasant. Some peasants chose not to receive their full allotment, for which they were obligated to pay rent or redemption payments according to the values assigned to the land they received, but took instead a quarter allotment, which they received for free.

15. Engelgardt refers here to the Napoleonic invasion in 1812, which crossed through this territory and laid waste to it in particular.

16. "No. 301 of "Birzhevye vedomosti" for 1871 (November)." (A.N.E.)

17. *Vershok:* 1.75 inches, thus the crust of bread is about 4–8 inches square.

18. Orel Province was the next province southwest of Smolensk Province, which means that peasants could be traveling over one hundred miles in their search for crusts of bread.

19. A kite is a type of bird of prey.

20. *Arshin:* measure equivalent to 28 inches.

21. During the post-Emancipation period, there were several forms of "court" in the Russian village. Some (the so-called court of neighbors, family court, and court of elders) were informal and were made up of heads of household. These courts handled many of the disputes and acts of wrongdoing that occurred in the village. The Emancipation legislation also established a district, or volost, court for each district, which was made up of peasant judges from villages in the district and which was to decide civil disputes according to customary law. In this instance Engelgardt's steward seems to be referring to one of the informal courts in the village community. See Peter Czap, Jr., "Peasant Class Courts and Peasant Customary Justice in Russia, 1861–1912," *Journal of Social History* 1, no. 2 (1967): 149–79; and C. A. Frierson, "Rural Justice in Public Opinion: The Volost' Court Debate, 1861–1912," *Slavonic and East European Review* 64, no. 4 (October 1986): 526–45.

22. In Russian households the stove was a large structure that took up an entire corner and had shelves or ledges on it where people could sleep.

Letter II

1. This letter appeared in the June 1872 issue of *Notes of the Fatherland*, 161–82.

2. The artel was a labor association that peasants often formed to undertake group work for hire, whether as agricultural workers, factory workers in town, or hired laborers in local manufactories. Engelgardt deals with them extensively later in the letters. See Joseph Bradley, *Muzhik and Muscovite: Urbanization in Late Imperial Russia* (Berkeley, 1985); Robert Eugene Johnson, *Peasant and Proletarian: The Working Class of Moscow in the Late Nineteenth Century* (New Brunswick, N.J., 1979); and Timothy Mixter, "Of Grandfather-Beaters and Fat-Heeled Pacifists: Perceptions of Agricultural Labor and Hiring Market Disturbances in Saratov, 1872–1905," *Russian History* 7, pts. 1–2 (1980): 139–68.

3. *Osmina:* about 3 bushels.

4. Shneidersha was a popular entertainer and Dusot's a famous restaurant for the elite in St. Petersburg.

5. Again, establishments for wealthy members of society in the capital.

6. *Shtof:* unit of liquid measure equal to 1.23 liters.

7. A *sazhen* is just less than 84 inches, so the regulation called for removal of the tavern from the volost administrative offices by a matter of several yards.

8. The volost was the smallest administrative unit in post-Emancipation Russia, similar to a district or canton. The administrative offices were where the volost clerk worked and where sessions of the volost court were likely to be held. The regulation for removing the tavern from close proximity to the volost offices reflected the widespread concern among educated Russians and policymakers that volost officials and judges were often susceptible to bribes of liquor.

9. *Letitsines:* this was probably a term coined by the Russian chemical community to refer to highly volatile substances, drawing on the Russian verb *letit'* (to fly).

10. *Kulak:* village strongman, wealthy peasant in the village who had the financial means and the ability to wield power and influence in the community through economic assistance, moneylending, hiring labor, and so forth. Engelgardt discusses this phenomenon at length later in the letters. It is interesting to note that Engelgardt addresses this peasant by his name and patronymic, thus according him unusual respect.

11. Constable: the local police chief.

12. Redemption certificates: the notes serf owners received as compensation for the land granted to the peasants, who then had to redeem them through payment.

13. *Feldsher:* medical assistant, paramedic. For a study of public health in post-Emancipation Russia, see Nancy Mandelker Frieden, *Russian Physicians in an Era of Reform, 1856–1905* (Princeton, 1981); and Samuel C. Ramer, "The Zemstvo and Public Health," in *The Zemstvo in Russia: An Experiment in Local Self-Government,* ed. Terence Emmons and Wayne S. Vucinich (Cambridge, 1982), 279–314.

14. Engelgardt switches from *Aniuta* to the more familiar diminutive form *Aksiuta*.

15. "How she strokes her haunches and legs."

16. The zemstvo was a local board of self-government, introduced as one of the Great Reforms in 1864. It consisted of locally elected representatives of the peasantry, gentry, and townsmen. It handled, among other things, such public works programs as fire insurance, road and bridge repair, and construction of schools and hospitals.

17. Patronymic: in Russian, a person's name consists of the first name, the patronymic (the name of the father with a female or male ending), and the family name.

18. Peace mediator: official responsible for the execution of land-settlement agreements following the Emancipation.

19. Bast shoes: peasant-made shoes constructed of woven inner bark from lime or linden trees.

Letter III

1. This letter first appeared in the January 1873 issue of *Notes of the Fatherland,* 11–90.

2. Avdotia is describing two aspects of flax processing here. The first is removing the seeds from the stalk which in the United States was also called *rippling.* In Russia this was done by pulling bunches of dried flax stalks across a standing plank of wood with teeth carved in it, so that the seeds were caught between the teeth of the plank and fell off. The second was *retting,* in which the flax was either soaked in water or steamed in order to remove the sap that bound the fiber and the bark. This was an imprecise process that was judged not by any set time but, in this case, by Avdotia's eye. She had to be careful not to allow the flax to rot, while also not taking it out of the water or steam too soon. Once retted, the flax was broken into pieces in a process called *braking.* In Russia this was done on a piece of equipment that looked like a sawhorse with a wooden cleaver attached, which was brought down onto the flax, or on a simple inclined plank on which the flax was laid and then beaten. The next steps, *scutching* and *hackling,* broke the fibers down further and separated them into coarse and fine fibers in preparation for spinning.

3. Engelgardt is switching back and forth between the more formal *Stepan* and the diminutive *Stepka.*

4. Gymnasiums: high schools based on a program of classical education.

5. Stepan's experience was not unusual. Peasant men often went off to the city to work but returned to their families in the village in case of illness or old age.

6. Engelgardt used clover in his system of crop rotation in order to prevent the rapid depletion of nutritive elements from the soil.

7. Engelgardt is referring here to the much-discussed goal of teaching the peasants respect for statute law, especially in regard to private property.

8. For a discussion of peasant attitudes toward wrongdoing, see Cathy A. Frierson, "Crime and Punishment in the Russian Village: Rural Concepts of Criminality at the End of the Nineteenth Century," *Slavic Review* 46, no. 1 (1987): 55–69.

9. Kassian was a figure in Russian folklore who passed up a peasant whose cart was stuck in the road, whereas Nicholas stopped to help him. For this reason, a holiday named for Kassian was celebrated only once every four years, while Nicholas had two each year (I. M. Sokolov, *Russian Folklore,* trans. Catherine Ruth Smith [Detroit, 1971], 455–56).

10. Because they had been on small amounts of feed all winter.

11. That is, when you try to innovate by introducing a fancy new breed.

12. The old men Engelgardt is referring to were wise old men or sorcerers of the village who used chants to exorcise such curses.

13. *Pud:* weight equal to 36 pounds.

14. Tver: a provincial capital city north of Moscow and northeast of Smolensk.

15. The steward is reminding Dema that he could be flogged for failing to meet his obligations.

16. Avdotia is thus justifying the peasant women's practice of exchanging sex for food.

17. Korobochka, a character from N. Gogol's novel *Dead Souls,* was a female landowner who was exceedingly greedy, masculine, and tight with all of her possessions.

18. The question of peasants felling lumber in gentry forests was a source of constant irritation and public outcry. Students of customary law paid special attention to this divergence in the concept of property held by educated Russians and peasants. See Cathy A. Frierson, "Rural Justice in Public Opinion: The Volost' Court Debate, 1861–1912," *Slavonic and East European Review* 64, no. 4 (October 1986): 532.

19. *Kasha:* mushlike hot cereal.

20. One of the duties of the volost administration was collecting taxes and redemption payments.

Letter IV

1. This letter first appeared in the February 1874 issue of *Notes of the Fatherland,* 269–333.

2. Grackles: another name for the jackdaw, considered the first bird of spring in this area of Russia.

3. These are three levels of the judicial system to which Engelgardt as a landowner could have complained against a peasant. The first two were state appointees, usually from the gentry; the third was a court of peasant judges who decided cases according to customary law.

4. Engelgardt is referring here to the fact that the volost courts, made up of peasant judges, decided cases according to customary law and sentenced accordingly, while the justices of the peace largely followed the civil code and followed formal sentencing requirements. This was one of the sources of dissatisfaction with the decision to establish the volost courts, because many critics believed this confusion hampered the development of an understanding of law and the courts among the peasantry. See Peter Czap, Jr., "Peasant-Class Courts and Peasant Customary Justice in Russia, 1861–1912," *Journal of Social History* 1, no. 2 (1967): 176–77; and C. A. Frierson, "Rural Justice in Public Opinion: The Volost' Court Debate, 1861–1912," *Slavonic and East European Review* 64, no. 4 (October 1986): 526–45.

5. *Barshchina:* obligations paid in labor to the landlord under serfdom.

6. *St. Petersburg News.*

7. "Torbole, September 12. Afternoon.

"In the cool of the evening I took a walk. Here I am really in a new country, a totally unfamiliar environment. The people lead the careless life of a fool's paradise. To begin with, the doors have no locks, though the innkeeper assures me that I would not have to worry if all my belongings were made of diamonds. Then the windows are closed with oil paper instead of glass. Finally, a highly necessary convenience is lacking, so that one is almost reduced to a state of nature. When I asked the servant for a certain place, he pointed down into the courtyard. 'Quiabasso puo servirsi [You can take care of yourself down there!]' 'Dove [Where]?' I asked. 'Da per tutto dove vuol! [The whole place, wherever you want!]' was his friendly answer. Everywhere one encounters the utmost unconcern, though there is noise and lively bustle enough. . . ."

J. W. Goethe, *Italian Journey (1786–1788)*, trans. W. H. Auden and Elizabeth Mayer (New York, 1962), 25.

8. Petrushka was the name of Chichikov's valet in Gogol's *Dead Souls*. It was also the nickname for a chamber pot. Engelgardt could mean either here.

9. Selifan was the name of Chichikov's lackey in Gogol's *Dead Souls*.

10. Because it costs too much to maintain them through the long winter months.

Letter V

1. This letter first appeared in the September 1876 issue of *Notes of the Fatherland*, 5–68.

2. Engelgardt's children have arrived to live with him on the estate.

3. Hundreder: minor village official.

4. *Kisel:* a gelatinlike mousse of cranberries and sugar.

5. Engelgardt comments on the lack of knowledge of the law among the peasants.

6. *Vedro:* 3.25 gallons, or 12.30 liters.

7. The term here is *krugovaia poruka,* the system established by the Emancipation through which the tax obligation for the entire commune lay with the commune rather than with individual households.

8. Again, Engelgardt is referring here to the volost court. He goes on to talk about the various jurisdictions of the volost court and the justice of the peace.

9. Engelgardt here offers advice to gentry farmers.

10. "A girl begins to receive a share of the wool and flax only from the time when she becomes useful in the household, for example, when she can gather hay for the pigs. The mother also receives a share for a boy only when he can do some kind of work." (A.N.E.)

11. "Relations between men and women among the peasants are established with the greatest simplicity. In the spring when the hired hands (men and women) gather, already within two weeks all of the relations have been established and everyone knows who is with whom. Usually, once relationships are established in the spring, they will be preserved solidly until the autumn, when everyone goes off in different directions knowing that they may never meet. A woman, furthermore, exercises the fullest freedom, but she must first abandon the one with whom she is involved and only then is she free to become involved right away with anyone she wants. There is no jealousy. But as long as a woman is involved with someone, she is inviolable for other men and any attempt by some man in this regard will be punished—his friends will beat him, never her. Therefore, men never look at a woman who is involved, until she parts with the one with whom she was involved and becomes free." (A.N.E.)

12. For a discussion of these and other cases where the women were involved, see Beatrice Brodsky Farnsworth, "The Litigious Daughter-in-Law: Family Relations in Rural Russia in the Second Half of the Nineteenth Century," *Slavic Review* 45, no. 1 (Spring 1986): 49–64. On the property rights of peasant women, see Rose Glickman, "Women and the Peasant Commune," in *Land Commune and Peasant Community in Russia: Communal Forms in Imperial and Early Soviet Society,* ed. Roger Bartlett (London, 1990), 321–38; and Christine D. Worobec, *Peasant Russia: Family and Community in the Post-Emancipation Period* (Princeton, 1991), 176–216.

13. Sack: approximately 275–300 pounds.

14. Garnets: dry measure, equal to 3.28 liters.

15. Engelgardt is referring here to the purchase of votive candles by members of the congregation, which they lit and placed before icons.

16. Gleb Ivanovich Uspenskii, Populist-realist author who was considered the most important writer on the peasant theme during these years. For a treatment of his life, see Richard Wortman, *The Crisis of Russian Populism* (Cambridge, 1967).

Letter VI

1. This letter first appeared in the March 1878 issue of *Notes of the Fatherland,* 5–42.

2. The Russian Imperial merchant marine had a tricolored flag, with white, blue, and red stripes.

3. The Russian army included two types of reserve status in addition to the standing army: unlimited furlough and temporary leave.

4. The Imperial Russian flag has a yellow field with a double-headed eagle in the center. The flag of Turkey was red with a crescent and a star.

5. General Mikhail Dmitrievich Skobelev, hero not only of Russian engagements with Turkey but also of conquests of territory in central Asia.

6. Children born out of wedlock would not necessarily have a right to a share of a household's land allotment.

7. *Arshin:* equivalent to 28 inches. Thus, the tavern is about 20 feet by 20 feet.

8. Tsargrad was the name by which the Slavs knew Byzantium or Constantinople. Engelgardt is referring again to the fact that the peasants confused the name of the city with a saint of their imagination, the Tsar of Hail (grad) who would protect them from hail damage to their crops.

9. Queen Victoria of Great Britain (1837–1901).

10. Again, Queen Victoria.

11. The Krnka and Berdan rifles were the first two breech-loading rifles supplied to the Russian troops, the former beginning in 1867, the latter in two issues: the Berdan I (1868) and the Berdan II (1870). Both the Krnka and the Berdan rifles were issued to troops during the Russo-Turkish War. See Joseph E. Bradley, *Guns for the Tsar: American Technology and the Small Arms Industry in Nineteenth-Century Russia* (De Kalb, Ill., 1990), 104.

12. The official report on this horse levy confirms Engelgardt's perception of significant wasted effort. Out of 25,773 horses examined in the district between May and November 1877, 14,694 were declared unfit for service (Gosudarstvennyi Arkhiv Smolenskoi Oblasti [hereafter GASO], fond 1, opis' 3, delo 360, l. 143).

Letter VII

1. The first installment of this letter first appeared in the January 1879 issue of *Notes of the Fatherland,* 101–42.

2. GASO, fond 1, opis' 5, delo 20, l.12 (report from Dorogobuzhskii District, March 28, 1881).

3. This was a traditional Russian greeting.

4. Peasants in Engelgardt's area referred to lower-rank policemen as "chicken

stealers" because they said they were likely to steal a man's last chicken to cover tax arrears or a fine.

5. Water meadows were those areas periodically flooded by rising waters of neighboring rivers and streams, in this region primarily the Dnieper, which were especially fertile and, thus, desirable.

6. For a discussion of these drinking patterns on a broad scale, see Patricia Herlihy, "Joy of Rus': Rites and Rituals of Russian Drinking," *Russian Review* 50, no. 2 (April 1991): 131–47.

7. "I know an example of the very same muzhiks, three veterans—artel people who were accustomed to working on a task together—after they settled in a village and took some land built a barn *together,* threshed in it *together:* today they thresh the grain which belongs to one of them, tomorrow that which belongs to another." (A.N.E.)

8. The repartitioning of peasant households was one of the most troubling phenomena of post-Emancipation rural life for educated observers. For a discussion of the causes that were suggested, see Cathy A. Frierson, "*Razdel:* The Peasant Family Divided," *Russian Review* 46 (January 1987): 35–52.

9. One of the suggestions in the air at this time was a law restricting family divisions in some way. Such a law was passed on March 18, 1886, according to which a son who wished to depart from his patriarchal household had first to get the permission of his household head, and then two-thirds approval of the communal assembly.

10. This peasant custom was one of the rituals of welcoming spring.

11. This concluding section of the seventh letter first appeared in the February 1879 issue of *Notes of the Fatherland,* 237–82.

12. That is, he does not owe any taxes or rent to either.

13. Recall that when a peasant took on a *krug* of the lord's land, he was agreeing to cultivate all three fields in the three-field system during one agricultural year, using his own horse and plough.

14. "One should say 'had the use of,' but we gentry landowners, even under serfdom were so used to saying 'peasant land,' 'the peasants own this land,' that even *having found out in the Emancipation Edict,* that this was 'our' land, out of old habit, still continue to make this error." (A.N.E.)

Letter VIII

1. This letter first appeared in the November 1880 issue of *Notes of the Fatherland,* 41–72.

2. TsGALI, fond 202, opis' 1, delo 34, l. 1.

3. GASO, fond 1, opis' 8, delo 13, l. 6, and fond 1, opis' 8, delo 23, ll. 1–21. These reports concern not only Engelgardt's movements but also those of his children, their guests, and any unfamiliar people who visited the estate.

4. In June 1878 a new semimilitary official was created in the rural police, the *uriadnik.*

5. Engelgardt is referring to the common practice among petty officials of demanding bribes of liquor to grease the wheels of the bureaucracy or simply to keep them off one's back.

6. It seems that *dentists* is used here as *butchers* would be used in English, that is, to connote crude bullies, and derives from the practice of punching the detainees in the mouth or pulling their teeth during interrogation. Among the peasants, the expression "to give your teeth a cleaning" meant to give someone a punch in the mouth.

7. During the 1870s, fire-prevention measures were a serious endeavor of the zemstvos and of the central government. Engelgardt is referring to several such measures, including decrees about the reconstruction of villages, supply of fire-fighting equipment, and efforts to ensure that there would always be water available in the village to use in the event of a fire.

8. *Fortochka:* a small window set into the upper corner of the larger window for the purposes of ventilation during cold weather.

9. "May trees: The birch branches which are put around the izba at Whitsunday are called May trees here. Churches are decorated with these same birch branches, and everyone comes to church on this day with bouquets of flowers. It is forbidden to put up May trees now." (A.N.E.)

10. Engelgardt is describing a spring celebration that was common throughout Russia. There are various interpretations of the Trinity rituals. In addition to the simple celebration of the arrival of spring, these rituals also were connected to ancestor worship and the veneration of trees as a symbol of fertility, dating to the pre-Christian era when the East Slavs practiced slash-and-burn agriculture as they colonized the forest. The fact that women were the primary actors in these rituals underscores their importance as fertility rites.

11. That is, he stays through the entire Trinity ritual, concluding with the "drowning" of the garlands in the river.

12. Engelgardt is referring to the plague scare of 1878, when plague broke out in Astrakhan and preventive measures were introduced in all areas considered at risk.

13. This was to signal to potential thieves that there was a guard.

14. For a discussion of changing policies toward the Jews, see Hans Rogger, *Jewish Policies and Right-Wing Politics in Imperial Russia* (Berkeley, 1986).

15. That is, where the Jews were trying to live discreetly.

16. Tenner: like the hundreder, a petty local official.

Letter IX

1. This letter first appeared in the January 1881 issue of *Notes of the Fatherland,* 171–200.

Letter X

1. This letter first appeared in the January 1881 issue of *Notes of the Fatherland,* 377–417.

2. TsGALI, fond 572, opis' 1, delo 37, l. 8.

3. *Chetvert:* 5.95 bushels.

4. This record is available in Engelgardt's two-volume journal in his personal archive in Moscow (TsGALI, fond 572, opis' 2, dela 19, 20).

5. For an extensive study of this phenomenon, see Ben Eklof, *Russian Peasant Schools: Officialdom, Village Culture, and Popular Pedagogy, 1861–1914* (Berkeley, 1986), esp. chaps. 3, 8.

6. Engelgardt is drawing here on the figures of two fish, the carp and the pike, in Russian folklore, where they represented the weak and the strong, the victim and the predator.

7. See Cathy A. Frierson, "Crime and Punishment in the Russian Village: Concepts of Criminality in the Late Nineteenth Century," *Slavic Review* 46, no. 1 (1987):

55–69; Stephen P. Frank, "Popular Justice, Community and Culture among the Russian Peasantry, 1870–1900," *Russian Review* 46, no. 3 (1987): 239–66.

8. Peasant households that did not have enough males of working age often took in, or adopted, boys or young men. The inheritance rights of these adoptees varied; hence, they may have felt more vulnerable and found the kulak's visions more appealing than did the more secure young men in the village.

Letter XI

1. This letter first appeared in the February 1882 issue of *Notes of the Fatherland*, 317–74.

2. The era of active counterreform is usually dated as beginning in 1881, under Alexander III, following the assassination of Alexander II on March 1, 1881.

3. That is, the peasants are waiting for the Tsar's merciful granting of a redistribution of all the lands in Russia, through which peasants would receive more land for free.

4. "*Notes of the Fatherland,* 1878, no. 3, and 1879, no. 2." (A.N.E.)

5. As opposed to the old edict that proclaimed the Emancipation in 1861.

Letter XII

1. This letter first appeared in the March 1887 issue of *Herald of Europe*, 147–83.

2. Rukopisnyi otdel, Pushkinskii dom, fond 577, opis' 1, delo 19, l. 68.

3. K. D. Kavelin was a prominent liberal historian and author of an important series of articles on the "peasant question" that appeared as a separate volume in 1882: *Krest'ianskii vopros. Issledovanie o znachenii u nas krest'ianskogo dela, prichinakh ego upadka i merakh k podniatiiu sel'skogo khoziaistva i byta poselian* (St. Petersburg, 1882).

4. The Peasant Land Bank was established in 1883 to assist peasants in purchasing land.

5. "The first series of my letters "From the Country" was printed under the pseudonym A. Buglim (the name of the village which I lived close to in the summer of 1863) in *St. Petersburg News* in 1863. The second series was printed in *Notes of the Fatherland* from 1872 to 1882, and then came out as a separate publication." (A.N.E.)

6. Engelgardt means that their allotment was not the maximum set for Smolensk Province at the time of the Emancipation.

7. *Tiaglo:* The tax burden for each working "soul," or one laboring unit, under serfdom.

8. Engelgardt is referring to the fact that peasants lit their homes with torches before the advent of kerosene and kerosene lamps.

Bibliography
of Related Works

Engelgardt

Archives

In Moscow: Tsentral'nyi Gosudarstvennyi Arkhiv Literatury i Iskusstva, fond 572: A.
  N. Engelgardt
In St. Petersburg: Rukopisnyi otdel, Pushkinskii Dom, fond 577: A. N. Engelgardt

Writings by Engelgardt

There have been seven editions of the collected letters:
Iz derevni. 11 pisem. 1872–1882. St. Petersburg, 1882.
Iz derevni. 11 pisem. 1872–1882. St. Petersburg, 1885.
Iz derevni. 12 pisem. 1872–1887. St. Petersburg, 1897.
Iz derevni. 12 pisem. 1872–1887. Moscow, 1937.
Iz derevni. 12 pisem. 1872–1887. Moscow, 1956.
Iz derevni. 12 pisem. 1872–1887. Moscow, 1960.
Iz derevni. 12 pisem. 1872–1887. Moscow, 1987.

Many of Engelgardt's other writings appeared as volumes of collected articles. These
include:

Izbrannye sochineniia. Moscow, 1959.
*O khoziaistve v severnoi Rossii i primenenii v nem fosforitov. Sbornik sel'sko-
  khoziaistvennykh statei A. N. Engel'gardta iz Batishcheva 1872–1888.* St. Petersburg, 1888.
Sbornik obshcheponiatnykh statei po estestvoznaniiu. St Petersburg, 1867.

The series of letters that Engelgardt wrote from Smolensk in 1863 appears in the 1897
edition of his *Iz derevni,* as do several other articles on agriculture and phosphates.

Biographical Materials

Biographical materials on Engelgardt consist largely of reminiscences and brief
sketches. Both the sketches written by his son, N. A. Engelgardt, and the one by A. I.
Faresov are particularly useful because they include lengthy quotations from letters in

Engelgardt's archive. His son's introductory essay to the 1897 edition of *Iz derevni* is also one of the best sources on Engelgardt's life on Batishchevo. While Engelgardt has attracted attention in the West primarily as a Populist, in the Soviet Union and Russia he has done so because of his contributions to science. The best discussion in English is Richard Wortman's.

N.a. "Aleksandr Nikolaevich Engel'gardt." *Liudi russkoi nauki. Ocherki o vydaiu-shchikhsia deiateliakh estestvoznaniia i tekhnika,* 698–704. Moscow, 1963.

Anzimirov, V. "Moe znakomstvo s A. N. Engel'gardt." *Khoziain,* no. 3 (January 21, 1894).

Budaeva, O. D. " 'Pis'ma iz derevni' A. N. Engel'gardta kak istoricheskii istochnik." *Sel'skoe khoziaistvo i krest'ianstvo nechernozemnogo tsentra RSFSR,* 81–92. Smolensk, 1976.

Engel'gardt, N. A. "Aleksandr Nikolaevich Engel'gardt i ego Batishchevoe delo." *Iz derevni. 12 pisem. 1872–1887,* 1–60. St. Petersburg, 1897.

———. "Davnie epizody." *Istoricheskii vestnik* 119 (1910): 529–56; "Iz davnykh epizodov." *Istoricheskii vestnik* 120 (1910): 89–116; "Davnie epizody." *Istoricheskii vestnik* 122 (1910): 123–44; 124 (1911): 42–68, 527–59, 844–71.

Faresov, A. I. *Semidesiatniki.* St. Petersburg, 1905. The sketch on Engelgardt originally appeared as "Vospominaniia ob A. N. Engel'gardt," *Vestnik Evropy* 4 (1893): 59–99.

Fortunatov, A. F. "A. N. Engel'gardt." *Russkaia mysl',* no. 4 (1893): 209–14.

Gerchikov, M. G. "Pamiati zabytogo khimika." *Priroda,* no. 10 (1932): 951–54.

Kotel'nikov, V. "A. N. Engel'gardt." *Khoziain,* no. 3 (January 21, 1894): 38–41.

Mertvago, A. P. *Ne po tornomu puti.* St. Petersburg, 1900.

Metelitsyna, P. "God v batrachkakh." *Otechestvennye zapiski* 252, no. 9 (1880): 71–112.

Modestov, A. P. *Ocherki po istorii agronomii v zhizneopisaniiakh zodchikh i stroitelei razumnogo zemledeliia.* No I. Moscow, 1924.

Musabekov, Iu. S. "Pervyi russkii khimicheskii zhurnal i ego osnovateli." *Materialy po istorii otechestvennoi khimii. Sbornik dokladov na vtorom vsesoiuznom soveshchanii po istorii otechestvennoi khimii 21–26 aprelia 1951 g.* 288–302. Moscow, 1953.

Nechuiatov. P. Ia. *Aleksandr Nikolaevich Engel'gardt. Ocherk zhizni i deiatel'nosti.* Smolensk, 1957.

Perlin, B. "Pervyi russkii agrokhimik." *Krai nash smolenskii,* 250–61. Smolensk, 1954.

Sharapov, S. F. *A. N. Engel'gardt i ego znachenie dlia russkoi kul'turi i nauki.* St. Petersburg, 1893.

Wortman, Richard. *The Crisis of Russian Populism.* Cambridge, 1967.

Related Works

The following bibliography includes general works that deal with questions raised by Engelgardt in his observations of life on and near Batishchevo. This is not meant to be exhaustive; Populism alone would require a bibliography far beyond the scope of this list.

Anfimov, A. M. *Ekonomicheskoe polozhenie i klassovaia bor'ba krest'ian evropeiskoi Rossii, 1881–1904.* Moscow, 1984.

———. *Krest'ianskoe khoziaistvo evropeiskoi Rossii, 1881–1904.* Moscow, 1980.

————. *Krupnoe pomeshchich'e khoziaistvo evropeiskoi Rossii.* Moscow, 1969.

Bartlett, Roger, ed. *Land Commune and Peasant Community in Russia: Communal Forms in Imperial and Early Soviet Society.* London, 1990.

Becker, Seymour. *Nobility and Privilege in Late Imperial Russia.* De Kalb, Ill., 1985.

Billington, James H. *Mikhailovsky and Russian Populism.* Oxford, 1958.

Blankoff, Jean. *La Société russe de la seconde moitié du xixe siècle.* Brussels, 1974.

Blum, Jerome. *Lord and Peasant in Russia from the Ninth to the Nineteenth Century.* Princeton, 1961.

Brooks, Jeffrey. *When Russia Learned to Read: Literacy and Popular Literature, 1861–1917.* Princeton, 1985.

Druzhinin, N. M. *Russkaia derevnia na perelome, 1861–1880 gg.* Moscow, 1978.

Efimenko, A. I. *Issledovaniia narodnoi zhizni. Vypusk pervyi: Obychnoe pravo.* Moscow, 1884.

Eklof, Ben. *Russian Peasant Schools: Officialdom, Village Culture, and Popular Pedagogy, 1861–1914.* Berkeley, 1986.

Emmons, Terence. *The Russian Landed Gentry and the Peasant Emancipation of 1861.* Cambridge, 1967.

Emmons, Terence, and Vucinich, Wayne, eds. *The Zemstvo in Russia: An Experiment in Local Self-Government.* Cambridge, 1982.

Farnsworth, Beatrice, and Viola, Lynne, eds. *Russian Peasant Women.* New York, 1992.

Field, Daniel. *The End of Serfdom: Nobility and Bureaucracy in Russia, 1855–1861.* Cambridge, Mass., 1976.

————. *Rebels in the Name of the Tsar.* Boston, 1976.

Gleason, Abbott. *Young Russia: The Genesis of Russian Radicalism in the 1860s.* New York, 1980.

Hamburg, G. M. *Politics of the Russian Nobility, 1881–1905.* New Brunswick, N.J., 1984.

Hoch, Steven L. *Serfdom and Social Control in Russia: Petrovskoe, A Village in Tambov.* Chicago, 1986.

Hourevich, Isaac A. *The Economy of the Russian Village.* 1892. Reprint. New York, 1970.

Itenberg, B. S. *Dvizhenie revoliutsionnogo narodnichestva. Narodnicheskie kruzhki i "khozhdenie v narod" v 70-kh godakh xix v.* Moscow, 1965.

Ivanits, Linda. *Russian Folk Belief.* Armonk, N.Y., 1989.

Jelavich, Barbara. *Russia's Balkan Entanglements, 1806–1914.* Cambridge, 1991.

Kahan, Arcadius. *Russian Economic History: The Nineteenth Century.* Edited by Roger Weiss. Chicago, 1989.

Kavelin, K. D. *Krest'ianskii vopros. Issledovanie o znachenii u nas krest'ianskogo dela, prichinakh ego upadka i merakh k podniatiiu sel'skogo khoziaistva i byta poselian.* St. Petersburg, 1882.

Kingston-Mann, Esther, and Mixter, Timothy, eds. *Peasant Economy, Culture, and Politics of European Russia, 1800–1921.* Princeton, 1990.

Koz'min, B. P. *Russkaia zhurnalistika 70-kh godov xix veka.* Moscow, 1948.

Kravchinskii, S. M. *The Russian Peasantry: Their Condition, Social Life, and Religion.* New York, 1888.

Leikina-Svirskaia, V. R. *Intelligentsiia v Rossii vo vtoroi polovine xix veka.* Moscow, 1971.

Leont'ev, A. A. *Krest'ianskoe pravo. Sistematicheskoe islozhenie osobennostei zakonodatel'stva o krest'ianakh.* St. Petersburg, 1909.

Lewin, Moshe. *Russian Peasants and Soviet Power.* Translated by Irene Nove. Evanston, Ill., 1968.

Ministerstvo Gosudarstvennykh Imushchestv. *Doklad vysochaishe uchrezhdennoi komissii dlia issledovaniia nyneshnego polozheniia sel'skogo khoziaistva i sel'skoi proizvoditel'nosti v Rossii.* St. Petersburg, 1873.

Pearson, Thomas S. *Russian Officialdom in Crisis: Autocracy and Local Self-Government, 1861–1890.* Cambridge, 1989.

Robinson, Geroid T. *Rural Russia under the Old Regime.* New York, 1949.

Smirnov, A. *Ocherki semeinykh otnoshenii po obychnomu pravu russkogo naroda.* Moscow, 1878.

Spasibenko, A. P. *Pisateli-narodniki.* Moscow, 1968.

Tenishev, V. V. *Pravosudie v russkom krest'ianskom bytu.* Briansk, 1907.

Teplinskii, M. V. *"Otechestvennye zapiski" (1868–1884). Istoriia zhurnala. Literaturnaia kritika.* Iuzhno-Sakhalinsk, 1966.

Thorner, Daniel, ed. *A. V. Chayanov on the Theory of Peasant Economy.* Homewood, Ill., 1966.

Todes, Daniel P. *Darwin without Malthus: The Struggle for Existence in Russian Evolutionary Thought.* Oxford, 1989.

Trudy Kommisii po preobrazovaniiu volostnykh sudov. 7 vols. St. Petersburg, 1873–1874.

Utkina, N. F. *Pozitivizm, antropologicheskii materializm i nauka v Rossii (Vtoraia polovina xix veka).* Moscow, 1975.

Venturi, Franco. *Roots of Revolution.* Translated by Francis Haskell. New York, 1960.

Vilenskii, B. V. *Sudebnaia reforma i kontrreforma v Rossii.* Saratov, 1969.

Volin, Lazar. *A Century of Russian Agriculture: From Alexander II to Khrushchev.* Cambridge, 1970.

Vtoroe otdelenie Sobstvennoi E. I. V. Kantseliarii. *Otchet po glavnomu komitetu ob ustroistve sel'skogo sostoianiia za deviatiletie 19 frevralia 1861 po 19 fevralia 1870 g.* St. Petersburg, 1870.

Vucinich, Alexander. *Darwin in Russian Thought.* Berkeley, 1988.

———. *Science in Russian Culture, 1861–1917.* Stanford, 1970.

———. *Social Thought in Tsarist Russia: The Quest for a General Science of Society, 1861–1917.* Chicago, 1976.

Vucinich, Wayne, ed. *The Peasant in Nineteenth Century Russia.* Stanford, 1968.

Walicki, Andrzei. *The Controversy over Capitalism: Studies in the Social Philosophy of the Russian Populists.* Oxford, 1969.

Wallace, Donald Mackenzie. *Russia.* London, 1912.

Worobec, Christine D. *Peasant Russia: Family and Community in the Post-Emancipation Period.* Princeton, 1991.

Yaney, George L. *The Systematization of Russian Government: Social Evolution in the Domestic Administration of Imperial Russia, 1711–1905.* Urbana, Ill., 1973.

Zaionchkovskii, P. A. *Provedenie v zhizn' krest'ianskoi reformy 1861 g.* Moscow, 1858.